BONATTI

ON

NATIVITIES

Treatise 9 of Guido Bonatti's
Book of Astronomy

Translated by Benjamin N. Dykes, Ph.D.

From the 1491 and 1550 Latin Editions

The Cazimi Press
Minneapolis, Minnesota
2010

Published and printed in the United States of America
by the Cazimi Press
621 5ᵗʰ Avenue SE #25, Minneapolis, MN 55414

© 2010 by Benjamin N. Dykes, Ph.D.

ISBN-13: 978-1-934586-14-3

PUBLISHER'S NOTE:

This reprint of Treatise 9 of Guido Bonatti's *Book of Astronomy* has been excerpted from the out-of-print 1st edition, published in 2007. The text reflects the original pagination for each Treatise, and has not been revised or updated to reflect new translation conventions or citations from more recent translations. The Table of Arabic Terms has been removed (a more recent version can be found at: www.bendykes.com/reviews/study.php).

Students should also consult my three-volume *Persian Nativities*, which contains translations of five important works of medieval natal astrology, several of which were sources for Bonatti's own work.

Dr. Benjamin N. Dykes
The Cazimi Press
October, 2010

TABLE OF CONTENTS

Book Abbreviations:

Abu 'Ali al-Khayyat: *The Judgments of Nativities*   *JN*

Abū Ma'shar: *Liber Introductorii Maioris ad Scientiam*   *Gr. Intr.*
                         Iudiciorum Astrorum (Great Introduction to
                         the Knowledge of the Judgments of the Stars)
                         On Historical Astrology: the Book of Religions   *OGC*
                         and Dynasties (On the Great Conjunctions)
                         The Abbreviation of the Introduction to   *Abbr.*
                         Astrology
                         The Flowers of Abū Ma'shar   *Flowers*

Al-Biruni: *The Book of Instruction in the Elements of the*   *Instr.*
                         Art of Astrology

Māshā'allāh: *De Receptione (On Reception)*   *OR*
                         De Revolutionibus Annorum Mundi (On the   *De Rev. Ann.*
                         Revolutions of the Years of the World)

Pseudo-Ptolemy: *Centiloquium (Centiloquy)*   *Cent.*

Ptolemy   *Tetrabiblos*   *Tet.*

Sahl ibn Bishr: *De Electionibus (On Elections)*   *On Elect.*
                         De Quaestionibus (On Questions)   *On Quest.*
                         Introductorium (Introduction)   *Introduct.*

'Umar al-Tabarī: *Three Books of Nativities*   *TBN*

Vettius Valens: *The Anthology*   *Anth.*

Table of Figures

TREATISE 9:
NATIVITIES

On nativities and their accidents, and other things which seem to pertain to those nativities, in general and in particular

Preface

Since it seems almost the entire purpose of astrology [deals with] two things, namely with nativities and with revolutions (but first of all with nativities, and secondarily with the others), to me it seems fitting and very appropriate to explicate faithfully, with an honest intention and the whole affect of my mind, what divine goodness has presented to me (according to what my tiny knowledge can lay bare) for the usefulness of those who are eager; and to follow in the footsteps of our predecessors, namely according to the abilities of Ptolemy, Abū Ma'shar, Hermes, 'Umar, Abu 'Ali, al-Kindī, Jirjis, Dorotheus, and of others who applied themselves both generally and in particular for our benefit in this work.

Chapter 1: An excuse why this Treatise was put off until now

Someone (of those wanting to study) should not wonder, nor should any hostile person (nor a maledictor or detractor) rise up, if the Treatise on nativities is placed after all the aforesaid Treatises, even though nativities precede all the named accidents in the other Treatises. Because even though a nativity (together with the native's accidents) comes first, still, of the knowable things taken together it is found more weighty and powerful. And therefore this Treatise rightfully should have been placed after all the other knowable things stated before. For it cannot be known by the crude, nor by those who must be introduced or in a certain manner have been introduced or by the great masses,[1] nor by any others except by the wise and the advanced. And therefore it is put after some other Treatises, because *they* can be known by less knowledgeable

---

[1] *Exuberatis.*

people. However, here it is not so. For no thing from the luminous circle[2] is found more powerful than a treatment of nativities. For through nativities it is necessary that all the native's accidents–which ought to happen to him naturally from the hour of the nativity up until the end of his life–be known; and likewise something may be said about him after his death.

Chapter 2: That two things are principally looked into, for the being of every man

Wherefore, two things are principally looked into for the being of any man (namely a first [beginning] and a second [beginning]). I believe[3] it will be fitting in this heading to make mention of each one (namely first[4] concerning the first, second concerning the second), and in which things it might be influential (even if I touched somewhat on these things elsewhere), and in what they differ, so that, of the things which will be stated, the order may be more rightly understood (since it is from God, because whatever is from God, is ordered).

---

[2] *A luminari circulo.*
[3] Reading *credo* for *crede.*
[4] Reading *primo* for *primus.*

PART 1

[On the first beginning]

Therefore[5] the start of the first beginning is the falling of seed into the womb, after which a fetus is generated–not suddenly, but in time. Whence, if the hour is had (which tends to happen in few [cases]), by that beginning is known what is going to be regarding that conceived child up until the hour of his exit from the maternal uterus. And the accidents of that conceived child will be according to the disposition, and according to the nature [or condition] of the surrounding stars, which will signify the accidents of the body up until it may be ensouled;[6] and [the accidents] of the body and soul immediately after the soul is infused, and onwards, while it remains in the uterus.

Because after the seed is injected into the womb, arrangement, variation, enlargement, increase, the composition of the members and their natural division, take place in it (and the nutritional adjustment of like to like[7]), concerning which certitude cannot be had (as it can be with respect to a nativity). For indeed the nativity is wholly an internal end, but its cause is an external end; indeed its operation is both an internal and external end.[8] For the beginning of

---

[5] The following sections seem to echo themes in *Tet.* III.2, but they are more expansive (even if occasionally convoluted).

[6] *Animetur.*

[7] *Similibus similium nutrimentalis adaptatio.* I believe Bonatti is referring to the interaction between the fetus and mother.

[8] Bonatti's argument, as usual, is stated incompletely but is very interesting, and offers a philosophical reason not to worry about conception charts. To put it briefly, Bonatti is arguing that a conception chart is like an electional chart, not like a nativity. The distinction he makes is between phenomena that are (a) "externally" dependent on something else for their being (or are the intended *result* of something else's will), and those that are (b) relatively self-contained and independent, and which will *themselves* to be. (a) The fetus is the external result of something else (i.e., the result of the parents' action). Therefore, while we can cast a conception chart that will show us the development of the fetus, we should think of such charts as being like electional charts: the parent's conception is like an action whose result we want to track. But we cannot track the results of the action/election beyond what it is the nature of the result to be. I cannot track the result of an election indefinitely, especially if the situation's nature changes after the success or failure of the election. Now the fetus's being is caused by the parents' action, and its development is determined by the external, ongoing factors of the environment of the womb: therefore a conception chart, like an election, would only pertain to the immediate development of the type of being the fetus is, *qua* created-by-parents. A conception chart can only show what a fetus will be as a *fetus*, not what it will be as a *native*. (b) On the other hand, a native is a different type of being. A native is a self-directed being who naturally wills himself, or whose will tends to actualize what he himself is. In life he will respond in this or that way, in accordance with the principles determined in the figure of the nativity. Therefore the natal figure shows what the *native* will be, and does not reach

the nativity is certain–the other [beginnings] are untrustworthy; wherefore if the falling of the seed into the womb is a complete beginning, the beginning of the nativity would already seem to be superfluous. However, the falling of the seed can be said to be an incomplete beginning, and likewise the other [beginnings] which are prior to the nativity. Nevertheless, knowledge of them can be had by a question, just as it seems a business transaction is renewed, [or] just as a [legal] case is renewed after the sentence, by means of an appeal.[9]

And if certain pretenders and detractors might say that the falling of the seed into the womb is the beginning for all accidents of the native up to the end of his life (which is manifestly contrary to all truth, and it agrees with falsity [to say] that the seed of a man makes a [legal] appeal[10]), it is not as they say: for no whole (or whole-like) part can advance [or grow] some thing without the aid of another; for incompleteness does not make for nobility. For one form cannot be in diverse materials, I reckon. Of those [individual] things which have a connection to each other, one can be destroyed without the other, before they are connected.[11]

---

back to the native's qualitatively different being as a fetus. Finally, because the native is self-directed but has to engage with the world, performing this or that project and encountering this or that thing, Bonatti says the native is both an internal and external end in the *operation* or *working out* (*operatio*) of what is prefigured in the nativity.

This argument is also interesting for two other reasons. First, it gives a philosophical reason for why transits before birth (insofar as they pertain to the *native's* future life) and like techniques are a dead end. Second, because a living native is both an internal end (because of the nativity) and an external end (because of interaction with the world), it offers a way of understanding how a fated life could also take advantage of horary and electional astrology. What is fated is what is prefigured in us, and it is also fated that some external events will affect us. But perhaps the interaction with the world provides us just enough opportunities, or "footholds," if you will, to take advantage of external circumstances that are not themselves prefigured in the nativity. Living, therefore, is a mixture of fate combined with real (even if unrealized) opportunities.

[9] Bonatti seems to mean that one should ask about unborn children by horary questions. By his analogy he is arguing that pregnancy is an ongoing process like a legal case or an ongoing business relationship. Just as one may hire an astrologer to check on the prospects of the ongoing legal or business process, so one may hire an astrologer to check up on the baby's progress–but only *in utero*. For more on this notion of an "appeal," see Tr. 6, Part 2, Ch. 4; Tr. 7, Part 1, Ch. 15.

[10] *Quod semen hominis appellatur.* This underscores the earlier point that the fetus is the development of the seed, while the native's life is the development of the native. A seed cannot go to court; a native can.

[11] *Numero eorum quae habent ad invicem connexionem unum potest tolli sine alio antequam connectantur.* Translation uncertain. Bonatti seems to be saying that (a) the fetus is not a distinct human being in the way the mother is. For example, having a baby is an accident of the mother, because she is a native. But being inside the mother is not an "accident" of the fetus because the fetus is not an independent native–its being is different. (b) When two essentially independent beings are connected, one can be destroyed without the other; but the fetus

For indeed, the falling of the seed is like a journey to the accidents of the one being born; the pouring [out of the amniotic fluid] is like a door; the nativity is then the entrance to [those accidents]. But it is superfluous [to say] that what can be had by one, or comes to be by one, comes to be by many; for it is not of the intention of Nature (who is always intent on what is better), to impede or complicate herself.

On the second beginning

The other beginning, namely the second one, is in respect of the accidents of the native from the hour of his nativity up to the end of his life. Whence these two beginnings differ in this, because the first is in respect of the accidents of the conceived child from the hour of the falling of the sperm up to the hour of the nativity–and in that hour, its disposition expires. Indeed the second one is more effective and true and noble than the first one in the whole being of the native (even though the form may be caused just like it is caused by matter); and therefore it is considered more noble from the hour of birth up to the end of his life.

Whence it is necessary at the hour of the nativity that all and every one [of the accidents] which are going to come to the native be had [in it]. Wherefore [this] principle is said to be the most certain; and the nativity is said to be such a beginning that it comprehends the accidents of the native taken as a whole, which does not happen in any one of the other [beginnings].

And it is a complete beginning, for which nothing is missing for the composition of the number of members,[12] wherefore in the nativity is found self-sameness[13] and certainty, and one and the same cause (therefore, not diversity); [but] in the other [beginning] is found a diversity of causes. And therefore the diversity of causes[14] diversify the effects, and they are multiplied according to how the causes are diversified and multiplied. For the purpose of the completion of the conceived child in the uterus, many things are aggregated together (and likewise diverse ones) into one thing, before he is born. But what is

---

cannot live without the mother. Therefore they are not independent beings with the same status (whether as biological creatures, or astrologically). This is to underscore his point that we should not treat the fetus (and its conception chart) as we do an actual native (and its nativity).

[12] I believe Bonatti is saying that it is complete because all of the houses (the "members"), and therefore all the areas of life, are contained in it.

[13] *Idemptitas*.

[14] Reading *causarum* for *effectuum*.

aggregated, is preserved through the one nativity alone (which is the peculiar property of the intention of Nature, who, insofar as she is in herself and from her own intention, always intends to prefer the more worthy and the better).[15]

And perfection makes for nobility: wherefore, while the conceived child remains in the uterus, it is in motion; and what is in motion, is not in a limit or in an end, but it is on a path,[16] namely in the operation of something incomplete which is conjoined to motion. However, if it is in a limit, it is in a perfection (for a limit or perfection, and a path or motion, are contraries of one another). Whence perfection cancels motion. For the conceived child is in the uterus; it is on a path until the umbilical ties[17] are severed in natural order—and then it is in a limit, wherefore it is already perfected or completed, and it has ceased to be on the path of the conceived child.

Then starts another beginning, namely the second one, which is the life of a man, in which it grows, is increased, is diminished, and breaks free. Nor can a child be called "perfected" before he is ensouled by a rational soul, since that is the first perfection. And knowledge and virtue are the second [perfection]. Indeed in a nativity each can be found, even if perhaps not everywhere nor in all ways blessed. But in the falling of the seed no perfection can be found; indeed the falling of the seed is an unperfected thing, from which many things are absent. Of something unperfected it cannot truly be said to be perfected (because something is missing from it).

And this beginning is called the being of a man, because the native then begins to use the five natural corporeal senses, which he could not use freely while in the uterus (and the delay of that is obviously sensed). And [the native's] growth employs even certain other accidents which he did not use (like speaking, laughing, weeping, and the like).

The being of the native is even aided by the virtue of the stars having power at the hour of the nativity in his qualities, even if it might seem to certain idle people that the stars do not help anything in the making of the native (which is far removed from the truth). For the stars aid the conceived child in perfecting

---

[15] I have personified Nature in this sentence, but Bonatti may also have in mind the Aristotelian view of the individual nature of something as being its own source of growth, self-preservation, and motion. This is in accord with his statement that a native is an internal end.

[16] Recall Bonatti's image of gestation as a "path" above.

[17] *Cotilidones.* Unknown word, but here and below Bonatti makes it clear he means the umbilical cord.

himself, and after the perfection, by leading him healthy from out of the maternal uterus.

And just as they helped him by informing[18] him after the falling [of the sperm] in the uterus before his rise [out of it], so they help him in nourishing [him] after the nativity. And since the truth of the matter conceals itself, it is necessary for you (at the hour of the infant's exit from the uterus) to observe the condition of the stars so that you may understand the quality of the body and soul of that native: like nourishment through the Lords of the triplicity of the Ascendant, [and] indeed through the direction of the Lords of the bounds. And through this you could prognosticate for him the status of the life and everything of his being as long he lives, according to the truth of the natural course [of things]; and to arrive at those things concerning which one would make mention about the diversities of nativities—and I will do this below in its own place and time, by means of the dissimilar accidents, and by the natural path of truth.

Of whatever kind was the condition the stars (and their dispositions) at the hour of the nativity, such will be all things of the native's being from his nativity up until the end of his life. Because the condition of the stars and their dispositions (with respect to being of the native and his dispositions) are like something containing; and the being of the native and his dispositions are like something contained; and the contained is moved by what contains. Whence the disposition of the stars moves the dispositions of the native, and draws them to his own being, unless perhaps free will works against that.

For the diversities and dissimilitudes are many, so that all things which come forth from the many stars by means of an intimately connected reason,[19] seem practically infinite—whose investigation seems to pertain more to what is natural than to the astrologer; therefore it must be left for what is natural (even though the astrologer cannot cross this with a dry foot without making some mention of them),[20] wherefore it cannot be fully expressed easily by his intention.[21]

---

[18] That is, by helping to provide form to his inchoate matter.

[19] *Ratione*, implying a rational principle to astrological effects.

[20] Again, whence we get the saying in English that one must "get one's feet wet" by trying something out, even if we are not able to fully engage in it.

[21] *Quoniam de levi sua intentio exprimi plenarie non posset.* Bonatti seems to be saying simply that the great variety in the possible effects of the planets on natural things is so complicated that even if we had the intention of addressing it, we would hardly be able to do so.

Chapter 3: How the being of the native should be examined

Now[22] you must see by what method (according to each kind of prognostication and according to the figure of its extent) the being of the native can be examined and openly grasped, and the powers of the stars over these things can be narrated, and by a natural path (as it pertains to the astrologer) the accidents of the native are truly comprehended, in order to reach the understanding of truth which we intend, both in particular and in general.

And since particulars are in universals in a particular way, according to the nature of each, it will be looked at below concerning them in its own place and time. Nor does it seem appropriate that a distinct discussion be had here on every one of the places of the figure. But concerning the Lords of the dignities, and which of them would prevail in this matter, and what is their peculiar nature, let it be stated in the required order that pertains to them, and let them be distinguished according to the turning around of the *at-tasīrāt*[23] (which belongs to the acting of the stars of heaven) rather than of those signifying the virtues of nativities, in the natural order, together[24] and step by step, following the successive significations of the houses. And by a subtle investigation it can be known more certainly, together with those things which are going to come to the native for the whole time of his life from the hour of the nativity, until his last day.

But what things are to be investigated first (in the aforesaid accidents)? It seems to me more fitting, in an inquiry into these accidents, to make the first teaching of the investigation of the degree of the ascendant of the nativity, then [on] the rest in order, as is proper.

Chapter 4: On the investigation of an unknown ascending degree

In order that your mind may be at ease in the relieving of a certain doubt (which most often seems to happen) concerning the finding[25] of an uncertain degree of someone's nativity (as exact as we can be concerning it), it is fitting, as I remember having said to you above (following the rules of the ancient sages,

---

[22] The following paragraphs either copy or adapt someone else's text. The style simply does not match Bonatti's usual one.

[23] Lat. *alachir*. This word (التسييرات) is spelled *athaȝir* in many medieval texts. It derives from the Greek *aphesis*, and pertains to primary directions. See al-Qabīsī, IV.11.

[24] Reading *iunctim* for *iunctatim*.

[25] Reading *inventione* for *intentione*.

and likewise that it seemed to me), that a special chapter should be added so that you can be truly made certain about the degree of the Ascendant of any sign and of any nativity.

And since the nativity is the first accident which happens to a conceived child after his full term and the severing of the umbilical cord, it is necessary for you to be rendered certain about the degree of his Ascendant, so that you could avoid all error, and even to assure the native about all of his accidents for the whole time of his life. And I want[26] you to know that the discovery of this matter is going to be of a most exact inquiry, even more so than may be found written in the books of the ancient sages–not that they were ignorant, but they left it to the industry of the wise.

What is the degree of the Ascendant of a nativity

But the degree of the Ascendant of a nativity, is the degree of the sign which is on the eastern line when a child is born, the umbilical cord having been severed. Nor is he said to be born immediately as he begins to appear from out of the maternal uterus, nor to be born when he has wholly gone out from it; but he is said to be born when two-thirds of him have appeared from out of it, and the remaining one-third remains hidden, naturally, without prolonging the time in his going out.[27]

And if you were to put down his Ascendant immediately when his last one-third goes out, not much perceptible error will fall in your work, nor will it impede perceptibly. If however some hindrance were to supervene, which would impede the natural method of being born by two complete thirds (and with the [last] one-third remaining to come out), which by a great effort of your will you could discover, you will have what is sought: for the degree which was then on the eastern line is called the Ascendant of the nativity (the aforesaid [points] about the appearance of the infant having, however, been observed).

The method of discovering the aforesaid degree

The method of discovering this matter, as the authority of our predecessors advises, is this.[28] For you will take the hour of the exit of the infant from the

---

[26] Reading *volo* for *nolo*.

[27] *Naturaliter sine tractu temporis egrediendo.*

[28] This is the technique of finding the *an-namūdār* (Lat. *animodar*, Ar. النمودار from al-Qabīsī IV.3; see also al-Bīrūnī, *Instruction* §525). Al-Bīrūnī seems to translate this as "indicator," but it seems to be a word of art of unknown origin (perhaps Persian). It is based on *Tet.* III.3.

maternal uterus just as best and most certainly as you can, with an astrolabe or any other instrument fit for this, like a quadrant or water-clock,[29] or any other instrument by which the hours are discerned (but with an astrolabe you would be able to be better certain than with any of the others); nor however with this could you be wholly assured to a fine point without hesitation; whence in order to remove every hesitation of doubt, and so that a certain and constructive[30] reckoning may be had, and so that you can [be assured] to a fine point concerning the aforesaid (from which you would have the hour of the nativity as near as you could), through yourself or through the instigation of another (either of midwives or the like), and so a certain and examined calculation could be exhibited to you, you will calculate the planets to the not-very-certain hour, and you will verify their places,[31] and the twelve cusps, and you will erect the figure according to the ascensions of the region in which you are, and you will then take the degree of the conjunction [of the luminaries] nearest to the nativity (if the nativity were conjunctional) or, if the nativity were preventional, the degree of the prevention (namely [the degree] of the luminary which was above the earth at the hour of the prevention).[32] Then you will look at the *al-mubtazz* in that degree, by domicile or by exaltation or bound or triplicity or by relationship with the Sun,[33] in the figure which you have erected for this.[34] Which if all of the aforesaid significators were impotent, impeded and made unfortunate, you would then use the Lord of the face.

---

[29] *Horologium.*

[30] *Constructiva.*

[31] *Loca.* In this case "places" seems to mean the exact degree, not the sign.

[32] Some authorities would have taken the position of the Moon–e.g., *TBN*, p. 6 (although Bonatti implied it is only in the search for the *hīlāj* that 'Umar means this: see Part 2, Ch. 1).

[33] In *Tet.* II.3, Ptolemy says "by phase or configuration." A phase or *phasis* exists when a planet makes (within seven days before or after the nativity) a morning or evening appearance, changes direction, or comes to a station. According to Schmidt (see forthcoming edition of *Tet.* II.3) "configuration" is not a synonym for "phase." So either Ptolemy is adding "configuration" (i.e., an aspect to the Sun) as a sixth member of the list, or else a configuration or aspect could be used in lieu of a planet making a *phasis* (since such planets are less common).

[34] Here Bonatti does not necessarily seem to want us to find a weighted-point *al-mubtazz*, because he includes the planetary phases of these rulers to the Sun. Perhaps he wants us to pick the planet with the best overall testimonies, taking into account all of these factors. That would accord rather well with Ptolemy (*Tet.* III.3), who also recommends that we look to see which of the rulers are most angular. But it is unclear from the text whether we are supposed to find the *al-mubtazz* in the chart of the *syzygy* and then look at its longitude in the natal figure, or find the *al-mubtazz* by looking at the rulers' condition in the natal figure alone. The same ambiguity is found in his other account, in Tr. 4, Ch. 8.

A teaching on the discovery of the aforesaid degree

The teaching of which matter is this: you will see if the Lord of the domicile were to aspect the sought degree (namely of the prevention or the conjunction), or [if] he were presently[35] in it (because the Lord of the domicile is to be preferred to all other significators). Which if this were not so and the Lord of the exaltation were to aspect it, he will be preferred to the Lord of the domicile and all the other significators. But if neither of them were to aspect, nor were in it, and the Lord of the triplicity were to aspect or were in it, you will consider him. Indeed if he did not aspect, you will observe the Lord of the bound by means of the aforesaid conditions.

Nor however would you judge according to this, unless first you were to see the strengths of all of these: because you will have to observe him who had more strengths in the aforesaid degree, unless the aspect of another works to the contrary. If however all the aforesaid planets (or many of them) were to aspect the aforesaid degree equally, he who has more dignities or strengths in it will be called the significator; and if they were in diverse degrees or minutes, and were different in number,[36] you will take the one whose number of degrees (in the sign in which he is) is nearer to the degree of the angle (if it were in an angle), or nearer to the Sun (if it were oriental). Which if it were not so, see which of them were nearer to the first or last degree of the bound in which it is, and you will put that one first before the others. But if all were equal in strength and dignity, you will put that one first who was nearer by aspect or presence.

Then you will look to that *al-mubtazz* over the degree of the conjunction or prevention, to see to which of the degrees of the cusp of one of the angles it is[37] nearer (namely of the Ascendant or the 10th, or the 7th or the 4th). Which if the degree of the planetary *al-mubtazz* were nearer to the degree of the cusp of the Ascendant than to the degree of one of the other angles, and the number of the degrees (which he had traveled through in the sign in which you were to find him) were equal to the number of the degrees of the sign of the Ascendant discovered for the ambiguous nativity (which you had first discovered by your consideration or by the instruction of another), that will be the Ascendant sought. If however they were different, then throw away that ambiguous degree of the Ascendant, and make the Ascendant like to the number of the degrees of

---

[35] This suggests that we are to look at the rulers' conditions in the natal chart.
[36] I am not sure what Bonatti means by this distinction.
[37] Reading *fuerit* (sing.) for *fuerint* (pl.).

the planetary *al-mubtazz* over the degree of the conjunction or the prevention; and construct the rest of the houses according to it.

If however it were closer to the cusp of the 10th house, make it the degree of the 10th house, and construct the angles and the rest of the houses according to that. You will give judgment likewise concerning the 7th and 4th.

Then you will discover, through your most subtle investigation, at what hour and at what minute of the hour that degree which you have so examined was ascending; or the degree of the cusp of some one of the angles (namely the 10th or its nadir, or the nadir of the Ascendant) was ascending–because that will be the considered hour of the nativity. And you must calculate the planets for that, and construct the houses according to the ascensions of the region in which the nativity was; and this will be its natural Ascendant–I say this, if you were to begin from the Ascendant. Indeed if you were to begin from the degree of the 10th house, you will begin from the beginning of Capricorn, and you will operate according to the direct circle, always by reducing the Ascendant into equal degrees; or you will find [it] according to the circle of the region, by beginning from the start of Aries up to the sought degree.

However, you have the degree of the conjunction from the degree in which the conjunction of the luminaries was. Indeed you would not be able to discover the degree of the prevention so easily. For according to Ptolemy it will be necessary for you to know the degree of the luminary which was above the earth at the hour of the prevention; wherefore that will be the degree sought. If however one of the luminaries were on the eastern degree and the other in the western degree, the eastern degree is preferred, and it will be the degree of the prevention.

Indeed Papiensis[38] said that the degree in which the Moon was at the hour of the falling of the seed in the womb, will be the degree of the Ascendant of the nativity, and conversely.[39]

Chapter 5: On the narration of the divisions of nativities, and of certain accidents of theirs

Our most reverend predecessor Ptolemy, wanting the accidents of nativities to be divided up according to a natural approach, took up this method of

[38] Undoubtedly Johannes Papiensis, who has been mentioned before.
[39] The fact that Bonatti tacks this point onto the end of his discussion, suggests that he does not give it much weight, but rather he includes it for information's sake.

division. For indeed he said that whoever wanted them to be divided naturally, will find what pertains to practicing this work.[40] For he said that certain accidents are those which happen before birth, and even after birth.

Before birth, like speaking about the brothers: because it is possible that certain ones [of them] exist before the birth of the native, from the same parents, and certain ones will be born after him. And certain [accidents] which come in that same hour of birth (and these are not one and the same, but diverse). And he said that the accidents which happen to the native in the hour of birth, which the astrologer intends to know, are many and diverse, like speaking about males and females; and whether the woman giving birth will give birth to twins (or even more), or not; and on monstrous forms, and about those who did not thrive.[41] And he spoke about accidents which happen after birth: they are to declare concerning the life, concerning which a rule is given, in two ways: one according to quantity,[42] the other according to quality.[43]

For indeed quantity is not varied except according to how it is given by the *hīlāj* and the *al-kadukhadāh*; for either it is long or short or in the middle. Indeed quality is varied in many ways, according to the dispositions and directions of the Lords of the bounds of the figure of the nativity. For one is good, another bad; one easy, another laborious; one large, another small; one miserable, another hoarding; one for the good, another for the bad; one chaste, another religious; one sinful or wanton; a certain one is in stealing and pillaging, one in making money and preserving, another in dissipating and devastating; one in ruling, another in serving; one in praise, another in blame; and by many other, practically innumerable means. The qualities of the life of natives are varied according to the diverse accidents of men, just as they come down from the diversities of the diverse motions of the supercelestial bodies, and by the actions of men and their free wills (as will be spoken of sufficiently below, in its own place and time).

---

[40] This is a paraphrase of portions of *Tet.* III.4, where Ptolemy simply seems to say that it will be obvious that some predictions pertain to the pre-natal state, some to the post-natal one (as Bonatti goes on to summarize in what follows).

[41] *Creverunt.* Ptolemy says "those who go unnourished," referring to a variety of cases in which children do not or cannot take nourishment (not, for example, infant exposure): see *Tet.* III.10.

[42] I.e., the length of life.

[43] I.e., all of the "qualities" or characteristics of the native's life given a descriptive delineation, like health, marriage, social status, *etc.* Ptolemy is therefore dividing his delineations and predictions into the following groups: (a) prenatal events; (b) events pertaining to the birth; (c) postnatal events, of which there are (c1) the length of life [quantity]; and (c2) concrete areas of life [quality].

Then [according to Ptolemy's order of topics] to speak about the form and shape of the native, then about the infirmities and impediments happening to the body, then about the qualities of the soul and about its accidents, then about the fortunes and misfortunes of the native, likewise about his kingdom and exaltation and loftiness, then about his works, then about his marriage and the period of time to be spent with the spouse, then what would happen to him from children, and from his close relationships with men, and about friends, and about his pilgrimages; lastly to judge the manner of his death.

And certain ones of the sages followed in his footsteps. I however, not so much by means of a contrary approach (even if a different one), but tending[44] toward the same end, will make mention to you concerning all things (or most of them) which pertain to the accidents of the nativity, following the succession of the houses and their significations, beginning from the first up to the twelfth, so that the work of nativities may be rendered easier, and you may succeed more handily in pursuing what you intend.

Chapter 6: On the causation of natives' spaces of time in the maternal uterus

The spaces of time of conceived children in the maternal uterus are caused by the dispositions of the supercelestial bodies, according to their three principal differences—which are the greater, the middle, and the lesser; to which certain other middles (among these) are subordinated.

For if you were to see the Moon in the upper part of her epicycle, going from the east to the west, in the hour of the falling of the seed into the womb;[45] or at the hour of a question made after conception, it is signified that the infant's space of time in the maternal womb is the greater one, which consists of 283 days from the hour (namely of the falling of the seed) up to the hour of birth. If however you were to find her in the lower part of the epicycle, going from the west to the east, it signifies that the stay was the middle one, which consists of 273 days—and this if, in the question, the Moon were distant from the degree in which she was at the hour of the fall of the seed, or from the degree which was then ascending, by exactly 90°. If however she were distant by more or less, it signifies that the circular motions will not be completed and then it was a certain other space of time in the middle between these (namely

---

[44] Reading *tendens* for *tendentem*.
[45] Bonatti means the Moon's location in the conception chart. See below.

between the greater and the middle). But if the Moon were right in the degree of the Ascendant of the falling of the seed, then it is signified that the space of time was the lesser one, which consists of 258 days.

Which if she were above the earth, distant from the east or from the west by more than 5°, it will be a certain other space of time in the uterus, in the middle between these (namely between the middle and the lesser). But if the Moon were directly in the opposition of the degree ascending at the hour of the fall of the seed, you could then be off by one month. Whence 'Ali said,[46] that in order to avoid that error, you should take the degrees which there are between the setting degree and the degree of the Moon, and double them, and divide by 24; and how many were to come out will be the days, and how many were to remain below 24, they will be the hours (because the Moon passes through one degree in two equal hours, according to her average course). Therefore, add these days and these hours to the hours of the lesser space of time, and what was collected together, will be the sought stay. Then you will subtract this stay from the days of the nativity, and you will have what you intend. If indeed it were an intercalary day, then add 5 hours and 59 minutes and with that which came to you within the tables, and calculate the Moon.[47] For the degree in which you were to find her then, will be the place in which she was at the hour of the fall of the seed. See, therefore, which degree will then be ascending; because it was the Ascendant at the hour of the fall of the seed.

Which if the Moon were below the earth, tending from the east to the west,[48] then you will take what there is between the ascending degree and the Moon (in terms of degrees and minutes), and divide by 24 as was said, and add to the middle space of time, subtracting what is collected from the days and the hours of the nativity, and with that which were to remain within the tables, and calculate the Moon to that hour; and according to the place in which you were to find her then, you will find the Ascendant of the falling of the seed, as was said above.

On the narration of the four species or varieties of nativities

It was said above that the species or varieties of nativities are four. Now we must make mention of each of them individually.

---

[46] Bonatti must be referring to 'Ali ibn Ridwān again, as I do not find this in al-Rijāl.
[47] *Et cum eo quod tibi devenit intra tabulas, & aequa Lunam.* I am not sure what Bonatti means here.
[48] This should probably read "the west to the east."

For as the ancient sages testify, the first of them will be that of abortions, who are born practically dead or half-dead, or of which life is not lengthened enough that they can take in any nourishment.

Indeed the second is that of those who take nourishment, but life does not last in them long enough that any perceptible benefit might follow[49] from it.

For indeed the third of them is [that of] those who take in nourishment and live through a month or years, but do not go beyond the years of childhood; and if they were to go beyond them, still they will not reach long life.

Indeed the fourth is that of those certain ones who take in nourishment, and life lasts in them until they reach their youth[50] (and sometimes they reach old age). And another [group] of these is subordinated to this, namely those who reach a decrepit age and die from old age (even though this happens to few, of which my uncle was one, whom I saw die without an obvious mishap, except that his vital spirits went away, a corpse having been left behind; for he had 120 years), concerning all of whom I believe will be looked at in an appropriate order.

And even though I said above I was going to open up my wings in this Treatise, and was going to show my powers, still I want you to understand my words well. For the business of nativities is a very high and subtle one, being in need of examination; whence I will not assume the highest form of expression, lest perhaps it might impede; nor a wholly humble one, lest perhaps you rubbish it; but a middling one, so that you might better succeed in pursuing what you intend and not judge that I had not observed what was promised to you.

---

[49] *Sequantur.* In this Treatise especially, Bonatti routinely uses the verbs *sequor* and *consequor* ("follow, pursue") in the opposite way he should. The object followed or pursued should be in the accusative, and the subject doing the following should be in the nominative. Thus if benefit (*utilitas*, the subject) follows the nourishment (object), he should say *sequatur...utilitas*, but he makes it read as though natives *pursue* the benefit, saying *sequantur...utilitatem*. It is possible that he means that natives seek benefit, but it sounds unnatural and this way of speaking does not always work in his uses of *sequor* below.

[50] *Ad iuventum.* "Youth" (*iuventus*) for Bonatti lasts roughly from age 20 to 40.

PART 2

Chapter 1: How one must look concerning the four species of nativities, in order

Mention having been made above that the distinctions of nativities are four (according to their four determinations in the first part of this Treatise which preceded this one, to which this one is subordinated), it now remains to speak in this second part about all of these in order; and first about those [natives] whose life does not endure in them long enough that they might take any nourishment.

The knowledge of which matter is that you should look at the degree of the Ascendant of whatever nativity, and its Lord; also the Lords of the triplicity of the degree of the Ascendant; and at the other angles and their Lords, even the degree of its luminary[51] and their[52] Lords.

And Abu 'Ali said that you should look likewise at the Lords of the triplicity of the Sun [by day, and the Lords of the triplicity of the Moon by night],[53] and likewise at Jupiter, and Venus, and the diurnal and nocturnal planets (in accordance as the nativity is diurnal or nocturnal). You should even look at the Part of Fortune and its Lord; likewise the Lord of the conjunction or prevention which was before the nativity itself.

Then you will look at the planet which was stronger than the rest in the aforesaid places, or in some[54] of them, and you will see whether it is only one, or if there were two or three. Which if there were only one, and he were cadent from the Ascendant or only from the angles, and one of the malefics were with him in the same degree, impeding him, or the degree of the Ascendant were impeded (namely so that one of the malefics is in it, not having dignity there), or [one of the malefics] were to aspect it by a square aspect or from the opposition, it signifies that the native will die before he takes any nourishment. You may say the same if the degree in which the luminaries were, were impeded.[55]

---

[51] I.e., of the sect ruler (the Sun in diurnal nativities the Moon in nocturnal ones).

[52] This must mean "of the other angles and of the luminary who is the sect ruler."

[53] Following *JN*, Ch. 1.

[54] *Aliquibus*, lit. "any" (plural).

[55] The procedure here suggests that we are *not* looking for a compound *al-mubtazz*. Moreover, it seems we are looking for extreme weakness, since Bonatti is looking to see if the *best* planet of all of these is severely weakened (or the Ascendant afflicted, *etc.*).

Indeed Ptolemy seems to have felt something different from that which the other sages felt, though not something contrary.[56] For it seemed to him that if the luminary whose authority it was, were impeded, and the degree of the Ascendant, and the Lords of the degrees in which the luminaries were, receded from the angles, the native will not taste anything until he dies. And he said that the hour of this matter[57] will be when the luminaries reach a malefic.

However, other ancients said that if all three Lords of the triplicity were to recede from the angles, and the luminaries were to recede, and their Lords, and the conjunction or prevention and its Lord were to recede, then the native will not taste anything until he dies; or the native will not be a human, or he will be of that minority[58] who are born with some unnatural signs, like those who have more limbs than they ought to, or are missing them, or they have them transposed, like I have often seen, of which certain ones were missing arms, others even hands, others feet, others legs, others had backwards knees, others were missing eyes; and I saw a certain one who had three arms, and another who had a hip-bone and leg in the place of an arm, and another who did not have an anus (and there was a certain foolish lay surgeon who wanted to make one for him, and he was so foolish that he perforated him below with a certain iron [instrument], and so killed him). And likewise in my own time there was a certain monster who was two people above the navel, and below it only one; and a certain one had one head, and from there below there were two bodies. Or the native will be of those who are born with some brute animal, as sometimes happens; like with a monkey or cat[59] or the like; or the mother would give birth to a monstrous thing, or the native himself will be a brute animal.

Which if it were so, and the aforesaid significators were all cadent as was said, and some one of the malefics were to impede the Lord of the Ascendant or the Moon or the *al-mubtazz* over the aforesaid places, or the *al-mubtazz* himself were a malefic, he will be a rough forest animal (like a wolf and the like),[60] not wanting to associate with others and especially with men. Indeed if

---

[56] This seems to be a generalized statement based on *Tet.* III.9-10, as I do not see Ptolemy saying this all in one place. Medieval astrologers tended to want to harmonize differing accounts, especially if Ptolemy was involved. This statement brings to mind a passage in Lilly (*Christian Astrology* III, p. 568), where he sides with the majority of authorities against Ptolemy, adding (in Latin): "It is stupid to believe one man over others, without a demonstration."

[57] I.e, the death of the infant.

[58] *Partibus*, i.e., the "portion" of births in which this happens.

[59] *Musipula* (translation from DuCange).

[60] Here is an ambiguity. Ptolemy also speaks of natives being *like* certain animals in behavior; and that is probably what Bonatti means here.

benefics and malefics were in charge (and especially if Mercury had some dignity in these places), he will be of those who associate with men, as ʿUmar says (like dogs and the like).[61] And my mother (who seemed to be a truthful enough woman), said that in her own time a certain woman gave birth to a cat.[62]

On the second species or distinction

The second species or distinction is that you should look at the ascending degree and the rest of the angles, and their Lords; even the degrees of the luminaries and their Lords, and the Lords of their triplicity (in accordance as the nativity were diurnal or nocturnal), even the Lords of the triplicity of the ascending degree, and the Part of Fortune and the conjunction or prevention which was before the nativity itself, and the Lords of the triplicity in which they were to fall; Jupiter also and Venus; and you would see the planet which is stronger in these places by the multitude of dignities,[63] which is called the *al-mudābit*.[64] If it were cadent from the angles, and one of the malefics were in charge over them, and there were some distance between the *al-mubtazz* and the malefic, it signifies that the native would take some nourishing, and he would live until the *al-mubtazz* reaches the malefic (or he to it), by body or aspect, that will first happen to him degree by degree; for then it signifies that the native will die after so many days or so many months or so many years.

If the malefic were impeded in an angle, and in a fixed sign, they will be years according to the quantity of degrees of distance which there is between the *al-mubtazz* and the malefic. If however it were in a succeedent, and in a common sign, they will be months. Indeed if in a cadent and in a movable sign, they will be days. But if it were in an angle and in a common sign, it will subtract one-sixth of those years. Indeed if it were in a succeedent, and a movable sign, it will subtract one-fourth of those

---

[61] *TBN*, p. 2.

[62] *Gattum* (translation from DuCange). One wonders if perhaps animal stories like this could have been invented by women having unwanted children, who needed a reason to kill the child afterwards (perhaps with the cooperation of the midwife). After all, the category we are dealing with are infants who die immediately.

[63] Clearly this is an *al-mubtazz*, as he says in the next sentence; but whether by weighted or equal points is unclear.

[64] Lat. *almudebit*. This word must be from the Ar. *dābit* (ضابط) which means a governor or official. I have not seen this word used before.

months. And if it were in a cadent in a movable sign, it will subtract one-third of those days.

Which if it were a benefic instead of a malefic, and it were in a cadent in a common sign, it prolongs the days by one-sixth. If however it were in a cadent and in a fixed sign, it prolongs them by one-fourth. But if it were in a cadent, in a movable sign, it prolongs them by one-third.

You may say the same about the ascending degree (and likewise about the degree in which the Moon then was), if it is joined with a malefic.

And if all of these (or many of them) were cadent from the angles, he will even taste food, but he will not be nourished. If however some one of the Lords of the triplicity of the Ascendant were in the cusp of the angle of the Ascendant, or of the 10th or 11th or 5th, or Jupiter or Venus were there, and it were free from impediments and from the malefics, it signifies nourishing, but not in a determinate way (namely whether it is going to be long or short), unless according to other testimonies which signify nourishing.

And if the aforesaid significators were impeded, look at the Lords of the triplicity of the Part of Fortune, and judge according to their nature [or condition], and according to how the Sun were to aspect the Part. You would say the same about the Lords of the triplicity of the conjunction or prevention. You could even say likewise if the Moon were besieged by the two malefics (of which one is in the first and the other in the seventh),[65] because his life will be short.

When these things will come to pass

Indeed, to know the time and hour when these things ought to come to pass, the degree of the Ascendant must be directed to the body of the impeding malefic, or to its square aspect, or to its opposition, by giving a day or a month or a year to 1°, according to how they were to signify days or months or years. And if the native has already passed through one year, you will consider next according to profections (namely by giving one year to every 30° by equal degrees, and a month to [every] 2° 30', and a day to every 5'; and an hour to

---

[65] I.e., in the first or seventh signs or places.

approximately every 12"); and when the number were ended, then the native will perish.

And 'Umar said,[66] look even in that hour to certain benefics, to see if they are in angles or in the optimal places, [namely, in] their own dignities,[67] or [look] to the planet who is more worthy in the degree of the Ascendant and the Part of Fortune,[68] because this signifies, according to the quantity of his strength and weakness, that the native's life will reach to years or months or days, according to the quantity of the donation of that planet from its own lesser years.

And he said, perhaps they will be days according to what Dorotheus thinks:[69] if the Lords of the triplicity of the Ascendant (namely the first and second and third[70]) were cadent, it signifies that the native will not be nourished (and especially if Saturn were in an angle in nocturnal nativities, and Mars in diurnal ones). And the hour of his death will be when the profection of some other year were to arrive at the angles, if the malefic were in the angle, when the year comes to one of the angles ([so] that the light of the square aspect of the malefic is there); and if the native were not dead in the first year, then he does what belongs to him.[71]

And ['Umar] said, it is thought in the *Book of Likenesses*,[72] wherefore if there were two *al-mubtazz*es, and one of them were impeded, the native will die, and the other would not be able to suffice [to keep the native alive]. Likewise if

---

[66] *TBN*, p. 3.

[67] Bonatti says "in the best places from their own dignities," but 'Umar says "in the best place, namely in their own dignities." I follow 'Umar here. This departs from my earlier statement that an "optimal place" suggests a whole sign which is in aspect to the rising sign, but perhaps this meaning is idiosyncratic to 'Umar.

[68] 'Umar's text reads somewhat differently and alludes to profections: "or the planet who is more worthy [with respect to / the more worthy of] the degree of the Ascendant, and the year and the Part of Fortune" (*gradu ascendentis, & anno atque parte fortunae*). The use of the ablative means either with respect to all three, or the better of the three–in either case, we are obviously supposed to compare the Lord of the Ascendant, and the Lord of the profected Ascendant of the year, and the Lord of the Part of Fortune (in the natal figure). Bonatti makes it seem as though we are to look for a compound *al-mubtazz* derived from all three together, which is not the intent of 'Umar's Latin translator.

[69] *TBN*, p.3. I am not quite sure to what passage in Dorotheus 'Umar is referring.

[70] 'Umar only mentions the first two Lords, and does *not* mention the third.

[71] 'Umar does not have this last (and ambiguous) phrase, but breaks off the sentence with "if he were not dead in the first year." This passage is ambiguous in both sources (Bonatti is virtually quoting 'Umar verbatim). There is a lot of "if" and "when" talk, but no conclusion. I have punctuated the sentences as best I can, and I believe it means that if the native is not dead in the first year, we are to look for a profection of the Ascendant to an angle *if* a malefic is in it.

[72] *In libro similitudinibus.* I do not know what book this refers to. See *TBN*, p. 4.

there were three [Lords],[73] and one of them were impeded, even though the other two are strong, that the native will last but his life will not be prolonged. Even if they were four, and one were impeded, or two, and the other were useful, again the child will remain longer, but his life will not be prolonged. If however three were impeded, even if the other is strong, the native will not live[74] (unless a strong benefic were to aspect the significator of that nativity); and the more strongly so, if the Moon were impeded and not received (if however she were free and received, it signifies the prolongation of life with regard to its shortness).

On the third species or distinction

Indeed the third species or distinction is that there is no *hīlāj* or *al-kadukhadāh* for the native from his own nativity, but the Lord of the Ascendant and the luminaries and the Lords of the domiciles[75] in which they were, are free from the aforesaid impediments (namely retrogradation, combustion, the corporal conjunction of the malefics, and their square aspect and opposition), and [free from] the Lords of the domiciles in which the malefics are, even if they were cadent from the angles or from the Ascendant, or they were impeded in the angles:[76] it signifies the staying of the native in the world and his nourishing, but his life will not be prolonged; and it will hardly or never come to be that it will be prolonged beyond twelve years, but he will die beforehand according to the quantity of degrees which are between the Lord of the Ascendant and the angle from which it[77] is cadent.[78]

And ['Umar] al-Tabarī said if the nativity were according to what we have said, we will put off speaking about such a nativity until the Ascendant reaches

---

[73] *Domini*, according to 'Umar, who now omits *al-mubtazz*.

[74] Here 'Umar stops—the rest of the passage seems to be Bonatti's own addition.

[75] 'Umar simply says "their Lords," which indicates the domicile ruler.

[76] 'Umar states it somewhat differently: "if [these significators] are free from the malefics, and from retrogradation or combustion, or cadent [but] free from the degrees of the malefics and their opposition or conjunction, also by the rulership of the malefics in them." I am unclear on exactly what 'Umar might mean by the latter phrase, but we would get an alternative reading if we read *domino* (Lord) for *dominio* (rulership): "also by the Lord of the malefics in them."

[77] Reading *fuerit* (sing.) for *fuerint* (pl.).

[78] This last predictive technique is not given by 'Umar in this passage.

one orb (namely [an orb] of twelve years),[79] namely [giving] one year per each sign (and this, on account of the cadence[80] of the significators).[81]

And he said, for as often as the orb of the Ascendant were to reach the bodies of the malefics, or the square aspect or opposition of any of them, it will be feared for him until the Ascendant runs through one orb. And he said, whenever it were to transit one orb, we will direct for him from the Ascendant, [giving] one year to every degree by the ascensions of the region in which the nativity was, until it arrives at the malefics, as was said in another species.

On the fourth species or distinction

Indeed the fourth species or distinction is like when the native has a *hīlāj* and *al-kadukhadāh*, and the aforesaid significators[82] are free–namely, the ascending degree and its Lord, and the Lord[83] of the triplicity of the degree of the Ascendant, and of the rest of the angles,[84] and their Lords, and the degree of the luminaries and their Lords, and Jupiter and Venus and the Lords of the domiciles in which they are; and the diurnal and nocturnal planets (according to whether the nativity were diurnal or nocturnal), and the Part of Fortune and likewise its Lord; and the Lord of the conjunction or the prevention which was before the nativity, and the planet who is the *al-mubtazz* in these places.[85]

On the discovery of the hīlāj[86]

The discovery of which matter is that you would seek it from the Sun in diurnal nativities; which if you were to find it the first[87] or eleventh or tenth, it will be fitting to take the *hīlāj* from it (whether it is in a masculine or feminine

---

[79] I.e., by profection of the Ascendant completely around the nativity, hence one "orb" or circle. The native's life (signified by the Ascendant) would be fundamentally affirmed or denied by its return in the twelfth year, because it will have circled back to itself.

[80] *Casum*, lit. "the falling."

[81] This parenthetical remark is Bonatti's.

[82] 'Umar calls these the "Lords of the nourishment," and refers the reader to the prior passages. The list here is Bonatti's.

[83] *Dominus.* Note that he mentions only one Lord.

[84] This suggests he means "the Lord of the triplicity of the rest of the angles," since their domicile Lords are mentioned next.

[85] Again, note Bonatti does not say "of" these places, suggesting again we are not looking for a compound *al-mubtazz.*

[86] *Ylem.*

[87] 1491 gives the neuter or masculine for the first of these, but employs numerals for the rest. I will follow this lead and treat them all as indicating whole sign houses, unless the text reads otherwise.

sign). Indeed if it were outside these places, in the seventh or eighth or ninth, and in a masculine sign, it must be put down as the *hīlāj*.

And 'Umar said,[88] know that the Sun or the other places[89] which are used as the *hīlāj* could not be a *hīlāj* unless the Lords of the domiciles (or exaltations or triplicities or bounds or faces) were to aspect them (according to how it seemed to Abu 'Ali concerning the Lords of the faces).[90] If however the Lords of one of those dignities did not aspect, the Sun will not be fit to be the *hīlāj* nor the Lord of that dignity.[91] (You will pronounce likewise concerning the Moon in the day and night; and concerning the Part of Fortune and the ascending degree, and even the degree of the conjunction or prevention.)

Again, if the Sun were not fit to be the *hīlāj*, you will take the *hīlāj* from the Moon; which if you were to find her in an angle or in a succeedent, and in a feminine sign, and one of the Lords of one of the four[92] aforesaid dignities were to aspect her, she is fit for this, so she would be the *hīlāj*.

And if the nativity were preventional, then the *hīlāj* is to be sought from the Part of Fortune. If however it were conjunctional, seek it from the ascending degree (which will signify [the *hīlāj*] if one of the aforesaid significators were to aspect it or the Moon)[93]–and it is to be put before the Part of Fortune if it were so. If however one of them did not aspect it, it will not signify the *hīlāj*.

Which if the ascending degree were not then with the *hīlāj*, you will look at the Part of Fortune: which if it were with the *hīlāj*, or with the degree of the Ascendant of the nativity, it will be *hīlāj*; if however not, not.[94]

Which if neither of them could be the *hīlāj*, seek it then from the degree of the conjunction (if the nativity were conjunctional) or from the degree of the prevention (if it were preventional). However, 'Umar seemed to want that it be sought from the degree in which the Moon was at the hour of the prevention in this case.[95]

---

[88] *TBN*, p. 5.

[89] *Loca.* The context suggests this indicates the exact locations of the other candidate *hīlāj*es.

[90] That is, 'Umar does not mention the faces, but Abu 'Ali does ("the five essential dignities," *JN*, p. 4).

[91] By "dignity," Bonatti means the *hīlāj* as a kind of rulership over the native. See the following paragraph.

[92] Bonatti is quoting 'Umar, who does not use the Lord of the face.

[93] This parenthetical remark is Bonatti's.

[94] I do not know what Bonatti means by being "with" the *hīlāj*, since the *hīlāj* is what we were seeking (and 'Umar does not say this). But perhaps, on the basis of his prior remark, he means "with the Moon," who was the favored nocturnal *hīlāj*.

[95] *TBN*, p. 6.

Which if again, one of the aforesaid significators did not aspect the aforesaid degrees, then the *hīlāj* will be made useless, and the native will have a short life.

And if one of them *were* to aspect the degree [of whatever *hīlāj*], he himself will be called the *al-kadukhadāh* and the giver of years. But of all of the aforesaid significators (namely the Lord of the domicile, and the Lord of the exaltation, and the Lord of the bound and the Lord of the triplicity), he who is closer to the degree by aspect or by conjunction will be the *al-kadukhadāh* or giver of years, whether the aspect were in front or behind.[96] If however all were to aspect equally, that one will be called the *al-kadukhadāh* who is stronger in his own place, and were to have equal dignity (namely, exactly one). If however one of them were to have more dignities than the others, he will be called stronger than the rest, and he will have to be preferred to all, provided that he aspects the aforesaid degree, even if the distance between the degree of the *hīlāj* and the other one of the aforesaid significators (who did not have but one dignity in the degree of the *hīlāj*) were the lesser one.[97]

On the certifying of the years of the native and his life

Indeed, after you were to establish, and you were made aware of, the *hīlāj* and the *al-kadukhadāh*, you could be made certain about the years of the native and his life (and concerning his life, namely, whether it is going to be long or short, healthful or dangerous), and you could be made certain about his good or bad accidents, and his prosperities, likewise about his adversities. For the *hīlāj* signifies the root of life, the *al-kadukhadāh* the number of its years; wherefore the status of the life is taken from the *hīlāj*, the giving of years is taken from the *al-kadukhadāh*; but still, neither of them suffices for giving life to the native without the other. For, just as a man alone does not suffice for generation, neither does a woman alone suffice for conceiving or begetting; for one cannot beget without the other.[98] For the *hīlāj* gives life formally, the *al-kadukhadāh* gives it effectively.[99]

---

[96] I believe that by "in front," Bonatt means "in a later degree," so that the *al-kadukhadāh* is moving toward the degree of the aspect. By "behind" he means "in an earlier degree," so that the *al-kadukhadāh* is moving away from the degree of the aspect.

[97] In this paragraph Bonatti seems to be relying more on Abu 'Ali than on 'Umar. 'Umar also seems to favor aspects to the bound in which the *hīlāj* is.

[98] This is Bonatti's paraphrase of a comment inserted into 'Umar's text by his Latin translator: "And know that '*hīlāj*' utters a term which, in Latin, can be called 'wife,' and likewise '*alcochoden*' utters [a term which can be called] 'husband' from this signification; because just as a woman cannot rule her own house well without the help of a husband, so in the matter of

Again on the certifying of the years of the native

However, if you would see the years of the native and their number, you will consider the disposition of the *hīlāj* and the *al-kadukhadāh*, and you will see how many years are attributed to the native. You will even see if years would be given to him through the *al-kadukhadāh* or through another, just as sometimes happens.[100] Because if they are given through the *al-kadukhadāh*, it will be plain what you must do. Indeed if they would be given to him through another, you will see whether the years of the *al-kadukhadāh* are equal to the lesser or middle or greater [years of that planet] (which happens most rarely in this), or [whether they are] a little less.

And you will see in which of those years the *hīlāj* arrives at the bodies of the malefics, or to the places[101] in which they were in the nativity, or to their square aspect or the opposition; or to the Tail of the Dragon, or to the degree in which [the Tail] was in the nativity, or to the square aspect of the place in which the Moon was in the nativity (or to its opposition), namely by giving one year to each degree according to the degree of that region[102] (and [provided that] one of the benefics did not project its own rays to the bound in which the *hīlāj* reached the impeding malefic)–it signifies that the native will die in that year or month or day, namely at the hour in which the arrival of the *hīlāj* to the aforesaid places[103] (or to some one of them) is perfected.

But if the aforesaid years were not equal to the years of the *al-kadukhadāh* nor similar to them, and the *hīlāj* were to arrive at the impeding malefic (as was said) or to the aforesaid places,[104] without the aspect of any one of the benefics, the native will be burdened by the most powerful impediment, so that one will practically lose hope that he will not be imperiled; and he himself will fear the

---

the *hīlāj* it does not suffice to signify the years of the native without the authority of the alcochoden."

[99] This last statement recalls two of Aristotle's causes or types of explanation. The "formal" cause states *what* something is, the "efficient" or "moving" cause states what actions cause it to be. The idea here seems to be that the *hīlāj* is responsible for the native being a human in such a way that his life is established, while the *al-kadukhadāh* acts to preserve that life for a certain number of years.

[100] 'Umar alludes to "another place" which can act as the *hīlāj*, but does not say what it is. I do not know what planet Bonatti might mean, although I suspect it is something like the *al-mubtazz* of the whole figure.

[101] *Loca.*

[102] I.e., by oblique ascensions.

[103] *Loca.*

[104] *Loca.*

same, that he would die. In the end, however, he will escape it, unless perhaps he will be imperiled by error. But if a benefic were to project its rays to the *hīlāj*, the native will be burdened then, but one will not have to fear so much about him then.

Chapter 2: On the diversity of opinion which exists concerning the *hīlāj*

However, there was diversity on the *hīlāj* among the wise, even if not contrariety. Because it seemed to Ptolemy that the *hīlāj* is not to be sought in the 8th, because the Ascendant does not have any help in it,[105] and it is a dark place,[106] nor does it aspect [the Ascendant]. However in the 9th it is otherwise, because it is of the triplicity of the Ascendant[107] and of its kind, and because the Sun rejoices in it, and it is [the Sun's] foundation. Which if the Sun were in the 9th in someone's nativity, and he were otherwise well disposed, the native will have a good and likewise honest life, and one of good durability.

Indeed to Dorotheus it seemed that the *hīlāj* is not to be sought from the 8th, nor from the 7th, unless it is in masculine signs.[108] And he said that if the Sun were in these two houses [domiciles?], he is not fit to be the *hīlāj* in feminine signs, because his strength is weakened in them, and made effeminate. And it seemed to him that the Sun would be *hīlāj* in nocturnal nativities in places opposite these masculine signs.[109]

But Ptolemy did not make mention of the sex of the signs, wherefore it seems fitting to me that you observe the opinion of Dorotheus if you can, for it is safer; but the opinion of Ptolemy is not to be thrown out.

If however the Sun, in diurnal nativities, were not in masculine signs in the aforesaid places, he will not be fit to be the *hīlāj*. Then it will be necessary for you to seek the *hīlāj* from the Moon. Which if you were to find her in one of the angles or the succeedents, she will be fit to be the *hīlāj*, nor will you care about the sex of the signs (namely whether they are masculine or feminine); however, in the nativities of women she will be more useful in a feminine sign; in the nativities of men, in a masculine sign. And in this all agree: that the Moon is fit to be the *hīlāj* in the 3rd, because she rejoices in it, and it is her foundation.

---

[105] *Tet.* III.11. Lat. *eo*, signifying a place or sign.

[106] *Locus.* Here, *locus* (house) is distinguished from *locum* (exact position).

[107] Again, which would only be guaranteed when using whole-sign houses.

[108] *TBN*, p. 7.

[109] Again, Bonatti is following 'Umar's text, which is somewhat confusing on this point.

However, concerning the 9th there was a difference [of opinion] among them): for to Dorotheus it seemed not to be certain that the Moon could be the *hīlāj* in this place,[110] because she is impeded then; indeed to Ptolemy it seemed that she could be the *hīlāj* in the 9th, but it is necessary for her to be in a feminine sign.

And 'Umar said that if the Moon were not in these places, and the nativity were conjunctional, the *hīlāj* will be sought from the degree of the Ascendant of the nativity. Indeed if it were preventional, it would be sought from the Part of Fortune (which is called the "Ascendant of the Moon"); and you will put the degree of the Ascendant last. And the sages put the Part of Fortune first in a prevention, because then the Moon is in the full amount of her whole light from the side which we see of her, and she is in charge of the whole night. In conjunctional nativities however, we must begin from the Ascendant, because then the Moon is deprived of all of her light.

But if the *hīlāj* is sought from the Part of Fortune, and it were to signify [the *hīlāj*], and it were in the angles or the succeedents of the angles, you will not care whether it is in a masculine or feminine sign. Which if you were to seek [the *hīlāj*] from the Ascendant of the nativity, nor were the Ascendant impeded, even if the Part of Fortune is not there, still it will be the *hīlāj*. And 'Umar said[111] you will not care whether it is cadent from the angles or not, because the Ascendant itself will be[112] an angle. And he said there is nothing in [the Ascendant] which must be sought which is feared concerning the condition of the other places of the *hīlāj*–namely from what is profitable or improfitable. For it is possible, like if the aforesaid places[113] are in places of profitability,[114] for the Ascendant does not cease being in [a place of] profitability.

And ['Umar] said, indeed if the Sun or the Moon or the Part of Fortune or the Ascendant were not appropriate for the *hīlāj*, look at the conjunction or the prevention which was before the nativity, to see which of them the Sun or the Moon or the Lord of the Ascendant (or others of the benefics) were to aspect, and to see [if] it were in an angle or a succeedent to an angle–it will be the *hīlāj* (nor will you care whether the sign is masculine or feminine).

---

110 I.e., the 9th. See *TBN*, p. 9.

111 *TBN*, p. 10.

112 'Umar says it is "in" an angle, which suggests that the degree of the Ascendant is in an angular *sign*.

113 *Loca*.

114 Omitting *vel improfectus* here, which belongs earlier in the sentence. 'Umar says simply, "For it is possible, like if the aforesaid places are in profected [advanced] places."

On the knowledge of the al-kadukhadāh

And if you knew the *hīlāj* and you wished to know the *al-kadukhadāh*, who is called "the divisor," you will consider the said four significators (namely the Lord of the domicile in which the *hīlāj* is, the Lord of the exaltation, the Lord of the bound, and the Lord of the triplicity), and the one of them you were to find more fit, make him the *al-kadukhadāh*, beginning from the Lord of the bound: which if you were to find him projecting his own rays to the bound itself, put him [down] as the *al-kadukhadāh*. Which if you did not find [him] thus, look then at the Lord of the domicile and operate through him just as you did with the Lord of the bound; then through the Lord of the exaltation, [and] afterwards through the Lord of the triplicity. Which if you were to find none[115] [of them] fit for this, you will use, lastly, the Lord of the face (even though his signification is weak). And may you understand this if their dignity[116] were the same and equal (namely, that of any of them).

If however all were to aspect equally, and one of them were to have more dignities than one, he who were to have two will be preferred to another having only one; and he who were to have three, will be preferred to one having two, and he will be said to be stronger. If however, all were equally strong (in terms of dignities or testimonies) he will be preferred who is in an angle or in a succeedent. If indeed they were all in an angle or in a succeedent, he will be called stronger who is closer to the cusp of an angle or of a succeedent. Indeed if they were equal in strength and dignity in the place of the *hīlāj*, and they were equally in an angle or a succeedent, he who is in his own dignity will be preferred to another who is peregrine or his own lesser dignity than [the other].

But if all were equally equal in all of the aforesaid strengths, he will be preferred who is oriental. And if all were oriental, he will be preferred who is closer to the Sun, whether cosmically or heliacally rising (provided that he is not combust). And if the Sun were in the eastern line, he will be preferred to the rest of the significators. And if one of the planets were in the Ascendant, or in the 10th, not distant from the line of the cusp by more than 3° ahead or more than 5° behind,[117] make him a participator with the *hīlāj*, whether he has dignity

---

[115] *Neuter*, lit. "neither."

[116] That is, if they had the same number of dignities in the place of the *hīlāj* (see below). We do not look yet to see what kinds of dignities the Lords have in their *own* places. Note also that in this situation 'Umar (whom Bonatti is following) does not seem to assign points to each *kind* of dignity, but each dignity itself seems to count as a single one.

[117] I believe that by "ahead of," Bonatti means "in an earlier degree than the cusp's"; by "behind," he means "in a later degree than the cusp's." See my Introduction.

there or not; but if he were to have a dignity there, he will be stronger than one who is outside the aforesaid places,[118] even if their dignities are equal; and not to mention if it were equal, or rather if the one not present were to have one dignity, or even two more than him.[119] However he who is present will be stronger in the aforesaid places, as I said. If however he did not have a dignity there, his participation will be weak and not particularly successful.

And [Dorotheus said][120] if some one of the three [superior] planets were oriental, and it were in the *kasmīmī* of the Sun, or before its own second station, or after it by a space which it could travel in seven days, and it were to have some dignity in the place of the *hīlāj*, and it were otherwise well disposed, the *hīlāj* and *al-kadukhadāh* could be found from it, unless the Lord of the bound of the degree of the *hīlāj* works against it.

And it seemed to Ptolemy that an aspect[121] is one strength of a planet [for purposes of] the *hīlāj* and the *al-kadukhadāh*, and that a planet who had three dignities, even if he does not aspect, is stronger than him who had only one and did aspect; nor however does this contradict the other philosophers who said that he who had one will be stronger if he were in the aforesaid places; because he understood [this to be] about those aspecting and not about those present in the places. And he said that that planet is more worthy (so that he would rule) who were to have more dignities in the Ascendant, and in the places of the luminaries, and in the Part of Fortune, and[122] in the degree of the conjunction or prevention which was before the nativity. And he said that if there were some planet who had dignity in three or four places (or at least in two), we will set him up as the *al-mubtazz* over the nativity.[123]

---

[118] *Loca.*

[119] In other words, it is better to be in a good place with one dignity, than outside it with two dignities.

[120] This passage is a poor paraphrase of 'Umar, who attributes this material to Dorotheus and specifically mentions the three superiors only. Dorotheus's view is based on the concept of a *phasis*: he means that if one of the superiors will make a station or change direction, or make an appearance outside of the Sun's beams (i.e., be visible) within seven days before or after the nativity, and it is in the bound of "[one of] these three," it will be the "governor" of the nativity. 'Umar's own text reads: "Dorotheus said that Saturn and Jupiter and Mars, if they were pertaining-to-arising, or with the Sun in one degree, or in one of the stations, or before these places [*loca*], or after [the nativity] by seven days, while they thence had some testimony in the *hīlāj*, [the superior in question] will govern or be in charge of the *hīlāj*." I note that Dorotheus specifically says we cannot use these planets if they are so close to the Sun that they cannot rise within the time specified (i.e., what is usually called "combust").

[121] Refer above to the ambiguity in Ptolemy's doctrine.

[122] Reading *et* (with Ptolemy) for *vel* ("or"). Bonatti is following 'Umar (*TBN*, p. 13).

[123] This seems to mean the *al-kadukhadāh*, but note that this phrase anticipates other designations for a planet authoritative over the nativity–the "significator of the native," for

On the knowledge of the years of the native

After this[124] we will look at the place of the *al-mubtazz* in order to know the years of the native: which if it were oriental and in an angle, and in addition he were in his own *haym* (as a masculine planet in a masculine sign, and above the earth, and a feminine one in a feminine sign and below the earth)[125] and it were in own of its own aforesaid dignities (which are domicile, exaltation, triplicity, [bound],[126] and face–as it seemed to certain people concerning the face), and it were in the Ascendant or in the 10th, and in its own *haym*,[127] then it will give its own greater years.

And Abu 'Ali said[128] that if the Sun were the *hilāj*, and were in Aries or Leo, nor did one of the Lords of his five dignities aspect him, he himself will be the *hilāj* and the *al-kadukhadāh*. It is likewise concerning the Moon if she were in Taurus or Cancer, with the aforesaid conditions.

And Ptolemy said,[129] if however if it were oriental and in a succeedent to an angle (and especially in the eleventh), and in one of its own aforesaid dignities, and were free from impediments, then it will give the middle years. Which if it were in the cadents, even if it is otherwise free, then it will give its own lesser years. If indeed it were cadent, and were otherwise impeded (namely retrograde, or in the opposition of one of its own domiciles or its own exaltation; or it were peregrine, or besieged by the two malefics) then it will give months instead of those years; or perhaps it will give weeks instead of months. But if it were combust in addition to one of the aforesaid impediments, it will signify, and it will give, hours instead of those years; or at most it will signify days. Abu 'Ali esteemed all of the angles to be equal in giving greater years; and all of the succeedents in giving middle years; indeed the cadents in giving lesser years.

---

instance, and others which we will see soon. This formulation also suggests that perhaps the *al-kadukhadāh* is meant to be the "Lord of the Geniture" or the *al-mubtazz* of the figure itself– see for instance, the material on character traits in the 12th House, Ch. 2.

[124] I believe this is based on *JN*, p. 5–but Abu 'Ali does not mention *haym*.

[125] This sentence and parenthetical remark is based on 'Umar, who nevertheless breaks off by saying, "above the earth, *etc*." Bonatti seems to be emphasizing a best-case scenario, i.e., *hayyiz*: (a) the planet being in a sign of its own gender; and (b) if feminine, below the earth in a diurnal figure and above it in a nocturnal one; or if masculine, above the earth in a diurnal figure and below it in a nocturnal one.

[126] Adding *terminus* from 'Umar.

[127] Note that Bonatti repeats this condition.

[128] *JN*, p. 5.

[129] This must be based on a pseudo-Ptolemy.

When the planets increase years

Indeed, after you come to know the *al-kadukhadāh*, who is called the giver of years, see whether he is aspected by one of the planets or were joined corporally to it. You will even see whether he to whom he is joined, or the one who aspected him, is a benefic; and by what aspect it aspects him: because if it were to aspect him by a trine or sextile aspect, and it were a benefic, and that benefic were made fortunate and strong, it will add its own lesser years to him, and so many months as are its middle years. If however it did not receive[130] him, however, by the aforesaid conditions, it will add its own lesser years to him, and besides that so many days as are its own lesser years. You may say the same if it were to receive him from a square aspect or the opposition. If however that benefic were impeded, it will add months to him according to the number of its own lesser years.

When planets decrease years

Indeed if it were a malefic who aspected him, and it aspected him from a square aspect or from the opposition, or were joined corporally to him, it will subtract [from] him from its own years, according to the number of its own lesser years. If however it were made fortunate and strong, it will subtract [from] him only according to one-third[131] of its own lesser years.[132]

And Mars is of greater harm than [any] other of the malefics. Indeed Mercury is convertible, because if he were with those increasing, he will increase the years of the native according to the number of his own lesser years. Indeed if he were with those decreasing, he will take away the same amount.

On the Head of the Dragon and its Tail

Indeed al-Kindī said,[133] the Head of the Dragon, if it were with the *al-kadukhadāh* by 12° before or after, that it will subtract one-fourth of the years

---

[130] Reading *reciperit* (sing.) for *reciperint* (pl.). I am not exactly clear who is supposed to be receiving whom, so I have decided to say "it" (the benefic) is receiving "him" (the *al-kadukhadāh*).

[131] Reading *partem* for *partes*.

[132] Bonatti confirms this formulation in the delineation of the mother's longevity below. It is clear that when planets take away years, they take away according to the number of *their own* years, not according to whatever years are signified by the *al-kadukhadāh's* greater, middle, and lesser years.

[133] Bonatti must be referring to the unnamed astrologer in al-Rijāl, p. 155.

[of the *al-kadukhadāh*]–which however I have not proven (that I remember); [but] regarding the Tail, it is so. And it[134] harms more if it were with the Moon than with another of the significators.

The years of the native are even altered otherwise, and they are given out of the virtue of someone's nativity by his own children coming after him ([or] of those, the one who survives), just as the years are altered by means of the revolutions after nativities. And on this you will find it stated below in the chapter on the father.[135]

On the direction of degrees to planets, for knowing the accidents of the native

After you were to discover the number of years of the native's life which are signified by the *al-kadukhadāh*, and you wished to know about the accidents of the native and about his condition, direct his *hīlāj* to the rays of the malefics, from the square aspect and the opposition, and from their corporal conjunction in one sign, and even from their trine or sextile aspect. And you will give one year to each degree of distance which there is between them, up to the completion of their conjunction, minute by minute, by the degrees [of oblique ascension] of that region (and a month to every 5', and six days to every minute, and one day to every 10", and one hour to every 25 thirds[136]).

And see when the *hīlāj* were to arrive at the rays of the malefics, or to the degrees in which the malefics (or their rays) were at the hour of the nativity: because if the *hīlāj*-significator or the *al-kadukhadāh* were then badly disposed, the accidents of the nativity will be burdened, and horrible things will come to be. Which if the *hīlāj* were to arrive at some one of the malefics, or to one of the aforesaid places to be feared, nor did one of the benefics project its own rays to that place, and that year was the last one of the years of the native which were given to him by the *al-kadukhadāh*, the native will die in that year, and in that month and that day and that hour, by such a death as the giver of years signified for him in his own nativity. If he survived up until he ought to, that is, that he was not overcome by an accidental death (as often happens), and more strongly and certainly and infallibly so if the malefic were to impede the Lord of the Ascendant of the nativity, and the Lord of the Ascendant of the revolution of

---

134 Bonatti means the Tail.

135 See the chapters below in Part 3 on the 4th house, where Bonatti says a father's longevity may also be given by techniques applied to his children's (i.e., the native's) figures.

136 I.e., where a "third" is a further subdivision of every second into 60 portions. If 1 day = 10 seconds, then 1/24 of a day (i.e., one hour) = 10/24 seconds = .416 seconds. .416 x 60 = 25 "thirds."

that year, and the Lord of the profection of the same—or he and another malefic were to impede all of the aforesaid significators; nor will there be but one remedy there, that is, if the malefic were in a greater latitude, or in a lesser one, than the *hīlāj* is, so that they will not block each other by a straight diameter, so that the deviation of one from the other is more than 1° (unless perhaps it is by divine miracle); but if the their deviation were as I said, he will not die except perhaps through the fault of those going astray, or a force of nature should come; still, he will be imperiled by a danger like death.

You will even employ the fixed stars which are of the nature of the impeding malefic, in their own latitudes, just as you employ the impeding malefic [above]. And you should not make your direction unless you were to look first at the latitudes of the planets and of the fixed stars, as I said.[137]

However, in other years, if the *hīlāj* were to arrive at the aforesaid places without the projection of the rays of any benefic, the condition of the native will be burdened, and horrible contrary things will happen to him (not, however, dangerous ones). But if a benefic does project its own rays to that place, the native will not be impeded by a serious impediment. And however often the *hīlāj* were to arrive at the benefics, or to the places[138] in which they were (or to the places[139] in which their rays were) at the hour of someone's nativity, without the projection of the rays of some malefic, so often will prosperous and even pleasing things happen to him. If however a malefic were to project its own rays to it, it will subtract from the goodness (however it will not subtract much; still, according to more and less in accordance with how he were disposed). Likewise, whenever the *hīlāj* were to arrive at the malefics or to the places[140] in which the malefics were (or their rays) at the hour of the nativity, without the projection of the rays of some benefic, so often will contrary and horrible things happen to him, and his condition will be made worse. Which if a benefic were to project its own rays to the aforesaid places,[141] it will subtract from the malice of the malefic, in accordance with how it were disposed. Which if the *hīlāj* were to arrive at a malefic [who had been] impeding at the hour of the nativity, or to any aspect of his, nor did the malefic receive it by perfect reception, and the malefic himself were impeded, it signifies the death of the native in that year, as is said elsewhere.

---

137 This passage shows Bonatti recommends figuring planetary latitude in primary directions.
138 *Loca.*
139 *Loca.*
140 *Loca.*
141 *Loca.*

**Chapter 3: That all of the planets are givers of years,
but not all are preservers of them simply; but rather sometimes
they are killers, certain ones naturally, certain ones accidentally,
[and] likewise the Head and Tail**

All of the planets are givers of years (and even the Head and Tail of the
Dragon), but following a different organization; but not all are custodians or
conservators of [years] simply; but rather certain of them are naturally killers
(obviously Saturn and Mars, and the Head and Tail of the Dragon). And even
certain others [are] killers besides the rest, even if not naturally so, but more by
accident (and there are thirteen)–so that all of the killers are seventeen, namely
the aforesaid four [which kill] naturally, and the other thirteen [which kill] by
accident–certain ones by time, certain ones by the position of places.

[5] For the Sun kills by corporal conjunction, and by the square aspect,
and by opposition.

[6] The Moon likewise kills by corporal conjunction with the Sun,
whether she is the *hīlāj* or not (unless she is in the *kasmīmī* of the Sun);
and when she is in his square aspect or in his opposition.

[7] The Moon even kills if she were to arrive at the degree of the Ascendant of the nativity without the aspect of a benefic (if she were the *hīlāj* in
the nativity), and it was the degree of the Ascendant of some revolution:
then the native will perish, because her [nature] is inimical to the Ascendant on account of the difference of the nature of each. For the
Ascendant is friendly to the Sun, and is of the nature of heat and of the
day. And the Moon is unfriendly to the Ascendant, and she is friendly to
its nadir (namely the 7th), and is of the nature of cold and night. And one
is inimical to the other, and they are contrary to each other.[142]

[8-9] Indeed the Head of the Dragon and its Tail kill on account of their
compression [or stricture] in the sectioning of the circles, when the *hīlāj* is

---

[142] Refer back to Tr. 7, Part 1, Ch. 11.

joined to one of them in the nativity or the revolution, unless the benefics were then to aspect the degree of the *hīlāj*.[143]

[10-12] And you may understand the same about the degree which was the 12th house (namely, at the hour of the nativity), or the 6th, or the 8th.

[13-14] *Cor Tauri* and *Cor Scorpionis* act likewise on account of the overflowing abundance of heat prevailing in them.

[15] Indeed Mercury kills if he were corporally joined to one of the malefics or in its square aspect or in its opposition, without perfect reception (or without the aspect of some benefic), and he were in the degree which was the Ascendant at the hour of the nativity, or he were joined to the *hīlāj*, or were in its square aspect or in its opposition (indeed not with benefics).

[16] Even the *hīlāj* kills if it is joined with the degree of the nadir of the Ascendant of the nativity.[144]

[17] You could say the same about the Moon if she is joined with that degree, and that it is more so if the planet whose degree you were directing to the *hīlāj* were badly disposed at the hour of the nativity–it kills.

Even certain other degrees kill, which you would direct to the *hīlāj*, if they were badly disposed. Whence 'Umar said[145] if the direction were completed at the end of a sign, with half of the lesser or middle or greater years of the *al-kadukhadāh*, it kills.

And ['Umar] said[146] if the disposition is changed from the *hīlāj* out of the bound of a malefic, into the bound of a malefic, it kills in the entrance of that malefic.

And he said,[147] know that it seemed to Ptolemy that the Moon is always directed to the rays of the malefics and the benefics, in order to know the condition of the body in health and infirmity, and for the condition of the

---

[143] Here Bonatti is counting the Nodes again, this time as killers by location.
[144] I.e., with the cusp of the 7th.
[145] *TBN*, p. 18.
[146] *TBN*, p. 18.
[147] *TBN*, p. 18.

mother.[148] And the Part of Fortune [is directed] for knowing the acquisitions of the native (namely his riches or poverty). And the Sun for knowing the condition of the father or [the native's] kingdom. The Midheaven for knowing the condition of his kingdom and profession. And he said that it seemed to him that the direction of the Midheaven should be by the ascensions of the right circle. Again, it seemed to him and others generally, that for knowing his condition one should direct from the degree of the Ascendant, according to the division of the bounds, to the rays of the benefics and the malefics. Like if the divisor[149] and dispositor were a benefic, it will signify health and the safety of the body in the division or disposition, and his good condition (of whatever circumstances it was), and [that period of time] will be of a greater and better condition, and of a better complexion, than his own predecessors. And this will happen, however, in kings and the wealthy and great men more so than in small men and paupers, or low-class and middle-class men. And better and more strongly than that, if the rays of some benefic were present; and by however much the benefic were of a better condition, by that much will his condition be better. If however the divisor or dispositor were a malefic, and the division were found in the rays of some malefic, it signifies the bad condition of the native in that division or disposition; it even signifies infirmities and the bad mixture[150] of the complexion of his body, according to the nature of that malefic, and according to his disposition; and however much worse his condition was, so much will its disposition be more burdensome in that time; and worse than that is if the rays of another malefic were present.

Which if the divisor or dispositor were a malefic, and the rays were a benefic's, or the divisor were a benefic and the rays were a malefic's, the condition of the native will be middling: that is, the native will be sometimes healthy and sometimes infirm, sometimes wealthy and sometimes poor, sometimes having abundance, sometimes being in need, sometimes losing, sometimes acquiring, sometimes putting his affairs in order, sometimes devastating or ruining them, sometimes a miser in things he does not need, sometimes generous in things he should not spend.

If however that benefic were impeded, his condition will come down more on the side of adversity, more so than to the side of prosperity. Indeed if the

---

[148] See further information on directing significators in Part 3, 12th House, Ch. 10.

[149] In this context the "divisor" or "dispositor" is the Lord of the bound through which the degree of the Ascendant is directed. But in other places he says the "divisor" may be the *al-kadukhadāh* or perhaps some other planet that is directed. See below, Ch. 6.

[150] *Discrasiam*, i.e., an imbalance in the native's natural complexion of humors.

malefic were well disposed, his condition will come down more on the side of prosperity than adversity.

Chapter 4: On the knowledge of the direction of the rays of the planets to the *hīlāj*

If you wished to direct the degree of some planet to the *hīlāj*, so that you might know the life of the native and his condition for the whole time of his life, and his disposition with his accidents, see whether the Sun or Moon is the *hīlāj*, or whichever other of the planets or degrees [is]. Because it is necessary for you to consider the disposition of the rays of the planets, and their projection to the *hīlāj*, and to look to the place of the planet or the degree which was the *hīlāj*, and to see in what place or in what degree it was, by equal degrees and their minutes. And when you have done this, see which of the planets projects his own rays to it[151] by whatever aspect it was (or by opposition), by equal degrees and their minutes, and reduce them into equal degrees by the ascensions of the region: and those are called the rays of that planet. Then we must look to see in what degree of that sign [the planet] is, and reduce them into degrees of ascensions, and this will be called the degrees of the body of that planet. You will even discover the Ascendant and the rest of the houses by degrees of ascensions of that region.[152]

And many of the ancients worked according to this method, and especially those who followed in the footsteps of Dorotheus, who was one of the few more proven ones who applied themselves to this work. Nor was this contrary to the opinion of Ptolemy, even if perhaps it might seem somewhat different from his; but it was an easier method, and therefore many of the ancients followed in [his] footsteps.

An example of such a matter is this. Let it be put that the *hīlāj* is in the seventeenth degree of Leo, and the planet whose direction you intend to carry out is in the twenty-eighth degree of Pisces. The seventeenth degree of Leo (in which the *hīlāj* is) must be directed to the twenty-eighth of Virgo, to the rays of the aforesaid planet (whether he is a benefic or malefic, provided that the benefic is a killer, which sometimes happens). Then you will subtract the ascensions which

---

[151] *Ipsum* (masc.), i.e. the place where the *hīlāj* was at the nativity.

[152] Bonatti's description here means that we ought simply to subtract the oblique ascension of one body or degree, from the other. This is much simpler (as he acknowledges) than the more complicated version at the end of this Treatise (Ch. 15 of the 12th House).

there are in the straight line[153] of the degree of the *hīlāj* from the ascensions which are in the straight line[154] of the twenty-eighth degree of Virgo, where the opposition of the killing planet is; and the degrees which would remain are so many years of the native, absolutely–which are 41.[155] Likewise you will see if some one of those adding years, adds; or if one of those subtracting [them] diminishes something from those years, and you will judge the number of years of the native's life according to that–concerning which I will tell you below when the direction of the planets according to bounds is treated.

Indeed 'Umar said that Ptolemy worked by another method, but, however, it was not contrary to this, even though it seemed different from it. Perhaps it seemed more difficult to some.[156] For I say that Ptolemy's intention was following the disposition of the Lords of the bounds, and following the division of their disposition in them. For he said that all rays are congregated in the [central] point of the earth, and they become one thing;[157] and that it is necessary for us to know the diversity of the rays according to the site of the place, beginning to operate on the rays by the longitude of the planets from the angles by the ascensions of the city in which we were, and by the ascensions of the right circle. And if you were to do so, and you were to order the places[158] of the planets, you will direct the *hīlāj* and the ascending degree according to these longitudes, as was said. And if you were to see it arrive at benefics, judge good; and if you were to see it arrive at malefics, judge the contrary, according to how you were to see their conditions and their strengths or weaknesses, and their fortunes and misfortunes–and this, if the *hīlāj* were from the 10th up to the 7th, according to the succession of signs. Indeed if it were between the 7th and the 10th, these things will come to be backwards, namely against the succession of the signs, namely by subtracting the ascensions of the degree of the *hīlāj* from the ascensions of the degree of the malefic, if it were in the aforesaid places to which you were directing, even though certain people seem to want something else.

And concerning the Head of the Dragon, you may understand the same: that is, if you were to direct the *hīlāj* to the Head, whatever kind of *hīlāj* it was,

---

[153] *In directo.* I am somewhat unsure of the exact meaning of this.

[154] *In directo.* See above.

[155] The number 41 refers to the number of ecliptical degrees, not the degrees of oblique ascensions. We would have to have a terrestrial latitude for the birthplace to calculate the ascensions.

[156] See *Tet.* III.11, and Hand's note to *TBN*, p. 21.

[157] *Tet.* I.24.

[158] *Loca.*

whether the degree of the Ascendant, or the degree of the Moon, or another, you will direct backwards, namely against the succession of signs, by subtracting the ascensions[159] of the degree of the Head from the ascensions of the degree of the *hīlāj*. Indeed to the Tail you will direct according to the succession of the signs, just as I told you above; and you will give years according to the number of the degrees of distance.

And if the *hīlāj* were to arrive at the western degree, or to the degree of a malefic who was between the 10th and the 7th (to which you directed the degree[160] of the *hīlāj*), then the native will die–unless a strong benefic were then to aspect that degree from a trine or sextile aspect, and with reception: because then it will not kill, but the native will be endangered by a danger similar to death; and if he did not watch out for himself, then he will die by the required command [of the planets], even if the error is moderate.

Chapter 5: On the number of malefics and benefics

The ancient sages said the malefics were four; it seems to me, however, that they can be said to be seven. Because even though they said they were four, still they did not seem to have excluded others. Whence I say that there can be seven: namely, two naturally (as Saturn and Mars), indeed two accidentally (as the Sun and Mercury), one by misfortune (as the Moon), two again by location (as the Head of the Dragon and its Tail).[161]

Namely, the Sun [is accidentally a malefic] when it is joined with Mars or in his opposition, or in his square aspect without perfect reception. And Mercury, if he were combust or in the aforesaid aspects [of Mars or Saturn][162] aforesaid aspects, with reception or without reception.

And the Moon [is a malefic by misfortune] if she were made unfortunate, as was said in the chapter on the impediments of the Moon.[163] (And ['Umar] al-Tabarī said, if these[164] were congregated above[165] Venus with-

---

[159] Reading *ascensiones* for *ascendens*, as above.
[160] Reading *gradum* for *gradus*.
[161] Here Bonatti adds the Moon, going beyond 'Umar's list of six.
[162] Bonatti simply says "their," but 'Umar (from whom this passage is taken) specifies Mars and Saturn.
[163] See Tr. 5 (5th Consideration) for the conditions that make the Moon "malefic."
[164] 'Umar says, "these six," referring to Mars, Saturn, the Nodes, the Sun, and Mercury.

out the aspect of a benefic, then the native will be a eunuch. Which if the primary Lord of the triplicity of Venus were strong, this will profit him; without this, however, in addition to what he has suffered he will be full of labor, in need of food for his belly all the days of his life).

Indeed the Head of the Dragon [is a malefic by location] if it were with malefics, and likewise the Tail if it were with the benefics.

Indeed the benefics are eight:

Namely, four naturally (as Jupiter, the Sun, Venus, and the Moon);

Two accidentally (as [1] Mercury, if he were joined corporally with them or to one of them, or in their trine or sextile aspect with reception, or without reception, or in the square aspect or opposition with perfect reception–and if one of the malefics did not impede him without reception); and [2] Mars and Saturn, if both were made united by body, that is if both were in the same minute, in the domicile or in the exaltation of one of them, or in two of their lesser dignities, or even if there were 5' or less between them (but with Mars going toward Saturn); but in other places they are not made benefic unless they were received by a benefic, but their malice will lie hidden. And therefore it is said that the two malefics joined together, make one fortune.

Indeed two locally (as the Head, by increasing with benefics, and the Tail by diminishing with malefics).

And they are called benefics because they aid the works of the virtues and even the operations of nature. And therefore Jupiter and Venus are called benefics, because always they do this, each one of them according to its own power. And Saturn and Mars are called malefics naturally, because each of them by his own nature always strives to harm and impede the works of virtues and the operations of nature. Indeed the others behave in both ways.

---

[165] This probably means "elevated above." This situation would be exceedingly rare, and perhaps 'Umar simply means, "the more of these, the worse." Or, it could refer to the Hellenistic "overcoming."

And may you know that it is said by the jealous and the ignorant, that all external goods are goods of a benefic;[166] but they are prejudiced, because they do now know what others know, nor do they love knowers, nor knowledge (because nothing is loved except what is understood).[167]

Chapter 6: On the knowledge of the life of the native and its condition, according to the Lords of the bounds

Indeed to know the condition of the life of the native and his disposition according to the division of the bounds of the planets, it is necessary that you first consider the projections of the rays of the planets; then you will direct the *hīlāj* and the its degree, just as was said above, which I will yet repeat for you [here]:[168]

For if you wished to direct the *hīlāj* to one of the planets or to its rays, you will consider how many degrees of distance there are between them, according to the ascensions of the region of the nativity by the oblique circle,[169] and you will give one year to each degree, and one month to every 5', and six days to every minute according to this method.

For you will begin from the first minute of Aries both for the *hīlāj* and the degree of the planet or its ray to which you were directing, and you will subtract the lesser from the greater; and that which is left over will be the distance or longitude which there is between them; then you will give a year to every degree; and so on with the others just as I have told you now.

And 'Umar said that you would always direct the degree of the Ascendant in nativities so that you could know the being [or condition] of the native's life, because [the degree of the Ascendant] is the "divisor" which is called the *jārbakhtār*[170]–of the operation of which, even though I have taken it briefly from the ancients, I give you such a teaching: that is, that you see the ascending

---

[166] *Bona fortunae.* I think Bonatti is trying to say that good things can even come out of conventional evils, as we see in the planets; and so we should not adopt a crude, black-and-white view of conventional goods and evils in this world.

[167] I am not sure of the origin of this phrase, but it sounds as though it might be from Aristotle or Plato.

[168] For more on primary directions in nativities, see Part 3, 12th House, Ch. 10.

[169] I.e., by oblique ascension.

[170] Lat. *algebutar*, from Ar. الجاربختار (al-Qabīsī, IV.14), origin unknown. According to al-Qabīsī, this refers to the primary direction of the Ascendant through the bounds, not the Ascendant itself. But al-Bīrūnī (*Instruction*, §521) agrees with Bonatti, also calling it the "divisor," i.e., the Ascendant itself.

degree and its minute, of whose bound it is, and how many degrees of that bound were above it by the oblique circle, for the purpose of ascending.[171] Because that planet who is the Lord of that bound, will dispose the life of the native from the day and hour of his nativity up until so many years and so many days and so many hours, as are those degrees (and their minutes and seconds). Then you will subtract the ascensions of the last degree of that bound from the ascensions of the last degree of the following bound and its minute, and you will give one year to each degree of that which was above it; and one month to every 5', and six days to every minute. And the Lord of that bound will dispose the life of the native according to what his condition was; and his disposition [will last] for so many years, and so many months, and so many days. Then you will subtract the ascensions of the last degree of the second bound from the ascensions of the last degree of the third bound, and you will give one year to every remaining degree which was above it, and so on, as was said above. For the Lord of that bound will dispose the life of the native for so many years, so many months and so many days; and you will work thus from bound to bound up to the end of the signs, insofar as the life of the native lasted. And you will always consider the condition of that planet whose bound it was, because according to what his condition was (good or bad or middling), so will the life of the native be disposed, unless another would impede. Which if the work of direction were to come up to the end of Pisces, you will start from the beginning of Aries, and do as I said.

If the division were with a benefic

However, if you were to find the division (to which you directed) [to be] with one of the benefics (or in its rays), without the aspect or the presence of one of the malefics, and the *jārbakhtār* or divisor were a benefic, the native will be in a good and praiseworthy condition in those years, and in tranquility and the goodness of his life, and likewise in the increase of matters; and this will last until the degree of the direction reaches a malefic or its degree. If however a malefic were to aspect, it will subtract from that goodness according to what his malice was, unless those degrees were his dignity. Indeed if he were to have a dignity there, it will impede less.

---

[171] *Ad ascendendum.*

If the division were with a malefic

And if this were one of the malefics, without the aspect of a benefic, and the divisor of those years were a malefic, the native will be in a bad and detestable condition in those years, and he will be in distresses and griefs and tribulations and sorrows, and evils will find[172] him, and the diminution of [his] affairs, and need. If however a benefic were to aspect, it will subtract from the malice according to what its goodness was. And if these degrees were its dignity, it will profit more.

If it were the dignity of many planets

If however many planets were to have dignity there, and they were to aspect that place, he who had more dignities or strengths there will be more worthy in the disposition of that time. Indeed if one were to have one dignity, and he were to aspect, and another were to have more and did not aspect, each will be a participator and worthy [in the] disposition; and each of them will dispose the life of the native, namely according to his good or bad condition, just as was said above.

---

172 Reading *invenient* for *inveniet*.

PART 3: On the Form and Shape of the Native's Body–and Likewise on its Accidents, Generally and in Particular, and on the Qualities of the Soul and What is Connected[173] to It

It was spoken above (in those [Parts] which have preceded this Part) about the determinations or species of nativities, and what are connected to them; and how many years and how much a space of life is attributed to every native. It is fitting to make mention, in this Part, of the accidents and the form and shape of the native's body, both in particular and in general, and on the qualities or accidents of the soul.

Chapter 1: On the form and shape of the native

And so, if you wished to know this, you will consider the Ascendant in someone's nativity, and its Lord, and you will see which of the planets were the *al-mubtazz* in it, and according to the form and shape which it attributes, and according to the shape which the ascending sign attributes to the native.

You will attend to [this] future form generally, because natural action is according to the necessity of the form, but [also] by conjecturing from the signification of the planet to the sign, and [from the signification] of the sign to the planet, and from the added essence of [natives'] ancestors, because from similar causes are produced similar effects. And this could last until the seventh generation of their descendents; and whichever descendent could give something of his own essence to his own descendents up to his own seventh generation, however according to more and less, both in one and in another of its individuals; because a person proceeds from another person, for [a person] is an individual substance of rational nature.[174] The same being [or nature] can be in the species of the human; nor does it seem discordant that individuals of a species bear the likeness or appearance or complexion from mothers more so than from others of their ancestors, since they are nourished from the maternal humors in their uteruses, even though the members are organized by the paternal seed; for it is necessary that it follow the necessity of matter.[175]

---

173 *Adiacentibus.*
174 *Naturae*, not *esse.*
175 Like most of Bonatti's theoretical statements, this passage is hard to understand, and has no clear astrological application.

And because the truth of all the world's forms or shapes, [and] of the two kinds of humans, cannot be stated or described simply (unless perhaps by an extremely long speech, generating weariness for the reader), it is necessary that you consider, from your own industry and likewise discretion, the admixture of the significators (both planets and signs) and of the places of the circle, coming together to attribute a form and shape to the native.

Indeed every thing which is appointed[176] for this, is appointed so that it might do what is given to it by the appointer. For you will not find someone [to be] simply Saturnine or Jovial or Mercurial or Solar or Venereal or Martial or Lunar, [i.e.,] who is free of the signification of all the others so that none [of the other planets] would play a role in him. And even the sign puts some of its own influence[177] into it, and likewise the position of the place[178] in the circle of signs; and, as I touched on above, the essence of the [family-] relations. Whence Ovid: "Often the son tends to be like the father."[179]

Therefore, consider the planetary *al-mubtazz*[180] in the hour of the nativity of him whose accidents you wished to know, and the ascending degree of that nativity; and you will take the signification of the form and shape of the native's body from the one which was then the ruler.[181] And it seems fitting to me first to make mention of the form of the native's body (on account of its density) rather than the qualities of the soul, by reason of certain accidents which will appear in its combination,[182] which naturally precede the qualities of the soul. However, the qualities of the soul do not appear so obviously as do the qualities of the body, but those things which he acquired from the stars after his creation and nativity, gradually and step by step, are perceived (which combined his body together, which we see appearing).

---

[176] In this sentence Bonatti repeats the verb *instituo* three times, which I have translated as "appoint." But it also means "establish, put in place, arrange," *etc.* One might think that by the "appointer" he means God.

[177] *Partes*, lit. "parts, portions."

[178] *Loci positio.* I am unsure what Bonatti means by this, if he is only speaking of the rising sign.

[179] I do not know the source of this quote in Ovid. But it was used in the 12th century as a reason for levying penalties on the children of promiscuous priests.

[180] Here we see one of Bonatti's ambiguous statements about the *al-mubtazz* or significator of the native or the nativity. Perhaps he means the *hīlāj* or the *al-kadukhadāh?*

[181] *Dominator.* This probably means we are to take the stronger of the *al-mubtazz* of the Ascendant and the aforesaid *al-mubtazz* "of the hour of the nativity."

[182] *Coadunationem. Adunatio* in other medieval texts is often a synonym for a conjunction or aspect.

Chapter 2: On those things which are outside the body, which are not of its substance nor of the substance of the soul

Indeed other things existing outside the body (like gaining wealth, marrying, begetting, and the like) tend to happen over a long time after the aforesaid, all of which naturally can and ought to be known from the hour of the nativity and its Ascendant (but by accident or by habit, sometimes nature[183] tends to be taken away). Whence it is necessary for this purpose, so that we might know them, that we consider the stars which are in it[184] or aspect it, and likewise [to consider] the condition of the Moon rightly, just as will be stated below about each one in particular, in its own place. For the operations of nature are diversified in many ways. For they are diversified by the planets and the fixed stars, by customs, by nourishment, and by the locales of the regions, by preservation[185] and the like; all of which will be useful to know (if it were possible).

We are even able to know each one of the knowable things better when we know its cause; for indeed the act of cognition is in the cognition of what is cognized or cognizable; for a place is owed to every commixed body, according to the person and the disposition of what is operating; because the perfection of a matter is taken up from its totality, since operating is more noble than an action which follows the one acting. Whence, through the actions of the supercelestial bodies their more noble effects or operations come to be. For indeed the stars regulate the inferior corruptible things taken together, namely every individual nature; wherefore [in one sense] the operations of the stars are the same in terms of their reference;[186] indeed according to the operations, they are diverse. Wherefore, the forms and shapes of the bodies of natives are comprehended by the nature of the shapes of the Ascendant, and from the planets and their conjunctions with others, and from the signs, and from the fixed stars appearing in these places.

---

183 Reading *natura* for *naturae*.
184 *Eo...illud.* This must mean, "the ascending sign."
185 *Conservationibus.* I am unsure what Bonatti means by this.
186 *Secundum rationem.*

Chapter 3: On the form and shape of the native's body, and first on that which Saturn bestows[187]

If Saturn were the sole significator of the nativity, without the aid or admixture of another, and he were oriental in the world and from the Sun, Ptolemy said that the native will of temperate size and middling thickness, being honey-colored; his hair will be black, but it will be dense on his chest; the hair on the head curly [or wavy]. Concerning his complexion, coldness and moisture will prevail.

If however he were occidental in the world and from the Sun, he will be thin, blackish, with a small body, having straight and thin hair on the head, with a fitting combination of his bodily members. His eyes will be black, and dryness will prevail in his complexion.

And Dorotheus said it signifies a very hairy man on the body, with joined eyebrows. And ad-Dawla said Saturn gives a man a swarthy nature, making hair sparse in the beard; he will have a gray color, sometimes a thin chest, rough and unkempt hair on the head, having sores or fissures in his heels.

On the participation of Jupiter with Saturn

And if Jupiter had participated with Saturn, it signifies a man having a face not truly white, whose color will be chestnut or olive, but with a praiseworthy comeliness. His eyes will be blackish, of medium size, but comely; his stature will be more than average, and he will be half-bald, some of his teeth not truly white, the hairs on the head semi-curly and with a chestnut color; his [body] hair totally black, and they will be between thinning and dense—and this, if each of [the planets] were oriental.

If however one were oriental and the other occidental, they will be somewhat below this. If indeed each were occidental, it will be much below this.[188]

On the participation of Mars with Saturn

Indeed if Mars were a participant with Saturn, it signifies a man not very straight, half-thick, whose color is blackish, a certain unsightly redness partici-

---

[187] This chapter and those following contain a mixture of opinions from various authorities (often taken from al-Qabīsī II). I will give specific citations only when Bonatti mentions their source, or as needed.

[188] See Bonatti's parenthetical comment below.

pating. He will sometimes have some unsightly *palestras*[189] on his face; his [body] hair will be half-sparse, the hair on the head not very black, but rather they will participate with a certain obscure redness.

On the participation of the Sun with Saturn

Which if the Sun were a participant with Saturn, it signifies a man having an average stature, coming down rather more on the side of largeness than on the side of smallness; whose color will be practically imitative,[190] so that it will seem as though it could participate with every other color, but rather more with blackish. And he will be of a more comely stature than with any of the other planets; and he will be semi-fleshy,[191] having semi-thick eyes, and a semi-full beard, chestnut or honey-colored hair on the head, between semi-curly and long. And the Sun will add something of fatness to the body and form of the native, and beauty–more so than the rest of the planets.

[General comments on the planets]

Moreover, if the Sun were oriental in the world, and even the other planets if they were oriental in the world or from the Sun, and were participants with Saturn, they add something in the size of the native's body. And if they were in their own first station, they aid natives' bodies in making them stronger and more vigorous than at other times. Indeed if they were to have transited the first station, the aforesaid will be moderated, and they will come to be lesser [or smaller] according to how much more they were remote from it. And were they to approach the second station, they will make natives' bodies weaker. But if they were to fall into combustion, they will take away the beauty and form of natives' bodies, and will make them burdened and impeded, and likewise wretched [or miserable]. And even the places[192] and degrees in which the significators or dispositors of the natives (and the Moon) are, make for the

---

[189] Unknown word, but perhaps related to *palea*, "chaff," as though there are fleshy flaws like warts on the face. A *palea* also refers to the wattles on a rooster, and *palear* the loose skin on an ox's neck. Or, it could be related to *palleo*, referring to pale discolorations.

[190] *Aemulus.* This term will appear several times below. This word means "striving, emulating," and seems to refer to a kind of indeterminate color.

[191] *Semicarnosus. Carnosus* means "fleshy," and is applied to succulent vegetation; it is also the second word in many medical terms pertaining to flesh (like muscles). But I cannot be sure whether Bonatti means "muscular" or "fleshy" (tending towards pudginess). I will translate this term simply as "fleshy."

[192] *Loca.*

disposition of the form and shape of the body of any native, and his complexion, according to the nature and complexion of the signs in which those places[193] or those degrees are.

Indeed if the significator had no latitude in the hour of the nativity, so that it is in the degree of its own *jawzahirr* or in its opposite, it signifies that the native will be thin. If however the latitude were great, he will be fat. Indeed if it were between a great and small [latitude], he will be fleshy, and light in pace, and easily carrying burdens with that fleshiness. And if it were between the greater and middle latitude, it will be adding in fleshiness up to fatness, according to the approach to the greater latitude, and remoteness from the middle.[194] And if it were between the middle and lesser [latitude], he will be diminishing in fleshiness according to its remoteness from it, and its approach to the *jawzahirr*, until it reaches thinness.

And these things will happen more strongly so if the Ascendant were at the end of the sign or around it, and the Lord of the 10th house [domicile?] were occidental. And if the Lord of the Ascendant and the other significators were in the nearer longitude, they make for fatness. And if they were in the farther longitude, they make for thinness. If however the latitude were southern, that is, so that the significator is from the point of its own *jawzahirr* up to its opposite from the southern half (which are 179° or less) the native will be light in pace, as 'Ali testifies;[195] and his lightness will be according to more and less, insofar as its latitude were greater or lesser or in the middle; because that half[196] is hot and dry, for which reason it lightens those things together which are perfected in it. If however it were northern, namely from its Tail[197] up to the *jawzahirr* (so that the distance is 179° or less), he will be heavy and burdened in his walk, and slow of motion: because this half has more coldness and moisture, by which it aggravates those things which, taken together, are perfected in it–and this according to more and less, insofar as its latitude is greater or lesser.

And may you know that the first station and retrogradation, make for fattening up; indeed the second station and direct motion make for thinning down. Nor should it be concealed from you that the relationship of [one's] predeces-

---

[193] *Loca.* In this case, it would seem the places are being identified with the degrees.
[194] I.e., in terms of that particular planet's greatest possible latitude, and half of that.
[195] This may be 'Ali ibn Ridwān.
[196] I.e., southern ecliptical longitude.
[197] Again, we seem to be dealing with each planet's own particular *jawzahirr*; Bonatti is calling one of these points the "Tail" by analogy with the Moon's Nodes.

sors[198] sometimes (or rather often) makes much for the fatness and thinness of the native, insofar as it precedes, and likewise for fleshiness.

On the participation of Venus with Saturn

If however Venus were a participant with Saturn, it signifies the native is going to have such a bodily form, namely that his color will be practically blackish or honey-colored, or olive (but comely); and the hair on his head will be neither truly gray nor truly chestnut. His face will be practically round, his whiskers medium, his eyes will be praised for beauty by the majority of those seeing them; their blackness [being] greater than if Saturn alone were the significator; having becoming hair on his head. And he will more often be semi-fleshy.

On the participation of Mercury with Saturn

And if Mercury were a participant, it signifies that the native will be of a blackish color, having a half-raised forehead, a semi-long face, likewise the nose; semi-handsome eyes (coming down more to blackness than to another color); a black and thin beard, semi-long fingers, and he will be of suitable stature.

On the participation of the Moon with Saturn

Indeed if the Moon were a participant with Saturn, it signifies that the native will be said to have a white color; however his whiteness will be neither clear nor true. It will be in some sense tinged cloudy, with some kind of admixture of redness. And he will have beautiful eyebrows, black eyes, a round face, fine stature (and comely enough); and he will have a fitting coordination [or combination] of his members.

(You may understand this always in any of the aforesaid planets, if any of them were well disposed. If however they were badly disposed, all of these things will be below what was said, according to the quantity of the impediment of any of them. And it will signify that the native will be deformed, inept, stinking, horrible, and of a vile appearance, and have a disordered composition and coordination of his own members. And however much it were Saturn (or he who participated with him), whether in the aforesaid places or the ones to be

---

[198] *Parentela praecedentium,* i.e., ancestors.

stated below, by that much more will it be increased in the deformity and likewise the form and shape of the native's body.)

Moreover, the sages said that the Moon helps the form of the native and his shape, in the mixture of the complexion, and makes him thinner than Saturn will make him if he were the sole significator (and more so if she were being separated by conjunction from any [planet], or by aspect, or by conjunction more, and she is joined to Saturn); and this according to more and less, insofar as it were illuminated by her own body, or her elongation were greater from him, until she would then transit the projection of his rays upon her rays.

Chapter 4: On that which the quarters of the circle of signs perform in the disposition of the form and shape of the native's body, and first concerning the first quarter

And even the quarters of the circle of the signs operate and make for the disposition of the form and shape of the body of any native. For the first quarter (which is from the beginning of Aries up to the end of Gemini), which is called the spring one, makes for the goodness and improvement of the form of any native's body. Whence, if the Moon and all the other significators were in that quarter at the hour of the nativity, they will help the form and shape of that native by increasing the beauty of his body, and the fitness of his stature and its goodness, and the comeliness of his eyes; and they will give him a suitable fleshiness; in whose complexion (according to Ptolemy),[199] heat and moisture will prevail. If however only certain ones of them were in it, they will perform the aforesaid according to how they were found in it. The ones that are in other quarters will operate according to the nature of those quarters in which they remain.

On the second or summer quarter

Indeed the second quarter (namely, which is from the beginning of Cancer up to the end of Virgo), makes for the goodness and the improvement of the form and shape of any native's body. Whence if the Moon and all the other significators were in that quarter at the hour of the nativity, they will help the form and shape of that native's body, by giving him a temperate quality of the body, and a medium size of stature,[200] and a suitable fleshiness, and a largeness

---

[199] *Tet.* III.13.

[200] *Atque staturae mediocritatem et quantitatem.*

of the eyes (not, however, unsightly); a thickness and curliness of hair on the head; in whose complexion (according to Ptolemy) heat and dryness will prevail. If however only certain ones of them were in it, they will perform the aforesaid according what their nature was. The ones that are in other quarters will perform the aforesaid according to the nature of the quarters in which they are found.

On the third quarter, namely the autumnal one

Indeed the third quarter (namely, which is from the beginning of Libra up to the end of Sagittarius), which is called autumnal, makes for the goodness and improvement of the form and shape of any native's body. Whence, if the Moon and all the other significators were in that quarter at the hour of someone's nativity, they will help the form and shape of that native's body by giving him a honey color, a stature somewhere between average and thin, round [or full] shoulders, something more than is necessary (but not, however exceeding measure); suitable eyes for his form, and average hair on the head; in whose complexion, cold and dryness will prevail. If however only certain ones of them are found in it, they will perform the aforesaid in accordance as it proceeds from their nature. But those who appear in the other quarters will operate according to the nature of the quarters in which you will find them.

On the fourth, last one (namely the wintry one)

Indeed the last quarter (namely which is from the beginning of Capricorn up to the end of Pisces), which is called wintry, makes for the goodness and improvement of the form, indeed the shape, of any native's body. Whence, if the Moon and all the other significators were in that quarter at the hour of someone's nativity, they will help the form and shape of that native's body by giving to him a color verging on blackness, and a fitting and temperate quality and size of the body; and straight, thin hair on the head; and a fit assemblage of his members; [in] whose complexion coldness and moisture will rule. If however only certain ones of them were to remain in it, they will perform the aforesaid in accordance with how it would proceed from their nature. Indeed those who will be found in other quarters will operate according to the nature of the quarters in which they are found.

Chapter 5: On other aids to the forms and shapes of natives' bodies, besides the aids of the quarters

Again, Ptolemy said[201] that there are certain other aids which help the aforesaid, particularly according to the places[202] and sites in which they were found: and these are the signs which are likened to human shapes (like Gemini, Virgo, Libra, the first half of Sagittarius, and Aquarius). For they make for the symmetrical fashioning of natives' bodies, and even to the fit assemblage of the members. Whence if the Moon and the other significators were in them at the hour of someone's nativity, they will help all of these, and they will make native's bodies more suitable for exercising them, and more fit.

Indeed those signs which are not likened to the human form (as are Aries, Taurus, Leo, Scorpio, and the last half of Sagittarius, Capricorn, and Pisces), make for the goodness of natives' bodies: for they render the members (which are deputed to those signs in which the Moon and the significators are) stronger and more temperate, and more ready and fitting for the actions deputed to them.

Those which aid particularly according to largeness

Again, in the signs there are those which aid particularly the form and shape of the body of any native, and [aid] his members in making them big (like Taurus, Leo, and Virgo), because their forms are big in the heavens; but Taurus and Leo help them in making them likewise strong.

Those which aid particularly according to smallness

For indeed certain ones make for the smallness of bodies and members, like Cancer, Capricorn, and Pisces–because their forms are found to be small in the heavens; however they are smaller from the rear part than from the foremost part. Moreover, the first part of Aries, and the first part of Taurus, and the first of Leo, help the members of natives by making them more inclined and more fit in taking on fat. However the last half of each of them inclines to making natives' bodies thin.

Indeed the first half of Gemini and the first [half] of Scorpio and the first [half] of Sagittarius enable natives' bodies to be thin.[203] Indeed their last parts

---

[201] *Ibid.*

[202] *Loca.* Note how this is distinguished–albeit without explanation–from "sites" (*situs*).

[203] *Ad maciem suscipiendam corpora natorum abilitant.*

help in taking on fat. Again, Virgo, Libra and Sagittarius prepare natives' bodies for a temperate complexion of the body, and a good and fit assemblage of the members, without a doubt. Indeed Taurus and Scorpio and Pisces impede them and slacken them from a good mixture, even if perhaps the slackening does not exterminate [the mixture altogether]. For indeed it would seem fitting that you, from your own industry, together with the aforesaid, might perceive the aforesaid taken together, in a right and deliberate way, according to the more and less, according to the approach of the significators to the aforesaid places,[204] or their remoteness from them, according to how they were strong or weak, made fortunate or unfortunate, so that you could judge more truly and certainly and securely about the accidents of any native, according to the condition of his nativity; and skillfully [holding them] together in your mind.

Chapter 6: On the form and shape of the native which Jupiter bestows

If however Jupiter were the sole significator of the nativity, and oriental in the world and from the Sun (or either of them), it signifies that the native will be of a white color, fitting, and of moderate stature and average height, having white[205] (and fitting and comely) hair on his head. His eyes will be average, neither very big nor very small; in whose complexion heat and moisture will prevail. Indeed if he were occidental, his whiteness will not be so fitting as when he is oriental; he will have straight hair on his head, and he will be bald, [having] average eyes, average stature, in whose complexion moisture will prevail.

On the participation of Mars with Jupiter

Which if Mars were the participant, there will be some redness mixed into his color, and he will have eyes a little bit wider than if Jupiter were the sole significator. Which if Mars were oriental, he will have a sign [or mark] on his right foot. Indeed if he were occidental, he will have it on the left one (this rarely fails).

---

[204] Loca.
[205] This is probably what we would call "blonde."

On the participation of the Sun with Jupiter

But indeed if the Sun were the participant with Jupiter, it signifies that something of his whiteness will be taken away; however he will be more comely than if Jupiter were the sole significator, and his stature will be somewhat less than average, but suitable and comely. The hair on his head will have some curliness, and his eyes will have some orange.

On the participation of Venus with Jupiter

If however Venus were the participant with Jupiter, it signifies that the native will have a color coming down more to blackness; nevertheless more comely than [if] coming down more to another color; beautiful hair on his head, practically honey-colored; but it will not be of a determinate color, for its color will be imitative. He will have a handsome stature, a semi-round face, whiskers not long but comely, beautiful eyes—apart from the fact that their blackness will be something greater than what it ought to be (nor however will it be unsightly); a decent and handsome face, and he will be semi-bald.

On the participation of Mercury with Jupiter

For if Mercury were the participant with Jupiter, it signifies that the native will have a color not particularly differing from the original one; a semi-raised forehead, a semi-long face, and likewise the nose; comely eyes, not totally black; a black and sparse beard; semi-long fingers, a semi-slim body, an average stature, thin lips.

On the participation of the Moon with Jupiter

Indeed if the Moon were the participant with Jupiter, it signifies a man not truly white, with a certain not-true redness; comely eyebrows, eyes not truly black, sometimes one bigger than the other, or flawed; a round face; average stature.

On the participation of Saturn with Jupiter

And if Saturn is found to be the participant with Jupiter, it signifies the native is going to have a color somewhat more beautiful than honey-colored is; lowering his eyes to the ground when going along the road; crooked feet, and he joins them when he goes;[206] eyes not big; and joined eyebrows; skin not decent, practically dry; thick lips; veins appearing; a beard not thick; the hair on the head rough and unkempt.

If Jupiter were impeded, what form he contributes to the native

And if Jupiter were impeded in the nativity, and he were made unfortunate, and [in] a bad condition and badly disposed, it signifies the contrary of those things which were said. Which if he who was a participant with him were likewise impeded, there will be a greater defect again in the form and shape of the native's body, and a greater deformity. And by how much the impediment were greater, by that much will the deformity of the native be increased; and many contrary things will happen, just as was said above in the chapter on Saturn.

Chapter 7: On the form and shape of the native's body which Mars contributes

Indeed if Mars were the sole significator of the nativity, and he [were] oriental in the world (namely that he is above the earth)[207] and from the Sun (that is, that he rises in the morning before him), or either of them, it signifies that the native will be of an unhealthy color; and it will participate with a certain whiteness that is not very clear, and a certain redness that is not true.

And Ptolemy said that he will have a good size to his body, and fitting fleshiness; his eyes will be varied, the hair on his head thick and average; in whose complexion heat and dryness will prevail.

If Mars were occidental

And if he appeared[208] occidental, it signifies that the native will be of a red color, moderate stature, having small eyes, straight and thin hair on the head, however with a certain golden yellow; in whose complexion dryness rules.

And Māshā'allāh said that, concerning forms and shapes, it signifies a man who has a red color, red hair on the head, and round face, wide eyes, a horrible

---

206 What in English is called "pidgeon-toed."
207 Perhaps this is meant to exclude his being in the "oriental" quarter between the 4th and the 7th.
208 *Extiterit.*

look [or expression], [and] a sign or mark on the foot. Indeed Dorotheus said the same about his look.

However, Sacerdos said Mars gives a man to have a crooked body, it being semi-brown, and neither truly red, nor truly black, just as those who spend too much time in the Sun have, or who go for a long time in the heat; and the Martial man sometimes has red grains[209] on his face, and often wearing thin hairs in his beard, like a eunuch.

On the participation of the Sun with Mars

Which if the Sun were the participant with Mars, it signifies a man having a color not truly white, nor truly red, nor truly brown, covered with a kind of not truly red color, semi-bald and semi-wide, the stature coming down on the side of beauty and comeliness, the hair on the head coming down more on the side of grayish more so than another color; the eyes not truly black.

On the participation of Venus with Mars

Indeed if Venus were the participant with Mars, it signifies a man having a semi-red color with a certain suitable whiteness; an average and handsome stature; much hair on the head, and decent; a semi-round face; average whiskers; decent eyes, their blackness will be greater than it ought to be, but not inappropriately so; well fleshy, so that he could be said to be semi-thick;[210] his face will be lively.

On the participation of Mercury with Mars

Indeed if Mercury were the participant with Mars, it signifies a man having a semi-slender body, an average stature, a color coming down more to the color of Mars than to another (unless the conjunction of other planets works to the contrary); a beautiful beard (even if sparse and small); thin lips, and likewise the nose.

---

[209] I believe this means "freckles" (*grana rubea*).
[210] Reading *semigrossum* for *semigrassum*.

On the participation of the Moon with Mars

Indeed if the Moon were a participant with Mars, it signifies a man having a beautiful color, and white, which a certain mixture of semi-redness; semi-wide eyes; beautiful eyebrows; a practically round face; a decent stature.

On the participation of Saturn with Mars

On the other hand, if Saturn were the participant with Mars, it signifies a semi-thick man, not very straight, having an unsightly color sharing in a certain redness with blackness mixed in; sometimes having certain not-comely markings on the face; semi-sparse body hair; hair on the head tinged between black and a certain obscure redness.

On the participation of Jupiter with Mars

If however Jupiter were the participant, it signifies a man having a color a little bit blush, semi-wide eyes; having a sign on one foot.

All of these, I say, if Mars and his participant were well disposed and of good condition. If however they were of bad condition and badly disposed, say the contrary just as was said above in the chapters on the others.

Chapter 8: The form and shape of the native's body which the Sun bestows

If however the Sun were the sole significator of the nativity, and he were oriental in the world, it signifies a man having a color between saffron and almost black, covered by a certain redness or imitative [color] (and according to certain people, it signifies a white color); an average stature, and sometimes coming down on the side of being larger rather than to being smaller; a beautiful and comely stature, even bald.

And Dorotheus said, if you wish to know the shape of the Sun and the Moon, know that it will be just like the shape of the planets that are with them. And he said if the Sun were in the Ascendant in someone's nativity, there will be a sign on the native's face; he will have hair on his hair between saffron and the participation of a certain redness; eyes a little saffron.

Indeed if he were occidental in the world, it signifies a man having a stature more than average, an imitative color, flaxen and long hair on the head, and sometimes a little curly.

On the participation of Venus with the Sun

Which if Venus were the participant with the Sun, and she were well disposed, it signifies a man having an average and beautiful stature; a commixed color of whiteness and redness, semi-clear and comely; much, and suitable, hair on the head; it will seem in the front part to want to participate in a certain baldness (however he will not be truly bald); an almost rotund and happy face; not large whiskers; beautiful eyes; fleshy so that he could be said to be almost fat.

On the participation of Mercury with the Sun

Indeed if Mercury were the participant with the Sun, and he were well disposed, it signifies a man having a honey color; and his color will participate with the color which will be signified by the planet aspecting him, or who were corporally joined with him; having a beautiful beard, but not big nor overly thick; semi-wide and decent eyes.

On the participation of the Moon with the Sun

And if the Moon were the participant with the Sun, and she were of good condition, it signifies a man having a beautiful and decent color with a certain semi-clear whiteness, and with an admixture of some redness; beautiful eyes; and beautiful eyebrows; a round face.

On the participation of Saturn with the Sun

Which if Saturn were the participant with the Sun by a good condition, it signifies a man having an average stature, and suitably comely; a honey color; semi-wide eyes; semi-fleshy; chestnut or honey-colored hair on the head, and curly in a certain way.

On the participation of Jupiter with the Sun

Indeed if Jupiter were the participant with the Sun, it signifies a man having a honey or olive or chestnut color, which is practically the same with some kind of whiteness mixed in, and decent enough; a fitting enough stature; eyes a little bit saffron; hair on the head verging in a certain way to curliness.

On the participation of Mars with the Sun

If however Mars were the participant with the Sun, it signifies a man having blackness, but verging on redness, little far from an imitative color; a stature following the average one, and comely; semi-thick hair on the head, almost gray; semi-wide eyes.

Chapter 9: On the form and shape of the native which Venus bestows

And if Venus were the sole significatrix of the native, and she were oriental in the world and from the Sun, it signifies a man having (as Ptolemy says) a beautiful and decent color, more so than the color which Jupiter bestows; and his face will be soft, adorned more like the face of a woman than a virile one; he will have a handsome and decent stature; eyes blackish, likewise comely.

And Māshā'allāh said that, of the shapes of men, it signifies a white man tending to a shading of blackness; and from thence it will seem more suitable, having a beautiful stature; beautiful eyes, whose blackness is somewhat greater than is found in others, but still suitable; beautiful hair on his head; a round face (but not big, nor the whiskers).

And Dorotheus said that it signifies a man having a beautiful face; beautiful eyes whose blackness will be more than it ought to be; much beautiful hair on the head; dense, white, complete with a redness [or blush]; in whose complexion moisture prevails. But if she were to appear[211] occidental, the things she signifies will be below the aforesaid; [and] coldness will prevail in his complexion.

On the participation of Mercury with Venus

Which if Mercury were the participant with Venus, and he were well disposed, it signifies a beautiful and comely man; having a beautiful color; having a somewhat raised forehead; a long face, likewise the nose (and sometimes a thin one); beautiful eyes not totally black; and long fingers.

And Sacerdos said [it signifies] one having a slender body; average stature; a beautiful but thin beard (nor small); sometimes having thin lips.

---

211 *Extiterit.*

On the participation of the Moon with Venus

Indeed if the Moon were the participant with Venus, and she were well disposed, it signifies a man having a beautiful color of whiteness and redness mixed through; semi-black eyes; beautiful and pleasing eyebrows; and a beautiful and average stature; but a round face; sometimes having one of the eyes somewhat larger than the other, or even defective.

On the participation of Saturn with Venus

Which if Saturn were the participant with Venus, it signifies a man having a honey or blackish color, but having a suitable comeliness of his color; hair on the head between silver and honey-colored; and from them he will have a suitable and decent quantity of them; a semi-round face; medium whiskers; beautiful eyes whose blackness will be of a suitable magnitude; and he will be semi-fleshy.

On the participation of Jupiter with Venus

And if Jupiter were the participant with Venus, it signifies a man having a blackish and decent color; beautiful hair on the head (but it will be imitative in color); a beautiful stature and one blessed by beauty (for beauty is a harmony of parts, with a certain sweetness of color); a semi-round face; medium whiskers, and decent; beautiful eyes; however it will seem their blackness is somewhat greater than it ought to be; however it will not detract from their beauty; a very beautiful face; and he will be semi-fleshy.

On the participation of Mars with Venus

If however Mars were the participant with Venus, it signifies a man having a suitable color, commixed of a certain whiteness and redness; a beautiful and average stature; much decent hair on the head; average whiskers; a semi-round face; beautiful eyes (their blackness superabounds somewhat, though it is not unbecoming), semi-thick [in body], having a cheerful face.

On the participation of the Sun with Venus

Indeed if the Sun were the participant with Venus, it signifies a man having a beautiful color commixed with redness and whiteness, not very clear; an average and beautiful stature; beautiful and decent hair on the head; a happy face, almost semi-round, semi-fat; beautiful eyes.

Chapter 10: On the form and shape of the native's body which Mercury bestows

If however Mercury were the sole significator of the nativity, and he were oriental in the world or from the Sun, and otherwise well disposed, it signifies a man having a honey or chestnut or olive color; the members fit enough, coordinated together; small eyes; average hair on the head, both in quantity and in color; in his complexion, heat will prevail. Which if he were occidental (namely in the world or from the Sun), it signifies a man having a saffron color with a certain admixture of blackishness; thin; having a meager voice; hollow eyes whose pupil will be goat-like,[212] coming down on the side of a certain redness; in whose complexion dryness will rule.

On the participation of the Moon with Mercury

But if the Moon were the participant with Mercury, and she were oriental in the world, and from the Sun,[213] and otherwise well disposed, it signifies a man having a beautiful color, in which whiteness will prevail with a mixed-in redness; beautiful and benevolent eyebrows; eyes not totally black; a round and decent face; a fitting and beautiful stature; indeed if she were occidental, what she signifies will be less than this; and the more so if the Moon were impeded.

On the participation of Saturn with Mercury

Indeed if Saturn were the participant with Mercury, and oriental, it signifies a man having a practically blackish color; the forehead somewhat elevated; an average face and likewise the nose; semi-decent eyes verging on blackness; a sparse and black beard, average fingers; a fitting stature. Indeed if he were occidental, the things he signifies will be below the aforesaid.

---

[212] *Caprina.*
[213] Note that the Moon would be waning, which is usually understood negatively.

On the participation of Jupiter with Mercury

Which if Jupiter were the participant with Mercury, and he were oriental, it signifies a man having a color coming down more on the side of a certain comely blackness; imitative hair; a semi-round face; average and suitable whiskers; beautiful eyes in which blackness will prevail; a suitable and beautiful face; a decent stature; and he will be semi-fleshy. Which if he were occidental, the aforesaid things he signifies will be below this.

On the participation of Mars with Mercury

And if Mars were the participant, and he were oriental, it signifies a man having a color determined more to a certain untrue redness, with an admixture of a certain untrue whiteness (rather than to another color); a sparse and small beard (not however unsuitable); thin lips and likewise the nose; an average stature; often a slender body.

On the participation of the Sun with Mercury

Indeed if the Sun were the participant with Mercury, and he were oriental in the world, it signifies a man having a color like honey; an average and beautiful beard (even if thin); decent and semi-thick eyes. If however he were occidental in the world, all the things he signifies will be below the aforesaid.

On the participation of Venus with Mercury

And if Venus were a participant with Mercury, and she were oriental in the world or from the Sun, it signifies a man having a beautiful and decent color; a long face, likewise a long and thin nose; a high forehead; beautiful eyes not totally black; long fingers; a beautiful and decent stature.

And Sacerdos said a slender body, an average stature; a beautiful but thin beard (not however, short); sometimes having thin lips. And if Venus were occidental, all the things signified will be below the aforesaid.

Chapter 11: On the form and shape which the Moon bestows upon the native

Indeed if the Moon were the sole significatrix of the nativity, and she were oriental in the world or from the Sun, and otherwise well-disposed, it signifies a man having a white color commixed with a rosy red; verging on thinness; benevolent eyebrows; eyes not totally big; a round face; a wholly beautiful stature.

On the participation of Saturn with the Moon

Which if Saturn were the participant with the Moon, and they were well disposed, it signifies a man having a color verging on whiteness, but not a true [whiteness], and the whiteness will have a commixture of a certain redness; beautiful eyebrows; black eyes; and round face approaching thin; an agreeable stature [and] a fitting coordination of his limbs. If however they were badly disposed, they signify the contrary of those things which were said, for indeed the native will be of a vile appearance, nor will his members be fitly assembled; and by how much more they (or either of them) were made unfortunate, by that much more will the native be unfit and deformed and vile and horrible.

On the participation of Jupiter with the Moon

If however Jupiter were the participant with the Moon, it signifies a man having a color not truly white, with a clear admixture of redness; beautiful eyebrows; beautiful, semi-black eyes; a round face; agreeable stature; one of the eyes sometimes defective.

On the participation of Mars with the Moon

If indeed Mars were the participant with the Moon, it signifies a man having a beautiful color; beautiful eyebrows; semi-wide eyes verging in a certain way on blackness; an agreeable stature; a semi-round face.

On the participation of the Sun with the Moon

But if the Sun were the participant with the Moon, it signifies a man having a decent color with a certain agreeable whiteness and redness; beautiful eyebrows and beautiful eyes; a round face.

On the participation of Venus with the Moon

On the other hand, if Venus were the participant with the Moon, it signifies a man having a color produced of whiteness and redness, and very beautiful;

decent eyebrows, eyes not truly black; an average and beautiful stature; a round face; suitable eyes, even if they are not wholly equal.

On the participation of Mercury with the Moon

Lastly, if Mercury were the participant with the Moon and he were well disposed, it signifies a man having a color commixed of an agreeable whiteness and redness; beautiful eyebrows; semi-black eyes; a round face with a decent proportion; a decent stature and set all around with beauty.

C3   C3   C3

All of these things which were said about the forms and shapes which the planets bestow upon natives–may you know them to be common to each sex. For may you know [that] such things ought to happen in the way they were otherwise said, if the planets were made fortunate and well disposed; if indeed it were the contrary, you will judge the contrary according to the quantity of the contrariety.

Having considered all (and individually) the things which were said about the planets and the rest (as I have touched on for you above), and with your discernment, and their own roles having been introduced by conjecturing, with the help of our Redeemer Jesus Christ, you should even know something else that sometimes impedes the natural course of nativities, of which it is necessary for you to beware–that is, that the years of natives are changed in the nativities of children, practically according to how they are changed in the revolutions of years (just as will be touched on below, when it is treated of the matter of fathers).[214]

---

[214] See the material in the 4th House, Chs. 1-8.

ON THE FIRST HOUSE

Chapter 1: On the qualities or accidents of the native's soul

Mention having been made in the preceding about the form and shape of the native's body, and about his accidents, I think we must speak next[215] about the qualities or accidents of the native's soul itself, and write about them according to our abilities: first about rationality (about both the more worthy and the more noble), and subsequently about the sensible and the vegetable.[216]

Therefore it must be said that that which properly pertains to reason and intellect is known through Mercury;

However, what is of the vegetative and perceptive [parts of the soul] is truly apprehended through the luminary whose authority it is. And if the nativity were diurnal, [it would be] only through the Sun; indeed if it were nocturnal, through the Moon and through the planet with which she is joined; and he who were to have *al-'insiraf*[217] (or even contrariety[218]) with her, or *al-'ittisal*[219] (whether conjunction or application).

However we cannot arrive to the cognition of it by one path alone, but by different ones. For there are six ways, of which:

The first is the consideration of the condition of the Moon and Mercury.

---

[215] Much of what follows is based on *Tet.* III.14.

[216] This statement reflects Aristotle's psychology, which describes three parts of the soul: the rational, the sensible (which includes appetites and certain emotions, and movement), and the vegetable (responsible for growth and the ability to take in nourishment). But note that Bonatti also approves of Abu 'Ali's statement that while the Ascendant and the Moon pertain to the body, the Lord of the Ascendant and the domicile ruler of the Moon pertain to the soul (below, 6th House, Ch. 4)–the idea being that just as these planets rule the Ascendant and the Moon's position, so the soul rules the body.

[217] Lat. *Alithirat*. I am taking this to be the same as the term in Tr. 5 (4th Consideration), which Bonatti defines as "separation or disjoining."

[218] This probably refers to Bonatti's own concept of contrariety (Tr. 3, Part 2, Ch. 16), which is identical to al-Qabīsī's "resistance" (*al-i'tirād*). To be technically faithful to the definition, three planets would have to be involved. See the definition in Tr. 3, Part 2, Ch. 16. But his inclusion of several very different types of planetary aspects or conjunctions suggests that he wants to be as inclusive as possible.

[219] Lat. *Alitisal*. See Tr. 5 (4th Consideration)–this term means "conjunction," as the text immediately makes clear.

The second is the consideration of the signs in which they are (namely one or more).

The third is the consideration of the Lords of those signs [in which the Moon and Mercury are].

The fourth is the conjunction of the planets in the figure at the hour of the nativity.

The fifth, what is the peculiar signification of each of the planets which is a participant[220] in the figure of that nativity which the astrologer intends to consider.

The sixth is the consideration of the angles and their Lords, because the aforesaid significators (likewise the signs) in which the qualities of the soul (and likewise the accidents) are, aid and help much.

Whence, the significators are to be considered; and the signs in which they are must be considered; and likewise the angles.

On the three superior planets[221]

If the three superior planets were oriental from the Sun, or from the Lord of the Ascendant, or they were in the Ascendant or in its angles, or in the "facing" of the Sun or the Moon or the Lord of the Ascendant, they make the soul liberal[222] and capable of freedom, stern[223] and sure of his own counsel; great

---

[220] Does this mean a participant of the planet which has overall mastery of the chart?

[221] I have moved the section on the fixed signs, which appeared here, to its proper position with the other triplicities below. The reader will note that the text goes back and forth between different types of planets and conditions; moving the section on the fixed signs at least makes the text flow more smoothly.

[222] *Liberalem. Liberalis* is an important sociological and moral term, referring to qualities assumed to be in free people (i.e., not slaves or serfs): free, honorable, kind, noble, gentlemanly, beautiful, generous. The "liberal arts" are supposed to ennoble the mind and improve us morally without being immediately practical in the way that manual trades and hourly labor (which are relatively unfree professions) are.

[223] *Atrocem.* Again, this links social position with moral qualities: exalted and powerful people (whose position parallels that of the superior planets) are expected to be less sentimental and harsher than peers in the lower classes. Nietzsche's *Genealogy of Morals* is a good essay on the traditional assumptions that link social and moral (and health) status.

and open, exalted,[224] and bringing his own thoughts into the open, but not very discreetly.[225]

On the signifying stars[226]

And if the stellar significators were in their first station, and they were appearing[227] fortunate and strong (and more so if they are found around the cusp of the 10th house), they will announce [that] the soul of the native will be a thinking[228] one, and a steward [or dispenser] of goods, and of good memory, and of good capacity [or comprehension]; and of good intellect; stable, quiet and immovable; magnanimous, cannot be converted, not deceitful, and lawful; investigating [and understanding], a lover of works, a true expounder of dreams, and very experienced in such and similar things.

On the three inferior planets

Indeed if the three inferiors were to remain in the aforesaid places, and they were occidental,[229] direct and strong, and particularly in nocturnal nativities (even though in diurnal ones they [signify] something less than this), they will make the native's soul weak, easily changing from proposition to proposition; faint-hearted and unfortunate; false; slow and sluggish to understand [things by acquaintance] or [exercising] the intellect; timid and quaking with fear, a lover of great tempests of falsity; gladly remaining alone.

---

[224] Reading *exaltatam* for *exalatam*.

[225] Note that the superior planets will do this, but only if they are in the relevant places of the nativity (i.e., with respect to the Ascendant or its Lord, or the luminaries–and then probably only the luminary whose authority it was).

[226] I.e., the planets–probably only the superior planets, based on the passage's placement here.

[227] *Existentes.* The sentence reads awkwardly, but "appearing" does not seem to add anything to the sentence except to emphasis what we ought to look at their condition in the heavens.

[228] *Cogitatricem. Cogito* does not merely mean "to think" (as in Descartes's *cogito, ergo sum*), but to plan, meditate, intend. This implies an orientation in the soul towards goals, and meditating and reflecting on actions.

[229] This does not quite make sense. Normally when the inferiors are "occidental" of the Sun (i.e., rising after him), they are stronger and better. Since this seems to mirror a passage in *Tet.* III.14 which says that planets that are retrograde and in their "settings" will have just the qualities listed here, I am tempted to say that "occidental" should be translated as "pertaining-to-sinking." But even so, I do not see how pertaining-to-sinking and being "strong" and "direct" go together or how these in combination could produce this list of traits. My educated guess is that either Bonatti's text or his source text should read, "and they were pertaining-to-sinking, and *not* direct *or* strong…"

Indeed Ptolemy seemed to say that if the three superiors were in the opposition of the Sun (namely in the middle of retrogradation), then they are hidden in the beginning of the day. If however they were united with the Sun, then they are hidden in the beginning of the night (this is true), and then they become weaker than they could [ever] be, and they make the soul vile [or low-class] and of little goodness.

And if [the superiors][230] were pertaining-to-arising,[231] or in their first station, they are strong, and make the soul strong. And if they were retrograde, they are weak, and make it inert. And if they are in their second station, they make it average. If however they were direct and oriental, they are stronger, and make the soul strong and skillful at exercising its strengths.

On Venus and Mercury

Concerning Venus and Mercury, [Ptolemy] said that if they are in their first station and the nativity were diurnal (or they were in their second station and the nativity were nocturnal), then they are middling, and make the soul average, neither good nor bad, but fit to be inclined to both the good and the bad.

Abu 'Ali seemed to say[232] that if they are in their first station and the nativity were nocturnal (or in the second station and the nativity were diurnal), they are most strong, and make the soul strong. And if they were in the middle of their direct motion, they are weak, and make the soul weak, nimble, and easily changing itself from proposition to proposition; fainthearted and unfortunate, and loving faintheartedness, and freely spending time alone.[233]

---

[230] At first one would expect this sentence to refer to the inferiors (since they were introduced as being occidental before). But the inferiors are not oriental when in their first station, neither are they supposed to operate as well when they are oriental (as Bonatti attests several times).

[231] Orientales. Here again, Bonatti and his text distinguish being orientalis and being in the first station, which are typically counted as phases. So I have read orientalis here as "pertaining-to-arising."

[232] I am not sure of Bonatti's source here.

[233] In order of best to worst, we seem to have: (a) first station and nocturnal makes strong; (b) second station and diurnal makes strong; (c) first station and diurnal makes average; (d) second station and nocturnal makes average; (e) middle of direction motion (i.e., combust) makes weak. It is unclear to me how much stock Bonatti puts into these statements.

On the three superiors

If however the aforesaid three superior stars were in their second station, and they were in the 10th, around its cusp.[234]

Indeed Venus and Mercury, when [1] retrograde, if they were to enter under the rays of the Sun, or they were under them (and it were a diurnal nativity), or while [2] direct, [if] they were to enter under the aforesaid rays, or were[235] under them (and the nativity were diurnal), they will make the soul of the native pure, intelligent, gentle; but it will not have a perfect memory; avoiding and fleeing labor; and it will be an inquirer into secret things; a subtle investigator of hidden things (and especially of the sciences, like of nigromancy, magic, and other profound and hidden sciences); it will even fare well in some wondrous and lofty things, like the judgments of the stars and the expounding of dreams, and things like these.

[On the fixed signs]

For if they (namely the significators and the angles) were in fixed signs, they make these accidents or these qualities come into the soul: wherefore they make it benevolent, upright, legal, not deceitful, not lightly changing, stable, many troubles, sustaining many labors; and many efforts, able to understand and talented, true and rigid; and bringing about what it wills; very free [or pure] from malices; and defending itself well from pleasures. [The soul will be] a collector of things which it sees or hears, and of words (both of vile and valuable things), letting go of nothing or very little of them, committing [them] to memory; jealous in useful matters, and especially in the sciences, for it does not want to be outdone by others in them; a lover of honor and of things concerning which praise is acquired; and to a good extent contentious in lawful matters; passing beyond the talents of other souls, changing [only] with great difficulty from proposal to proposal.

On the common signs

If however the Ascendant and the aforesaid significators were in common signs, on account of their multiformity and mutation they will make the soul multiform, slow and reluctant to act, difficult to be understood appropriately,[236]

---

[234] This sentence ends abruptly, but it seems to draw on *Tet.* III.14, end of p. 57.
[235] *Extiterint.*
[236] *Debite vix cognoscendam.* This seems to mirror Ptolemy's "hard to grasp."

easily loving, and lightly leaving love behind; unstable, cunning, wanting now this, now that, persevering in few things well; and it will be expert at gaining the knowledge of music; easily repenting for things both good and bad; however it will be of a manifest intellect.

On the movable signs

Indeed if they were in movable signs, they will make the man stay gladly in cities, and associating with others (on account of the mobility of those signs); they make [the soul] loving matters of communities and guilds [or societies]; likewise striving for praise; and they make it a ponderer of divine things; and it will be of a praiseworthy character [or talent], and ready to move itself toward those things which it ought;[237] an investigator into matters; and liberal and of a good opinion toward practically everyone indifferently; and caring for (and noticeable in) the judgments of the stars.

On the stars disposing the soul of natives

Again, the Moon and Mercury are to be considered, [to see] whether they (or those in whose domiciles or exaltations or bounds or triplicities they are) are in the aforesaid places, or in their own peculiar dignities, or in their own sects:[238] because then they make the native's soul great [or generous], open, the peculiar characteristics of which will be free, prosperous and faring well, nor could this be disappointed unless something against [its] nature mitigates this. And the more so, if one and the same significator were the Lord of the places in which the Moon and Mercury are, or it is associated to them,[239] or at least one of them were to have al-'ittisal with the Moon. If however it were otherwise than was said–that is, that the aforesaid stars (namely one of the five other planets) are not the rulers of the places (namely of both the Moon and Mercury, or one of them), nor are they associated to them nor to either of them–you will look around to see to which one of those two one of the others approaches more; because the soul of the native will be disposed according to how it (namely Mercury or the Moon or the one associating to them) is disposed.

If however the aforesaid five planets were outside of their own dignities, or were otherwise badly disposed, they will signify, and will make, the soul of the

---

[237] *Et ad ea quae debuerit apta se movere.*
[238] *Aym.* Reading "sect" with Ptolemy, here and below as appropriate.
[239] This means "in aspect." Ptolemy probably means "by whole-sign aspect."

native contrary to what was said. Wherefore its qualities will be rough and hidden and imperfect, without prosperity.

Indeed Baruch[240] said that the stellar ruler of the places in which the Moon and Mercury are, or those which were elevated over them,[241] will make the native's soul perform rigid and harmful works (I say this, if they were malefics or made unfortunate), and [they will make] the native perform unjust things, and the soul of that native will be easily moved to rule over others, willing to harm them; nor will it be reformable through its own power of discernment; nor will it seem troublesome to wound others, but it will be delighted in this.

But if those impeding in the places of the stars were malefics who are in the sect contrary to them, they will make the native's soul weak and detestable, and easily changing from one proposition to another (and more likely to a bad one than to a good one); and for such a reason misfortunes will happen to the native with torments harming him. The same means by which the native's soul becomes inclined toward the aforesaid, [will be that] through which it will become joyous in doing well to others, and inclined toward the good, if the benefics were significators, and he[242] free from impediments, and nothing impeding were elevated above them.[243] Then it will please the native's soul to do well for others; and it will delight in this; nor however will something troublesome result from acting well, but [rather] benefit and good praise.

But if the benefics themselves were the significators, and the malefics were elevated above them,[244] it will not be the same nature for the native's soul with the aforesaid, for it will be altered, and the qualities of the native's soul will be soft and benevolent, not rigid, not rough, but rather quiet. However, I will tell you what will happen to the native from this, because on account of his humbleness and evenness and softness and quiet, and benevolence, and abstinence from doing bad, and [his] pity and the delight which he has in men, he will be reviled and spurned by them, and be blamed, and be accused when he is guiltless and innocent; and they will think[245] to fear evil things which are

---

240 Unknown astrologer, but the name is Jewish.
241 This must refer to the Hellenistic "overcoming." See Introduction and footnote to Tr. 3, Part 2, Ch. 20.
242 *Ipse.* Perhaps Bonatti means "if *one* of the benefics were the significator, and *he* were free." Ptolemy treats this matter using only plurals.
243 *Tet.* III.14 says, "when these stars have nothing in superior position to [or "overcoming"] them." This refers to the Hellenistic "overcoming." See Introduction and footnote to Tr. 3, Part 2, Ch. 20.
244 This refers to the Hellenistic "overcoming." See Introduction and footnote to Tr. 3, Part 2, Ch. 20.
245 Reading *credent* for *credentur*, otherwise the *temere* (to fear) would be more awkward.

spoken falsely about him, and discernment will be found in practically none or very few, in excusing him;[246] nor will his words be listened to; and he will be reputed in all cases to be practically nothing (even if he ought to be praised and well reputed as being genuine, and his counsels[247] will be found to be sound); and many false pretexts will be imposed on him. And friends will easily leave him, practically without cause; and by how much more he will be of service, by that much less will he be thanked, and his service reputed as nothing; and men will often strive often to harm him, not to mention others, but even those whom he were to serve better; and often in all those things concerning which he gets involved, it will go unluckily for him.

This is the manner through which the qualities of natives' souls are generally known and prognosticated. However, concerning the particular qualities which must come about according to the nature of the stars or planets, we must look individually below.

Chapter 2: On the qualities of a native's soul coming about in a particular way according to the nature and significations of the stars

Having already spoken about the qualities generally happening to the native's soul, we must but make mention of the particular qualities belonging peculiarly to them, which tend to happen to the native's soul according to the natures of the stars and their qualities.

On the signification of Saturn if he were the sole dispositor
of the qualities of the native's soul

You may say, therefore, that if Saturn were the sole ruler or dispositor of the qualities of the native's soul, and were the *al-mubtazz* of the places in which the Moon and Mercury were,[248] and were oriental in the world and from the Sun, and [he were] in the angles, and is otherwise well disposed, nor impeded, according to Ptolemy it will make the soul of the native a lover of just and good men; and of solid and profound counsel; confident in its own counsel; a disputator; bearing labor; not always using truth, for it will not be but that it will

---

[246] Reading *in eius excusatione* for *in eius excusationem.*
[247] Reading *consilia* for *consimilia.*
[248] By "and," Bonatti is equating this "sole ruler or dispositor" with an *al-mubtazz*. It seems to mean Saturn would rule the places the Moon and Mercury are in, by domicile or exaltation or bound or triplicity (see above), which would suggest an *al-mubtazz* by equal points.

keep something of its own malice to itself; loving enrichment; desiring to have dignities; not well observing its own promises, nor remaining firm in them; gladly gathering up treasure; jealous; hiding its own secrets from others.

If Saturn were of bad condition

And if Saturn were found to be to the contrary of these things which were said, and were detestable in his own condition or in the place in which he appeared, it will make the soul of the native low-class, unclean, fainthearted in knowledge; confident only in its own counsel, nor however will it know what kind of counsel it is, always believing itself to be deceived in the counsels of others; jealous; timid and not brave; abhorring to associate itself with men; a lover of concealment and mourning; unfortunate, cunning, shameless, difficult, a deceiver, loving no one, malevolent, never knowing for the time of its life how even to apply its own goods [so] that it may rejoice in them or because of them.

If Saturn were neither good nor bad

Indeed if Saturn is found not totally well nor totally badly disposed, you will pronounce the qualities of the soul will be according to his condition. But if he were to come down more towards freedom than impediment, you will judge the good to be less removed; if however more toward impediment than to freedom, the bad less removed.

On the signification of Saturn if Jupiter were joined with him

Which if Jupiter is joined with Saturn, and he were of good condition and well disposed (namely oriental in the world and from the Sun), and he were in the angles, it will make the soul of the native just, gladly honoring old and decrepit men; and it will be of sound counsel, freely succoring others and helping them; having good knowledge; a giver of gifts, generous, patient, quiet, intelligent; a lover of friends and desiring philosophy.

If Jupiter were badly disposed

If however his disposition were contrary to the aforesaid, it will make the native's soul inexperienced in doing well, unintelligent in matters, and gladly devoted to and conversant with and delighting in diabolical words; and loving hypocrisy,[249] pretending to spend time gladly in the houses of prayer, when inwardly the contrary is found; even predicting future things[250] without the knowledge of letters; not inclined to delightful things, abhorrent of having children; in no way wishing to have friends, desiring to live in places removed from [other] habitations, not wanting to keep company with men. And although he is foolish, sometimes having words similar to the words of a wise man; not seeking honor, nor caring about being praised, rather choosing evils than goods, and adhering to them gladly; weak and malicious; and if he were exercise good things at some time, quickly repenting of them; difficult, and not loving quiet.

If Jupiter were neither well nor badly disposed

Indeed if Jupiter is found in a disposition which is neither wholly good nor wholly bad, it will make the native's soul of such qualities as the kind [in which] his condition is found. Which if his condition were to come down more on the side of good than bad, the qualities of the soul will come down more on the side of good than bad. But were his condition to come down rather on the side of bad than good, it will make the qualities of the soul to come down more on the side of the bad than the good. And you could always prognosticate according to his condition.

On the signification of Saturn if Mars were joined to him

If however Mars were joined to Saturn, and he were of good and praiseworthy condition, namely in the angles, and oriental in the world and from the Sun, nor impeded, as Ptolemy says it will make the native's soul–on account of the malice of both–not understanding what it ought to understand; miserable; an imbecile; harming; laborious; faint-hearted; hardly ever (and with great, quaking fear) attempting [anything]; lacking reverence, grave, an impostor; and if it contained great-heartedness in itself, practically criticizing everything; having no organized method in itself; and with a certain hypocrisy against its own bellicose nature, pretending to be timid in all things; but still pretending the contrary, and therefore it will be said to be bellicose (when it is a child of great fear); loving confusions, jealous with the worst jealousy, a traitor, persevering in its own malice, nor easily moving away from it; a laborious native, and gladly making others to be full of labor; loving pretended sanctity; having hatred for kings,

---

[249] *Hypocrisem.* I.e., pretended sanctity, not merely inconsistency.
[250] Or, "preaching future things."

princes, regents, great men, and all of his betters; boasting about victories that belong to others, or ascribing them to himself; having nothing profound in the good; full of rusticity, grave in tolerating,[251] unjust, gladly harming men and hating them, esteeming them little and despising them (nor will it be altered or changed from the things said above, but it will always persevere in them); getting himself involved concerning trades and many and diverse other things, and persevering well in none of them.

If Mars were in a condition contrary to the aforesaid

Indeed if Mars were in a condition contrary to what was said, it will make the soul of the native a plunderer, and making the native a besieger of roads; Mars will even make it have the worst qualities, not knowing God, nor even revering Him; neither fearing, nor loving; gladly making money through unlawful [or immoral] means, a blasphemer; disturbing, nor truly loving anyone, given to thievery, a traitor, deceiver, killer, shameless,[252] impure, bad, sacrilegious, a nigromancer, the native committing homicide against his own,[253] a fornicator, violator of tombs, and generally worthless [or vile] in all things.

On the signification of Saturn if Venus were joined to him

Which if Venus were joined to Saturn, and she were of good condition and well disposed, and were oriental in the world and from the Sun, and likewise in the angles, it will make the soul of the native peaceful, benevolent, faithful, modest, abstaining, taking counsel, a lover of knowledge, abstaining from impurities, loving God, and fearing [Him], and holding Him in reverence.

If Venus were in the contrary condition

If however Venus were in a condition contrary to the above said one, it will make the soul of the native have a bad [way of] holding back,[254] and bad opinion, and bad law; immodest, unclean, irksome, jealous, abhorring women, inclined toward unseemly and unclean sexual intercourse, (like the horrendous and despicable sodomitical type, and the like, and with old and dirty men);

---

[251] *Rusticitate plenam ad tolerandum gravem.* This is unpunctuated in 1491 and 1550, but it seems to be best broken up into separate phrases.

[252] *Impudicam.* This adjective has connotations of being unchaste, immodest, and dirty.

[253] *Sui ipsius.*

[254] Lit., "be of bad reception" (*receptionis*). I choose the above translation because the traits Bonatti lists have to do with excessive sexuality.

concerning women, choosing a vile and deformed one, not caring about a beautiful one, and sometimes permitting himself to be deceived by women; segregating himself from all others, confident only in his own counsel; a fornicator in every shameful and perverse fornication; ignorant, adulterous, shameless and delighting in shameful things; impure, accomplishing his own impurity more likely with his own blood-relatives than with others; getting aroused with regard to shameful venereal acts and [those] against nature (not only with rational beings but with the brutes); and proud, low-class, accursed, a scoundrel, concealing his own thoughts from others, not holding God in reverence, despising dreams and other secret things, involving himself in nigromancy and many other different things.

On the signification of Saturn if Mercury were joined with him

And if Mercury were joined to Saturn, and he were of good condition, and well disposed, and were oriental in the world and from the Sun, and likewise in the angles, nor otherwise impeded, it will make the soul of the native an inquirer into the laws and legal affairs; and investigating nigromancy; a lover of medical science; a deliberator on hidden things, and hiding itself from others; a sophist, a nigromancer; showing himself to perform wonders in the presence of men (and without their presence); of good talent; an easy expounder of things that must be expounded, a good investigator of things to be investigated; but having an acute bitterness in himself; a lover of understanding of practically all works; and from thence it will go well for him.

If Mercury were badly disposed

If however the disposition of Mercury were contrary to the above-said, it will make the soul of the native turbulent, jealous, full of labor, annoying to men (and especially to his own blood-relatives); nor will he be inclined to see them; pained at their good things, rejoicing at their evils, a lover of sorrows, seeing fantasies in the night (because of which he will be disturbed); a deceiver, traitor, concealer of his own business dealings, adhering gladly to nigromancy; nor will usefulness follow from thence, but its contrary.

Chapter 3: On the signification of Jupiter if he were the sole significator or dispositor of the qualities of the soul

If Jupiter were the sole dispositor of the qualities of the native's soul, and it was such that he were the *al-mubtazz* over the places in which the Moon and Mercury were, and were oriental in the world and from the Sun, likewise that he were in the angles, and otherwise well disposed, nor impeded, it will make the soul of the native just, generous, magnanimous, even, modest, and making the native famous; benevolent, liberal, calm, gentle, distinguished, reverent, and having great thoughts of his own works; amiable to men, gladly doing good, a conductor of matters and knowing how to establish rule,[255] and the like.

Which if Jupiter were in a condition contrary to the aforesaid, it will make the soul of the native weak and hidden, without a good intellect; wasteful, demoniacal and exercising his services in diabolical things; and of evil opinion, deceitful and to be watched out for; loving delights and strong desires; stubborn, disdaining and ignorant of knowledge; he will be wanting to liken himself to the other things said above, but much less so.

On the signification of Jupiter if Mars were joined to him

And if Mars were joined to Jupiter, and he were of good condition and well disposed, namely oriental in the world and from the Sun, and he were in the angles, in no way impeded, it will make the soul of the native cunning, an appeaser; gladly litigating, and enjoying itself in controversies; bellicose and an arranger of wars; and one who conducts armies (and especially of those of which justice were a part); most strong, humbling himself before none; loving revenge and to overcome others, nor wanting to placed under (or lying under) anyone; wanting to promote himself to dignities and rulerships; nor ignorant of the truth of matters, seeking honor and thanks, and thence pursuing prosperity; prudent, easily provoked and a liar; enjoining many people to many things.

If Mars were to appear in a condition contrary to the aforesaid

Indeed if Mars were to appear in a condition contrary to the aforesaid, it will make the soul of the native a blasphemer, shameless, a malicious divulger of his own words and his own secrets and those of strangers; apprehending things that must be apprehended, expounding things that must be expounded; a despiser of

---

[255] *Regimina facere scientem.*

others, having pretended sanctity, proud, a deceiver, disobedient; making the native lying, a plunderer, a cutter of roads, a rapist,[256] losing his own things, a man of evil words, throwing things into confusion, low-class, unfaithful, unstable, of ill-repute and bad advice; unintelligent, easily changing from one proposition to another, appearing [to be] of different qualities, nor will a definite manner of living be easily found in him.

On the signification of Jupiter if Venus were joined to him

If however Venus were joined with Jupiter, and she were of good condition, and well disposed, namely oriental in the world and from the Sun, likewise in the angles, free from impediments, it will make the soul of the native polished, simple, without malice, loving professions[257] and the investigations of things; strongly desiring games, song, dancing, feasts, and drinking parties; and it will be of good capacity and good opinion, and good counsel, reverent, loving God and serving Him, full of labor in love of Him; humble, intelligent, obliging, gladly having leisure time for the reading of books and for thinking about things; temperate with respect to venereal acts; and acting according to his law; a lover of his own blood-relatives; desiring honor and a good reputation; just and honest.

If Venus were impeded

Which if Venus were in a condition contrary to the aforesaid, it will make the soul of the native easily provoked, and its anger will be of the likeness of a woman's anger; unintelligent, and especially wasteful in the affairs of women; libidinous, a wooer[258] or uncompliant, or easily being witty [or alighting on] on a stupid matter, or a giver [of gifts], doing wrong, a decorator of the body, ignorant of friends, extolling himself; not very free of trouble among men (for he will blush in their presence); permitting himself to be hindered for a trifling reason; having a feminine sense, competent in matters pertaining to Church

---

[256] *Raptorem. Rapio* means "to snatch or take by violence." Its field of meaning covers violent plundering, laying waste, and seduction. Bonatti could simply mean that the native will try to take things at will; but since he has already mentioned highway robbery, he could also mean a rapist.

[257] *Magisteria.* This might also mean that the native loves to have skills and be a master of something.

[258] *Procam.*

oversight[259]–if he were to stick to them, he will prevail, loving them; faithful, ignorant of malicious things; leading the way in other matters, and a concealer of them; submissive in all of his own acts, both in serving others and in his own particular affairs; honorable, but in all of his own works he could be said to be other than commendable.

On the signification of Jupiter if Mercury were joined to him

Indeed if Mercury were joined to Jupiter, and he were of good condition and well disposed (namely made fortunate and strong, oriental in the world and from the Sun), and he were in the angles, nor otherwise impeded, it will make the soul of the native fit for syllogizing, doing geometry, reading books (gladly spending leisure time devoting himself to them), and expert in every area of mathematics, a sermonizer, versifier, compliant, an arranger [of things], a lover of associations, exhibiting sound counsel, a good quality and good opinion and good belief; having a bountiful and good skill [or character], and gladly and quickly finishing well all things which he were to begin; and if he were to stick to medicine, very proficient at it, and honor and a fitting usefulness following from thence; and the native will be called on that occasion by kings and great men and the wealthy and the noble, and they will gladly submit themselves to his care; loving God and holding Him in reverence and fear; a lover of blood-relatives and neighbors; having riches; a rational lover of the sciences.

If Mercury were in a condition contrary to the above-said

Indeed if Mercury were in a condition contrary to what was said, and he were impeded, it will make the soul of the native stupid, ignorant, unintelligent, and talkative in his speaking, often and more often deceived; and he will readily lose the small bit of sense he has; impetuous, wishing to stick to divine things, but not knowing how to do it; bitter,[260] proud in persevering in his stupidity; reputing himself wise, putting himself in the service of another; disorganized in his own actions and movements; verbose, of a public appetite[261] (for he will not know how to hide those things he feigns [or pursues]); however there will be some kind of memory, even of some doctrine.

---

[259] *In rebus ad ecclesiasticam censuram pertinentibus.* The *censura* especially refers to moral oversight, so perhaps the impeded Venus makes him interested in moral and sexual laxity.

[260] *Amaribundam.*

[261] *Publicique appetitus.*

Chapter 4: If Mars were the sole significator of the qualities of the native's soul

Which if Mars were the sole significator or dispositor of the qualities of the native's soul, and he were of good condition and well disposed, namely oriental in the world and from the Sun, and in the angles, nor otherwise impeded, it will make the soul of the native most strong, most powerful, easily provoked, spirited, a strong desirer of arms, indeed judging everything to [pertain] to arms, humbling himself to none, putting himself in danger of death for the sake of any matter; caring little or practically nothing for pecuniary wealth, destroying almost everything; wishing to be first in war, despising all things, wishing to bring violence into everything, confident of his own powers more so than all the rest of the world.

If Mars were badly disposed

Indeed if Mars were in a condition contrary to the above-said, it will make the native's soul proud, stupid, unintelligent, a whisperer, irritating, a blasphemer, garrulous, not reverent, a plunderer, a deceiver, a waster and destroyer of things, a delighter in the shedding of blood, rejoicing in the harm and detriment of others; abhorring blood-relatives, ignorant of his own Creator, not holding Him in reverence.

On the signification of Mars if Venus were joined to him

Indeed if Venus were joined to Mars, and she were of good condition and well disposed, namely oriental in the world and [from] the Sun, and she were in the angles, nor otherwise impeded, it will make the soul glad and joking, complying well, making the native good, likeable, even rejoicing and of a happy or quiet life with games; loving his partners, well disposed according to the complexion of the native's body; a fit form of the body; wanting to leap and loving dancing, and gladly engaging in them; adhering gladly to beautiful women and willingly spending time with them, and deliberating;[262] inclined to delights, and knowing how to manage a good life and praiseworthy life of them; easy in sexual intercourse, and pursuing benfit from thence; wise, modest, understanding what must be understood, knowing how to be on his guard against illicit and

---

[262] *Ratiocinantem.* Perhaps, given the context, Bonatti means "calculating," i.e., calculating to get what he wants from women.

unuseful and unrequired or dangerous things; but easily provoked to anger—meanwhile a jealous destroyer of his own matters by abusing men by sodomitical means, sometimes devastating their good qualities.[263]

If Venus were badly disposed

And if Venus were in a condition contrary to the above-said, it will make the soul of the native delinquent and remaining in the contraries of the above-said; for it will make it exceeding in the cultivation of venereal things, bending itself now to one quality, now to another; a blasphemer, liar, traitor both of what is his and what is others', and a deceiver; disgusting, strongly desirous of illicit things, desiring things lightly, and easily and quickly leaving what was sought; and one who deals in illicit and prohibited sexual intercourse, or a corrupter (like of nuns, virgins, and brides); disordered, cunning, sharp even in malices, and always striving in the qualities of its own vices; and on such an occasion easily falling upon many immodesties,[264] making the native of a low-class intellect, practically unintelligent, impetuous, freely committing shameless things, and eager to ornament his own body.

On the signification of Mars if Mercury were joined to him

Which if Mercury were joined to Mars and he were well disposed and of good condition, and were oriental in the world and from the Sun, and likewise in the angles, free, nor otherwise impeded, it will make the soul of the native to be of commingled and diverse qualities: for it will make it wise and able, a lover of things to be loved, an understander of things to be understood, knowing how to rule, easily changing from one proposition to another, desiring to arrive quickly to what was proposed, sometimes (or rather often) gladly engaging in bad things, cunning, a traitor, astute, unstable, raging,[265] having a shallow intellect, a deceiver, loving feigned sanctity, stubborn, a shapeshifter,[266] delighting in quarrels and discords, a great inquirer into any and all matters; however, in all of these reprehensible things it will go unluckily for him; loving those like himself and profiting them gladly and helping them; hating those inimical to him, and intending to harm them in every way, knowing well how to do it.

---

[263] *Bonitates,* lit., "their goodnesses." Perhaps "their virtues."
[264] Reading *inverecundias* for *verecundias.*
[265] *Furibundam.* But *furibundus* also means "inspired," i.e., filled with prophetic inspiration. But Bonatti probably means the former.
[266] I.e., good at lying or concealing true intentions.

If Mercury were in a condition contrary to the above-said

And if Mercury were in a disposition contrary to the above-said, it will make the soul of the native appearing to know something, when it knows practically nothing; for it will be unintelligent, practically foolish, pretending to be obedient when his obedience is not something [done] by [true] obedience, but rather by a certain kind of foolishness; quickly repenting of all which he has done or undertaken, nor knowing how to choose a good portion of them; wanting to be called wise when he knows practically nothing; a deceiver, disorganized, a destroyer, observing no right order in his motives [or movements], robbing,[267] a liar, cunning, a good-for-nothing, speaking falsely, a perjurer, loving discords and controversies, low-class; still, he wants to be called honest; a blasphemer, plunderer, eager to misuse roads and dig under walls, performing incantations, a traitor, killer or murderer; a nigromancer; and not holding God in reverence.

Chapter 5: If Venus were the sole significatrix of the qualities of the native's soul

Indeed if Venus were the sole significatrix of the qualities of the native's soul, and she were of good condition and well disposed, namely oriental in the world and from the Sun, and were in the angles, nor otherwise impeded, it will make the native's soul just, humble, and likewise quiet, intelligent, having riches, and using them in a good way; suffering injuries, deliberating wisely in matters, loving games, leaping and dancing; abhorring impieties, holding God in reverence, inclined to know professions; bestowing a beautiful form and a good quality to the native; dreaming good dreams; likeable, reverential, doing good, prospering; nevertheless lazy in all of these; a wooer; making the native effeminate, and likening his qualities to women's qualities; not spirited,[268] nor even well acquainted [with that] nor making the native magnanimous [or of great and famous soul], but rather his name will practically not exist among other names; and making him rush easily into the majority of his professions.

---

[267] *Latronissam.*
[268] Where "spirited" has the Martial connotations mentioned above.

On the signification of Venus, if Mercury were joined to her

And if Mercury were joined to Venus, and he were of good condition and well disposed, oriental in the world and from the Sun, and he were in the angles, nor otherwise impeded, it will make the soul of the native a lover of professions and sciences, and especially the *quadrivial* ones; and of good skill [or character], a versifier, inclined to music, loving all commendable things; in the same way it will strongly desire delights [or frolics], and be well-suited to them; operating commendably; and it will make him likewise a lover of quiet, and delighting in [those things], glad, loving his own friends, likewise intelligent and having a good law and good worth; a lover of horses; and entering on a straight path and deviating in nothing; gladly learning more, both by himself and from others, and willingly applying himself in learning; an imitator of the ways of good and honest men, likening itself to the souls of the just, eager in making public speeches and fit in speaking, likeable, temperate in the quality of the soul, calm, magnanimous, a helper to those in need. However, he is made faulty in strongly desiring to take advantage of boys and committing shameful deeds with them, wanting to prefer them to women; and he will be jealous.

If Mercury were badly disposed

If however Mercury were of bad condition and badly disposed, namely in the contrary of what was said, it will make the native two-tongued, speaking evil, sly, duplicitous, astute, a liar, deceiver, false, a traitor, perjurer, throwing things into confusion, considering all evil things deeply and wholly,[269] evil in all things, loving no one, loved by no one, a deceiver of women; and if a woman were born [it will make her] a suffocator and destroyer of her own children, blaming and condemning others; and doing all evils which it can; wanting to all things and trying them; however sometimes (even if rarely) to the good, but more often or rather mostly to the bad; freely committing shameful acts, and ought to be blamed in many things; however sometimes he will be found at fault, even if he might not commit it now; but this will happen to him because of his own evil habit of committing guilty acts.

---

[269] *Profunde ac radicitus.*

Chapter 6: If Mercury were the sole significator of the qualities of the native's soul

If however Mercury were the sole significator of the native's soul, and he were of good condition and well disposed, namely oriental in the world and from the Sun, and were in the angles, nor were he otherwise impeded, it will make the native's soul have many good qualities and sciences, a sharp mind [or skills], and a good intellect; a good memory for ancient things and recorder of experiences; an advocate of natural things,[270] and an understander and expositor or interpreter of them; a doer of good, a deliberator and investigator of the sciences, able to learn the *quadrivium*, and an evaluator[271] of goods, and a good and true and secret concealer of things that must be concealed.

If Mercury were in a condition contrary to the above-said

Which if Mercury were in a condition contrary to the above-said, namely that he is of bad condition and badly disposed, it will make the native's soul low-class, a deceiver, gladly making others go astray, confident in its own counsel, having a shallow and quick motive, easily changing from proposition to proposition, ignorant, false, a liar, unstable,[272] disorganized in its own qualities, unfaithful, not holding God in reverence; disobedient, unjust, employing falseness in all things and through all things.

If Mercury were joined to any of the aforesaid

Which if Mercury were joined with any of the aforesaid, of whatever condition you were to find him, he will be converted to the nature of him with whom he will be joined, and you will judge [that] the qualities of the soul are going to be according to the disposition and condition of [the other planet], whether [the condition] were good or evil.

What each of the planets will do in the qualities of the soul, if they were contrary

Indeed if any one of the other planets were joined with any one of the other planets, and one were well disposed and of good condition, the other badly disposed and of bad condition, it will not signify such qualities of the soul as the

---

270 I believe this means natural phenomena, i.e, in terms of natural science.
271 Reading *existimatricem* for *extimatricem*.
272 Reading *instabilem* for *stabilem*.

kind stated above, but they will be between each of the participants (or wise in the nature of each)[273] through a certain middle signification between those extremes, neither truly good, nor thoroughly evil.

Chapter 7: On what is signified by the luminaries concerning the qualities of the soul of the native, and first on the Sun

Concerning what is signified by the luminaries concerning the qualities of the soul, a rule is given to each, at variance with the others' rules, but not contrary to them. For since the Sun has the natural signification of religion, and the qualities of the soul would seem to pertain to religion, he has participation in the qualities of the native's soul with the dispositor of those qualities. Whence if he were of good condition at the hour of the nativity, and well disposed, namely in the world and in the angles, and he were joined with the dispositor of the qualities of the native's soul, he will help [the soul] in making [it] more discerning, more mindful,[274] and separating itself from unjust and illicit things; likewise greater and more powerful, having a better and more faithful law.

If the Sun were of bad condition and badly disposed

Which if the Sun were in a condition contrary to what was said, it will help the dispositor of the qualities of the native's soul (if he were joined to him) in making [the soul] miserable, having bad qualities, base in its harm, full of labor, confident in its own counsel, doubting strangers, stupid, grave and having a wicked will against others, nor going easily away from its own vices.

Chapter 8: On what is signified by the Moon concerning the qualities of the native's soul

Indeed to the Moon is given signification over the qualities of the body and soul, but not individually concerning the qualities of the native's soul like the others; but she has the significations of other things, by means of her own supports,[275] to aid according to what her disposition is: namely [if] good, to the

---

[273] *Sive sapientes naturam utriusque*, although *utriusque* technically means "one of two."
[274] Reading *remororem* for *remorem*.
[275] *Habet tamen aliorum significata suis adminiculis.*

good; [if] bad, to the bad. Whence Ptolemy said in [the *Tetrabiblos*],[276] if the Moon were in the bending[277] places (that is, the beginning of her reversion to the circle of the signs when she is in her own greater elongation from it, namely to the north or to the south), it will help the qualities of the soul, and will make them change suddenly. If however the Moon were in one of the two Nodes (or in the places of the transiting of the Moon's circle through the path of the Sun), it will help the qualities of the native's soul so that he might employ more quickly the ones which he ought to employ.[278] Moreover, if the Moon were above the earth, increased in light, or it were her fullness[279] or in the opposition of the Sun, it will help the qualities of the soul in making them truthful and revealed [or open], and proper[280] in those things which are necessary. And if she were below the earth, or decreased in light, under the rays of the Sun, it will help the qualities of the soul in making them more hidden, or coming into action less, and [that] they will be less quick.

On the things signified by the Moon if she were joined to planets from their dignities

Indeed, to know the things signified by the Moon with the planets (which she bestows on the native) when she is in their dignities, look at her place in the circle in nativities, to see in whose domicile or exaltation or in two of the other dignities she were.

> For if she were in one of the aforesaid dignities of Saturn, joined to him by aspect or by conjunction, it will make the soul of the native sad, full of labor, foolish in inquiring into living; anxious, cold [or frigid], and it will make the native cold unless Saturn were then oriental–for then the condition of the native will be improved.

> But if she were in the dignities of Jupiter, joined or applying to him, it will make the native magnanimous, having a commingling with kings and great men; religious and fortunate; he will be praised by all in his actions.

---

[276] Lat. *Alarba*, Arabic for "the fourth," obviously referring to the *Tetrabiblos*. The passage is from the end of *Tet.* III.14.

[277] Reading "bending" with Ptolemy for *anectatis*. The next clause explains what these "bendings" are.

[278] In other words, Bonatti is describing (a) the points at which the Moon's latitude is greatest from the ecliptic, and (b) the Nodes, i.e., where she crosses the ecliptic. بدر

[279] Lat. *Bederem* (1550) and *bederez* (1491). This is the Full Moon (Ar. *badr*, بدر).

[280] Reading *idoneas* for *iconeas*.

If however she were in the dignities of Mars, conjoined or applied to him, it will make the native's soul bold, a lover of quarrels, loving labor and pilgrimages, gladly commingling with bellicose men, and acquiring good from thence.

Indeed if she were in the dignities of the Sun, and she were joined to him or applied by a good aspect, they will make the native's soul to be making him mix with kings, great men, and high men; or he himself will be one of them. If however she were applied to him by a bad aspect, it will make [the soul] to be making the native to be of a bad condition, and a short life and many infirmities.

Indeed if she were in the dignities of Mercury,[281] joined or applied to him, it will make the soul of the native clever, ingenious, wise in contentions, fortune and good following as a consequence from them.

---

[281] Both 1491 and 1550 omit Venus.

ON THE SECOND HOUSE

Chapter 1: On the signification of the prosperity and substance of the native, and on its acquisition

Having spoken in what has preceded about the form and shape of the native's body, and about the qualities of his soul, it remains to make mention concerning the substance of the native, and his prosperity; likewise whence the native would acquire it, and how, and in what part of his life, since it comes to be after the nativity, happening among the rest of the principal things, and [is] more necessary for the native.

For indeed, Ptolemy said[282] that we ought to get the kind of, and how, and whence substance will come to the native, from the Part of Fortune [alone]; nor is it contrary to his saying what 'Umar and Abu 'Ali said, because Ptolemy made a general statement. Indeed others followed in his footsteps, but they added certain things (which in his times were proven) affirming his statements, not being contrary to them.

The knowledge of arrival of his substance, is that you look at the Part of Fortune and the planetary *al-mubtazz* over the degree in which it is; and at its strength and weakness; and at the planets which are conjoined with the *al-mubtazz* in the hour of the nativity, or those which are elevated above it according to the aforesaid way,[283] [and to see] whether it were of his sect or not. Wherefore, if the *al-mubtazz* over that place were of good condition and well disposed, namely made fortunate and strong, free from impediments, you could judge the native is going to be overflowing with many riches—and more so if the aspect of some benefic were to intervene (and especially Jupiter, both in the day and in the night; or the Sun in the day, or the Moon in the night).

And if that significator of substance were Saturn, or Saturn were the *al-mubtazz* over it, and he were of good condition as we said, it will signify the native is going to acquire riches through heavy labors or from great buildings.

If however if were Jupiter, it will demonstrate the native is going to attain riches from offices [or duties] and the bearing of burdens, both extraordi-

---

[282] *Tet.* IV.2.
[283] This sounds like Hellenistic "overcoming." See Introduction and footnote to Tr. 3, Part 2, Ch. 20.

nary (as are the deputyships of fortresses, the office of a judge, or others by means of honor [or respectability) and ordinary.

But if Mars appeared as the significator of the native's riches, you will have no doubt they will increase from the raising of armies and from ruling, both of cities and of others.[284]

Indeed if the Sun were the significator of the native's substance, it will bring riches to him from the discovery of raw gold, either not planned out or bought for a low price. And if the Sun were in the fourth, he will find it underground.

Likewise if Venus were the significatrix of the native's substance, it will make him aggregate substance from women or from donations.

Still, if the native were to acquire money, and Mercury were his significator, it will announce riches are going to arrive to the native from merchants and mercantile dealings, and from scientific[285] industry.

On the other hand, if the Moon were to signify the native's substance, it will adduce it to him from unexpected silver or from journeys or sailing or the managing of merchandise.

Again,[286] if Saturn were the *al-mubtazz* over the Part of Substance, and Jupiter [were] conjoined to him, and more strongly so if it were in the angle of the

---

[284] *Aliorum.* This could also mean, "other things."

[285] "Scientific" should be taken in the broad medieval sense, as any kind of specialized knowledge of the types signified by Mercury.

[286] The summary of Ptolemy resumes. For the sake of comparison, Ptolemy says: "But in particular, when the star of Kronos [Saturn] gains familiarity with the Fortune pertaining to Possessions, if it should be configured with Zeus [Jupiter], it procures inheritances–and especially when this should happen upon the upper pivots while the star of Zeus chances to be in a bicorporeal *zōidon* or possessing the application of the Moon. For then, after having been taken up for adoption, [the natives] inherit from one another. And should the stars of the same sect themselves chance to assume the testimony of the rulerships, [the natives] retain the possessions unreduced; but if the stars of the opposite sect have superior position over [or "overcome"] the lordly places [i.e., the places of the rulers of the Lot of Fortune] or post-ascend them [i.e., are succeeded], they bring about reductions in the belongings–the general time being taken through the inclination of the stars productive of the cause to the pivots and the post-ascensions." By "inclination," Schmidt takes Ptolemy to mean how close

Ascendant, or in the 10th, or in another good place, in a common sign–it will signify inheritances which will come to the native from foreign parts,[287] which he will inherit, and especially through women; and more so if Jupiter were to have al-'ittisal[288] with the Moon; and again more if the planets which were of the sect of the significators of substance were in her conjunction[289]–and it will even be signified by this that the inheritances will remain in the native's possession. Indeed if one of the planets who was not of their sect (but of the contrary one), is elevated[290] over the al-mubtazz, or follows him from the neighboring [sign],[291] it signifies that the native will lose what is acquired by the aforesaid means, nor will they remain in his power for very long. You could tell when these things (which were spoken concerning substance or its loss) ought to happen, through the aforesaid significators: for these things will happen when they arrive at the angles of the figure of the nativity, for example by means of their distance from the angles–this [distance] having been considered, years or months are signified.

Indeed ['Umar] al-Tabarī[292] said if you wished to look (namely, into the matter of the native's substance), look at the second from the Ascendant of the nativity, and see which of the planets is in it, and [look at] the Lord of the second and the Part of Substance and its Lord; also Jupiter and the Part of Fortune, and likewise its Lord. Then look at the al-mubtazz over these places,[293] whether it were one or more,[294] and after this look to see what kind of condition the al-mubtazz has, whether it is free from impediments (namely made fortunate and strong),[295] and see how it behaves with the Lord of the Ascendant, whether they aspect each other or are joined together corporally; and whether with reception or not (because reception signifies the effecting of the matter); or they are joined from the opposition or square aspect (because these

---

it is to the angles–the closer, the faster the effect. I note that Ptolemy does not specifically endorse primary directions here (as Bonatti does), but perhaps he had it in mind.

[287] *Extraneis.* Note that Ptolemy simply says "others" (Gr. *allotria*).

[288] *Ytisal.* I.e., a conjunction (see also quote from Ptolemy above).

[289] This last clause is obviously based on *Tet.* IV.2: "And should the stars of the same sect themselves chance to assume the testimony of the rulerships…"

[290] This refers to the Hellenistic "overcoming." See Introduction and footnote to Tr. 3, Part 2, Ch. 20.

[291] *De propinquo.* I.e., the sign rising after it. See the quotation from Ptolemy.

[292] *Tiberiades. TBN*, pp. 57-58.

[293] *Loca.*

[294] Again, an indication he is not recommending a compound *al-mubtazz.*

[295] Everything else in this paragraph (except for the final clause about judging according to what you see), is due to Bonatti. 'Umar does not specifically mention the Lord of the Ascendant or particular aspects.

signify the detriment of the matter); and judge thus according to what you were to see concerning substance.

However, Abu 'Ali[296] seemed to want it that you should look (in the matter of prosperity and the substance of the native), to see whence it would come to him, and its multitude or scarcity, from the Lords of the triplicity of the sign in which is the luminary whose authority it is,[297] just as will be said below. And so that I might more easily explain this: which if they were in the angles, namely made fortunate and strong, they signify the native's prosperities and riches in all the times of his life; and especially if they were in the first 15° in front of the cusp of whatever angle (namely of those degrees which go toward the cusp of the angle, not of those which have already gone across the angle)[298]–but more in the seventh than in the fourth, more in the tenth than in the seventh; more again in the first than in the tenth. Wherefore then his accidents will be made more prosperous. Even by how much more they were near the cusp, by that much more will his standing and prosperity and fortune be greater and more praiseworthy. And if they were after the aforesaid 15° up to the end of the angle,[299] by how much more they were removed from the angle, by that much more will his prosperity and fortune be below this.

Therefore, you will consider all the above-said which I have already told you must be considered, namely all the aforesaid methods and all the aforesaid significators: which if you were to find all of them made fortunate and strong, and free from impediments (which hardly or never tends to happen), you could judge the native is going to have immense and inestimable riches; and his prosperity and status will be sublime and most excellent, to such an extent that it could never be resisted but that he would be promoted to rulership over the whole world, of whatever family or condition he was, even if the native is found to be of the lowest stock; and he will remain in that for all the times of his life; unless perhaps one of the fixed stars which I listed for you above diminishes this somewhat (or even *Cor Leonis*), namely in the Ascendant or in the 10th, be it

---

[296] *JN*, pp. 11*ff*.

[297] I.e., the ruler of the sect: the Sun in diurnal charts, the Moon in nocturnal ones.

[298] For example, let 5° Leo be on the cusp of the Midheaven. Bonatti means that the planet will be stronger between 5° and 20° Leo, because these are approaching the cusp of the angle by primary motion, but have not yet passed it. Once they have passed it, they will be "falling" away from the cusp and therefore be "cadent."

[299] To continue the example above, Bonatti now means any planets between 20° Leo, through the end of the sign and up to wherever the cusp of the 11th is.

found by 1° before the line or by 3° after it;[300] for it will increase the sublimities to be practically immense; however, ultimately it will end them in evil (unless a strong benefic were to aspect [the fixed star] from a trine or sextile aspect), wherefore it signifies the native is going to die a bad death, or at least he is going to fall from all of this dignities and powers and sublimities. If however the benefic were to aspect, it diminishes the malice of *Cor Leonis* by one fourth. But if a malefic were to aspect, it will increase its misfortune.

And if all of the aforesaid significators did not appear sound and free, but [only] a portion of them, you could judge the prosperity and status of the native to be strong, and his riches to be overflowing, according to the quantity which was sound.

Therefore I will render the individual [factors] individually, so you may rightly discern the prosperity of the native, and his riches and status.[301]

If you wished to know the prosperity and substance of the native

Whence, if you were to erect the figure of someone's nativity, and you wished to know his prosperity and substance, first look at the Part of Fortune, for it is preferred to the Part of Substance: because the Part of Fortune signifies the native's substance, prosperity, and status, and his whole condition; indeed the Part of Substance is attributed to riches alone.

And see in whose domicile or exaltation or bound or triplicity you were to discover it to have fallen, and consider which of the aforesaid significators[302] is stronger in that place by the multitude of dignities or strengths, because he will be called the *al-mubtazz*,[303] and will be the significator of the native's prosperity and substance, and his condition. Wherefore if it were in the Ascendant or in another[304] of the angles, or in one of his own domiciles (and especially in the one in which the Part of Fortune is), free from impediments (namely fortunate and strong), it will signify the prosperity of the native, and his gain [or advantage], and likewise that a great quantity of riches is going to arrive. And if the Lord of the Ascendant or one[305] of the benefics were to aspect him, and the one

---

[300] By "ahead," I believe Bonatti means "in an earlier degree than the cusp"; by "after" he means "in a later degree than the cusp."

[301] I.e., because the above considerations are only general.

[302] I.e., the Lords of the dignities mentioned.

[303] It is unclear whether this is by equal or weighted-points, but I suspect equal points.

[304] Reading *alio* for *angulo*.

[305] Reading *aliqua ex fortunis* ("one of the benefics") for *ex aliqua ex fortunis* ("[the Lord] of one of the benefics").

aspecting were free from impediments, namely made fortunate and strong (and the more so if the aspect were a trine or sextile; and more again if it were with reception), his substance will be increased by half of the total. Indeed if it were the Lord of the exaltation, it will be increased by one-third, but it will be with greater fame. If however it were the Lord of the bound, it will be increased by one-fifth. And if it were the Lord of the triplicity, it will be increased by one-seventh. Indeed if it were the Lord of the face, it will be increased by one-twelfth. If however the aspect were from the square or from the opposition, it will be much less than this (and the more so and worse, if the aspect were without reception).

If the Lord of the domicile did not aspect, or were impeded

If however the Lord of the domicile did not aspect, or were impeded, then look at the Lord of the exaltation; which if he were impeded, look at the Lord of the bound. Indeed if the Lord of the bound were impeded, look at the Lord of the triplicity; which if you were to see him impeded, look lastly at the Lord of the face–and speak about whichever one of them, and about what is signified by him, just as I have told you now. Indeed if the Part of Fortune and all of the aforesaid significators were impeded (and especially the *al-mubtazz* over the place of the aforesaid Part), you will firmly announce it is going to be the contrary of those things said (which you found); and according to the same method in a bad way,[306] you will predict according to what was judged above in the good one.

If the Part of Fortune could not be the significator of the substance of the native

Indeed if the Part of Fortune could not be the significator of the native's substance or riches (and of his condition), nor the planet who was the Lord of the domicile in which it was (or of the exaltation or the bound or the triplicity, nor even of the face, nor the *al-mubtazz* over that place), then look at the Part of Substance, and you will see in whose domicile (or one of the aforesaid dignities) it were to fall; and you will consider the *al-mubtazz* over that place, according to the method which I have told you for the Lord of the domicile. Because such a planet will be the significator over the prosperity and substance of the native.

---

[306] *In mala parte.*

If the Part of Substance could not be the significator of the substance of the native

Which if the Part of Substance (nor even the planet in whose dignity it was) could not be the significator of the native's prosperity and substance, look at the second and its Lord, or at a planet which is in it. Which if one of the benefics were in the second, or joined with the Lord of the second from a trine or sextile aspect, it will signify the native is going to acquire much substance (and more so if the benefic were Jupiter). If however it were the Sun in the day, his signification will be below what is signified by Jupiter. Indeed if [it were] the Moon in the night, it will be below what is signified by the Sun. Indeed if it were Venus, it will be below what is signified by the Moon.[307]

If [neither] the second [sign], nor its Lord, nor a planet which is in it, could be the significator of the substance of the native

And if the second [sign] or its Lord, or a planet which is in it, could not signify the substance of the native, look then at Jupiter, who naturally signifies substance. Which if you were to find him in the second, judge confidently that the native is going to be affluently overflowing in riches–according, however, to the disposition of Jupiter–nor is he ever going to fall into poverty at any time; and more strongly so, if Jupiter were the Lord of the Ascendant. [A Proposition] of al-Mansur goes along with this: "he will never be a pauper or needy, the Lord of whose nativity is Jupiter"[308]–and again more so and more sublimely so, if the Ascendant were Sagittarius, and Pisces the 4th house [domicile?]; for it does not receive the contrary.[309]

Which if Jupiter were impeded, so that he could not be the significator of the aforesaid, and the nativity were diurnal, then look at the Sun; which if he were in some good place from the Ascendant, free from impediments, namely made fortunate and strong, it signifies the native is going to attain money or substance–but this will be below what is naturally signified by Jupiter.

Indeed if the nativity were nocturnal, then look at the Moon; which if she were in the second, namely made fortunate and strong, free or in another good

---

[307] The idea here seems to be that the wealth conferred by the benefics in such a situation (in or ruling the second) follows this descending order: Jupiter, the Sun, the Moon, and Venus. Note that by the luminaries' being out of sect, their ability to produce their significations is weakened.

[308] Proposition 13 of the *Chapters of Al-Mansur.*

[309] *Non enim recipit hoc contrarium.* I think Bonatti simply means it cannot be the other way around–one cannot have Pisces rising and the 4th Sagittarius.

place from the Ascendant, it will signify great riches that are going to come to the native; however what is signified by her will be below what is signified by the Sun.

If neither the Sun nor the Moon could signify the native's substance

Which if neither the Sun nor the Moon could signify the substance of the native, then look at the planet who is the *al-mubtazz* over the place in which is he who was the *al-mubtazz* over the place in which was one of the aforesaid Parts (namely of Substance or Fortune),[310] and make him the significator of substance. Which if he were fit for this, he will signify the native is going to acquire much substance; but what he signifies will be below what is signified by the Moon.

When that planet could not be the significator of the native's substance

Indeed if such a planet were not fit to signify the substance of the native, look at the planet in whose domicile the Moon is; which if it were in the Ascendant, or in the 2nd or in the angles, or in another good place from the Ascendant, and were free from impediments, made fortunate and strong, it will bring in much money for the native; however what it signifies will be below what is signified by the aforesaid *al-mubtazz*.

If the planet in whose domicile the Moon is, cannot be the significator of the native's substance

However, if that planet could not be the significator of the native's substance, look at the planet who is in the 2nd: which if it were free from impediments, made fortunate and strong (and more so if it had some dignity in the 2nd, or it were a benefic), it will signify the native is going to attain money in a good quantity; however what it signifies will be below what is signified by the planet in whose domicile the Moon is.[311]

---

[310] I.e., take the *al-mubtazz* of the *al-mubtazz* of *either* the Part of Fortune *or* the Part of Substance. Zoller reads this as indicating a compound *al-mubtazz* over *both* the Part of Substance and of Fortune at the same time. But the text clearly states that we are looking for the *al-mubtazz* of the *al-mubtazz* of only one of them (though it does not specify which one, but probably the Part in the better condition).

[311] Bonatti has already considered planets in the 2nd (or rather the second sign) above, but it could be that this consideration here pertains only to wealth–the earlier example, which focused on the benefics and luminaries, would have combined wealth with general prosperity.

If the planet who is in the 2nd could not be the significator of the substance of the native

If however the planet who is in the 2nd could not be the significator of substance, then see if the Lord of the Ascendant and the Lord of the 4th domicile[312] were the same planet–because he will be deservedly called the significator of the native's prosperity and substance; which if you were to find him free, namely made fortunate and strong, you would have it as settled that the native will amass much money just as equally well as if a benefic were in the 2nd.

When the Lord of the Ascendant and the Lord of the 4th is not the same planet

If however you did not find this, look then at the Lords of the triplicity of the house of substance: which if you were to find all of them free (namely made fortunate and strong), it will be signified that riches will come to the native in abundance, in accordance with what his condition was, or enough beyond it. If however only two of them were sound, riches will come to him in two parts of his life, but not in the third. But if only one of them were sound, riches will come to him only in a single one-third of his life, but not in the others. Which if none of them were sound, riches (however much there is of this) will never come to him; however, riches could come to him by means of other causes than the aforesaid ones, namely by the ones to be spoken of below.

If the Lords of the triplicity of the house of substance
could not be the significators of the native's substance

And if the aforesaid Lords of the triplicity of the house of substance could not be the significators of the native's substance, then look at the Lords of the triplicity of the sign in which the Sun is (if the nativity were diurnal) or the Lords of the triplicity of the sign in which the Moon is (if the nativity were nocturnal), and judge according to what I told you about the Lords of the triplicity of the house of substance.

---

[312] I translate *domus* as domicile here because by whole signs this would guarantee that at least either Mercury or Jupiter could fill this role. If quadrant houses were meant, and we assume that one of the signs is intercepted, then no planet could fill this role. Note that this would imply that "domicile" and whole sign houses ought to be implied for the others.

If the Lords of the triplicity of the sign in which the Sun or Moon is,
could not signify the native's substance

Indeed if the aforesaid planets could not be the significators of the native's substance, nor were they fit for this, then look at the Lords of the triplicity of the Ascending sign, and judge concerning them according to what you judged concerning the said Lords of the triplicity of the Sun and the Moon; but what is signified by them will be below what is signified by the Lords of the triplicity of the Sun (in the day) and the Moon (in the night).

If the Lords of the triplicity of the ascending sign could not signify the native's substance

If however the Lords of the triplicity of the ascending sign were not fit to signify the substance of the native, then look at the sign in which the Part of Fortune is, and [look at] its Lord;[313] which if he were in the second or in another good place from the Ascendant, free from impediments, namely made fortunate and strong, he will be the significator of the native's substance and his prosperity; and will bring in a suitable quantity of substance for him. However, what is signified by him will be less than what is signified by the Lords of the triplicity of the Ascendant.

If the Lord of the sign in which the Part of Fortune is,
could not signify the native's substance

Indeed if the Lord of the sign in which the Part of Fortune is, could not be the significator of the native's substance, then look at the sign in which the Part of Substance is, and its Lord; which if you were to find him in the 2nd, or in another good place from the Ascendant, free, namely made fortunate and strong, put him as the significator of the native's substance, and the giver of it. For what he signifies will be comparable to what is signified by the Lord of the sign in which the Part of Fortune is; for it will vary little from it.

If the Lord of the sign in which the Part of Substance is,
could not signify the native's substance

And if the Lord of the sign in which the Part of substance is, could not be the significator of the native's substance, then look to see if the Sun were on the

---

[313] But this planet was already examined and–by hypothesis–rejected above.

line of the 10th house, by 2° ahead or 5° after,[314] and with the Moon going toward him from the left, from his [or her] trine or sextile aspect;[315] and the Lord of the house of substance were in his own domicile or exaltation, going to the conjunction of the Lord of the Ascendant, or to his trine or sextile aspect; and the more so and more strongly so if Jupiter were the Lord of the house of substance. Because this will signify that the native will have a great name, and great fame, and be very powerful. If, however, with this situation, the significator of substance were other than Jupiter, substances will come to him to an immense degree, but they will not be together with exceeding fame. Which if 19° Aries were the 10th house, and the Ascendant were 25° Cancer, and it[316] (or at least the Sun and Jupiter)[317] were free from the malefics and their Lords, the name of that native will be exalted, and will be greatly expanded, and his fame will be broadcast through the whole world.

And Ptolemy said[318] a certain word which seems to differ from the consideration of this house, but it does not depart from the opinion.

For he said that if the planetary rulers of the domiciles[319] or signs which give children (which will be described below in a chapter on the topic of children) were in the places proper to them (which are namely the 10th and the 11th, the 1st and the 5th),[320] and they were oriental,[321] the native will be powerful and have a great name.[322]

---

[314] I believe that by "ahead of," Bonatti means "in an earlier degree than the cusp's"; by "after," he means "in a later degree than the cusp's." See my Introduction.

[315] This must mean either that the Moon's body is approaching his sinister sextile or trine (cast forward in the order of signs), or she is casting a sinister trine or sextile toward his body from an earlier sign. It is unclear to me which is meant.

[316] This seems to refer to the putative significator of substance.

[317] Bonatti puts this at the end of the clause (following "and their Lords"), but it seems to belong here, based both on the "best explanation" principle and Bonatti's usual style.

[318] The following paragraphs are in error, because the following discussion derives from the chapter on children (*Tet.* IV.6), where Ptolemy says the following conditions will make the native's *children* prosper or suffer–it has nothing to do with the native's own substance. But Bonatti had a somewhat good reason to suppose it pertained to the native, because of an ambiguous word choice in his Latin edition of *Tet.* The word *natus* literally means "the one born," and virtually always refers to "the native," i.e., the person whose nativity we have. But in this excerpt from Ptolemy, Plato of Tivoli says, e.g., "the *natus* will be powerful and have a great name," where *natus* would normally be taken to refer to the native himself. But this could–and should–be read as: "the one born [*to the native*] will be powerful and have a great name." I do not know why Plato of Tivoli used *natus* instead of *filius* ("child"), since Ptolemy's Greek clearly says "child" and "children."

[319] I translate *domorum* as "domiciles" because Ptolemy clearly means signs.

[320] Ptolemy mentions the 10th, the 11th, and "the stars in the diameters to these"–i.e., the 4th and the 5th. He does not mention the Ascendant.

If however they were occidental[323] [and] in the place of the sect contrary to them, the native will be poor and unknown.[324]

If however the aforesaid rulers of the places taught [to you here], and the Part of Fortune, were in the Ascendant, or with the Lord of the Ascendant, the native will live until he takes a wife; and he will be loved by his parents; and will be made their heir.[325]

If however it were not so, or they were contrary to each other,[326] or were to aspect each other from the square aspect or the opposition, the native will be a litigator, and will accumulate the greatest hatred regarding his parents, and will treat them badly; nor will he succeed to their inheritance.[327]

If the aforesaid planets could not be significators of the native's substance, nor were the Sun in the 10th

Which if [neither] the Lord of the sign in which the Part of Substance is, nor the other aforesaid planets, could be the significators of the native's substance, nor were the Sun in the 10th by the method which I have told you, then look at the planets with which the aforesaid significators are joined, or who are elevated over them[328]–that is, who precede the others in the conjunction of the *al-mubtazz* which I have told you; or who were northern [in latitude] from it; because they will be the significators of the substance of the native, and especially that one among them who is stronger in dignity or fortune–but what he signifies will be very much below what is signified by the planet in whose domicile the Part of Fortune is.

---

[321] *Orientales.* According to Schmidt, Ptolemy's *anatolikos* here means "rising before *or* after the Sun, provided that it is not under the rays nor retrograde."

[322] Again, this actually pertains to children–the *children* will be famous and notable.

[323] *Occidentales.* According to Schmidt, Ptolemy's *dutikos* here means "under the rays of the Sun, within 15° of him."

[324] Again, Ptolemy is actually referring to the native's own children.

[325] Again, the children will be dear to the native and inherit *his* estate.

[326] This could be taken either as indicating the opposition, or as being in signs which do not aspect each other.

[327] Again, this refers to the native's *own* children being troublesome.

[328] This could refers to the Hellenistic "overcoming." See Introduction and footnote to Tr. 3, Part 2, Ch. 20.

If the aforesaid planets (with which the significators were joined)
could not signify the native's substance

Indeed, if the aforesaid planets could not be the significators of the native's substance, then look at the *al-mubtazz* over the aforesaid places, or [over] one of them; which if [the *al-mubtazz*] were free from impediments, namely made fortunate and strong, it will signify the native's substance; but what it signifies will be lower than all the aforesaid significations.

Which of the said significators should be preferred to the others

Indeed, of the said significators, the principal and stronger ones are the Part of Fortune, the Part of Substance, the 2nd and its Lord generally (and more in the matter of substance); and likewise Jupiter, who, even though he may not always be stronger than the others, still, in the signification of substance he is always more general than all the others.

If all the aforesaid significators were impeded

Which if all the Lords of the aforesaid domiciles, and all the aforesaid significators were so impeded that not one of them could signify the native's substance, then look at the Lords of the exaltations (nor is this [going to be] a repeat statement). If however the Lords of the exaltations were impeded, look at the Lords of the bounds. Indeed if the Lords of the bounds were impeded, look at the Lords of the triplicities. But if the Lords of the triplicities were impeded (which would be astonishing and unheard-of), look lastly at the Lords of the faces, and judge by them, just as you would have judged for any of the others, as I have touched on above.

If the malefics were the significators of the native's substance

And you should know that if the malefics were significators of the native's substance, even if they should be found well disposed, still they will not convey so much good as the benefics do. Indeed if they were made unfortunate and badly disposed, they bring in the contrary, and poverty, intolerably. Indeed if you were to find a malefic in the 2nd, or the rays of a malefic which did not have dignity there, without the presence or aspect of a benefic, or even in one of the aforesaid places signifying substance, or those significators of substance were impeded, you will expect and have to judge the contrary of those things which were said.

If the benefics were the significators of the native's substance

Indeed if the benefics were strong, they will exhibit the great good of the native; if however they were impeded, little good.

Chapter 2: Whence the native will acquire substance or money, and by what means, and in what part of his life

Lastly indeed, the planet and the place signifying whence the native would acquire substance, and by what means, and in what part of his life, and in what part of time, must likewise be looked at. Therefore, after you were to find the significator of the native's substance, consider into what house you found him to have fallen; for you will announce–according to what is signified by that house, and even according to what is signified by the planetary *al-mubtazz* over that house; and likewise according to what is signified by the planet found in that house–whence and by what means substance[329] ought to come.

Chapter 3: In what time of his life, and in what part, the native would acquire substance

Indeed, you could weigh carefully [and know] in what time and in what part of his own life the native will acquire substance, by the Lords of the triplicities. For the first will draw substance in the first part of the native's life, the second in the second, the third in the third; and so you could judge each of them is going to exhibit wealth for the native in that one-third part of his life, according to how you were to find them fit for this. Which if you were to find all of them well disposed, the native will rejoice in the advantage of substance for the whole time of his life. Indeed if you were to find only two of them made fortunate, you will predict he is going to attain substance in two parts of his life. But if you were to find only one of them made fortunate, you could affirm substance is going to arrive in the single one-third of his life deputed to that significator.

---

[329] Reading *substantia* for *substantiae*.

Chapter 4: Why the ancients avoided certain ones
of the said significators

The ancient sages, not because they were ignorant, but because they avoided labor, operated (in the matter of the signification of the native's substance) only by the Lord of the Ascendant, the Lord of the second, the Part of Fortune, the Part of Substance, and their Lords, likewise Jupiter–leaving practically all the other things touching on this to the efforts of the wise. And this tended to happen often enough, [so] that it is not judged rightly by the astrologers, to a fine point, regarding the matter of substance. Because they do not care to consider the other significators, except for those I have told you [just] now. However, you can see, if you want to consider rightly, that the riches or substances of natives do not always come down exactly according to what is signified by [the brief list above]. For we see certain greatly wealthy men, some more wealthy, others wealthy, some moderately wealthy, some neither wealthy nor poor, some moderately poor, some poor, some poorer, some very poor, some beggars, some more beggarly, some most beggarly, some always abounding, some always in need, some sometimes abounding (and the same ones sometimes in need), some who get out of need with great labor, some who escape it with ease, and the like; which does not happen except by the significators listed above, and because of their dispositions and what falls together with that (even if the [significators] which [the ancients] use are more principal).

Whence you could judge regarding the native's prosperity and substance, according to how you were to find them. And [you could] pronounce on his adversity according to their succession and order (which I showed you), according to how you were to find them made unfortunate; because just as the aforesaid significators of substance (if they were made fortunate and strong), bring [substance], so if they were made unfortunate and weak and badly disposed, they take it away; and they will convey trouble and misery and labor and sorrow and poverty. Therefore be industrious and wise, so that you may know how to consider all these.

You will even consider if the Part of Fortune were with the Moon in nativities, and Jupiter were to aspect it, and the nativity were diurnal; or Venus were to aspect it, and the nativity were nocturnal; because it will signify the good rearing of the native (and more strongly so if the Part of Fortune were in a good place from the Ascendant).

Likewise, you will look at the disposition of each one of all of the aforesaid significators (namely the Lords of the triplicities, and the others). For if one of the Lords of the triplicity were well disposed, and the Lord of [the Part of] Substance or the Part of Fortune (or its Lord) were badly disposed, he will detract from the Lord of the triplicity;[330] and the reverse, according to his own condition.

And if the significator of the nativity[331] were in a masculine sign in diurnal nativities, and in a feminine one in nocturnal nativities, nor were he otherwise impeded, his strength will be greater, and his testimony more affirming the truth concerning good rearing, whether the native's life is long or short.

Chapter 5: Whence and because of what reason the native would acquire substance

Having looked (in what has preceded) concerning the acquisition of the native's substance, and the accumulation of its quantity, we must look from this point on [to see] whence the native will acquire it, and by what means, and for what reason.

Therefore you will consider the Lord of the house of substance, or any other significator of it you were to find, and you will see into what house [domicile?] you were to find he had fallen; and likewise with whom (from among the planets) you were to find him joined: because that will signify what kind and whence the native is going to acquire money.

For if it were in the 1st, just as I remember having touched on for you in the Treatise on what is signified by the twelve houses (by way of repeating the same), it signifies that the native is going to acquire substance from his own person, namely by his own industry, with little worry and little labor; or by one of the reasons which are signified by the 1st house [domicile?].

---

[330] Reading *triplicitatis* for *termini* ("bound").
[331] It is unclear what Bonatti means by this.

If the significator of the native's substance were in the 2nd

If however it were in the 2nd, he will find it because of his own substance, like the use of his own possessions and his own goods; and merchant dealings and other arts which are employed with money, and the like; or because of one of the reasons which are signified by the second house [domicile?].

If the significator of substance were in the 3rd

And if it were in the 3rd, he will find it because of brothers or sisters, or neighbors not related to him, or short journeys (which are of two days or less), or because of his own relatives or relatives by marriage [who are] lesser him in riches and power and likewise age, or who consider him their elder, or because of one of the reasons which are signified by the 3rd house [domicile?].

If the significator of substance were in the 4th

Indeed if it were in the 4th, he will find it because of fathers or uncles or fathers-in-law, or other ancestral blood-relatives older and of greater age than he; or from the use of merchant activities of lands or houses or things which are dug up from the ground; or perhaps he will find a treasure underground (even though this happens most rarely); or from the use of furnaces and the like, or because of one of the reasons which are signified by the 4th house [domicile?].

If the significator of substance were in the 5th

And if it were in the 5th, he will acquire substance because of children, and magnates carrying out the affairs of kings, or because of moderate journeys (which I consider from two to four days), or because of banquets or drinks which are sold in taverns or like places; or because of games and the like; or because of one of those things which are signified by the 5th house [domicile?].

If the significator of substance were in the 6th

Which if it were in the 6th, he will acquire it because of male or female slaves, or servants, or small animals which are not ridden (like sheep, goats, pigs, dogs, birds and the like), or because of one of those things which are signified by the 6th house [domicile?].

If the significator of substance were in the 7th

But if it were in the 7th, he will acquire it because of women or partners or enemies, or because of one of those things which are signified by the 7th house [domicile?].

If the significator of substance were in the 8th

Indeed if it were in the 8th, he will find it because of the dowry of women or their goods, or the goods of partners or enemies, or because of someone's death, or goods which are inherited by the dead, goods owned by a woman apart from her dowry, or because of one of those things which are signified by the 8th house [domicile?].

If the significator of substance is in the 9th

But if it were in the 9th, he will acquire it because of religion or the religious, or because of long journeys like the ones merchants and others traveling far tend to make, and the like, or because of one of those things which are signified by the 9th house [domicile?].

If the significator of substance were in the 10th

If however you were to find it in the 10th, say that he will acquire it because of a king, or a profession or magistracy or office or other lay dignity, like a generalship, or a civil authority, and the like, or because of one of those things which are signified by the 10th house [domicile?].

If the significator of substance were in the 11th

On the other hand, if it were in the 11th, he will find it because of friends or the soldiers or household members of the ruler,[332] or by means of business deals, or lending, and harvests; or he will acquire it from an unexpected fortune coming to him, or even because of matters concern-

---

[332] Reading *regiminis* for *regimine*.

ing which he has the hope of making money; or because of one of those things which are signified by the 11ᵗʰ house [domicile?].

If the significator of substance were in the 12ᵗʰ

Lastly, if indeed it were in the 12ᵗʰ, he will acquire it because of prison or the incarcerated, like sometimes guards of the incarcerated tend to do, or one who has released the incarcerated from their prisons for the sake of making money; or because of hidden enemies, or great animals, or some low-class and detestable duty, and from thievery, or because of one of those things which are signified by the 12ᵗʰ house.

These are all the things signified by the twelve houses, which you have above in the treatment of the twelve houses; it is not necessary that I repeat all of them to you.

Chapter 6: By what means the native will acquire substance

We must [now] look at the means through which the native will acquire substance. For indeed you will consider the significator of substance, whether it is the Lord of the Part of Fortune, or the Lord of the Part of Substance, or the Sun or the Moon, or one of the Lords of the triplicities or whichever other one of the aforesaid (from the said significators) it was.

[If Saturn were the significator of substance]

Wherefore if Saturn were the significator of the native's substance, and he were of good condition and well disposed, free from impediments, namely made fortunate and strong, and joined with the benefics, and he were in the angles or the succeedents of the angles, the native will acquire substance and riches from the said labors or the like, by law[333] and by licit and suitable means. If however he were impeded, namely made unfortunate and weak, retrograde or combust, or joined with the malefics, cadent from the angles, and of bad condition, and badly disposed, the native will

---

[333] *Phas.* This term means both divine and moral law, not simply what is written in a legal code.

gather substance more likely through wickedness[334] than otherwise; even by means of deception and lying, and likewise by pilfering [or something clandestine].

If Jupiter were the significator of substance

Indeed if Jupiter were the significator of the native's substance, and he were of good condition and well disposed, namely made fortunate and strong, free from impediments, the native will collect riches by law and by licit and praiseworthy means. Indeed if he were impeded and of bad condition, badly disposed, namely made unfortunate and weak, retrograde or combust or joined with the malefics, and cadent from the angles, the native will acquire substance sometimes through law, sometimes through wickedness, sometimes by licit means, sometimes by illicit means.

If Mars were the significator of substance

Which if Mars appeared as the significator of substance, and he were of good condition and well disposed, namely made fortunate and strong, free from impediments, the native will apply himself to the acquisition of substance by licit and non licit means; nor will he care much whence it comes to him, provided that he can get it. For he will say it is good to extort money everywhere, "a *denarius* in the purse, a peasant in the ditch."[335] If however he is found [to be] of bad condition and badly disposed, namely made unfortunate and weak, impeded by the said impediments, he will investigate the paths of acquiring money by law and wickedness, by robbery, by the cutting of roads, by arson, by the illicit shedding of blood, and by every means by which he could, and from whomever, not considering sex or rank or dignity.

If the Sun were the significator of substance

Indeed if the Sun were to signify the native's substance, and he were of good condition and well disposed, free from impediments, namely made fortunate and strong, the native will acquire substance by licit and required and reputable means. Indeed if he were impeded, and of bad

---

[334] *Nephas*, the antonym of *phas*. I will translate these terms as "law" and "wickedness" respectively below.
[335] *Denarius in bursa, rusticus in fossato.* This must be a medieval Italian saying.

condition, and badly disposed, he will acquire it by all means that he can, practically not caring whether by law or wickedness; however he will know how to whitewash his wickedness, so that it will not appear so openly as badness would.

If Venus were the significatrix of the native's wealth

Which if Venus were the significatrix of the native's substance, and she were of good condition and well disposed, namely made fortunate and strong, the native will aggregate substance (namely riches) in a praiseworthy way and by licit means. If indeed she were found in the contrary condition, he will make use of it in a reprehensible way, and in which lies are committed; nor will he be despised for taking such advantage.

On Mercury and the Moon

With Mercury and the Moon, however, it is not like the others. For whichever of them were the significator of the native's substance, it will signify the native is going to acquire substance according to the condition of, and what is signified by, he with whom [Mercury or the Moon] were joined. Indeed if [Mercury or the Moon] were joined to none of them, and [Mercury or the Moon] were the significator of substance, it will show the native will acquire substance through the bearing of small merchandise, and by short journeys.

And always let it be your concern [to see] if the planetary significator of substance were joined with one of the planets: because he with whom he were joined, will interpose in one of his roles. For if the significator of substance were good, and were joined with a good [planet], his goodness will be increased; if however it were bad and is joined with a bad one, his malice will be increased. Indeed if it were a benefic and is joined to a malefic, his goodness will be decreased. Indeed if it were a malefic and is joined to a benefic, his malice will be decreased.

Chapter 7: At what age or in what part of his life the native is going to acquire substance

Lastly we must see at what age or in what part of life the native is going to acquire substance. To certain ancient sages it seemed that you should consider the Lords of the triplicity of the Sun in the day, the Lords of the triplicity of the Moon at night; to certain ones it appeared differently, according to how their opinions pleased them. I however do not contradict their statements, but still I neither agree wholly with these [people] or those [people], nor do I dissent from them. However, it seems to me that the one who is more powerful in some matter, is by nature more powerful in the judgment of his effect. For the Lords of the triplicity of the house of substance seem to signify it more effectively and more naturally than the others do.[336] And so it seems more fitting that the Lords of the triplicity of the house of substance should be preferred to the other significators in the signification of the time (or in what part of life) in which the native or querent is going to have or acquire substance.

For if the first of them were of good condition and well disposed, he will acquire it in the first one-third of his life; in the other two, he will be in need. If it were the second one, he will acquire it in the second one-third part of his life; in the other two, he will be in need. Indeed if it were the third one, he will acquire it in the last one-third of his life; in the other two he will be in need.

If however so many as two of them were made fortunate, the third not, he will acquire it in the thirds deputed to them; in the other one he will be in need. For if the first and the second were made fortunate, he will acquire it in the first and second one-thirds of his life; in the third he will be in need; if it were the first and the third, he will acquire it in the first and last one-third of his life; in the middle one he will be in need. If it were the second and the third, he will acquire it in the second and third part of his life; indeed in the first one he will be in need.

If however they were all made fortunate, he will acquire it, and it will abound for the whole time of his life. Indeed if they were all made unfor-

---

[336] Remember that in Hellenistic astrology, the triplicity rulers of the luminary whose authority it is, indicate general eminence and prosperity, not strictly monetary wealth (as the triplicity rulers of the 2nd would indicate here).

tunate, he will be in need for the whole time of life, and he will always spend time in misery.

And if the *al-mubtazz* over the place of substance were other than a Lord of the triplicity of the house of substance,[337] see whether he is oriental or not: because if he were oriental, it will signify substance in youth (that is, in the first half of the native's life). If however it were occidental, it signifies [it] in the last half of the native's life. Whence, you will make him a participator in the signification of the time of the acquisition of substance, with the Lord of the triplicity of the house of substance. Indeed if they both were to agree in the good, substance will be increased in that time, and will be made more than could be signified by only one of them. If however they were to disagree, the signification of [something] better will be decreased, nor will there be so much substance for the native as what it ought to be at that age.

Chapter 8: When other significators will increase or diminish the substance of the native, with the Lords of the triplicity of the house of substance

Likewise you will consider the significator of the native's substance (of whatever sort [the significator] is), and you will commingle his virtue with the virtue of the Lord of the triplicity of the house of substance who is the significator of the time in which the native is going to acquire substance. Which if they were to agree, and they were of good condition, it will be increased then, and in that part of the native's life, and it will become more abundant. If however they were both of a bad condition, it will be diminished in that time more than it seems it ought to be diminished, and the native will become more needy. Indeed if one were made fortunate and the other weak, the goodness of the fortunate one will be less. Indeed if the more worthy significator of substance were made fortunate, and the other unfortunate, the goodness of the good one will be diminished, and the quantity of substance will be signified to be less. But if one were unfortunate and the other fortunate, the malice of the bad one will be diminished, and the scarcity of substance will be signified as less.

---

[337] To me this suggests an *al-mubtazz* by equal points, or else in a more general sense. If it were an *al-mubtazz* by weighted-points, it would have to be at least the Lord of the domicile or exaltation, in which case this rule would always apply.

And Abu ʿAli said[338] (concerning the signification of the time of the native's substance) that if the Lords of the triplicity of the luminary (whose authority it is) were all sound, free from impediments, and they were in the angles, it signifies the prosperity of the native for all the days of his life taken together. And more so, and more strongly so, if the significator of substance of that time were in the degree of the cusp of the angle; and by how much more he were elongated from the angle up to the full amount [the end] of that house, by that much will his prosperity and fortune be something less, according to his elongation from the angle, by gradually diminishing a certain [amount].

If however the first Lord of that triplicity were free, and the second and third were impeded, it signifies the fortune of the native and his prosperity to be in the first one-third of his life; in the second and third one-thirds of his life, he will be in need (as was said). Which if the second one were sound and the first and third were impeded, the native will prosper in the second part of his life; in the first and third (one-thirds) he will be in need. If however the third one were made fortunate, he will prosper in the last one-third of his life; in the first and second (one-thirds), he will be in need.

Which if the first Lord of the aforesaid triplicity were impeded, and the other two sound, it signifies the impediment and bad condition, and his detriment in the first one-third of his life, but not in the others. Indeed if the second one of the same triplicity were impeded, and the others sound, the native will be impeded in the second one-third of his life, not indeed in the others. If indeed only the third were impeded, it signifies his impediment in the last one-third of his life; but he will prosper in the other [one-thirds] of his life. And if all the said significators were impeded, it signifies the evil and detriment of the native, and his neediness for the whole time of his life, and the decrease of his life, just as was said above concerning the Lords of the triplicity of the house of substance.

Nevertheless, if in addition to these misfortunes there were benefics in the angles, and the malefics were cadent, and the luminaries well disposed, the malice of the malefics will be decreased, and the native will almost always prosper, nor will his life be diminished because of it. You could say the same if the Lord of the Ascendant and the Moon were in angles, free from the impediments of the malefics, or if they applied to planets in the angles (and better and more strongly so, if reception[339] were to intervene).

---

[338] *JN*, p. 11.
[339] Reading *receptio* for *deceptio*.

If the Lord of the Ascendant were to apply to the luminaries, or they to him

If however the Lord of the Ascendant were to apply to the luminaries, or they to him, and [the Sun][340] were in Aries or in Leo, and the Moon in Taurus or in Cancer when he [or she] were to apply to the Lord of the Ascendant; or the Lord of the Ascendant were in his own domicile and in his exaltation when he were to apply himself to the luminaries; or one of them were in two of its own lesser dignities when one were to apply to the other (as was said), it signifies the native's fortune and prosperity for all the times of his life together, unless the Lords of the triplicity of the house of substance were to work against it. For if the Lords of that triplicity were impeded, they will take away something from his disposition, and his prosperity and fortune will be somewhat less than this.

If the Part of Fortune and its Lord were oriental

Which if the Part of Fortune and its Lord were oriental, and free from the impediments of the malefics, and they were in the angles, and aspected the Ascendant, and the benefics were to aspect them, it signifies the native's prosperity and his fortune will be durable; and the increase of the goodness of his life; and its firmness and constancy and vigor. And if the Moon were in [her own] domicile or in exaltation, safe from the malefics, and were not impeded, it signifies the native's exaltation, and the greatness of his name. If however the said significators were cadent and impeded, it signifies the native's life will be full of labor and of little usefulness; and more so if they did not aspect the Ascendant.

Which if benefics and malefics together were to aspect the Part of Fortune and its Lord, and [the former][341] were in angles, they will judge the mediocrity of the native's fortune and prosperity. Indeed if the Lords of the triplicity of the Ascendant were joined to planets in the angles, and they[342] were cadent from them, they will signify the native's fortune and prosperity, but after labor and exhaustion. You may say the same about the Lord of the Ascendant, if he were joined to a planet in an angle, and in its domicile or in its exaltation, and [the Lord of the Ascendant] were cadent and in his own descension. Indeed these

---

[340] The text omits *Sol*, but that is clearly what is meant.
[341] I take this to refer to the benefics and malefics. In all cases here, we are apparently concerned about significators of substance or the native are joined to planets in an angle. But I grant there is some ambiguity throughout.
[342] I.e., the Lords of the triplicity of the Ascendant.

are true, unless the aforesaid significators of substance worked to the contrary (or one of them), because every one of them interposes his portions according to how he is disposed. Indeed if he were well disposed, he will increase what is signified by the benefics in the good, and will decrease what is signified by the malefics. If however he were badly disposed, he will increase what is increased by the malefics in the bad, and will decrease what is signified by the benefics.

Nor should you forget to consider the aforesaid significators–how all of them are disposed. Because if they were all well disposed, the native's prosperity will be increased, and his fortune will be augmented. Indeed if they were all badly disposed, the native's prosperity and his fortune will be decreased. But if the more principal significators were well disposed, and the less principal ones were badly disposed, his prosperity and fortune will be decreased, and he will profit less. Indeed if the more principal ones were badly disposed, and the less principal ones were well disposed, their misfortune will be decreased, and will harm less.

If the nativity were diurnal or nocturnal

You will even see whether the nativity is diurnal or nocturnal. For if it were diurnal, you will look to the Lords of the triplicity of the sign in which the Sun is, as was said above. If however it were nocturnal, then you will look to the Lords of the triplicity of the sign in which the Moon is. Which if they were in angles, namely made fortunate and strong, and the benefics were to aspect them (and better and more strongly so, if the benefics were to receive them), it signifies the prosperous and happy fortune of that native.[343] Which if they were in the succeedents of the angles, they will judge a middling amount of fortune. If however the malefics were in the angles, and the benefics were in the succeedents, it signifies the neediness of the native, and his labor in the first half of life; but in the last one, fortune and a good condition. If however the benefics were in angles, but the malefics in the succeedents of the aforesaid, they will judge the contrary. Indeed if they were in the native's cadents, they will signify his misfortune and bad condition, and a life full of labor, unless the said significators worked to the contrary.

---

[343] Again, the triplicity rulers of the luminary whose authority it is, show general prosperity, not solely financial well-being.

When the house of substance is looked at

Likewise, look at the domicile of substance, which is the second sign from the Ascendant;[344] and [look at] the second sign from the domicile[345] in which the Part of Fortune is; and likewise the second sign from the domicile in which the Sun is (in diurnal nativities) or from the domicile in which the Moon is (in nocturnal nativities). And see if one of the malefics were in one of the aforesaid places.[346] Because if the native had other good significations, this signifies their decrease and [that of] his good condition. Indeed if he did not have other good significations, it signifies the fall of his prosperity, and the detriment of fortune, and a bad condition, unless that malefic were to have a domicile or exaltation or two other lesser dignities there.

And Abu 'Ali said[347] that if the Sun did not aspect the Part of Fortune or its Lord, or [the Lord] the Sun (in diurnal nativities) or the Moon (in nocturnal nativities), it signifies detriment, and the decrease of the native's fortune and his prosperity.[348] You could say the same about the Moon if she were besieged by the malefics, both in diurnal and nocturnal [nativities]. Likewise the *al-kadukhadāh* signifies the same, if it were cadent from the angles or from the Ascendant, and in a bad place from it, and in the aspect of some malefic. Indeed if you were to find the malefics in angles, and the benefics in the succeedents of the angles, it signifies the native's labor and his impediment at the beginning of his life; but prosperity and good at the end. You could judge this same thing if the Sun (in diurnal nativities) [or] the Moon (in nocturnal ones) is being separated from the malefics and is being joined to the benefics. You may speak likewise about the Lords of the triplicity of the luminary whose authority it was, if they were cadent from the angles or from the Ascendant, and they were joining themselves to planets appearing in their own domiciles or exaltations (or in two of their own other dignities).

---

[344] Here is a definitive statement that the "house of substance" is a *domicile*, and not a *place*.

[345] In this section at least, I will translate *domus* as "domicile," since that is how he defines the "house" or "domicile" of substance here.

[346] Here a "place" means the sign.

[347] *JN*, p. 25.

[348] Abu 'Ali's statement is slightly different, saying this will be so if the Part of Fortune or its Lord did not aspect the *Ascendant* or the luminary whose authority it was.

If the planet who is the significator of substance, is oriental

You will even consider beyond this, if the planet who is the significator of substance is oriental and above the earth: because then it will signify the fortune and good of the native, and his prosperity in the beginning of his life. Indeed if it were occidental and under the earth, then it will signify it at the end of his life.[349] Which if it were oriental under the earth, or occidental above the earth, then it will signify it in the middle of his life.

Chapter 9: On what is signified by the places of the circle

Indeed the places[350] of the circle signifying the times, are these: for the Ascendant and the second [sign] signify[351] the beginning of the native's life up to the end of his adolescence. Indeed the tenth [sign] and the eleventh [sign] signify youth [or young adulthood] up to the end of mature age. Indeed the seventh [sign] and eighth [sign] signify from the end of youth up to the middle of old age. However the fourth [sign] and fifth [sign] signify from the middle of old age up to the end of the native's life. And Abu 'Ali said[352] the Part of Fortune signifies the beginning of life, its Lord the end.

And any one of the aforesaid significators signifies the condition of the native in its own time, according to how it is disposed at the hour of someone's nativity.[353] And if you knew the accidents through those things which you have perceived regarding the dispositions of his significators at the hour of his nativity, when and at what time they ought to be prosperous and useful, or fortunate or the contrary, or laborious or unfortunate or unlucky; and you saw the direction of the rays of the planets to the places[354] signifying his fortune or misfortune, and you saw the distance which there was between them (in terms of signs, degrees, and minutes), and you saw at what times of his life good or bad things ought to happen to him through those significators–then look at the Part of Fortune, which you will direct to the bodies of the benefics and malefics, or their rays. And if you were to see [the Part] joined to a benefic (and especially

---

[349] *JN*, p. 25. The following sentence is Bonatti's.
[350] *Loca. JN* (p. 25) is clear that these are signs, not quadrant houses, and I have translated accordingly.
[351] Reading *significant* for *significat*.
[352] *JN*, p. 25.
[353] The rest of this paragraph is based on *JN*, pp. 25-26.
[354] *Loca.* But his specification that we are looking for exact distances indicates he means the exact locations of the benefics and malefics.

to Jupiter or Venus), then judge the good condition of the native. If you were to see it joined to the malefics (and especially to Saturn or Mars), you could judge the contrary, unless the aforesaid significators worked against it; for when the benefics or their rays come to it, and the significators[355] are joined to benefics or their rays,[356] his prosperity and his fortune and good will be increased twofold. Indeed when the malefics or their rays come to it, and the significators are joined to the malefics and their rays, his misfortune and evil and labor will be increased twofold, and his goods will be diminished. If however the Part of Fortune were joined with the benefics, and the significators with the malefics, or it with the malefics, and the significators with the benefics, what is signified by each is decreased, you will not doubt.

For what reason the native is going to acquire money

Having seen, in those [chapters] which preceded, whence the native would acquire substance, and by what means, we must see lastly for what reason he might acquire it.[357] And even though [this topic] might seem to want to be likened to those which have already preceded, still it is not the same as them, but something else.

If the Part of Fortune were in the dignities of Saturn

Therefore you will consider the Part of Fortune at the hour of the some-one's nativity: which if you were to find it in the domicile or the exaltation of Saturn, or in two of his other lesser dignities, and Saturn were joined to it or were to aspect it, it signifies that the native will acquire substance because of male or female slaves, and middle-aged men (namely in their fifties and older, up to the middle of old age), and low-class persons; and his fortune will be in them and in commingling with them; and what [Saturn] signifies will be stronger if the Part of Fortune were in [his] exaltation than if it were in [his] domicile or in the other dignities. Which if the Part of Fortune were in the angles, the fortune of the native will be raised up, and be greatly exalted.

---

[355] Reading *significatores* for *significatoris*.
[356] Bonatti is speaking about directing two different types of things: the Part of Fortune, and the significators of substance.
[357] These paragraphs on the planets are based on *JN*, p. 26.

If the Part of Fortune were in the dignities of Jupiter

And if it were in the dignities of Jupiter according to the aforesaid method, he will acquire it because of commingling [with] and working [with] great men and nobles, even bishops and the like, and other wise people, and his fortune will be in them and with them.

If the Part of Fortune were in the dignities of Mars

And if it were in the dignities of Mars according to the same method, he will acquire it because of the generals of armies, and bellicose men, and warriors,[358] and whose who delight in wars and the waging of wars; and his fortune will be in commingling with them.

If the Part of Fortune were in the dignities of the Sun

Which if it were in the dignities of the Sun according to the aforesaid method, he will acquire it because of commingling [with] and working [with] kings and other princes like kings; and his fortune will be in them and with them, and the like.

If the Part of Fortune were in the dignities of Venus

If however it were in the dignities of Venus according to the same method, he will acquire it because of women, eunuchs, and likewise effeminate men; and his fortune will be in them and with them, and the like.

If the Part of Fortune were in the dignities of Mercury

If however it were in the dignities of Mercury according to the same method, he will acquire it because of commingling with the wise and scribes, and even those doing business; and his fortune will be in them and with them, and the like.

If the Part of Fortune were in the dignities of the Moon

Indeed if it were in the dignities of the Moon according to the aforesaid method, he will acquire it because of commingling with those skilled in

---

[358] *Guerrariorum.*

law, and legal men; and his fortune will be in them and with them, and the like.

That the aforesaid will be signified by the aforesaid significators, however they are disposed

And know that whatever kind of condition the aforesaid significators had, and wherever the Part of Fortune was in their dignities, those things which were said will be signified naturally and according to their disposition, and according to their places[359] in the circle. For if they were in the angles and of good condition, and otherwise well disposed, and likewise the Part of Fortune, the increase of the native's fortune will be signified (and his prosperity). If however they are in the succeedents, they will signify the moderate fortune of the native. Indeed if they were in the cadents or otherwise badly disposed, the laboriousness, burden, impediment, and diminution of the native's fortune will be signified.

Chapter 10: On the same [subject], according to Abu 'Ali

Moreover,[360] another thing practically in the same vein, similar to the aforesaid (even if not simply for knowing the status of some native's life at the signified times), by the Lords of the triplicity of the Ascendant. For the first Lord of its triplicity signifies the beginning of the native's life, namely the first one-third of it. Indeed the second one signifies the middle, namely the second one-third of it. Indeed the third one signifies the end, namely the last one-third of it.

Which[361] if one of them were in its own domicile or in its exaltation, or in two of its other dignities, in the angles, joined to benefics, free from impediments, it signifies the good and prosperous condition of the native in the times of its own signification. If however it were in the succeedents, his condition will be somewhat below this. Which if it were in the cadents, it signifies his condition [will be] much below this. But if one of them were cadent from the angles (or in its own fall, or in its own descension,[362] or in a bad place from the Ascendant, or it were retrograde or peregrine, or combust or joined to malefics),

---

[359] *Loca.*

[360] See *JN*, p. 27.

[361] See *JN*, p. 27.

[362] This is one of the few places where Bonatti actually distinguishes "fall" and "descension" (detriment), instead of seeming to let one of them stand for either condition.

it signifies the native's bad condition, and his impediment in the times of its signification; but in the cadents it will be increased more.

Again more (and more strongly) will its impediment be increased, if the Lord of the Ascendant were impeded with the first Lord of the said dignity, or the Lord of the 10th with its second Lord, or the Lord of the 7th with its third Lord. If however the first Lord of the said triplicity were impeded, and the Lord of the Ascendant were sound (or *vice versa*), the misfortune of the impeded one, and the fortune of the sound one, will be decreased. Indeed if the second Lord were impeded and the Lord of the 10th sound (and *vice versa*), the misfortune of the impeded one and the fortune of the sound one will be decreased. But if the third Lord were impeded and the Lord of the 7th sound (or *vice versa*), the misfortune of the impeded one and the fortune of the sound one will be decreased. But if all were sound, their fortune will be increased, and the fortune of that native will be prosperous. Indeed if they were [all] impeded, his misfortune and bad condition will be increased.

You will even look at the Moon,[363] because she has a great signification over the condition of the fortune of any native. For if she were of good condition and well disposed, joined to the benefics, it signifies generally over the prosperity and fortune of any native, by adding to the goodness of the benefics, and detracting from the malice of the malefics.[364] Indeed if she were joined to the malefics, it signifies the native's adversity, and his bad condition, by adding to the malice of the malefics and detracting from the goodness of the benefics. Which if she were void in course, and in malign places in the circle, it signifies the native's impediment, and the adversity and detriment of his fortune.

You will even look at the Lord of the sign in which the Moon is.[365] If you were to see him well disposed and in a good place from the Sun (namely in his trine or sextile aspect), and he were otherwise made fortunate and strong, and well disposed, joined with the benefics (or they[366] with him), it signifies the good of the native and his prosperity. But if you were to see the contrary, you could judge the contrary.

---

[363] See *JN*, p. 27.
[364] This could also be read, "by adding to the goodness of goods, and detracting from the malice of evils." The same goes for the next sentence.
[365] See *JN*, pp. 26-27.
[366] Reading *ipsi* for *ipse*.

Chapter 11: Another practically extraordinary thing about the condition of the native

Indeed you will perceive the condition of a native's nativity by the Lord of the Ascendant of that nativity, and through his place in the houses [domiciles?] according to how you were to find him in one of them.[367]

For if it were in the 1st, it signifies that the native will be powerful among those near him, and those in his household, and those known to him, and among those of the same age.[368]

Indeed if it were in the 2nd, and were of good condition and well disposed, joined to benefics, and it were received, it signifies him to be fortunate in the acquisition of substance. Which if it were in the contrary condition, you will judge the contrary, and that he is going to be a destroyer of substance.

If however it were in the 3rd, it signifies him to be fortunate among his own brothers, or rather he will appear more fortunate; and that he will gladly make pilgrimage on short journeys (and sometimes ones of moderate length).

But if it were in the 4th, it signifies he is not malicious, and that he will be loved by his father (and good will follow from him), and by his older ancestors.

Which if it were in the 5th, it signifies that he will be happy in children, and because of them; and he will be loved by men in a good way.

Likewise if it were in the 6th, it signifies that he will be a man full of labor, involved in worries, and will have many infirmities.

In the 7th it signifies that he will be a man of quarrels, contentions, irascible, suing people,[369] permitting himself to be with women here and there, appearing to be taken in by *their* will.

---

[367] What follows is based on *JN*, p. 28.

[368] *Notos suos ac inter ipsos natus*, treating *natus* as a misspelling for *natos*. *Natus* has a connotation of age, cf. the relationships of age in the other houses.

But if it were in the 8th, it signifies that he will be fainthearted, a deceiver, crafty, sad, not caring about others, rejoicing in the inconvenience of others [and] suffering at their prosperities.

Indeed if it were in the 9th, it signifies that he will be a man of the sciences, a lover of them; he will even make many pilgrimages, and especially long journeys, loving to go on pilgrimage.

If however it were in the 10th, he will be a man gladly having dealings with kings and great men, and with whose who are fit for a kingdom, and wanting to conduct his life with them.

Indeed if it were in the 11th, it signifies that he will be a compliant man, of good dealings, loved by men, among which he will number many as his friends; having few children.

Lastly, if it were in the 12th, it signifies that his life will be heavy, full of labor, hindered; he could number many enemies but no friends; and if [he had] any [friends], most few.

Chapter 12: On the acquisition of substance, again according to Abu 'Ali

Another means of the acquisition of the native's substance, according to the opinion of Abu 'Ali, tending practically to a like end: for he said[370] that the 2nd domicile from the Ascendant must be looked at, and we must look at which planets are in it. For if benefics were in it, and the malefics (and likewise their aspects) were absent, and its Lord were free and in a good place from the Ascendant, and likewise from the Sun, it signifies the fortune of that native with substance and in substance. If however it were the other way around, it signifies the misfortune of the native with substance and in substance.

After this,[371] you will see whether the Lord of the Ascendant is joined with the Lord of the 2nd [domicile][372] from the Ascendant, because it signifies the

---

[369] *Causator*, lit. "someone who pursues causes." A "cause" is a case in court.
[370] *JN*, p. 28.
[371] *JN*, p. 28.

native is going to acquire a multitude of substance, easily–practically without weariness.[373] You will even look at the lighter of them, namely he who is in an angle,[374] because he will signify that quantity of money or substance is going to come from matters already known (as Abu 'Ali says), not things happening fortuitously. Which if [the lighter, applying planet] were in a succeedent, his acquisition will be below the aforesaid, but it will be of the good, and fair, and licit. If however it were in a cadent or in another bad or shameful place[375] from the Ascendant, the acquisition of substance will be from wherever he could acquire it, by law and wickedness; and he will be persistent in it, and greedy.

Which[376] if there were not a conjunction or application between them, then look at the Lord of the domicile of substance: which if he were in angles, free from impediments, and likewise the Moon, it signifies the native is going to acquire moderate substance. Indeed if it were in the succeedents, it signifies that there will be little acquisition of money for him. But if it were in the cadents, it signifies his labor and distress and burden in acquiring whence he might live; and he could hardly pursue it, and worse and more gravely so, if the Lord of the domicile were impeded by the malefics, or were joined to their aspects or rays.

Again,[377] you would look at the Lord of the Ascendant, and likewise Jupiter: which if one of them were joined to the other by body or by aspect, and they were made fortunate and strong, and of good condition and well disposed, it signifies the prosperity of the native's life and much acquisition of his substance; and more so and more strongly so if the one applying himself to the other were received. If however their condition was not such as I have said, what is signified by them will be below this which was said, according to the quantity of the decrease of their strength and goodness.

You[378] could say the same about the Part of Fortune and its Lord, if they were in good places[379] from the Ascendant, free from the malefics and from their rays.

---

[372] According to JN.

[373] Abu 'Ali adds that if the Lord of the Ascendant applies to the Lord of the second sign, then the assets are gotten by hard work–the distinction is between money coming to the native, or the native pursuing the money.

[374] Abu 'Ali says, if "this application is made from an angle." Since applications can only be made by a lighter planet, then if the application is made from an angle, then the lighter planet has to be in an angle.

[375] Abu 'Ali uses *domus*, undoubtedly referring to whole-sign houses.

[376] JN, pp. 28-29.

[377] JN, p. 29.

[378] JN, p. 29.

[379] Abu 'Ali says *domibus* (houses) not *locis* (places).

Likewise[380] concerning the Moon if she were in a good place from the Ascendant, aspecting it (and especially if she were received; and more strongly so and better if the reception were from a benefic). For the Moon has this prerogative, because if she were in angles or in their succeedents, increased in light and number,[381] and she were to commit her virtue or disposition to a planet receiving her,[382] it signifies the goodness of the native's fortune, and the multitude of his goods, and the abundance of things flowing to him.

Also,[383] look at the eleventh sign from the sign in which the Part of Fortune is: in which, if some benefic were there, it signifies the honesty of the acquisition of the native's substance, and his good method of acquiring it. Which if one of the malefics were in it, it signifies the contrary: namely, a dishonest method of acquiring it (nor will the native be ashamed by whatever means he can acquire it, provided that he can get it for himself); and often by injustice and from illicit things (and more strongly so, if the sign in which the malefic is, were its domicile or exaltation, or it had two of its other dignities there).[384]

You[385] will even see whether the said Lord of substance (or the Lord of the sign in which the Part of Fortune is, or the Lord of the eleventh sign from the sign in which the Part of fortune is), is entering combustion: because this signifies the destruction[386] of the fortune and prosperity of the native, and likewise of his substance and his good condition.

Likewise[387] you will look to see whether the Part of Fortune is joined with one of the benefics or were in their opposition or square aspect, and [whether] the malefics were cadent from it. Because this signifies the good fortune and prosperity of the native, and the increase of his substance. Which if it were the other way around, you could rightly judge the contrary.

---

[380] *JN*, p. 29.
[381] According to Holden, "increased in number" here means "in direct motion." But Bonatti uses it to mean "faster than average course," and his sources explicitly distinguish it from being direct or retrograde. See Tr. 7 (Part 1, Ch. 16; Part 2, 4th House Ch. 6 [citing 'Umar]; 7th House Ch. 9).
[382] Here Bonatti is either suggesting that a received planet commits its disposition to the receiver (which contradicts his explicit statements elsewhere), or else the Moon can commit to anyone simply by aspect, and the statement about reception is simply an extra, strengthening condition.
[383] *JN*, p. 29.
[384] I note that Abu 'Ali only mentions rulership by domicile and exaltation, and does not mention the other possibilities.
[385] *JN*, p. 29.
[386] *Diminutionem*, elsewhere described as "diminution" or "decrease." But combustion is harsher, so I have opted for the more correct "destruction."
[387] *JN*, p. 29.

You[388] will even consider whether the Lord of the Ascendant and the Lord of the domicile of substance are joined, or apply to each other at the same time, because this signifies the good condition of the native. If however they did not join themselves together by body or by aspect, and the benefics were cadent from the Ascendant and from the domicile of substance and from their Lords, it signifies the detriment of the native and his bad condition, and his laborious and suffering life, and neediness for all the times of his life, because of the fact that the Lord of the Ascendant and the Lord of the 2nd domicile (who naturally signify the advantage of the native and his wealth) are not joined nor are applied together.

These[389] things which were said, will happen as I stated them, unless the aforesaid significators of the native's substance (which are the Lords of the triplicity of the domicile of substance,[390] the Lords of the triplicity of the luminary whose authority it is, the Part of Fortune and its Lord, likewise Jupiter and the Part [of Substance][391]) worked against it. Which if you were to find these significators, or the majority of them (and especially the more authoritative of them, and who had more dignities in the places in which they were), in good places from the Ascendant, they will work against the malice of the aforesaid (namely, of the [malefic] planets who were in the eleventh sign from the sign of the Part of Fortune, of the Lord of the Part of Fortune, and of the planets to which they are joined or to whose conjunction they were, or in whose opposition or in square aspect they were).[392] If however you were to find them impeded in the places in which they were, they will work against their goodness, by taking away from them.

---

[388] *JN*, p. 29.

[389] *JN*, pp. 29-30.

[390] Abu 'Ali omits these.

[391] *Et eius pars*, lit. "and its Part." I take "its" to mean substance, since Abu 'Ali says "the Part of Wealth" (in Holden's translation).

[392] This unusual sentence is an elaboration by Bonatti for purposes of clarity (which ends up rather unclear). Abu 'Ali simply says that if the majority of the listed significators were in good places, *etc.*, it signifies "good circumstances for the native in assets and fortune, according to their place and motion."

Chapter 13: On the same [subject]

Furthermore,[393] you will see the Lord of the domicile of substance, or the planet who was the *al-mubtazz* over the substance of the native, and consider where it is.

For if it were in the 1st, it signifies that the native will acquire substance without labor and fatigue and worry, and more strongly and more fruitfully so if it were received by a benefic located in an angle or a succeedent.

And Abu 'Ali said if it were in the 2nd, it will be from something belonging to the native.[394]

And if it were in the 3rd, it signifies the badness of the brothers.[395]

And if it were in the 4th, it signifies the good condition of the parents, and [his continued living][396] in the house in which he is.

And if it were in the 5th, he said that he will have children [who are] known in the palaces of kings.

And if it were in the 6th, it signifies the flight of slaves and the loss of animals, especially[397] small ones.

And if it were in the 7th, it signifies the upheaval [or turning around] of things because of something unjust,[398] and the dispersion of the same, because of women and contentions.

---

[393] The following is based on Abu 'Ali, who omits any mention of the *al-mubtazz* or significator of substance.

[394] Abu 'Ali says, "from some known thing."

[395] I.e., the badness of their condition (according to Abu 'Ali), probably because the 2nd is the 12th from the 3rd.

[396] *Populationem.* Abu 'Ali says, "the continuance of the native in that house in which he was born."

[397] *Supple.* I am following Holden's Abu 'Ali.

[398] Abu 'Ali says, "the accumulation of things through unjust means."

And if it were in the 8th, it signifies the acquisition of things from what is left over by the dead; nor will he care how he makes money or how he spends it.

And if it were in the 9th, it signifies acquisition because of pilgrimages and the religions (from sects). And he said, that he will not care for any but hidden things, and his business will be from pilgrimages.

And if it were in the 10th, he will pursue substance from kings and because of them.

And if it were in the 11th, he will find substance from friends and business dealings and leasing, and from merchandise.

And if it were in the 12th, it signifies that he will earn money from prisons and enemies (especially hidden ones), and from every low-class and shameful work. And he said that he will be a thief and robber.[399]

---

[399] *Raptor*, following Holden's translation.

ON THE THIRD HOUSE

Chapter 1: On the matter of siblings of each sex, and on their multitude or scarcity

Having spoken in the preceding chapter about the native's substance and his prosperity, and by what means and whence he would acquire it, we must look in this present chapter concerning the matter of siblings and their condition, and concerning their multitude or scarcity, according to how we can know it; and even from what we should acquire their affairs.[400]

Therefore[401] you must look at the third sign from the Ascendant of the nativity of him whose nativity you intend to investigate; and the Part[402] of Siblings[403] and its Lord; look even at Mars, because he has participation in the signification of the matter of siblings. And likewise the Lords of the triplicity of the sign in which [Mars] is, and the planetary *al-mubtazz* over the aforesaid places (whether they were one or more); even the planets which are in them, or which aspect [the signs][404] from the opposition or from the square aspect, or even from others.

Wherefore[405] if benefics were in those places, or were to aspect [the signs] with a praiseworthy aspect (namely by a trine or sextile, whether they have dignity in them or not), or from the square (and they have a domicile or exaltation or bound or triplicity in them–but the bound and triplicity are below domicile and below exaltation), it signifies the good condition of the native's siblings, and their prosperity. If however they were to aspect from a trine or sextile aspect, and they had dignity in them, it signifies again the better condition of the siblings, and the increase of their prosperity. If however malefics were in them, or they were to aspect from a square aspect, or from the opposition, they will indicate the contrary of the aforesaid; and more so and more strongly so, if they did not have dignity in them.

---

[400] See also a similar discussion using the Part of the Number of Brothers from Tr. 8, Part 2, Ch. 6.

[401] This paragraph is drawn from *TBN*, p. 59.

[402] Reading *partem* for *patrem*.

[403] According to Tr. 8, Part 2, Ch. 6, it is taken in the day and night from Saturn to Jupiter, and it is projected from the Ascendant.

[404] *Ea*, referring to the signs. Abu 'Ali says "it," referring to the third sign.

[405] Based on *JN*, p. 31.

You[406] will even consider the third sign from the Ascendant of the nativity, [to see] if it was of those signifying more children (which are Cancer, Scorpio, and Pisces), and [if] its Lord in one of them. And [consider if],[407] between the Lord of the Ascendant and the aforesaid *al-mubtazz*, there were one of the 14 ways signifying the effecting and detriment of matters (which I described for you above in the Treatise on the Considerations which fall under judgments, *etc.*, which are said to be 16):[408] it signifies the native is going to have many brothers and sisters. You[409] could say the same if Mars were in a sign of many children, and the planet in whose domicile you were to find him [were] oriental, nor were the Moon in a sign of few children (because then she diminishes the number of siblings).

Chapter 2: On the masculinity and femininity of siblings

You will look[410] yet to see if the aforesaid places[411] were masculine signs, and the significators in masculine signs: because these will signify the majority of the siblings are going to be of the masculine sex. If however the aforesaid places[412] and aforesaid significators (or a majority of them) were in feminine signs, they will signify the majority of the native's siblings are going to be of the feminine one. But[413] if they were in signs signifying few children (which are Gemini, Leo, Virgo, Capricorn, and Aquarius), they will signify there is a scarcity of siblings for the native. Indeed the rest of the signs show a middling [amount].

Which if[414] the domicile[415] of siblings were a common sign, and its Lord were in a common and masculine sign, it signifies the native only has siblings from the same father. If however each sign were masculine, it signifies them to be masculine; if each sign were feminine, it signifies them to be feminine.

---

[406] See Abu Ali, p. 31.

[407] See *TBN*, p. 59.

[408] Tr. 5 (4th Consideration). 'Umar says there are 14 conditions or interactions, but Bonatti (following Sahl) uses 16.

[409] See *JN*, p. 31.

[410] See *TBN*, p. 59.

[411] *Loca.*

[412] *Loca.*

[413] See Abu Ali, p. 31.

[414] See *JN*, p. 31. But Abu 'Ali omits the consideration of being in a masculine sign. In fact the rest of this paragraph seems to be inspired by *TBN* (p. 59) and *JN* (p. 31), but Bonatti's version is either garbled or crafted according to his own ideas.

[415] Translating *domus* as "domicile," following Bonatti's lead above where he explicitly says we are looking at the third sign. Moreover, Abu 'Ali explicitly says "sign."

Indeed if one were masculine and the other feminine, it signifies they are masculine and feminine. If however the domicile of siblings were a feminine sign, and its Lord in a feminine sign, it signifies the native only has siblings from the same mother. Which if in addition Venus and the Moon were in feminine signs, it signifies only feminine ones. Indeed if the Moon were in a masculine sign and Venus in a feminine one, or *vice versa*, it judges the native to have masculine and feminine ones; and the more so if the Ascendant were of the signs signifying many children, and the Moon [were] in one of them. Again, I say that if the Ascendant and the domicile of siblings (or either or them) were a masculine sign, and their Lords (or either of them) and the Lord of the 4th [were] in them, and Venus and the Moon [were] in feminine signs, or *vice versa*, it signifies that the siblings will be of the same father as the native, and from the same mother.

You will even look[416] at the Lord of the Ascendant, and the Lord of the domicile of siblings, to see if they were to agree with each other or they were of the planets loving each other. For if it were so, or they were to aspect each other by a trine or sextile aspect, it signifies that there will be concord and love and good will between the native and his siblings. If however you were to find the contrary, you could judge the contrary and say they are going to be deceivers and grave enemies. Indeed if they were to aspect themselves from the square, it signifies that there will be some kind of friendship between them, but not perfect, even if reception intervenes.

Likewise[417] look at the Lord of the domicile of siblings, to see if he were combust or were entering combustion in nocturnal nativities: because it signifies a scarcity of siblings and their detriment and destruction; and more strongly so if the Moon is being separated from Saturn [in nocturnal nativities], with him appearing in an angle (or from Mars in diurnal nativities, with him likewise residing in an angle).

And Abu 'Ali said[418] when Mars enters combustion, it signifies a scarcity of siblings. And he said that if a malefic, peregrine planet[419] were in the third sign from the Ascendant, it will signify a scarcity of siblings and the death of the older siblings.

---

[416] See *JN*, p. 34. But Abu 'Ali adds that the corporal conjunction between the two signifies a "stable friendship."

[417] See *JN*, p. 31.

[418] See *JN*, p. 31.

[419] Abu 'Ali says a peregrine *or* malefic planet.

And 'Umar said,[420] look to see if the native or the siblings is of greater dignity, from the strength of the *al-mubtazz* over the Ascendant or the *al-mubtazz* over the domicile of siblings, because the stronger of them will be in charge.

And Abu 'Ali said[421] if Mars and the Lords of his triplicity were in a good place in the circle and from the Sun, it signifies the good condition of the siblings, also their fitness and prosperity, and a multitude of them. And if he were in his own descension, or were entering into combustion, and the Lords of his triplicity [were] in bad places, it signifies a scarcity of siblings and their weakness and bad condition. You would say the same if the Lords of the triplicity of the Ascendant were cadent; and if they were in signs of few children, they will signify a scarcity of siblings (and in those signifying it moderately, they will judge their moderate [quantity]).

Then[422] look at the Part of Siblings and its Lord, and see if they were to agree with the Lord of the domicile of the native's substance: because it will increase his virtue. Indeed if it were the contrary, the virtue of the Lord of the domicile of siblings will be reduced, but it will prevail over the Lord of the Part of Siblings, even if their virtues seemed to be of one quality, according to what the Lords of the triplicities do.

And 'Umar said,[423] look at the Lords of the triplicity of Mars (namely the first and the second and the third), and see which of them is stronger and of better condition: because he signifies the matter of siblings. For the first one signifies older siblings, the second one middle ones, the third one younger ones.

You[424] will even look at the Lord of the Part of Fortune, for if it were with the Part of Siblings[425] it signifies that the older brothers will hate each other.

Chapter 3: Who among the brothers would die first, or who would have a longer life

And ['Umar] said,[426] in order to know which of them will endure,[427] and which of them death will consume (and the rest of the things which happen to

---

420 See *TBN*, p. 59.

421 *JN*, p. 31.

422 See *JN*, pp. 31-32. But the phrase "with the Lord of the house of the native's substance" does not appear there, and may be an error.

423 See *TBN*, p. 59.

424 *JN*, p. 34.

425 Reading Part of Siblings (with *JN*, p. 34) for "Part of Fortune."

426 See *TBN*, p. 60.

427 See also the Part of the Death of Brothers and Sisters in Tr. 8, Part 2, Ch. 6.

them), look to see what there is between the Midheaven and the Ascendant: because if there were a benefic planet there, it signifies that children were born to his father before him, and they still live. And if there were a malefic there, it signifies that they have already died. Indeed if the benefics and malefics were in common signs, the siblings who remain or who have died, are two.

Likewise ['Umar] said,[428] look to those who are born afterwards, which is between the Ascendant and the angle of the earth. If there were planets in it,[429] brothers and sisters will be born after him according to the quantity of the stars [planets] which you were to find. Which if you were to find some of those planets in common signs, it doubles their number. If however there were malefics in it, it signifies their death. And if they were benefics, it signifies [their] durability.

And ['Umar] said[430] also the Sun and Saturn signify the father; indeed Venus and the Moon signify the mother. Likewise, he said the separation of the Moon from the planets (and especially from the Sun or from Saturn), signifies those who were born before him. Indeed the conjunction of the Moon with the other planets [signifies] those who will be born after him, and those who are younger than him.

And ['Umar] said,[431] you will also look at the Lords of the triplicity of Mars (namely the first and the second and the third), and you will take the stronger of them. (And the one who is of greater testimony, will be either the first [child] or the fourth [child] or the seventh [child] or the tenth [child], and understand this about the rest.) And he said that if it were in an angle, he will be the first [child] (or according to the number of the angles, just as was said). And he said that if it were in the Ascendant, he will be the first or fourth. Likewise he said if it were in the Midheaven, it signifies that he is the first or fourth or more. Again he said if it were in the seventh [angle], it signifies that he is the seventh or fourth or first. Indeed if it were in the fourth [angle], it signifies that he is the first or fourth. Moreover he said all of these places[432] signify according to the quality of the place; but this seems to me that it is a mistake of the writer.[433]

---

[428] See *TBN*, p. 60.

[429] I.e., in the space between the degree of the Ascendant and the degree of the 4th.

[430] See *TBN*, p. 60.

[431] See *TBN*, pp. 60-61.

[432] *Loca*.

[433] I do not see why Bonatti thinks a mistake has been made.

Indeed Abu 'Ali said,[434] look at the Lord of the triplicity of the Ascendant, which if it were in the Ascendant, he will be the first-born of his mother; and if it were in the Midheaven or in the angle of the earth, he will be the first or tenth;[435] and if it were in the seventh [angle], he will be the first or the seventh [child]. And he said that if it were not[436] in the angles, look at the planets which there are between the degree of the Ascendant and the degree of the Midheaven—which if they were benefics, it signifies he has living brothers; and if they were malefics, it signifies he had one, but they have died. And if there were neither benefics nor malefics,[437] say that he is the first-born of his mother.

Chapter 4: On the matter of siblings

Indeed Ptolemy[438] was of the opinion that the matter of siblings is found from the matter of the mother, by making mention of siblings from the *same* mother; nor did he care to make mention of the same father, because we are more certain that brothers are from the same mother than from the same father.[439] (Sometimes it happens not to be true, as is commonly thought.)

Ptolemy[440] seems to want that the 11th domicile signifies the mother just like the 10th does; and because the 3rd from the Ascendant is the 5th from the 11th (which signifies the mother, just like the 10th does), therefore the 3rd is the house given to the siblings of the native, and to the children of the same mother (because it is the 5th from the 11th).

---

[434] See *JN*, p. 32. Bonatti leaves out some details.

[435] Reading *decimus* (with Abu 'Ali) for *quartus*.

[436] Adding *non*, with Abu 'Ali.

[437] Abu 'Ali says "But if the fortunes *are* there, *but not* the malefic stars" (emphasis mine).

[438] *Tet.* III.6.

[439] The idea seems to be that since paternity can be hard to determine, one might have countless other siblings in the world without knowing it; therefore we will stick to siblings we are rather certain we have, because they have come from the same mother.

[440] Bonatti has misunderstood Ptolemy, but like his sources he had reasons to do so. The authentic Ptolemy says we should look at (a) the tenth sign *from the sign in which the maternal significator is* (i.e., that of Venus by day, the Moon by night), and (b) the sign *which succeeds* (a). But due to a misreading of Ptolemy's difficult Greek, later authors believed that Ptolemy meant the tenth sign itself, and the sign succeeding the tenth (i.e., the eleventh sign). Ptolemy does not mention the third sign at all. This meant that the medievals had three domiciles to work with: the tenth, the eleventh, and the third (which already signifies siblings). For them, this would have made sense, too, because the third domicile is the fifth from the tenth by derived houses—i.e., the (other) children of the native's mother. In other words, the misreading of the authentic Ptolemy still makes logical sense. Schmidt believes that this traditional misreading of Ptolemy is what is behind the traditional treatment of the 10th house as the mother, since the 10th never indicated the mother in Hellenistic astrology.

Whence the 10th and the 11th must be considered, in which, if benefics are found in either of them, they will judge a multitude of siblings and their prosperity (indeed if malefics were present, without a doubt you will pronounce the contrary of that which was said). If Jupiter were in [these places] (Venus in the day or the Moon in the night, both of which signify the purpose[441] of the mother), without the hesitation of doubt you may say this. Indeed if they[442] were to aspect Saturn from a trine or sextile aspect, and they were fortunate and strong, they will signify the goodness and the good number of siblings (however it will be below the aforesaid, nor will their condition be so prosperous). Indeed if they were badly disposed and they remained in the aforesaid places, or [the malefics] looked forward[443] from the square aspect or from the opposition, they will show the scarcity of brothers, and their weakness (and more strongly so if they were located under the rays of the Sun). Indeed if they or one of the malefics (Saturn for the first-born, Mars for those born later) are found in one of the angles (but more strongly in the Ascendant), they will judge scarcity and their bad condition. And Mars for the most part reduces their number through death.

And even though I touched on this for you above, again I say this: that if the planets which are the significators of siblings are well disposed, and they aspected the place of siblings from a trine or sextile aspect, it signifies that the siblings of the native will be skillful [or virtuous] and powerful and exalted among other men. If however the significators of siblings were in the contrary condition, the native's siblings will be found to be imbeciles and weak [or impotent]. Which if many malefics were to impede the significators of the siblings, they will signify the shortness of their life.

---

[441] *Causam.* This simply means that they are the significators of the mother and what she does.
[442] *Aspexerint Saturnus.* This does not make grammatical sense, and does not match Ptolemy. The other alternative is that Saturn should aspect "them." Either way, Bonatti or his source believes that a good aspect involving Saturn and either the relevant domiciles or the benefics will reduce the number and prosperity of the siblings somewhat.
[443] *Prospexerint.* This seems to be a reference to the Hellenistic doctrine which uses different words for aspects cast forward and backward in the signs. Ptolemy says, "if malefics have a superior position over [or "overcome"] them," i.e., if malefics are in the tenth sign from the benefics, thereby casting a square aspect forward by sign.

Chapter 5: On the masculinity of natives and siblings, according to Ptolemy

And Ptolemy said[444] the givers of masculine ones are masculine planets in their qualities of the world (that is, in their condition),[445] free from impediments; however the bestowers of female ones are the feminine ones.

And he made a certain statement which seems almost ambiguous (when it is not [really] so), that if the planetary significators [of siblings] are conjoined in the figure and are united to Saturn[446] (namely from a trine or sextile aspect), that the siblings will love and honor each other. If however they are not conjoined to each other, or they were to aspect each other from the square aspect or the opposition, the native will be a bringer of adversity.

Nor did he describe the reason why the significators of children must act in the matter of siblings.[447]

And [Ptolemy] said,[448] moreover, eastern ones impart first [older] siblings, western ones later [younger] ones.

And Abu ‘Ali said,[449] look at the planets which are between the Ascendant and the angle of the earth: which if they were benefics, it signifies that his mother will give birth again to children after him, and they will live. Indeed if they were malefic, then it signifies that she will give birth again, but they (who

---

[444] This paragraph represents a garbled paraphrase of *Tet.* III.6. Ptolemy says "male planets in the mundane sense" (in one of the oriental quarters of the chart) will give males, and female ones female ones (which must mean, feminine planets in occidental quarters). The statement about Saturn seems to be wrong: Ptolemy says the siblings will get along if planets giving them are in a harmonious aspect with the planet ruling the place of siblings (and if not, not)—it has nothing to do with Saturn.

[445] That is, by being in masculine quadrants (see *Tet.* III.6). This was clarified for me verbally by Robert Schmidt.

[446] The reason this statement is "ambiguous"is because Bonatti has read *Saturno* for the Latin Ptolemy's *signo* ("sign"), and has tried to fill in the conceptual blanks himself. The Latin Ptolemy actually says "Moreover, if in the figure the grantors or children are united to the *sign* signifying the matter of siblings…" Unfortunately, this is not even what Ptolemy himself says. Ptolemy says: "If the stars promising the siblings chance to be harmoniously configured with *the star that is lord over*" the whole-sign house signifying siblings. Normally I would simply correct Bonatti's Latin *Saturno*, but since he takes his misreading seriously and comments on it, I have let it stand in the text.

[447] This seems to be a reference back to the passage in Ch. 4, where Bonatti's understandable misreading of the ambiguous word *natus* impelled him to put material pertaining to children in the material on siblings. He is clearly aware that the reading of *natus* as "the native" (instead of "the one born [*to the native*]") is puzzling.

[448] *Tet.* III.6, a continuation of the same cite above. According to Schmidt (private communication), this means that for planets *within* a given quadrant, the ones that are *more* eastern will indicate older siblings, and those *more* western will indicate younger siblings.

[449] *JN*, p. 32.

will be born after him) will not live; or if his mother were to conceive, she will abort [or miscarry]; and if there were not [any] benefics or malefics, it signifies even that his mother will not conceive after the native himself.

And Abu 'Ali said,[450] look at the Lord of the domicile of siblings: which if it were in the Ascendant or the seventh, say the native does not have siblings; and if it were in the Midheaven, he has siblings older than him; and if it were in the fourth, he has siblings who will be born after him.

Again, I tell you that if the Moon were in someone's Ascendant, separated from the benefics, it signifies the good condition of the native's siblings (and especially of long-lived ones, and the good disposition of their life). And if she were separated from malefics, it signifies the detriment of the same, and the approach of their death.

Chapter 6: On the prosperity of the siblings

You will look for the prosperity and goodness of the siblings according to the Lords of the triplicity of their domicile (namely from the first and second and third): because the first one signifies siblings older than the native, the second one middle ones, the third one younger ones. For such will be the condition of the native's siblings, as what kind of condition the Lords of the triplicity of their domicile will have, at the hour of the nativity of him whose nativity you are inquiring into, and such things ought to be discovered.

For[451] if the first of them were of good condition and well disposed, it signifies the good condition of the elder brothers; if the second, of the middle ones; if the third, of the younger ones. For if the first Lord of the triplicity of the domicile of siblings were in its own domicile or exaltation, or in two of its other dignities, or in an angle, or in a succeedent, and in a good place[452] from the Sun and from the Ascendant, free from impediments, it signifies the good condition of the elder brothers, and their good disposition, and likewise exaltation and fame.

Which if [the Lord of the third domicile][453] were joined with one of the planets of a good nature (and well disposed, located its own domicile or

---

450 JN, p. 32.

451 JN, p. 33.

452 Reading loco for solo.

453 Per JN, p. 33. What follows pertains to the siblings generally, but Bonatti seems to have overlooked a few words in Abu 'Ali's text, since he simply says "he," as though the following still referred to the triplicity ruler. See too, that Bonatti follows this passage up by referring to

exaltation or in two of its other dignities), it signifies the increase of their prosperity and their exaltation, [and their] associating with and being recalled to memory by princes and great men, and nobles, and kings, and wealthy people fit for a kingdom. Indeed if it is joined with a malefic planet, not receiving him, or made unfortunate or cadent, or located in its own descension, or in some detriment of its own, it will judge their vileness and imbecility, and applying [themselves] with the most low-class persons, and spending time with them.

Indeed if the second Lord of that triplicity were so impeded, it will show the detriment of the middle siblings; if the third, of the younger ones—according to what was said about the older ones. But if the Moon were then void in course, it signifies the bad condition of the siblings, and their impediment.

And Abu 'Ali said[454] if the Head of the Dragon were in the domicile of siblings, it signifies the condition of the native is going to be below the condition of all of his siblings, and weaker than it. And if the Tail were there, it signifies that the condition of the native will prevail over the condition of all of his siblings. And if the Lord of the domicile of siblings were a benefic, and were free from the malefics and from impediments, or a free benefic were in the domicile of siblings, and were applied to an unimpeded benefic, it signifies the fitness of the siblings' condition, and of the native himself. Indeed if it were a malefic, and another malefic (or both malefics) were to aspect it,[455] and it were impeded, it signifies the bad condition of the siblings, and their detriment and destruction, and the evil of the native himself, and [his] impediment.

In order to know[456] whether the native or his siblings are of greater value, look at the Lords of the triplicity of the domicile of siblings, and at the Lords of the triplicity of the Ascendant. For whichever of them were of better condition and better disposed, he will be preferred, and will be in a better state and be more exalted.

---

the second and third triplicity rulers. These general statements could easily pertain to both the triplicity rulers and the Lord of the third domicile, but Abu 'Ali distinguishes them.
[454] JN, p. 33.
[455] This phrase could also be read: "Indeed if it were a malefic (or both malefics) and another malefic were to aspect him."
[456] JN, p. 34.

ON THE FOURTH HOUSE

Chapter 1: On the condition of the parents[457] and their accidents, and from what place of the circle it is taken

A narration on the matter of siblings having been set out in the preceding chapter, to me it seems fitting to make mention subsequently of the matter of parents, and from what place of the circle the matter of parents must be taken.

For 'Umar said[458] that you ought to look from the fourth sign from the Ascendant of the native's nativity, and from its Lord; also from the Part of Fathers,[459] and from the Sun and Saturn (from the Sun in the day, from Saturn in the night), from the Part of Fathers,[460] and from the sign of the fourth house,[461] we ought to look both in the day and the night.

For indeed you will see the place of each of these in the figure of the aforesaid nativity, and you will consider the *al-mubtazz* over the place of each of them, and that one of them which you were to find stronger, operate through him—namely by beginning from the Lord of the 4th house [domicile?],[462] then from the Part of the Father and its Lord, and so from the Sun (afterwards, from Saturn), indeed lastly from the planet which is in the fourth. For by that one through which you have operated, you could know the space [of time] of the life of the father of the native (and especially of the first-born), whether it is going to be long or short (and more unrestrictedly if the nativity of the father is not known: because the life of the parent varies in the aforesaid nativity, just as the

---

[457] *Patrum*, lit. "fathers." There is sometimes some ambiguity between the native's male relatives and his parents, in Bonatti's use of this word. I will translate it as context suggests.

[458] *TBN*, p. 61. 'Umar says we should look at the fourth sign, its Lord, the *al-mubtazz* over "these places," planets in the fourth, and "the significator" (which as Hand points out is probably the Sun or Saturn, depending on the sect of the chart). For the life of the father we direct the Part of the Father, the Sun, and the degree of the 4th.

[459] This is equivalent to the Part of the Father in Tr. 8, Part 2, Ch. 7.

[460] This second statement about the Part appears redundant, except (as I said) 'Umar wants us to direct the Part of the Father for his longevity and year-to-year status.

[461] This is an unusual statement–if Bonatti is using whole sign houses (following 'Umar), then why does he add "the sign of the fourth house"? Perhaps this statement is redundant, since he could mean "of the fourth domicile." But it could mean that he wants to incorporate both whole-sign and quadrant houses. Or, this could be a misread for 'Umar's "degree of the house of fathers."

[462] I cannot confidently use "domicile" in this section as I did for siblings, since Bonatti has spoken of the "sign of the fourth house," and the cusp of the 4th. If a sign is intercepted by quadrant houses, then a sign other than the fourth one could be the "sign of the fourth [quadrant] house," and the cusp could be on it.

years of the world and of nativities are varied by their revolutions, just as was treated above in the chapter on the form and shape of the native).[463] For indeed, the stronger of them will be he who is in an angle, not removed from the cusp of the angle by more than 3° ahead or 5° behind,[464] or who is in the succeedents (likewise not removed), or one of the Lords of the other four dignities of the degree in which it[465] is.

Indeed, after you were to see the quantity of the life of the father,[466] and you wanted to know what kind of condition his life is going to have, you will look at the degree of the Part of the Father and the 4th house, and the degree of the Sun (or Saturn), and you will look at him who is more fit to be the *hīlāj*, and direct him to the places of the benefics and the malefics. And according to how you were to see the quantity of his years (which are signified by the aforesaid *al-mubtazz*),[467] you will state the end of the life of the father of that native (which hardly or never is different from that which is signified in his nativity). And to know the truth of the condition of the father for every year, you will likewise direct[468] the degree of the profection of the father to the degrees of the benefics and malefics; and according to how you saw the condition of the said year of the profection (or even of a revolution), so could you judge about the condition of that father, and about the health of his body.

On[469] the knowing of his dignities and sublimities or honors. You will consider the Sun's *dastūrīya* by the diurnal planets (if the nativity were diurnal), which is signified by the planets who are oriental from the Sun. And if it were nocturnal, you will consider from Saturn's *dastūrīya* from the Sun in particular.[470]

---

[463] See Part 2, Ch. 2 ("On the Head of the Dragon and its Tail"), and Part 3, Ch. 13.

[464] I believe that by "ahead of," Bonatti means "in an earlier degree than the cusp's"; by "behind," he means "in a later degree than the cusp's." See my Introduction.

[465] *Ipse.* This must either mean, "in one of its *own* dignities," or "is a Lord over one of the dignities in which the *candidate al-mubtazz*es are." In one sense it doesn't matter, since being in one's own dignities and being a Lord over multiple places would both be routine considerations.

[466] See below. In Tr. 8, Part 2, Ch. 7, he also introduces the Part of the Death of the Father, which predicts the death of the father by profections.

[467] Here Bonatti is equating the *hīlāj* of the father with an *al-mubtazz*. This *al-mubtazz* or *hīlāj* is the planet described in the previous paragraph, which is chosen primarily by house placement.

[468] Based on *TBN*, p. 62. Omitting *ad*, which would read "direct…*to* the degree of the profection of the father to the degrees of the benefics and malefics. 'Umar does not combine the terminology of directions and profections as stated here, but only mentions directions.

[469] These statements are based on *JN*, p. 37.

[470] This is not what Abu 'Ali says, and perhaps there is an error in transcription. Abu 'Ali says to consider Saturn's *dastūrīya* from the *nocturnal* planets in a nocturnal nativity (just as we consider the Sun's from the diurnal planets in a diurnal nativity).

Which if there were *dastūrīya*, it signifies great dignities and great honors are going to come to the father. But if you were to find the contrary, you could judge the contrary.[471]

Chapter 2: On the time of the aforesaid

Indeed, to know at what time these things ought to happen, you will consider the Lords of the triplicity of the Sun (if the nativity were diurnal; if however it were nocturnal, you will consider the Lords of the triplicity of Saturn), and according to how you saw their condition (namely of the first one, the second one, or the third one), so will you pronounce.

Chapter 3: On the kind of death of the father

Which if you wished to look in the matter of the father's death, in its burdens or in its suitableness, you will consider the *al-mubtazz* over the matter of the father, namely to see if it is free from impediments: because this will signify that the father will pass away in his bed by means of a seemly death (and more so and more certainly so, if Jupiter or Venus is found in the 8th from the house [domicile?] of the father).

But if it were impeded, the contrary of that which was said will have to be suspected (and more so if Saturn or Mars were placed in the 8th from the house [domicile?] of the father). For if [the *al-mubtazz*] were impeded by Mars in the day or Saturn in the night, from the opposition or square aspect without the presence or aspect of one of the benefics, nor did the malefic receive it, this will signify the bad death of the father, and its severity. If however the malefic who impeded the said *al-mubtazz* were the Lord of the Ascendant or the *al-mubtazz* over the Ascendant, it signifies that the native will kill the father or will be the reason for his death.

---

[471] It is worth pointing out that (a) we do not know what Abu 'Ali considered *dastūrīya* to be; (b) 'Umar (*TBN*, p. 62) has his own version; and (c) Ptolemy's own definition (*Tet.* III.5) differed from some other Hellenistic conceptions. On this matter, Ptolemy says concerning the Sun, "when [the Sun is] surrounded by stars capable of doing good and by the those of the same sect, either in the same *zōidion* or in the next *zōidion*…and especially whenever morning stars are spear-bearers for the Sun…". He does allow spear-bearing for the Sun by Mars (in a succeedent sign), but because Mars is of the nocturnal sect, their mismatch in sect will contribute to mediocrity. See my Introduction.

Indeed for their getting along you will look at the *al-mubtazz* over the Ascendant and over the house [domicile?] of the father: which if they were to come together, and were concordant, it signifies that there will be concord and likewise benevolence between them (and more strongly so if they were to receive each other). Which if it were not so, and they were discordant, it will be signified that there are going to be discords and lawsuits and hatred between them. And 'Umar said[472] that you could then say he is not [a] legitimate [son]. And if the Sun were impeded by Mars in the day or by Saturn in the night, the father suspects that it will happen to him thus from the native. Likewise, if the Moon were impeded in the day from Mars or in the night from Saturn, he will not believe him, and will always suspect evil from him.

And 'Umar[473] even relates that certain sages said, that if the Lord of the Part of Fathers did not aspect the domicile[474] of children, nor did the Sun then aspect the Lord of the domicile in which he is, nor did the Lord of the Part of Fathers aspect [the Part], the native will not be the son of that father; but if either of them were to aspect, he will be legitimate.

Chapter 4: On the condition of the father and mother

Indeed, Abu 'Ali said[475] that if the nativity were diurnal, you ought to look from the Sun in the matter of the father; if however it were nocturnal, you ought to look from Saturn. And both in the day and in the night you ought to look for the father from the 4th, and the Part of Fathers, and their Lords.

(And again, Abu 'Ali said[476] that you ought to look from the 4th in the matter of the mother, just as in the matter of the father; and in the day and in the night from the Part of the Mother and its Lord—which is taken in the day from Venus to the Moon, and in the night the reverse, and it is projected from the Ascendant).[477]

---

[472] *TBN*, p. 63.

[473] *TBN*, p. 63. But Bonatti seems to have misread the first part of the list. 'Umar says, "But certain ones of the sages said that if the Lord of the *domicile* [not Part] of fathers, if it did not aspect the domicile of children, nor the Sun the Lord of his own domicile, nor the Lord of the Part of the Father [the Part]…".

[474] Reading "domicile," since aspects to houses are typically understood in a whole-sign sense.

[475] *JN*, pp. 34-35.

[476] *JN*, p. 35.

[477] Some material on the mother is here throughout Chs. 4-7. For more, see the 10th House, Ch. 3.

Indeed if you were to find the significators[478] of the father and the mother, or the Lords of the signs in which they are (or more of them), [to be] in the angles, or in their succeedents, and one of the benefics were in the domicile signifying the father, and the Lords of the triplicity of the domicile in which is the luminary whose authority it is, [are] sound and well disposed and in a good place in the figure of the nativity, it signifies the prosperity and good condition of the father, and his gladness, and a multitude of joy. Indeed if you were to see the contrary, you could judge the contrary about the condition of the father, and the durability of his misfortune and infirmity.

But if the Sun were in a good place of the figure of the nativity, and, I say, that he were of good condition and well disposed, and the Lords of the triplicity of the domicile in which he is were impeded and badly disposed, it signifies the good condition of the father, namely then at the time of the nativity–but in the future you will judge the contrary, indubitably. If however the Sun were impeded, and the Lords of his triplicity are found to be sound, it signifies the bad condition of the father and his impediment at the time of the nativity of the child, but in the future his good fortune and good condition and good disposition.

Chapter 5: On the condition of the father by direction

If however you intended to know the condition of the father (what kind it is going to be, and what kind his disposition is going to be) according to a direction, [then] if the nativity were diurnal, direct from the place of the Sun and from the place of the Part of Fathers. If however it were nocturnal, direct from the place of Saturn and from the place of the Part of Fathers (as you do when you direct from the place of the Sun) to the bodies of the benefics and the malefics, and to their rays: because to that place will be borne[479] what is signified by the accidents of the benefics or the malefics, which are going to come to the father after the child's nativity; which, when they arrive at the body of some benefic or to its rays without the presence of a malefic or its rays, then it will signify good accidents and prosperities and advantages, and the health of his body; and things pleasing to the father ought to come (and more strongly so if

---

[478] Reading *significatores* (with Abu 'Ali) for Bonatti's *signum* ("sign"). In addition, while of course we are to look at the fourth sign (according to Abu 'Ali), the sentence would be ungrammatical if it read "sign."

[479] *Transumentur*, "to assume, adopt, take from one to another."

the Part of the Father and the Lord of the domicile in which it is, were in the angles or are found in their succeedents).

Indeed if it were to arrive at the body of some malefic, then it will signify the contrary of all those things which were said, and that infirmities and impediments and vile things will happen to the father (and the more so if the Part of the Father and its Lord were in places cadent from the Ascendant).

And Abu 'Ali said[480] that the same must be looked at in the matter of the mother, namely from Venus and from the Part of the Mother in the day, and from the Moon and from the Part of the Mother in the night. And he said that we ought to look at the degrees of the conjunction (and prevention)—which if the benefics were to aspect [the degree of the conjunction], and the malefics were cadent from it, it signifies the good condition of the father, and his exaltation. If however the malefics were to aspect it, and the benefics were cadent from it, it signifies his baseness. If however the benefics and malefics were to aspect it at the same time, it signifies the middling condition of the father. And he said that the sign of the conjunction and its Lord signify the causes[481] of the father; indeed the sign of the prevention and its Lord signify the causes of the mother.

And he said,[482] look at the fourth sign, because if Jupiter or the Sun or Venus were in it, or one of them were to aspect it by a praiseworthy aspect, it signifies the exaltation of the father[483] and his height and fortune. But if one of the malefics were in it, or were to aspect it by a bad aspect, without the presence or aspect of some benefic, or the fourth sign were the domicile or exaltation of the planet in whose domicile the Lord of the fourth [sign] is,[484] it signifies the weakness and cause of the father and his servitude. If however the same [afflicted] sign were Taurus or Cancer, it signifies the bad condition of the mother, and her weakness and the cause, and likewise her servitude.

---

[480] See JN, pp. 35-36 for this whole paragraph.

[481] *Causas*: his purposes, his undertakings, condition.

[482] See JN, p. 36. Bonatti's paraphrase is spotty and confusing. Abu 'Ali's instructions (deriving from Ptolemy) are: (1) if Jupiter or the Sun are in or aspecting the fourth sign, it is good for the father's status; if Venus or the Moon, it is good for the mother's status. (2) Malefics in or aspecting the fourth sign, without the aspects of benefics, is bad for the parents' status. (3) If this *afflicted* fourth sign is the domicile or exaltation of the Sun, it is bad particularly for the father's status; if of the Moon, for the mother's.

[483] Reading *patris* (with Abu 'Ali) for *matris*.

[484] See note above on Abu 'Ali. To be in conformity with Abu 'Ali, it should read: "*and* the fourth sign were the domicile or exaltation of the planet *whose authority it is, [then if it were the Sun's authority]*…".

And[485] if the Sun and the Moon were in movable signs, it signifies that the father will not be of the same stock as the mother, but one will be of a lower-class parentage than the other; and according to how they were in a more low-class or weaker place, it will signify a lower stock. For if it were the Sun, it will signify the father; if however it were the Moon, it will signify the mother.

And Abu 'Ali said[486] that the Sun (in the day; and the Moon in the night) signifies the causes of the parents at the time of the nativity of the child, and the Lords[487] of the domiciles in which they are, signify that which will be concerning the father in the future. And when the significators of the father–which are [1] the Lord of the domicile in which the Sun is (in diurnal nativities), and [2] the Lord of the triplicity and [3] its exaltation (and the Lord of the domicile in which Saturn is, in nocturnal nativities, and the Lord of the triplicity and its exaltation), [4] the Part of the Father, and [5] the Lord of the domicile in which it is (both in the day and in the night)–are[488] in their own domiciles or exaltations, free from the malefics, and the benefics were to aspect them, it signifies the exaltation and sublime dignity of the father, and the acquisition of substances. And the more so, and more strongly so, if the Part of Fortune and the Lord of the domicile in which it is, appeared fortunate and strong. And again more so, if in addition the Part of the Father were made fortunate, and its Lord–for by this it will be signified that the fortune of the father, and his dignity and honor, is of great durability and constancy after the nativity of the child.

You[489] will even look for the force[490] of the father, and likewise his value, in diurnal nativities, to see if some diurnal planet were in the *dastūrīya* of the Sun:[491] because this will signify the greatness and exaltation of the father's force (unless the nativity of the father works much against it; which if it were so, then the aforesaid would be diminished). If however [the figures of father and child] were to agree, they will be increased. But if the aforesaid significators (especially the luminaries) were impeded, and in bad places, void in course, in their own falls and descensions and detriments, it will signify the fall and impediment or

---

[485] See *JN*, pp. 36-37.
[486] *JN*, p. 37.
[487] Reading *domini* for *domui*.
[488] Reading *sint* for *sit*.
[489] Based on *Tet.* III.5.
[490] *Valitudine. Valetudo* derives from *valeo*, "to have power, to be hale and hearty." It usually has health connotations, but here Bonatti is using it to describe the father's ability to be strong and prevail (as he will below, with respect to the native's *valetudo* in his profession and actions. I will translate it as "force" to distinguish it from "power" (*potentia*) and "strength" (*fortitudo*), which Bonatti occasionally uses.
[491] See footnote above in Ch. 1 for Ptolemy's definition of *dastūrīya*.

detriment of the father, and his baseness, and his miserable life, and the decrease and loss of his goods; and more strongly so if Venus and Saturn were of bad condition and badly disposed. And again more if Mars were to ascend after the Sun, or Saturn after the Moon,[492] and the benefics did not aspect the Sun or Moon.

And[493] always look in the condition of the father, in the day from the Sun and the Lord of the domicile[494] in which he is, and from the Lords of his triplicity. Indeed in the night, from Saturn and the Lord of the domicile in which he is, and from the Lords of his triplicity.

And Abu 'Ali said,[495] know that the Sun and the Moon and the Lords of their domiciles, and the Lords of their triplicities, if they were in angles, free from the malefics and the impediments, it signifies the good fortune of the native's father and his mother. And if they were impeded and joined to malefics, and they were cadent and void in course, it signifies the bad condition of the native and of his parents, and the destruction of their matters.

Chapter 6: On the death of the father

And Ptolemy said,[496] look [at one in] whose nativity the Sun in the day were to aspect the Ascendant, and direct him to the bodies of the malefics and to their rays by degrees of ascensions, giving one year to each degree. And if the Sun did not aspect the Ascendant, and Saturn aspected, direct him just as you directed the Sun. Which if Saturn did not aspect the Ascendant, then direct the degree of the angle of the earth. Then look to see how much were to come to him in terms of years. Which if it were exactly that which was brought forth (how[ever] much it were), [i.e.,] what is signified by the planet who has greater dignities in the day from the Sun and from the Lord of the domicile in which he is (indeed in the night from Saturn and from the Lord of the domicile in which he were found); however in the day and night from the 4th and its Lord, and

---

[492] I.e., if Mars is occidental of the Sun or Saturn is occidental of the Moon–probably in charts of the respective sect.

[493] JN, p. 37.

[494] Reading domus for dominus.

[495] JN, p. 37.

[496] This is a reference to JN, p. 38; but it does not match Ptolemy's own methods.

from the Part of Fathers and its Lord, or near them, it signifies that his father will die in that same year.[497]

Chapter 7: On the death of the mother

And Ptolemy said,[498] look for the life of the mother from Venus (if the nativity were diurnal). Which if she were aspecting the Ascendant, direct her to the bodies of the malefics, and to their rays, by degrees of ascensions, giving one year to each degree. If however Venus did not aspect the Ascendant, and the Moon aspected it, direct her just as was said about Venus. If however the Moon did not aspect the Ascendant, then direct the degree of the 10th house. And begin in nocturnal nativities from the Moon (after [that], from Venus), then from the degree of the 10th house. After this, look ahead to see how much is brought forth for her in terms of years: which if it were equal to the years which are signified by the planet who had greater dignity in the day from Venus and the Lord of the domicile in which she is (and in the night from the Moon and the Lord of the domicile in which she were then to fall)–indeed in the day and in the night from the degree of the 10th house and its Lord, and from the Part of the Mother and the Lord of the same domicile in which it is, or near them–it signifies the death of the mother in the same year.

Chapter 8: On the knowledge of the years of the father's life

In order[499] to know the years of the fathers life if the nativity were diurnal, you will see if the Sun were in an angle or in a succeedent, and the Lord of the domicile or exaltation or bound or triplicity were aspecting him: because then you could take the *hīlāj* from him, whatever kind of aspect it was. However, if none of the planets were to aspect the Sun then, and the Lord of the face were to aspect him from a trine or sextile aspect, and he were otherwise of good condition and well disposed, you could take the *hīlāj* from the Sun and direct

---

[497] This is a confusing paraphrase of Abu 'Ali, who instructs us to: (1) determine the years based on primary directions; (2) find the planet with the most authority in the place of (a) the parent's planetary significator, (b) the significator's Lord, (c) the 4th, (d) the Lord of the 4th, (e) the Part of the Father (or Mother), (f) the Lord of the Part; (3) compare the years from the primary direction with the greater/middle/lesser years of the planet you have chosen. If the years given by (1) are close to those of (2), the father will die in the year specified.
[498] Again, *JN*, p. 38. See above notes for clearer instructions.
[499] See *JN*, p. 39.

[him for the life of] the father, and he who was the *al-mubtazz* over the degree in which the Sun is,[500] will be called the *al-kadukhadāh* and significator of the years of the life of that native's father.

But if what was said was not [so] for the Sun, then you will look at Saturn: which if you were to find him in one of the angles or the succeedents, and one of the Lords of the aforesaid dignities were aspecting him, you could then take the *hīlāj* from Saturn; and the planetary Lord of the dignity of that degree[501] will be the significator[502] of the years of the life of the father.

If however Saturn were not so disposed (as was said), then you will look at the Part of the Father: which if you were to find it in one of the angles or their succeedents, and one of the Lords of the aforesaid dignities were aspecting it, it will be the *hīlāj*. And the planet who was the Lord of that dignity and aspected it, will be the significator of the years of the life of that native's father.

And Abu 'Ali said[503] that if it were not what was said concerning the Part of the Father, look at the degree of the house of the father; and if one of the Lords of its dignities[504] were to aspect it,[505] that degree will be the *hīlāj*, and the planetary Lord of the dignity aspecting [it] will be the *al-kadukhadāh*.

Indeed if the nativity were nocturnal, you will begin to look first from Saturn, then from the Sun, after that from the Part of Fathers, lastly from the degree of the house of fathers.

And Ptolemy said[506] if the benefics aspecting the Sun or the Moon were to aspect the Part of Fortune in nativities, that it signifies the substance of the parents is going to last, and that it will be kept usefully. Which if you were to find the contrary of the aforesaid–namely that the benefics are not aspecting the Part of Fortune nor any of the luminaries (and more strongly so if the malefics were to aspect)–the native will not enjoy the goods of the parents, nor will they profit him.

---

[500] Abu 'Ali adds, "and aspecting the Sun…".

[501] I.e., of the degree in which Saturn is (provided that it aspects the degree, per Abu 'Ali).

[502] I.e., the *al-kadukhadāh*.

[503] *JN*, p. 39.

[504] Reading *dignitatum* for *dignitatem*.

[505] I.e., the degree itself.

[506] Based on *Tet.*, III.5. Ptolemy's instructions are somewhat different, and highlight the medieval confusion about the concept of spear-bearing (later known as *dastūrīya*). Ptolemy says we are to look to see what planets are spear-bearing for the luminaries, and if *these spearbearers* "are harmonious" with the Part of Fortune, then it will be good for the parent's assets and the native's inheritance.

Chapter 9: On the length or shortness of the life of the father

For the length[507] or shortness of the life of the father, you will look to see if Jupiter and Venus were joined to the Sun or Saturn ([and in a parallel way for the mother, if] Jupiter were joined with [the Moon or] Venus),[508] and the Sun and Saturn were so joined together in such a conjunction (namely corporeal or aspectual), that one is received by the other by mutual reception, and each of them is made fortunate and strong: they will signify the long life of the native's father. If however you were to see the contrary, you could judge the contrary, except that you could not be certain, to a fine point, of the length or shortness of the life of the father. However, one will more likely have to fear for its shortness than to hope for its length.

You could say likewise if Mars were northern[509] from the Sun or from Saturn, or he were oriental from Saturn and occidental from the Sun, or he were following them in the figure (that is, that one is in some domicile of some figure, and Mars is in the next domicile which immediately succeeds it), and likewise Saturn is joined with the Sun from a square aspect or from the opposition. If however it were a conjunction from the trine or sextile, the malice will be decreased (and more so, if reception would intervene). And if the Sun and Saturn were cadent from the angles, they will signify the unlucky condition of the father, and his weakness.

And Ptolemy said that if the Sun and Saturn were in the angles or in places ascending to the angles,[510] that they will signify the short life of the father. (Nor however is this contrary to that which Ptolemy said above – that if the Sun or Saturn were in the angles, they signify the [long] life of the father[511]–because there it is spoken of the *hīlāj*, [but] here it is spoken about the life after the *hīlāj*.)[512] Or [they signify] some detriment of his, or a harm similar or equal to it;

---

[507] Based on *Tet.* III.5.

[508] Bonatti nowhere else gives Ptolemy's instructions for the mother, but it seems that what is left of this sentence was a gesture in that direction; so I have supplied the missing bits of it based on Ptolemy, *Tet.* III.5.

[509] Ptolemy's instructions suggest that this really means being "in the tenth sign" from the sign of the Sun or Saturn (i.e., "overcoming").

[510] I.e., the succeedents.

[511] Ptolemy does not exactly say this, but it is consistent with his principles.

[512] This is not really right. Ptolemy is saying that if Mars is in the tenth sign from Saturn or the Sun, or Saturn and the Sun are in unaspecting signs or have a bad aspect, then the father will have an ailment or be injured or not live long–and if they are angular or succeedent, these ailments or his death will come more quickly. It has nothing to do with the *hīlāj*, and only pertains to situations where Saturn and the Sun are already afflicted in the ways mentioned.

and the more so if they were in the first[513] or tenth or the second or the eleventh (because these two angles[514] are faster[515] than the others). If however they were in the seventh or in the fourth, or in the eighth or the fifth, they will judge a less-short life of the father.[516]

But if Mars were to aspect the Sun from the square aspect or from the opposition,[517] it will signify either of two things to come to the father: namely a quick or sudden death, or the impending detriment of his eyes. Indeed if the aspect were from the 8th it will signify death (and more strongly so if the 8th were Scorpio). If however it were from the 6th, it will signify the aforesaid impediment (and more strongly so if the 6th were Virgo). Indeed if Mars were to aspect Saturn from the said aspects, it will judge the death for the native's father, or a fever with a very cold character, or mutilation, or burning, or harm by robbery. Which if the conjunction were from the 8th, death; if from the 6th, fever; if from the other places besides the 12th, mutilation; from the 12th, by robbery or by hidden enemies. But if Saturn and the Sun were joined by the aforesaid aspects without perfect reception, from whatever houses the conjunction was, they will announce the death of the father is going to be because of diseases (and especially cold ones).

---

[513] Reading all of these as signs or places, though Arabic numerals begin with *11*.

[514] I.e., the first and the tenth; the second and eleventh succeed them immediately.

[515] I.e., the lengths of time they *signify* go faster–it is not that the first and the tenth signs or houses *move* faster than the others. Ptolemy himself does not say that these places are "faster"; rather, he distinguishes between whether they show early death or ailments (see below).

[516] That is to say, the 1st, 10th, 2nd and 11th will make death more likely; but in the 4th, 7th, 5th and 8th, injury (rather than death) is more likely.

[517] I.e., by being in the tenth sign from the Sun. Ptolemy says: "For when the star of Ares [Mars] sees the Sun *in the manner we have said.*" See above.

ON THE FIFTH HOUSE

Chapter 1: On the matter of children and their condition

Even though it might have seemed to certain ancient sages[518] [that they should not] put a chapter on children first (since children follow after marriage), still it seems fitting to me, after a narration on parents, to make mention of children; nor is it in vain, since children are loved by parents more tenderly and deeply than spouses [are]; and the house [domicile?] signifying children in the sequence of houses [domiciles?], precedes the house [domicile?] signifying marriage.

Annuz[519] and Baruch[520] said, in the chapter on children (nor do they seem to have differed from the opinion of Ptolemy) that on the matter of children you ought to look at the tenth in the nativity of any native, and likewise the eleventh, the first and also the seventh; and see if one of the planets or other significators signifying children (which are Jupiter and Venus, even the Moon and Mercury and the Lord of the fifth, and the Part of Fortune and the Part of Children and their Lords) are found in the aforesaid places, or if one of those denying children (which are the Sun, Mars, and Saturn) were in them. For if one of the aforesaid significators of children (or some one of them) were in the aforesaid places, or in one of them, or even in the fifth, and they were made fortunate and strong, and one of the benefics were to aspect them by a trine or sextile with reception (or without reception), or even from a square with reception, they will signify the native is indubitably going to have children, unless that significator were with one of the fixed stars of the nature of Mars or Saturn, in the same minute. If however they were weak, they will judge there are going to be few children for him.

But if one of the aforesaid significators were not there, and the Part of Fortune or the Part of Children were there, and one of the malefics were to aspect it, it will deny children completely, whether they were weak or strong—unless perhaps one of the benefics were to aspect the malefic from a trine or sextile aspect, and with reception; or [the malefic] were with one of the fixed stars which are of the nature of Jupiter or Venus or the Moon, in the same minute

---

[518] Bonatti is probably speaking of 'Umar, who places the chapter on marriage before that of children.
[519] Unknown astrologer.
[520] Reading *Baruch* for *Baruth*, as above.

(nor should it be in Leo or Virgo or Libra or Capricorn or Aquarius, or in Taurus). However, this is varied in the signification of Mercury: because if he were in one of the aforesaid places, he will incline to the nature of him with whom he is joined.

And if one of the aforesaid significators signifying children were in one of the aforesaid places, and it were void in course, it signifies that the native will have only a single child.

Chapter 2: At what age the native is going to have children

You will even consider (if Mercury were to signify the native will have children) whether [Mercury] is joined to an oriental planet: because it will signify children in youth. If however the planet were occidental, it will signify them after youth. You could say the same about the Lords of the triplicity of Jupiter, because if the first were oriental, it will signify in youth; if the second one, in middle age; if the third one, in old age. If however all were oriental, they will signify at any age, but more in the first 25 years. Indeed if all [were] occidental, they will signify children for him after youth is completed.

Likewise[521] if the al-mubtazz over the house [domicile?] of children (or Jupiter, or the planet in whose domicile the al-mubtazz is) were oriental, or the Part of Children were in the Ascendant, it will signify that the native is going to have children in his youth.

Which if [there were] a planet appearing in the morning prior to[522] the Sun, far from him by three signs or more, or the Part of Children were in the 10th, it will signify children for him in his middle age. Indeed if it were occidental, or the Part of Children were in the 7th or the 4th, it will signify he is going to have children in his old age; and you will infer according to the rest of these houses.

Indeed Abu 'Ali said[523] that if the Part of Children were in the Ascendant, it will signify children in youth; if it were in the Midheaven, it will signify them in middle age; if it were in the 4th or in the 7th, it will signify them in old age. You however could connect all of their sayings, and thus by inference you could judge more rightly and securely.

---

[521] TBN, p. 70.
[522] I.e., "in an earlier degree."
[523] JN, p. 41.

Chapter 3: On the multitude or scarcity of children

But[524] for the multitude of children, you will look at Jupiter and Venus, and you will judge according to their condition. Indeed for [their] scarcity, you will look at Saturn and Mars, and speak according to what you see concerning their disposition. Indeed for a middling amount, you will find the Moon. However, you will speak concerning Mercury just as you were to see concerning him, as was said above.

If however the aforesaid places[525] were common signs (provided [they were] not of the sterile ones), and the significator of children were likewise in a common sign, it will signify he is going to have twins;[526] and of the sex which the aforesaid places or the aforesaid significators signify.

And if those places[527] were in signs which signify children (which are the watery ones, namely Cancer, Scorpio, and Pisces, which signify a greater quantity of children than the rest), it will signify[528] the native is going to have many children. Which if a planet signifying children were feminine, and the place[529] signifying them were a masculine sign, or *vice versa*, you will announce he is going to have children of each sex. And if the planet and the place[530] were of the same sex, they will judge[531] [that the] children will be of that sex of which they were.

And[532] if the givers of children were in the aforesaid sterile signs, or[533] the malefics were elevated above them,[534] or [the malefics] are the *al-mubtazz*es over the places signifying children, they will make an effort not to forsake the native having children.[535] Which if [the malefics] could not resist it but would [ulti-

---

[524] Based on *TBN*, p. 70, but deriving ultimately from *Tet.* IV.6.
[525] *Loca*. Note the connection with being a "sign."
[526] *Gemellos tantum. Tantum* usually means "as many as," or "exactly" or "only," but I do not know if Bonatti really means the native will never have anything but twins.
[527] *Loca.* But note here the places are "in" signs, not identified with them.
[528] Reading *significabit* for *significabitur.*
[529] *Locus,* now switching to the conventional masculine form.
[530] *Locus.*
[531] Reading *iudicabunt* for *iudicabuntur.*
[532] The beginning of this passage is roughly based on *Tet.* IV.6, but I cannot find an exact source. Bonatti seems to be drawing on several sources, including the Latin edition of *Tet.*
[533] The Latin edition of *Tet.* says "or" here; but Ptolemy himself says "and."
[534] This refers to the Hellenistic "overcoming." See Introduction and footnote to Tr. 3, Part 2, Ch. 20. Ptolemy himself says "and if they chance to have malefics in superior position to [or "overcome"] them." Plato of Tivoli reads this as "Which if the malefics were to conquer above them." So the Hellenistic method is to see if the givers of children have malefics in the tenth sign from their own.
[535] Ptolemy puts this more bluntly: "they do bestow, but not for good and not for long."

mately give] children, they will hardly or never permit him to have more than one child; and the father will see the death of that child, and he will not live long; and if he were to live, he will be unfortunate and troubled, and evils will find him. If however Mars and Saturn or the Sun were in the Ascendant or in the 10th or in the 7th or even in the 11th or in the 5th, or they were to aspect those places[536] without the conjunction or aspect of some benefic to the places, or to the aforesaid planets, or the Ascendant were a sterile sign, and the places[537] signifying children were sterile signs, this will signify that the native will not have children.

And Ptolemy said[538] that if the said malefics appear in masculine or sterile signs (even should the benefics aspect them), they will signify he is going to have no child, because masculine signs virtually speak against children, just like the sterile ones. But if they were in feminine signs, or those of many children, and the benefics were to aspect them, they will signify the native is going to have a child with some defect in his person[539] which he will suffer (for the feminine signs, just like the watery ones, bestow children), or that child will not have a long life but a short one.

But if a masculine or sterile sign were in one of the aforesaid places signifying children, [and] a feminine one or of many children in some other, it will signify[540] the native is going to have some children, whose friendship no men will aim to have, or rather they will totally abhor them; or the children will be aborted. And this will happen according to whether the majority of them were in one of the aforesaid natures (for if the majority were in masculine and sterile signs), or according to how, of those planets, one is stronger than another, or is elevated over him,[541] or they were greater in number, or they were stronger in those places; or according to whether, of them, the majority were oriental, or closer to the aforesaid angles, or going toward them by means of the aforesaid conditions, so the quantity of those significators will be greater.

And 'Umar said,[542] after this look at the sign of children and the sign of the *al-mubtazz* over the matter of the native's condition, and the Ascendant: which if they were signs of many children, the native will abound in children. If there

---

[536] *Loca.*
[537] *Loca.*
[538] *Tet.* IV.6.
[539] I.e., in his body.
[540] Reading *significabit* for *significabitur.*
[541] This must refer to the Hellenistic "overcoming." See Introduction and footnote to Tr. 3, Part 2, Ch. 20.
[542] *TBN*, p. 70.

were no concord between the *al-mubtazz* of the Ascendant and the *al-mubtazz* over the house[543] of children, and Jupiter were combust and Venus impeded, it signifies the native is going to be sterile, without children–and you will observe this for each sex).

And Ptolemy said,[544] but the particular matters of the children can be understood through an appraisal if we were to put down the planetary giver of children as an Ascendant;[545] for we will identify the particulars of the children taken together, just as they are generally known from a nativity.

Indeed ʿUmar said,[546] look at the planets who are the *al-mubtazz* over the house of children, whether they were one or many. Which if some one or more of them were to agree with the Lord of the Ascendant, the children will be good and just, loving their father; indeed if it were the contrary, they will hinder him. And he said[547] if the significator of children were a malefic impeding the Ascendant and its Lord,[548] the children will introduce diverse impediments to the father. And if it were to impede the Moon, they will heap diverse impediments upon the mother. And he said, indeed if the significators of children were sound, the children will be saved and will not die. And if the significators of children were impeded, the children will rarely be agreeable.

You[549] could say the same about the Part of Children: which if it were in the angles, or the succeedents of the 10th or the 4th, it signifies their multitude, and goodness and joy with them. If however it were in the other six places,[550] it will signify a scarcity of children and their quick death. Which if it were void in course,[551] it signifies the death of the native's first born, or perhaps his mother

---

[543] I am not sure if this should be "domicile," since the dignities of *al-mubtazz*es are determined by degree, implying a cusp.

[544] This passage is a direct quote from the Latin *Tet.* according to Plato of Tivoli (see *Tet.* IV.5).

[545] The Latin reads *in loco ascendentis*, which would normally mean "instead of the Ascendant"; but Ptolemy's text makes clear we should take the Latin to read "in the place of an Ascendant," i.e., *as an* Ascendant (which is what the Greek says), referring to derived houses. That is, the position of the (chief) planetary giver of children can be read as marking the 1st house of the children, reading derived houses from there.

[546] *TBN*, pp. 69-70.

[547] *TBN*, p. 71.

[548] Reading *malus impediens ascendens ac dominum eius* (with *TBN*, p. 71) for *multum impediens ac ascendens dominum eius*.

[549] *JN*, p. 40.

[550] Abu ʿAli mentions only the angles and the succeedents (leaving only four places), not mentioning the 10th and the 4th in particular. By Bonatti's count, the four angles and the succeedents of the 10th and 4th (i.e., the 11th and the 5th) leave six remaining.

[551] Abu ʿAli says, "if the Part of Children does not aspect good planets." (This is technically a misstatement, since Parts do not cast aspectual rays.)

will abort him, and she will be saddened concerning her children or because of children.

And Abu 'Ali said[552] that if the Lord of the Ascendant were applied with the Lord of the seventh, it signifies a multitude of children from concubines. If however it were applied with the Lord of the sixth, it signifies them from his own female attendants or slaves. You will even look at the Lords of the triplicity of Jupiter: which if they were in angles or in the succeedents of the angles, it signifies a multitude of children. (If however they were in other places besides the 6th and the 12th, in their own dignities, [and not][553] in the impediments of the malefics, it will signify a suitable quantity of children.)[554] But if they were cadent from the angles or otherwise impeded by the malefics, or they were combust, it signifies a scarcity of children, and their unfitness.

Moreover, Abu 'Ali said[555] if Jupiter and Mercury were in their own domiciles or in their exaltations, in the angles or in their succeedents, and the Lords of their triplicities were in good places from the Ascendant, not impeded (namely made fortunate and strong), they signify a multitude of children, and good and joy with them.

You could say[556] the same about the Part of Children if it were in good places, well disposed (namely that it is in angles or in their succeedents), because then it will signify a multitude of children, and their [good] condition and their good conversation [or interaction]. And if it were cadent from the Ascendant (and especially in the sixth or in the twelfth) it signifies a scarcity of children, and the shortness of their life. But if one of the benefics which was free (namely made fortunate and strong) were to aspect the Part from a trine or sextile aspect, and especially with reception, it will signify a great multitude of children. If however that benefic were to aspect the Part from the said aspects without reception, or from the square with reception, what is signified will be somewhat below the aforesaid (however it will be in a suitable quantity). If however it were to aspect it from the square aspect without reception, it will signify children, but what it signifies will be much below this. If however the benefic were impeded, or a malefic were to aspect the Part of Children (and more strongly so, if the aspect were from the square or opposition), what is signified by it will be weaker

---

[552] JN, p. 40.
[553] The text reads "or." It is unclear whether all of these conditions are supposed to obtain simultaneously.
[554] This comment is Bonatti's own contribution.
[555] JN, p. 40.
[556] Reading dicere for nicere. This paragraph is based on JN, pp. 40-41.

again, and it will indicate fewer children. Which if Jupiter did not aspect the Part of Children, and Venus were impeded by Saturn, you could announce the sterility of the native or the fewest children (and again more if, in addition, the Moon were impeded).

And Abu 'Ali said[557] that if Jupiter and Venus and Mercury were free from the malefics and retrogradation and combustion, the native will have many children. If however they were impeded by the malefics or were in their own detriment, or in their own descension or under the rays of the Sun, he will not have children (or if he will have them, they will die before their father).

You[558] will even look at the fifth: if a benefic were in it and its Lord were free from the aforesaid impediments, and it were to aspect the 10th house [domicile?], it signifies the native is going to have many, and benevolent, children. If however there were a malefic in the fifth and its Lord were impeded,[559] it signifies the scarcity of children and their hastened death (and especially if the impediment were in the 3rd or the 6th). Likewise if either the Sun or the Moon were impeded by the malefics without the aspect of some benefic, it signifies a scarcity of children, and the diminution of the substance of the native himself.

Chapter 4: On the time of children according to Abu 'Ali

Moreover, Abu 'Ali said,[560] by way of recounting the aforesaid, look at the planet who is more worthy in the significations of children: which if it were oriental, it signifies children in youth; if it were occidental, it signifies children in old age. And if it were in the 10th or 11th, it signifies children in youth; and if it were in the 5th or 8th or 9th, it signifies children in middle age. And if it were in the 4th or in the 7th, it signifies children at the end of life.

Moreover, he said[561] if the Part of Children were in the Ascendant, it signifies children in youth; and if it were in the Midheaven, it signifies children in the middle age of life. And if it were in the fourth or in the seventh, it signifies children at the end of life.

---

[557] *JN*, p. 41.
[558] *JN*, p. 41.
[559] Abu 'Ali says, "falling from an angle," i.e., cadent.
[560] Cf. *JN*, p. 41. Bonatti does not quite have it right. Abu 'Ali says: in the Midheaven or 11th, in youth; if in the 3rd, 9th, or 4th, in mid-life. He does not mention any other houses, but he does mention them in relation to the Part of Children (see below).
[561] *JN*, p. 41.

Moreover, he said[562] if Jupiter or Venus, in a revolution of years, were to arrive at the place of the Part of Children (or were to aspect it from a square aspect or the opposition), it signifies he is going to have children at that time (but Jupiter has greater signification in children). And likewise, if the year[563] were to arrive to the sign in which Jupiter or Venus was in his nativity,[564] it signifies children in that same year.

And he said,[565] look (in the coming-together of children to the father) at the planet which was more worthy in the significations of children, and at the Lord of the Ascendant; of which, if either of them were to make the other fortunate, it signifies their concord; and if one were to impede the other, it signifies discord and their enmity. (You, however, will turn your intention concerning this with industry and discretion, by reasoning from house to house, from signification to signification; for not all of the things which happen in these works can be written down individually; for effort would already be converted to nothing.[566]

---

[562] JN, p. 41.
[563] I.e., by profection.
[564] Reading *nativitate* (sing.) for *nativitatibus* (pl.).
[565] JN, p. 41.
[566] *Redigeretur enim studium iam in nihilum.* Bonatti's sense seems to be that if all the answers were given in cookbook style, the effort to gain experience would be devalued.

ON THE SIXTH HOUSE

Chapter 1: On the native's male and female slaves, and servants or domestics,[567] and on small animals which are neither ridden nor yoked, and on his infirmities and likewise diseases

Having spoken about the matter of children in the chapter which preceded this one, it seems fitting to me in this one to treat subsequently of the matter of male and female slaves, and servants or domestics, and small animals which are neither ridden nor yoked, and on the native's infirmities and his diseases, and to make mention of them.

For Abu ʿAli said,[568] concerning the affairs of male and female slaves or servants and attendants, you must look at the sixth [sign],[569] and likewise its Lord, and likewise Mercury and the Moon, and see if Mercury were oriental and in the Ascendant or in the 10th, joined to Jupiter by corporal conjunction or by aspect, in a movable or common sign; or if one of the luminaries or one of the other benefics were in the 6th or in the 12th; or if the Lord of the domicile of slaves were made fortunate, and were free from impediments, joined to Mercury in one of the angles; or if Mercury were free, joined with one of the benefics or seeking its conjunction; or if the Lord of the domicile of slaves[570] were in a good place from the Ascendant or were itself in the Ascendant, or were in the 6th, free from impediments (namely made fortunate and strong), joined to some benefic–because this signifies that the native will abound in male and female slaves, and servants, and household intimates and domestics, and that he will have good (and wealth and joy and usefulness) because of them and for them and from them.

But if Mercury were retrograde or combust, or joined with the malefics in a fixed sign, or seeking their conjunction, or one of the malefics were in the

---

[567] In this chapter there are a number of dependence-relationships referred to the 6th house. I will translate a few of the more obscure ones as follows: *famulus*, a servant or attendant, will be "servant"; *vernaculus*, a slave (especially a domestic slave) will be a "domestic"; *pedissequus*, a manservant or attendant, will be "attendant"; *familiaris*, an adjectival noun pertaining to servants, a household, and those who are familiar or intimate, will be "household intimate."

[568] Paraphrased from *JN*, p. 42.

[569] Abu ʿAli says "sixth sign," but Bonatti's text simply says "6th" (*sextam*). I will follow Abu ʿAli since Bonatti is so often concerned to quote or paraphrase him accurately.

[570] Bonatti says "the Lord of the house of fortune." But Abu ʿAli says "its Lord," in the context of the 6th. Therefore I have read "of slaves" for "of fortune."

domicile of slaves, or in the 12th, or the Lord of the domicile of slaves were a malefic, or were retrograde or otherwise impeded by the malefics, or were cadent from the angles or from the Ascendant, without the aspect of some benefic; or what was said about the Lord of the domicile of slaves were [true] of Mercury, or the Tail were in the domicile of slaves–this signifies a want of slaves, and their scarcity, and anger and sorrow and discomfort is going to come to the native because of them and by reason of them.

And Abu 'Ali said,[571] see the unsuitableness and impediment and profit of the native with slaves, [by looking] at the planet who is more worthy in the 6th domicile, and the Lord of the 6th [domicile], and at the Part of Slaves[572] and its Lord, and the planet who is in the 6th, and at Mercury, and the Lord of the Ascendant; and you will see if they make each other fortunate. Because if it were so, it will signify the native's success and goodness and concord with slaves. If however they impeded each other, you could judge the contrary. And according to what you were to see of the goodness or malice of each (namely of the Lord of the Ascendant and the other significators which were stated) in terms of the multitude of testimonies (obviously of good or evil), you will judge according to that. For if the Lord of the Ascendant were to behave well toward the significator of slaves, and the significator of slaves toward the Lord of the Ascendant, it will signify the goodness of each toward the other. If however they were to behave badly, they will judge the evil of each. Which if one were to behave well toward the other, and the other were to behave badly against him, one will seek good and the other evil from his contrary, so that one will be benevolent to the other, [and] the other will be judged malevolent to him.

Chapter 2: On flock-animals[573] and other animals which are signified by the 6th

Having looked concerning male and female slaves in the preceding, and concerning other things in what has preceded, now we must look concerning flock-animals and other beasts which are signified by the 6th house [domicile?], before we arrive at the infirmities of the native.

---

[571] A paraphrase of *JN*, p. 43.

[572] See Tr. 8, Part 2, Ch. 9.

[573] *Pecudibus*. A *pecus* is often associated with cattle, but it has the broader meaning of flock or herd animals like sheep, birds, *etc.* This form (gen. *pecudis*) refers to flock animals counted by the head (individually). The other form (gen. *pecoris*) refers to flock animals considered as a group or herd.

For it seemed to the ancient sages (with whom I agree in a friendly-enough way), that the matter of flock-animals (goats, pigs, and other animals, both two-footed and even four-footed, which are neither ridden nor yoked, and domestic and gentle birds), is taken from the 6th domicile.[574]

Whence[575] the 6th domicile must be looked at, and we must look at its Lord, and likewise Mars, and [see] how they are disposed, and in which places from the Ascendant they (or one of them) is found, and whether Mars is direct or retrograde (because he naturally has a signification over the aforesaid animals).

Whence, if [Mars] were in Aries or Capricorn,[576] in the Ascendant or in the 10th, or even in the 6th [domicile], and Jupiter or the Sun were aspecting him by a trine or sextile aspect, and he were otherwise made fortunate and strong, free from impediments, it signifies that the native will be fortunate in having a multitude of the aforesaid animals; and that good and usefulness and joy will follow from them and because of them. And the more so, if Mars were in one of his own dignities (he is even praised if he is in Leo), likewise if the 6th domicile is of the aforesaid signs, and its Lord in one of them, joined with one of the benefics or in its trine or sextile aspect: and this signifies that he will have wealth and profit from them, and that they will be multiplied for him and for his usefulness.

But if the 6th domicile were Taurus or Leo or Scorpio or Aquarius, and Saturn were in it, or were to aspect it from the opposition or by a square aspect,[577] it signifies that the native will be saddened and impeded because of the aforesaid animals, and he will suffer harm from thence (and more strongly so in Leo than in the others; less so in Aquarius).

And if Mars or Jupiter were to have a dignity then in the 6th [domicile], Saturn's hindrance will be greater, unless one of them aspects him from a trine or sextile aspect, and with reception, [and they are] made fortunate and strong.

And Abu 'Ali said[578] that if one of the signs of beasts were there, and the Ascendant were suitable,[579] and the Lord of the Ascendant were with Mars or in

---

[574] I do not know precisely which "ancient sages" he means. Again, Abu 'Ali associates animals with the 12th; 'Umar and Ptolemy do not mention animals at all. Bonatti goes ahead and treats Abu 'Ali as though he is talking about the 6th. I will use "domicile" for *domus* in this section, since Abu 'Ali clearly speaks of whole-sign houses here.

[575] See *JN*, pp. 43-44. But note that Abu 'Ali uses the 12th sign, not the 6th. The distinction between the 6th and 12th, and the reason for attributing animals to these places, is an interesting question. See my article, "How did animals get into the 6th?" (forthcoming).

[576] Abu 'Ali says, "in a quadrupedal sign, or even in a regal sign," thus Bonatti lists signs like Aries, and Leo, and uses Capricorn for Mars's dignity (below)..

[577] Probably by whole-sign aspects.

[578] Cf. *JN*, p. 44.

his aspects out of praiseworthy places, the native will love beasts and rejoice with them. Likewise if the Moon were in the aforesaid places, it signifies just as much as the Lord of the Ascendant does.

Chapter 3: On the infirmity of the native, and on his diseases

Having spoken on these things which have preceded in this chapter[580] about the native's male and female slaves, and on his small animals (and those which are not ridden), it now remains to speak about his infirmities and diseases.

And infirmity and disease differ. For an infirmity is an accident or weakness of the body that comes and goes away. Indeed a disease is an infirmity or accident of the body that comes and does not go away. Whence[581] it is necessary for you to consider that you ought to look, in the nativity of some native, at the Ascendant and its Lord, the 6th also and its Lord, the Moon, and the Lord of the domicile in which she is, and the planet which is in the 6th (if one is discovered there), even Mercury and the Part of Infirmities,[582] and at the planet in whose domicile it is (both for a native's disease and his infirmity), likewise the places[583] in which the aforesaid significators are.

Look[584] at the *al-mubtazz* over these places, and especially over the 6th house [domicile?], which signifies the infirmities of the native and his diseases. Which if [the *al-mubtazz*] were a benefic and there were a conjunction between it and the Lord of the Ascendant (and stronger than this if reception intervenes), it signifies the good health of the native, and his prosperity (if only his salvation from infirmities or diseases), and that his infirmity and diseases are few and light.

And 'Umar said[585] that he will be fortunate with animals and slaves and domestics, if the *al-mubtazz* over the foresaid places[586] were a benefic, or agreed

---

[579] Abu 'Ali is speaking about having one of the bestial signs rising–I do not know exactly how Bonatti is conceptualizing what is "suitable."

[580] This sentence suggests that Bonatti's own chapter headings do not match those of the editors of the 1491 and 1550 editions.

[581] See *TBN*, pp. 71-72.

[582] Bonatti gives two formulas in Tr. 8, Ch. 9. The first is the Part of Infirmities and Accidents and Inseparable Defects, which is taken in the day from Saturn to Mars, and in the night the reverse; and it is projected from the Ascendant. The second is the Part of Infirmities Both Separable and Inseparable, is taken in the day and night from Mercury to Mars; and it is projected from the Ascendant. I do not know which he means here.

[583] *Loca.*

[584] A paraphrase of *TBN*, pp. 72-73.

[585] *TBN*, p. 73.

with[587] the Lord of the Ascendant. If however the aforesaid *al-mubtazz* were a malefic, of whichever sort he were (of the aforesaid significators), and he were joined to the Lord of the Ascendant or were in one of the angles or the succeedents, impeding the Lord of the Ascendant (or the Ascendant itself), it signifies that the native will be surrounded and impeded by many infirmities and many diseases.

Which[588] if the *al-mubtazz* were Saturn, it signifies that his infirmities will mostly be because of cold and dryness; likewise they will be extended, as are cancer, being hunchbacked,[589] gout,[590] epilepsy, hyposarca,[591] anasarca,[592] morphew,[593] *elephantia*,[594] paralysis, and similar incurable illnesses (or nearly incurable, or very difficult to cure).[595]

But[596] if Mars were the *al-mubtazz*, and were in one of the angles, joined with the Lord of the Ascendant, [and] impeding him, it signifies that the native's infirmities and his diseases will arise from heat and dryness, like those which come to be from red cholera or even from blood, as do acute fevers, mania,[597] and abscesses which are not easily brought to maturity.

And 'Umar said,[598] [if] the Part *Azemena* (which is an inseparable accident),[599] with the Moon in the 9th and Mars in the 8th (in the nativity), were in signs of

---

[586] *Loca.*

[587] *Congruerit.* This verb can mean both "agree with" and "coincide," so I imagine if it were the same planet (and a benefic), it means good; likewise if the planets are of a similar positive nature (Venus and Jupiter; Sun and Moon, etc.).

[588] See *TBN*, p. 72.

[589] Probably related to a term used in biology ("gibbous"), ultimately derived from the gibbous Moon. It is a distended, rounded swelling. It can also indicate a tumor.

[590] Reading *podagra* for *prodagra*. A gout is a painful arthritis caused by excess monosodium urate crystals, often characterized by painful swellings of a joint (like the big toe).

[591] An extreme form of anasarca or dropsy, an accumulation of fluid under the skin, causing swelling.

[592] See previous note.

[593] *Morphea.* See Tr. 3, Part 1, Ch. 1 for this ailment.

[594] Probably *elephantiasis*, in which skin becomes very thickened, rough, and fissured.

[595] Note that all of these diseases involve processes of hardening, stiffening, and local accumulations, deposits, or swellings. This is typical of the Aristotelian phenomenon of the cold and the dry qualities. Dryness especially creates stiffness and inflexibility.

[596] See *TBN*, p. 73.

[597] *Frenesis*, maniacal behavior; from Gr. *phren*, the diaphragm, as a seat of emotion.

[598] *TBN*, pp. 73-74.

[599] In a parallel passage (*JN*, p. 44 n.82), Holden identifies a Part like this as being taken from Saturn to Mars by day (and by night the reverse), projected from the Ascendant: this is the same as the Part of Infirmities and Accidents and Inseparable Defects (see above).

severed limbs,[600] one of his limbs will be cut off by a sword. Likewise if the Part[601] were with the Moon in another quarter, and the Ascendant were impeded by some malefic, accidents will find the native in the limb of the sign in which the Moon is, or in the left eye in nativities of the day, and in the right eye in nativities of the night. And he said[602] if the luminaries were in conjunction or prevention, and the malefics were in the square aspect of the conjunction or prevention, and a malefic were to ascend, [then] later the native will lose the right eye from the Sun, and the left from the Moon. Moreover, if either luminary were impeded by a square aspect of the malefics, or their opposition, or were in its corporal conjunction, and[603] one of the benefics did not[604] aspect [the luminary], he will lose the eye signified by that luminary. If however each luminary were impeded, he will lose each eye.

And 'Umar said[605] if the Moon were impeded in the nativity (understand [by this, being impeded] by the malefics in some sign, without the rays of the benefics to that bound), that member which pertains to the sign in which the Moon is, will be destroyed. And he said[606] if the Moon were in signs which signify impediment in the eyes (like Cancer, Leo, Scorpio, Sagittarius, Capricorn, and Aquarius), it signifies the impediment of the eyes (and likewise the Ascendant).[607]

And he said[608] if the Moon were in Sagittarius, whether she were impeded by the malefics or not, an impediment will happen to him in the eyes, and blindness will be feared for him unless a [planet] (a benefic, you understand) were to aspect her.

---

[600] 'Umar uses whole sign houses, and only says "it is," not "they are." Likewise, he does not use the ablative with Mars, which is what one would expect if Mars were supposed to be in the 8th at the same time.

[601] Reading *pars* for *Mars* along with Hand and 'Umar, since the topic seems to be the Part of *Azemena*.

[602] *TBN*, p. 74.

[603] Reading *et* with 'Umar for Bonatti's *vel*.

[604] Adding *non*, with 'Umar.

[605] *TBN*, pp. 74.

[606] *TBN*, pp. 74-75.

[607] The Latin in 'Umar is ambiguous. Bonatti seems to think either that these signs by themselves (when rising) will cause eye problems, or else if one of them is ascending and the Moon is in it. The 'Umar text attaches *et ascendens* to the next sentence, speaking about the Moon in Sagittarius. Hand reads this as meaning "Likewise, when the Moon is rising in Sagittarius..." While this is grammatically possible, the word order is not quite natural. Bonatti may actually be right in his interpretation.

[608] *TBN*, p. 74. See previous note.

Which if the Moon were in Gemini or in Libra or Aquarius, [afflicted] by Mars, it signifies the rottenness of the eyes and their inflammation. And 'Umar said[609] [it signifies] leprosy, unless one of the benefics were to aspect her. But if she were impeded by Saturn in Cancer or Scorpio or Pisces, without the aspect of a benefic, it signifies cancers, gouts,[610] swelling [in the throat],[611] and white leprosy,[612] and sore throats.[613]

And ['Umar] al-Tabarī said[614] if the Moon were in the square aspect of the Sun, or with him in one sign (combust, you understand),[615] or in the square aspect of Mars, or in his opposition, the native will be burned by fire.

And[616] if Venus were impeded at the same time by Saturn or by Mars, and by the Sun, and Mercury, in someone's nativity, without the aspect of a benefic, the genitals of the native will be cut off. Which[617] if the Lord of the 8th were to aspect [the Moon] or the Lord of the 8th were one of the aforesaid, the native will die from the severing. Indeed if the Lords of the triplicity of the sign in which Venus then was, were made fortunate and strong and well disposed, dignity and honor will follow[618] the native from the severing. And if they were impeded, evil upon evil will follow from it, because he will fall into sorrow and distress because of it, and into labors and afflictions and depressions and detriments which he could not avoid. Which if it were a woman, she will not give milk for weaning[619] nor will she care about men nor want to do it with them, nor will she care about any venereal solace.

---

[609] *TBN*, p. 75.

[610] *Podagras*.

[611] *Bocium*. Perhaps he is referring to goiters.

[612] Reading *lepram albam* (with 'Umar) for *lepram albaras* (below, *albaras* or "white morphew" appears by itself). But I also note that (according to my online medical dictionary), our modern leprosy used to be called *lepra Arabum*, "leprosy of the Arabs." Perhaps further research will determine whether the Latin 'Umar manuscript might originally have said *albam* (white) or *Arabum* (of the Arabs).

[613] *Squinantes*. From Lat. *synanche*, derived from the Gr. *sunanchê*. This term has variously been called "squinancy," "squinsy," and "quinsy," as we also see in William Lilly's *Christian Astrology* III, p. 579.

[614] *TBN*, p. 75.

[615] This clarification is Bonatti's, not 'Umar's.

[616] *TBN*, p. 75.

[617] The following statement is Bonatti's.

[618] Again, Bonatti seems to invert the proper usage of *sequor*. 'Umar says the native will "acquire" (*acquiret*) these things.

[619] *Exuberabitur*. 'Umar, on the other hand, says her breast will be cut off–evidently in imitation of the Amazons.

And 'Umar said[620] if the Moon were in the first degree of the signs, or at their end, and the malefics (and especially Saturn) were to project their rays to that bound, he will love with the greatest love, and will be known publicly because of it. But[621] if Saturn were in the domicile of infirmities or were in the sixth from the sign in which the Moon then is, or he were in the opposition or in the square aspect of those places, it signifies the multitude of the native's illnesses coming from a cold cause (and more so if he were in a moist sign). Which if Mars were in the 6th [domicile] from the Ascendant or in the 6th [domicile] from the sign in which the Moon is, or in the square aspect or the opposition of those places, it signifies the multitude of the native's illnesses coming from a hot cause, and quickly coming to an end, to the good or to the bad. For if the Lord of the Ascendant or the Moon were to aspect Mars from a trine or sextile aspect, nor did they receive him, it signifies a determination to the good. If however they were to aspect him from a square aspect or from the opposition (or from any other one), and were to receive him, it signifies a determination to the bad,[622] and that he is more likely going to die because of those illnesses, than not.

And if the Moon and the Lord of the domicile in which she is, and likewise the sixth sign, were free from the malefics, it signifies the liberation of the native from his illnesses. Indeed if the Moon and the Lord of the domicile in which she is, and the Lord of the domicile[623] of infirmities were impeded by the malefics, it signifies a multitude of different illnesses of the native.

And Abu 'Ali said[624] if a malefic were in the Ascendant (and especially if it were Mars in diurnal nativities, and Saturn in nocturnal nativities), joined to the Sun or Moon, it signifies weakness of vision or the destruction of the eye. If however the luminaries were impeded by the malefics or by the Tail joined to them, it signifies weakness of vision or the destruction of the eye.

And he said,[625] if however the Moon were joined to malefics or were in their square aspect or opposition, and in a moist sign, it signifies that more infirmities

---

[620] *TBN*, pp. 75-76.

[621] *JN*, p. 44.

[622] The fact that things will be worse if they receive him, seems to be because they are formally inviting him into their house—and thereby allow him to do what he wants to do, which is to kill. Similar statements may be found in Tr. 6. Reception is good for the planet received (in this case, Mars)—it is not necessarily good for the native or for the planet doing the receiving.

[623] Reading "domicile," since Bonatti has specified the sixth sign above.

[624] *JN*, p. 45.

[625] Both Abu 'Ali's text and Bonatti's are ambiguous as to whether the malefic or the Moon is to be in the relevant sign. I have translated it as though it is the Moon.

of the native will be from cold and moisture. And if she were in a dry sign, it signifies illnesses from heat and dryness.

Chapter 4: At what age these things would happen

And if the planet who signifies the infirmities were oriental, the infirmities will be in the first half of the native's life. If however it were occidental, they will be in the last half of his life. And if it were in the Ascendant, they will be in the beginning of life. Indeed if they were in the 10th, they will be at the mature age of his life. Which if it were in the seventh, they will be in the decline of his life. Indeed if it were in the fourth, they will be around the end of his life.

You should even look at the condition of [the native's] significator,[626] because the illnesses will be according to its strength and weakness (namely, [they will be] weak or strong).

You will even see if the Part of Infirmities and the Lord of the domicile in which it is, were free from impediments: because that signifies the salvation and good health of the native, and his salvation from infirmities. If however they were impeded, it signifies infirmities and serious pains are going to come, and more strongly so if one of the benefics did not aspect them or at least one of them.

And Abu 'Ali said[627] (and it is true), for the Ascendant and the Moon are significators of the body; and the Lord of the Ascendant and the Lord of the domicile of the Moon are significators of the soul. And if the Ascendant and the Moon were impeded by the malefics, and their Lords were sound, it signifies the infirmity of the native's body and the good health of his soul. And if the Ascendant and the Moon were free from the malefics and their Lords were impeded, it signifies the good health of the body and the quaking fear and sorrow of the soul.

Indeed Ptolemy said[628] that we ought to consider the Ascendant and the 7th (and even the 6th, which naturally signifies infirmity because it has no friendship with the Ascendant). Likewise you ought to consider Saturn and Mars, and see how they are disposed: for if they were both (or one of them) in one of the aforesaid places, or they were to aspect [the place][629] from a square aspect or

---

[626] Perhaps either the *hīlāj* or the *al-kadukhadāh*.
[627] *JN*, p.45.
[628] See *Tet.*, III.13.
[629] I.e., *locum*.

from the opposition (from wherever the aspect arrived), it signifies that the native will be infested with many infirmities and impediments coming to him; and more certainly so, if in addition you were to find the Sun and the Moon impeded. And more strongly yet, if the impediment were in the angles or in their succeedents. And again more, if one of the aforesaid malefics were to aspect them[630] (or one of them). And again more, if those malefics were in the angles or in their succeedents and were to aspect them from the square aspect or from the opposition, and even from a trine or sextile without reception. And [those] illnesses will be weak, which are signified by the Ascendant or by the 7th or by the 6th or by the malefics themselves, according to how the *al-mubtazz* of the aforesaid places over infirmities was found, as was said above.

Chapter 5: In what limb the aforesaid will come

And illnesses will happen in that part of the body which is signified by the sign in which the aforesaid *al-mubtazz* were made unfortunate or impeded, and what things are signified by the *al-mubtazz* itself. Which if the *al-mubtazz* were to signify one part of the body, and the sign in which it is were to signify another, the aforesaid will happen in each member signified by them–like Aries, which signifies the head, Taurus the neck, Gemini the arms, and the rest; and Saturn the right eye, the spleen, the bladder, and the rest; Jupiter the right hand, the lungs, ribs, and the rest; Mars the left eye, and the left ear, the [male] genitals, and the rest; the Sun each eye (but more the right one), the face, and practically the whole right part of the body (and this because of his diurnality), *etc.*, Venus the buttocks, the liver, *etc.*; Mercury the tongue, the interior of the nostrils, *etc.*; the Moon the interior of the throat, the epiglottis, the stomach, *etc.*, in women the belly, private parts, and the whole left side of the body (on account of her nocturnality).

And Ptolemy said[631] impediments[632] will happen for the most part if the unfortunate stars (which are the occasion for them), were oriental in the figure or from the Sun. However, infirmities, for the most part (if not always) will come if the same stars (namely the unfortunate ones) were occidental either in the world or from the Sun, because there is a separation or distinction between

---

[630] I.e., aspecting the places of the luminaries (probably by whole sign, and even more if by close degrees).
[631] *Tet.* III.13.
[632] I.e., injuries (see Ptolemy).

each of these two. For *impediments* do not happen but once, nor do their pains last long; indeed *infirmities* either last forever, or they happen by going back-and-forth (namely, by intervals).[633] And he said, in matters through which particular accidents are grasped, when the peculiar figures are experienced and observed, and the qualities are discovered, there are infirmities and impediments signifying what was grasped in terms of the accidents which follow, and they will happen for the most part according to the similar positions of the stars in the qualities.[634]

For there will be a loss of vision in either eye if the Moon alone were impeded in the aforesaid angles (namely in an oriental or occidental one), and at that hour there were a conjunction or a prevention; or if she were in another figure with the Sun and were to have *al-'ittisal* (or she were in a trine or sextile aspect, or a square) with one of the stars which are likened to clouds–like the nebulous star which is in Cancer, and the Pleiades (which is in Taurus), and the point of the arrow of Sagittarius, also the tail of Scorpio, and what is around Adhafera[635] (and almost the cord or tresses of the parts of Leo), Regulus,[636] likewise [the Pitcher of] Aquarius. And if the Moon were impeded in one of the angles (namely the fourth), occidental from the Sun, and Mars and Saturn were oriental, also with the Moon going toward Mars and Saturn (or toward either of them); or the Sun were in the fourth angle and the said two malefics were to ascend before the Sun, or they were joined to him, and the luminaries were conjoined in one and the same sign, or they were opposite each other and the said two malefics were occidental from the Moon–impediments will happen to the native in each eye; and this will happen with some blow or a sword. And if it were in Aries or Leo or Sagittarius, this will happen because of fire. And if the said malefics (or at least Mars) were joined with Mercury, this will happen because of a battle or game which could in some way be likened to a battle. Or it will happen from something which will be moved unfairly against the native.

---

[633] Here Bonatti is emphasizing a new distinction: one-time impediments, and more chronic or recurring infirmities (to be added to the earlier "disease," which is a permanent illness).
[634] This last part is an awkward version of a passage in *Tet.* III.13. In Ptolemy it reads: "It is sufficient to arrange, for one of those [classes] laid out, an injury or ailment of such a kind as the places of the horizon and those of the *zōidia* begin to show, [also taking into account] the natures of the stars afflicting and being afflicted, and further more the natures of the stars configured with them. For, the parts of the *zōidia* surrounding the injured part of each horizon will indicate the part of the body that the cause concerns, and whether the indicated part can admit of injury or ailment or both, while the natures of the stars produce the species and the causes of the ailments."
[635] The cluster Coma Berenices, but in more recent times identified as ζ Leo.
[636] *Calbem.* From Ar. *qalb*, "heart," so Regulus (the heart of the Lion).

If however Mercury were joined with Saturn, this will happen from a running of water into the eye,[637] or from the torture of the eyes themselves, and the like. And[638] if the Moon were in the oriental half,[639] joined to Mars, and Venus joined to Saturn will be united with Mercury in the aforesaid way; and Mars were northern from her, or they were to aspect each other from the opposition, the native will not have his genitals, or will play the role with each sex, or will be born without an anus (or with its excessive constriction). And if it were a woman, she will not have her private parts like she ought to. And if Venus were to behave this way with Mercury, Mars, and Saturn, as was said, and Venus were seeking the conjunction of the Sun, and the luminaries were in masculine signs and quarters, and Venus and the Moon occidental (from the Sun, I say), also the malefics in following degrees and Venus and the luminaries impeded, and, Ptolemy said, if the native were male–he will be mutilated, or he will suffer impediments in his testicles (but especially if this were in Leo, Aries, or Scorpio, or Capricorn or Aquarius). But if it were a woman, she will be sterile, and perhaps she will not escape the impediments of one of the eyes.

You will even consider whether Mercury and Saturn are in the aforesaid angles with the diurnal luminary, [and] Mercury were retrograde, occidental,[640] going toward the conjunction of the Sun, and the Moon was in their conjunction (namely of Mercury and Saturn): because if it were so, it will signify the native is going to be a stutterer, and a holder of his tongue, but he will not be wholly deprived of speech. If however Mars is joined to them, it signifies he will hold his tongue less, even if he does not loosen it up entirely. If however Jupiter were to aspect, his tongue will be impeded little.

---

[637] I.e., cataracts.

[638] This passage (both in Ptolemy and in Bonatti) is complicated enough that it is worth quoting Ptolemy: "And if the Moon after rising should apply to the star of Ares [Mars], and if she along with the star of Kronos [Saturn] should apply to the star of Hermes [Mercury] while the star of Ares is in superior position [or "overcomes"] or diametrical, they become eunuchs or hermaphrodites or without holes and orifices. And with these things being so, when the Sun should also be configured, with the lights and the star of Aphrodite [Venus] being masculinized, and with the Moon waning and the malefics approaching in the post-ascensional degrees [later in the sign or in the next sign], the men become castrated or have their parts injured, and especially in Aries and Leo and Scorpio and Capricorn and Aquarius; the women become childless and sterile." Obviously this is a rare situation, and one wonders if this is a theoretical construct or has some experiential basis.

[639] Ptolemy seems to include only the eastern quarter from the Ascendant to the Midheaven.

[640] This probably means pertaining-to-sinking.

And Ptolemy said[641] that this will be known by the degrees of the direction which there are between him and the luminary whose authority it was. Again, if the aforesaid malefics were in the beginnings of the signs or near [them], it signifies that the native's impediments will be from the navel upwards. If however they were in the end of the signs, or near [them], it signifies that they will be from the navel downwards. If however the Moon were impeded in those places, you could judge the same.

Chapter 6: Again on the aforesaid impediments–where they will be, and for what reason they will come, according to Ptolemy

You[642] will even consider whether the luminaries are going to the conjunction of the said malefics (of Mars and Saturn), with them appearing in the angles, or [if] they were in their opposition; and with the Moon in the *jawzahirr* of one of them, or appearing in its Tail, or in the Head or in the Tail of the Dragon,[643] or in signs of infirmities (which are, as Ptolemy says, Aries, Taurus, Cancer, Scorpio, Capricorn): because this will signify that the native will be a hunchback or he will have some destroyed limb, or *azemena* will invade him, or lameness, crookedness,[644] or the shrinking [or shriveling] of some official limb. But if the malefics were joined with the luminaries, corporally or from the opposition, or from the square aspect, in the hour of the native, you could announce the same. Which if the said malefics[645] were in the 10th, and they were northern of the luminaries, or the luminaries were in the 4th, it will signify that these impediments and these infirmities will often come by accidents, often great ones from which follow the greatest and ultimate terrors, like drowning, falling into the hands of deadly enemies or desperate robbers, or [into the hands of] the cutters of roads who spare none, or a fall from or being trampled by a horse, or being gored by a bull, and the like. Which if Mars were northern from the luminaries, and he were the *al-mubtazz* over one of the aforesaid places, the aforesaid impediments will happen on the occasion of a fire or some burning or the infliction of great wounds. If however Saturn were northern, and he were

---

[641] I do not see this first sentence in Ptolemy, but the rest of the paragraph is based on *Tet.* III.13.

[642] *Tet.* III.13.

[643] This seems to be Bonatti's own addition. Ptolemy (*Tet.* III.13) speaks only of the Moon being at the equinoctial points (i.e., the Head and the Tail) or in the solstitial ones (i.e., the beginnings of Cancer and Capricorn)–see below.

[644] *Dislocatio.* Perhaps "dislocation."

[645] Reading *infortunae* for *fortunae*, following Ptolemy.

the *al-mubtazz*, impediments will happen which could happen to the native on the aforesaid occasions, by submersion or falling headlong, and paralysis.

Indeed[646] the impediments which happen more frequently–if the Moon is located in the two equinoctial points and in the two solstitial ones (if only the Moon and these signs were impeded)–are these: wherefore if she were in the vernal equinoctial point, then impediment happening to the native will be a peculiar morphew, and the particular spots will be white and leprous, and they are curable. And if she were in the summer solstitial point, it will be impetigo[647] or erysipelas, and the like. And if she were in the autumnal equinoctial point, it will be white morphew[648] and the like. And if she were in the winter solstitial point, happening more frequently, it will be a lentigo.

You[649] will even consider if the said malefics (Saturn and Mars) were in angles, joined with the luminaries (or with either of them), if they were oriental from them.[650] Because if it were Saturn, it will signify illnesses thinning the native down on account of the coldness of the humors, and drying his members, and wounds, and the native's body filled with infirmities: jaundice,[651] coughing, wounds of the intestines, and other hidden wounds, and certain other illnesses of the native, exterminating and drying out the body, and sometimes making it leprous. Which if it were a woman, she will grow ill in her private parts. Which if it were Mars, it signifies most often illness from a hot and dry cause, bloody and indeed stinking spit, soreness of the lung and of the windpipe artery,[652] the loss of sense, scabies, blisters of the lung and cavities,[653] things coming from inflamed and choleric blood; and impediments will even come to the native from wounds and cuts and burnings inflicted upon or done to him on account of his own illnesses[654] (and especially the hidden ones, like fistulas and hemorrhoids and the like, which are born in the body and grow), and hot, fiery ulcers will be present, and likewise ulcers which grow by corroding; and in

---

[646] *Tet.* III.13.

[647] An impetigo is a staph infection of the skin (often on the face), characterized by inflammation and pus whose discharge dries into a crust.

[648] *Albaras.*

[649] *Tet.* III.13.

[650] Ptolemy says, "west with respect to the Sun and east wth respect to the Moon"–i.e., the opposite of their usual improved positions oriental of the Sun and occidental of the Moon.

[651] Reading *ictericum* (with the Latin Ptolemy) for *hethicam*.

[652] *Tracheae arteriae.* Ptolemy says the native is liable to spit blood, so the medievals probably thought this was due to an internal leak from an artery in the throat.

[653] *Concavitatum.*

[654] This must mean bloodletting and other harsh treatments.

women, illnesses which come to them because of abortions and other incomplete [or improper] births.

You[655] will even consider Mercury: which if he were with one of the aforesaid malefics in one of the aforesaid places, and one of the benefics did not aspect them, it will assist that malefic in increasing its malice in deploying the illnesses and impediments, by increasing its malice in every kind of every illness.

The signs[656] even assist the said malefics in increasing their malice in illnesses. For if the Ascendant or the 7th (or the 6th), or the conjunction of the aforesaid malefics, were in Cancer or Capricorn, or Pisces or Leo, or Scorpio (which are signs of illnesses–but not the sole ones)[657] the aforesaid malefics will be assisted in illnesses which are increased by corrosion, like cancer, fistulas, impetigoes, and like things corroding the native's flesh; and leprosies. Indeed Gemini and Sagittarius help them in making epilepsy, or falling sickness, and the like. And if the aforesaid stars [planets] were in the last parts of the signs, it signifies that the infirmities of the native will be in his extremities, and this will happen on account of the impediments touching upon them, and on account of the uneven mixture of the humors–on the occasion of which there will be leprosy and gout [in the foot] and arthritis [in the hand][658] unless one of the benefics then aspects the malefics, or is joined to them corporally. And the infirmities and impediments which appear because of that will be serious and incurable.

And Ptolemy said[659] the same will happen if the benefics are united with them, and the malefics were elevated above them or [were] more strong.[660] If however the benefics were in their own dignities and stronger than the malefics[661] (which are the occasions for the operations [causing illness]), then the impediments will not be foul and shameful, but will be light; however this

---

[655] *Tet.* III.13.

[656] *Tet.* III.13.

[657] Ptolemy mentions the "terrestrial and piscine" signs, so Bonatti explicitly gives Leo and Scorpio as examples.

[658] *Podagra et chiragra.* Gout is an arthritis in the foot (Gr. *pod-*), so *chiragra* must be an arthritis in the hand (Gr. *cheir-*).

[659] *Tet.* III.13.

[660] This is not exactly what Ptolemy says. Ptolemy says that if the benefics are configured in such a way as to produce disease (i.e., by being in the first or seventh signs, in the proper type of sign, *etc.*), they will produce it if the malefics are "in power in superior position to [or "overcome"] them." Again, in Hellenistic astrology, for one planet to "overcome" or be in "superior position" to another means to be in the tenth sign from it.

[661] Again, Ptolemy speaks now of the benefics being in "superior position" to or "overcoming" the malefics.

will happen if the benefics were oriental [in the world].[662] And he said, for Jupiter conceals impediments and makes infirmities quiet down, namely with external aids (like physicians and even with money), and the more so if Mercury were with him. And he said Venus, however, will beautify the impediments, namely because on such an occasion the native will consecrate himself to God,[663] and thus he will be freed from impediments and infirmities–or at least she will alleviate [them], and sometimes she even makes them conceal themselves by means of the incantations of the just, or exorcisms, and divine pronouncements and experiences, and medicines, just as sometimes in dreams and by apparitions, like if it would seem to be said to him while sleeping, "Go to such a cross or to such a Saint, or to such a place, and you will be freed," and sometimes it happens thus. However, these things, even though they depend on faith, are not to be thrown away for that reason; for faith works much, and is powerful in every matter.

And he said,[664] if indeed Saturn were joined with Venus, this will be noted and manifest or their equivalent.[665] But if Mercury were with her, this will be with the advantage and wealth of the patient, which will come to him because of his illness.

Chapter 7: On the impediments of the soul, and on its infirmities and means

Mention having been made above of the infirmities of the body, and of its impediments, it now remains to look at something to be annexed [to the above] concerning the infirmities of the soul and its impediments.

And infirmities and impediments [of the soul] differ. For infirmities of the soul (as the astrologer takes them) are principally two: magnanimity[666] and pusillanimity;[667] and these two can hardly or never be cured, even if perhaps

---

[662] Ptolemy says that the illnesses may be curable "even if" the benefics are oriental. The reason oriental benefics could be a bad thing for the native, would seem to be that they are better disposed to cause the illness.

[663] Or, "makes a solemn promise" to God (vovet se deo).

[664] Ptolemy says something somewhat different: "though if Kronos [Saturn] is there, it will be with exhibition and public confession and the like; and if the star of Hermes [Mercury] is there with [Aphrodite (Venus)], it will be with aid and with a certain profit gained through the injuries and ailments by those who have them."

[665] Robbins says that according to a commentator, this refers to bringing the sick person to a public temple to be healed.

[666] Greatness of soul, generosity, high-mindedness.

[667] Timidness, faint-heartedness.

sometimes some people are cured of them. For the magnanimous man despises great things, the pusillanimous man esteems small things (as is said elsewhere).[668] Certain other [infirmities] are secondary, like ardor, sorrow, anger, and the like,[669] which are easily cured and removed from the soul, and they go away.

Indeed impediments of the soul usually do not go away, but they remain practically inseparably, like if the soul ought to be wise, following equality and goodness, [but] it is wise in an exceeding way, so that from that excess it is deceived; or it is less wise than it should be, so that it does not know how to beware of doing evil; or it is impetuous beyond what it should be, or less fearful [than it should be]. All of these, and like impediments, belong to the soul; and are such that they hardly or never go away from it.[670]

---

668 This seems to be Christianized version of Aristotle's original doctrine. For Aristotle, magnanimity is a good thing–it is a virtue. Such a man does not have admiration for great things, because he knows he is capable of so much that nothing much impresses him. The vice of excess associated with this virtue is vanity or undue pride, i.e., someone who falsely puffs himself us *as though* he can do great things. The vice of deficiency is indeed pusillanimity (or undue humility), i.e., someone who does not think himself worthy of good things. This gives us a vice-virtue-vice triad of vanity-magnanimity-pusillanimity. But undoubtedly due to the influence of Christian doctrine (which emphasizes humility and respect for a transcendant God), vanity and magnanimity came to be associated together in Bonatti's training. Under such a scheme, magnanimity becomes a kind of vanity or arrogance, pusillanimity remains a vice of deficiency, and the new virtue between them becomes some form of proper humility: magnanimity-proper humility-pusillanimity. Bonatti's statements make it clear that he views this arrangement as either describing a primary set of virtue and vices, or else they are an organizing principle for all of the *other* standard virtues and vices–as though they described a fundamental attitude about the world. He seems to think that these attitudes (whether the virtue or the vices) are so fundamental to a given human being that they can hardly ever really be changed. Rather, we must focus our moral improvement on their "secondary" forms (anger, *etc.*).

669 None of these by itself is an Aristotelian vice. But they are vicious states of the soul for the *Stoics*. Ardor (*alacritas*) and anger are examples of Stoic "desire," sorrow an example of Stoic "pain" or "distress." Nevertheless, it would seem that Bonatti's magnanimity and pusillanimity have to do with evaluation in general, with these others being particular applications– which would explain why the former are harder to cure, and the latter easier.

670 These "impediments" are other standard Aristotelian vices, and clearly they have to do with states of character formed by the "more and the less," so that the native has difficulty finding the correct mean between two extreme responses. The previous infirmities were more absolute, having to do with value judgment in general (and so seem more Stoic). Bonatti's classification, then, seems to be this. (1) *Infirmities* of the soul have to do with fundamental categories of value: either (1a) evaluation in general with respect to one's own self-worth and relation to the world, or (1b) with particular areas of life expressed as particular emotions (of which some are to be totally avoided). The former is hard to cure, the latter easier. But (2) *impediments* of the soul have to do with achieving the proper balance between extremes in certain emotions and attitudes, where there is a range of possible responses but it is difficult to get the emotion or response exactly right. These impediments are hard to cure, either

Whence you ought to look in the nativity of any native, to see what kind of condition belongs to Mercury and the Moon (since this signification concerns them), [and] show how they behave toward one another, and whether they are in the angles or in their succeedents; and whether they are joined with the malefics corporally or by aspect. Because if they were both joined together, or they were joined with the malefics[671] in the Ascendant, and the malefics were northern from them, or were to besiege them, or they were opposite them, this will signify the soul of the native is going to have many impediments. You could say the same if the *al-mubtazz* over the Ascendant were impeded by the said malefics by one of the aforesaid means.

However, the other qualities of the soul which are not thus[672] surpassed [in degree], nor subsist exceedingly low [in the soul], are said to be commendable and worthy of approval. If however the other qualities (which do not come to be by the aforesaid means, but on account of the excessiveness of the nature of the temperament) were to supervene, infirmities of the soul could be stated.[673] However, these things will happen to the irrational soul, and they will not happen to the rational one.

And certain illnesses sometimes happen which do not belong to the rational soul, even if perhaps they seem able to take up impressions in the appropriate part of the native,[674] as we see in certain epileptics, in whose nativities the Moon and Mercury are not united together, nor with the Lord of the Ascendant nor with its *al-mubtazz* (and [the *al-mubtazz*] was Saturn in diurnal nativities and Mars in nocturnal ones). And Ptolemy said, however, that he (namely Saturn in diurnal ones or Mars in nocturnal ones) will rule this quality.[675]

---

because of ingrained bad habits or the inherent difficulty of knowing exactly what the right response is. Examples of these states would be (1a) magnanimity or vanity, (1b) anger, (2) fearfulness. The proper states of the soul for each of these would be (1a) proper humility, (1b) lack of anger, (2) courage. Most of Bonatti's discussion below seems to pertain to (2) impediments.

[671] Reading *infortunis* for *fortunis*.

[672] *Modum.*

[673] Again, here Bonatti seems to distinguish infirmities from impediments, and suggests that natal delination is focused on *impediments* (which admit of degrees of excess and deficiency).

[674] *In parte apta nati*, reading *nati* for *nata*. Meaning somewhat uncertain. The idea seems to be that some illness belong to the irrational part, though they appear to belong to the rational— i.e., epilepsy belongs to the irrational soul, though seizures affect the speech and consciousness (which are classified as "rational").

[675] *Tet.* III.15. Ptolemy says a bit more: "Epileptics, for the most part, are all those who, when the Moon and the star of Hermes [Mercury] (as we said) are unconnected to each other and to the rising horizon, have the star of Kronos [Saturn] by day and the star of Ares [Mars] by night pivotal [angular] and scrutinizing the above figure." I take this last phrase to mean that Saturn (by day) or Mars (by night) are aspecting either the rising sign or the Moon or

And the illnesses which will then come over the soul will be called insanity and the like, [if] the nativity were nocturnal, and Saturn predominates over the quality (Mars in the day),[676] and the more so if the Moon and Mercury are not united together nor with the Lord of the Ascendant, and one of the aforesaid malefics is in an angle, and this were in Cancer or Virgo[677] or Pisces. However, Saturn will make people possessed by an evil spirit more, and Mars more raging. And [for Saturn], these things will happen because of the superfluous moisture abounding in their brains. And their occasioning will be the appearance of a malefic in the angles with the aforesaid quality–and the more so if Saturn were in his own being [esse][678] (or Mars in his own), elevated[679] above the Moon; with her next to [her] exit from under the rays of the Sun; and the Lord of the domicile in which she is, joined to Saturn (were the nativity conjunctional) or Mars (and the nativity is preventional); with [Saturn or Mars] staying in Sagittarius or Pisces. Indeed if Saturn and Mars predominate in nativities, and they were both the *al-mubtazz* over it, the aforesaid infirmities (epilepsy, insanity, mania and the like) will be incurable, but not very intense, nor will they be calmed very much.

Which if it were Jupiter and Venus instead of the aforesaid malefics, and they were in the Ascendant, the malefics in the 7th, the aforesaid illnesses will be curable, even if they often seem to be intensified. Which if only Jupiter is joined with the Moon, it signifies the illnesses are going to be cured, both by diet and by medicine, but [they will be] less severe. But if only Venus is united with the Moon, it signifies that it seems he can be cured by Psalms or exorcism or incantations, or the prayers of some saint, or intercessions, or divine prayers, and the like. Indeed if the aforesaid malefics were in the Ascendant, and Jupiter

---

Mercury. I take this to mean that epilepsy can be caused when both of the following conditions are fulfilled: (a) the Moon and Mercury are *neither* aspecting each other *nor* the ascending sign by whole-sign aspects, and (b) Saturn (in diurnal charts) or Mars (in nocturnal charts) is aspecting either the rising sign, the Moon, or Mercury (and the more so if it were more than one of them).

676 I have altered this sentence slightly. It appears prior to this sentence, out of place, and makes the conditions seem confusing. Bonatti writes: "Which if the nativity were nocturnal, then Saturn will predominate over that quality (Mars in the day)."

677 Reading *Virgine* with the Latin Ptolemy, for *Sagittario*.

678 I do not know where Bonatti is getting this word, and his elaborate paraphrase seems to be getting more jumbled. By *esse* here, Bonatti might mean that Saturn is in his own sect (either that it is a diurnal chart, or perhaps that he is above the horizon by day or below it by night). The reader should simply consult the much simpler instructions in *Tet.* III.15.

679 This must refer to the Hellenistic "overcoming," since it derives from Ptolemy. See Introduction and footnote to Tr. 3, Part 2, Ch. 20.

and Venus were in the 7th, with the aforesaid quality existing,[680] it signifies the aforesaid illnesses are incurable and intense, and very strong and obvious, and they are going to be loud and fearful, and that such infirm people will be unstable, nor will they be held back unless they are chained or incarcerated; and that they will say foul and shameful things both to their own people and to strangers, and will employ foul deeds, too. Indeed in the demonic infirmity, it will be said that its occasioning is a certain moisture which takes away sense, and after the taking away of sense it makes him rage (nor does it release him [from] the use of bodily sense): and thus while sometimes the spirits[681] are tortured, and even if sometimes they are not vexed, they will foretell future things; and sometimes such beings make an insult to men, and strike them, and do like things.

And there are other qualities of other stars assisting the aforesaid qualities. For if the Sun were with Mars in the aforesaid places, or in the angles (and particularly in the Ascendant or in the 7th), they will increase insanity. Indeed if Jupiter were to have a partnership with Mercury, epilepsy will be increased. Indeed Venus increases those things which are said above, by the aforesaid infirm people. Indeed if Saturn were to stay with the Moon in the aforesaid places, they will increase demonic passions and an abundance of harmful moisture; likewise they will add [or increase] harmful impediments of the rational soul, and its infirmities. And these aforesaid infirmities are those which tend to be cured by the care of the aforesaid qualities. Indeed, those which differ from the aforesaid (namely those which receive disposition in a non-rational soul, with increase or decrease) are considered in things happening naturally, and they will appear in each sex, for the avoiding and knowing of which it is necessary that we assume such a method by which we can arrive at a knowledge of them—namely, we should look at the Sun[682] to see if he is not united with the Moon, nor with the Lord of the Ascendant, nor is he in the Ascendant; and Saturn were in an angle in diurnal nativities (and Mars in nocturnal ones); and either of them were the *al-mubtazz* over the Ascendant, or over the domicile in which the Lord of the Ascendant is; and Mars or Venus were to aspect the Sun or Moon; and the Lord of the domicile in which the Moon is, were joined to Saturn (if the nativity were conjunctional) or Mars (if the nativity were preventional), and principally in one of the domiciles of

---

[680] This probably refers to nativities where Jupiter and Venus rule the quality.

[681] Reading *furia* (sing.) as *furiae* (pl.), to match the verbs.

[682] I believe this should read "Mercury," since this passage is drawn from Ptolemy, *Tet.* III.15 (who wants Mercury and the Moon to be in aspect).

Jupiter; and the aforesaid malefics were conquering[683] in the figure of that nativity; and the Moon and Sun are in masculine signs[684]–it signifies that the illnesses of the non-rational soul will be those exceeding natural measure in the acts of Venus, and he will employ them beyond the permission by Nature. Indeed, in a female native,[685] those things which are naturally permitted to her (the womanly nature having been transformed into a male one), she will be accustomed to them in a male way; but she will unduly get involved with those things which nature were to prohibit her.[686]

Moreover, if Mars (or Venus) [or both] appeared in a masculine sign, and in masculine quarters, in the nativity of someone, nor were one of the luminaries joined with them,[687] nor with the Lord of the Ascendant, nor with the Lord of the sign in which he (or she) was, it signifies that the male or female native will be exceedingly incited concerning venereal acts; and [the native] will put his intention in them, and will spend his time in them, and will commit the said foul acts against the permission of the law, gladly and indecently (if he were a man). If indeed it were a woman, she will be inclined to unnatural[688] venereal acts, and she will engage in them more than she ought to, [and] she will be commingled gladly and disgracefully with women. And Ptolemy said[689] if Venus alone were masculine, that which will be perpetrated thence will be hidden and will not be known. But if Mars [also] appeared masculine, it will be so open that sometimes women will have sex with them as though they were demonstrating them to be their own wives. If however they both were masculine, it will be something between both, namely neither totally open, nor totally hidden.[690]

Moreover, Ptolemy said[691] that if the same stars were in the contrary of the aforesaid (namely that only the luminaries appeared with the aforesaid qualities, in feminine signs), women will do those things which are natural to them, but

---

683 Ptolemy says, "When the malefics alone, then, assume the governance over the figure *in the stated manner.*" This could refer back to *Tet.* III.14, where Ptolemy speaks of the planets "which assume the governance over" Mercury and the Moon: this probably means their rulers by domicile, especially if there are aspects to Mercury and the Moon from them (also noted in III.15).

684 Cf. Tr. 5, the 131st Consideration, from here to the end of the chapter.

685 Reading *in nata* for *innata.*

686 *In nata vero, ea quae sibi naturaliter permissa fuerint, muliebri natura in virilem transmutat, eis modo virili assuescet, eis autem quae sibi natura prohibuerit, se indebitae admiscebit.*

687 For Ptolemy, these conditions pertain to the luminaries being in masculine signs.

688 Reading *innaturalibus* for *innaturalis.*

689 *Tet.* III.15.

690 This sentence does not appear in Ptolemy.

691 *Tet.* III.15.

men will commit what is contrary to their nature, and with softness and femininity of the soul, they will transgress natural things. If however only Venus were feminine, a woman will fill up exceedingly on unlawful venereal acts, and with anybody, so that she will deny no sexual intercourse, whether the intercourse is disgusting or against the law. However, men will be effeminate and soft, and very prone to venereal acts, nor will they prohibit someone from illicit sexual intercourse, nor from its foulnesses, except for this, that they will perpetrate it in secret. Moreover, if Mars appeared feminine, and not Venus (namely, of these two),[692] they will engage in fornication and foulnesses, and illicit, uncovered acts–and without blushing in the face, so that they will be reproached for excessive exposure.

The qualities of Venus and Mars [being both] oriental in the figure (namely from the Sun), assist detection in masculinity; and their evening and occidental quality (from the Sun) aids hiddenness in femininity. Likewise if even Saturn were with them, it assists them (namely the male and female native) to incur horrid things, rottenness, and great shameful thing, because its nature assists each one of these concerning [bad] morals.[693] But if Jupiter were with them, it will increase the beauty and decorum of matters, and a fit sense of shame. And if Mercury were with them, it will help the detection of matters and the hastening of what is going to be, and the multitude and increase of their kinds.

---

[692] Ptolemy makes both Venus and Mars feminized in this case.
[693] *De more.*

ON THE SEVENTH HOUSE

Chapter 1: On the native's marriages, and his partners, and his enemies openly opposing him

Mention having been made in the preceding chapter about the slaves and smaller animals and infirmities of the native, now we must immediately see about the marriage and partners of the native, and likewise his enemies openly opposing him.

Therefore you will consider in these [matters] the 7th and its Lord, and which of the planets is found in it (namely one or more), also the Moon and Venus, and likewise the Part of Marriage,[694] and the planet in whose domicile you were to find it. And you will look at the planet which is the *al-mubtazz* over these places, or over the angles of the figure of the nativity which you seek (and their succeedents),[695] and you will see if they are free from the impediments which have been frequently stated, and are made fortunate and strong.

Which if they (and especially the Lord of the 7th or the *al-mubtazz* over it[696]) were joined to the Lord of the Ascendant of the nativity or its *al-mubtazz*[697]–all or some of them, by a trine or sextile aspect, and the more so if reception intervenes, and [the Lord of the 7th] is lighter than the Lord of the Ascendant,[698] it signifies that the native will be married to a good and fitting woman, and with whom he will rejoice to his wishes. If however the aforesaid aspect were without reception, or the aspect were a square with reception, it signifies that the native will marry, but his marriage will be much below the aforesaid. If however it were a square without reception, it will be much more less than that again. But if the Lord of the Ascendant were joined to the Lord of the 7th, so

---

[694] Note Bonatti does not say whose version of this Part he prefers: see Tr. 8, Part 2, Ch. 10. In this case Bonatti is drawing on 'Umar, who calls it the *pars coniugii*.

[695] This is something new–perhaps the instructions offer this alternative on the theory that the angles (and the succeedents) tend to show areas of success and happiness in life, so that indications of a successful life will support the likelihood of marriage (marriage being considered a form of success).

[696] *Ipso.*

[697] *Eius.* Although Bonatti's Latin is ambiguous as to whether he means the *al-mubtazz*es over the Lords of these houses or the *al-mubtazz*es over the houses themselves, Bonatti's source seems to be 'Umar (p. 65), who clearly speaks of the *al-mubtazz* of the 1st and 7th, *not* that of their Lords. Therefore I have followed 'Umar.

[698] Bonatti is mixing up his general indications with his ideal case involving the Lord of the 7th, but the meaning is clear.

that he is lighter than him, it signifies the native is going to be desirous of copulating with women.

Indeed if the seventh sign were Cancer or Scorpio or Pisces, or the conjunction of the Lord of the 7th or its *al-mubtazz* with the Lord of the 1st or its *al-mubtazz* were in them or out of them, or one of them, it signifies the native is going to have many wives or a great abundance[699] of other women. Indeed if you were to find the contrary of that which was said, you could judge the contrary.

Which if Venus were then in an angle or in its succeedent, namely made fortunate and strong, and likewise the Lords of the triplicity of the sign which she then possesses, and she and they were oriental, it signifies the native is going to contract marriage in his youth, and he is going to be fortunate with women, and be loved by them. You would say the same if you were to find the Moon in the first quarter of her month, or in the third (namely in her separation from the Sun up to the half of her [increase of] light, or from the prevention up to the middle of its decrease), the which two portions (just as is testified by Ptolemy) are called "oriental"–however his marriage will be delayed somewhat more, and he will contract it with a young girl, and his fortune will be with women, however less than the aforesaid is.[700]

If however Venus were impeded (namely cadent or combust, or retrograde, or joined to the malefics), and the Lords of the triplicity of the sign in which she is were impeded, or she and they were occidental, or they were between the Ascendant and the 4th, or between the 7th and the 10th, or in the second quarter of the lunar month, or in the last one (the which two quarters Ptolemy calls "western"),[701] it signifies that his marriage will be postponed, and he will marry after youth, in his mature age, and to a little old woman; and he will be unfortunate because of women.

But if Venus were free (namely, made fortunate and strong), and were in an angle or in its succeedent, and the Lords of the triplicity of the sign which she were to occupy then, were impeded–it signifies that the native will be married with a good and suitable and decent woman; however, evil and detriment will

---

699 *Copiam.* An alternate reading would be: "or the great treasures [or resources] of other women." Bonatti probably means *copia* simply in terms of quantity, but the alternative reading is interesting.

700 That is, the Moon as an indicator is less good as, and more delayed than, the ideal condition of Venus at the beginning of the paragraph.

701 This quote comes from *Tet.* IV.5. Bonatti seems to be applying criteria originally pertaining to the Moon, to Venus.

follow because of the marriage. Which if only Venus were impeded, and the Lords of the triplicity of the sign in which she is, were free from impediments, it signifies the native is going to contract marriage with an unsuitable and disagreeable woman, but he will be made fortunate because of the marriage; and usefulness[702] and a suitable good will follow from it.

And Abu 'Ali said[703] if Venus were free from the malefics and impediments in nativities of women or men, and in fit places, it signifies a good and fit betrothal. If however she were impeded and in a bad place, it signifies the destruction and malignity of the betrothal.

Indeed 'Umar said[704] if Venus were exalted above Saturn from the 10th,[705] the marriage will be in middle age, in a time suitable for it, and the marriage will be in the middle (and likewise the children). If however Venus in someone's nativity were in a movable sign (and especially in Cancer or Capricorn), it signifies the firm stability of the native on one wife.[706] Indeed if the Moon and Venus were opposite each other, or in a square aspect, it signifies evil and impediment in the marriage. And if they were in Gemini or Virgo or Sagittarius or in Pisces, it signifies the native is going to contract marriage with more than one woman.

Chapter 2: On the native's manner of the venereal act

You[707] will even look to see whether Venus is in Aries or Scorpio, and Mars is in Taurus or Libra, because this signifies an excess of venereal cultivation is going to abound in the native, and impediment in his person,[708] and the destruction of his matters because of that.[709] Which if [1] Venus were in Capricorn or Aquarius, and Saturn were in Taurus or Libra; or [2] she were in Gemini or Virgo, and Mercury were in Taurus or Libra; or [3] Venus and Mercury were in Capricorn or Aquarius, and they were joined together, and one was seeking the conjunction of the other, it signifies the filthiness of the native's

---

[702] Reading *utilitas* for *utilitatem*. It could also read as "benefit."

[703] *JN*, p. 46.

[704] *TBN*, p. 66. Hand mistranslates this as "elevated." But at any rate, this probably refers to the Hellenistic meaning, i.e., that Venus is in the tenth sign from Saturn.

[705] In Hellenistic terms, this would have to mean that she is in the tenth sign from Saturn.

[706] This is a misquote of *JN*, p. 46. Movable signs show multiple marriages or relationships. This should read "fixed."

[707] *JN*, p. 47.

[708] I.e., his body.

[709] Abu 'Ali simply says that this configuration shows an abundance of wives.

sexual intercourse, and his being engaged in sodomitical vice; and he will delight more in the filthy sexual intercourse of men than in that of women.[710]

Indeed if Venus were in her own domicile or exaltation, a woman will be elevated above the native, and will predominate over him (and the more so if the Lord of the 7th were northern from the Lord of the Ascendant). If however she were in her own triplicity or bound, [the woman] will predominate over him, but much less. But if she were in her own face, they will predominate more again, and often less.

And 'Umar said,[711] indeed if Venus, and the Sun, and the Part of Marriage (or multiple significators of the native), and the Lord of the house of marriage were in Aries or Leo or Libra or Capricorn (which are those signifying stinking [or foul] intercourse), it signifies the native is going to be overflowing in sexual intercourse with a shameful and filthy overflowing.

Which if Venus[712] were corporally joined to Mars, or in his opposition or square aspect, and Mars were in Aries or Scorpio or Capricorn, it signifies that the native will be shamefully abusing, and with a shameful sexual intercourse— and the more so if Venus were in a masculine sign, because then he will be disfigured by that shameful vice of the sodomites. (If however she were in a feminine sign, he will be deceived by women.[713]) Indeed if it were a woman, and [Venus] were in a feminine sign, she will be insatiable and by means of an unsated sexual intercourse, and she will become a prostitute. If however she were in a masculine sign [in the nativity of a women], [the native] will abuse women and will be inclined to rub them, and she will even delight in being bent down over men.[714]

---

[710] Note that Bonatti has listed three types of planetary conditions, and then listed three sexual conditions. Abu 'Ali simply groups them all together and says it shows the native "will delight more in masculine intercourse than in feminine." But my sense is that Bonatti means to match the configurations with his sexual conditions in order, since Saturn is the typical significator of filthiness and shame, and Mercury tends to signify boys and sodomy: in that case, (a) Venus and Saturn in each other's domiciles signify filthiness; (b) Venus and Mercury in each other's domiciles signify sodomy; (c) Venus and Mercury together in Saturn's domiciles, signify filthiness *and* sodomy.

[711] *TBN*, p. 67.

[712] *TBN*. Hand appropriates Bonatti's own text for this passage on pp. 67-68. All of the following seems to pertain to Venus's being joined to Mars by conjunction, square, or opposition.

[713] Merely being deceived by women hardly seems to be an equal counterpart to being "disfigured" by sodomy.

[714] I do not know exactly what Bonatti means by being "bent down over men." This phrase does not appear in 'Umar.

And[715] 'Umar said,[716] if Mercury were the *al-mubtazz* over Venus and the Moon and the house of wives (of a portion of them or over more of them),[717] the enjoyment of the native will be in boys, and he will delight in deceiving them.

Chapter 3: Of what sort the native's wife is going to be

If however the Moon were combust and Saturn were to aspect her from the opposition or square aspect, nor did Jupiter aspect her, nor did Saturn receive her, it signifies the native is not going to take a wife.

If however the Moon were joined with the benefics from a trine or sextile aspect, and with her of good condition and well disposed, and with reception, it signifies the native is going to take a good[718] and useful and suitable, and fit wife. If however she were joined with the malefics, you will prognosticate the contrary.

For if she were joined to Saturn by a trine or sextile aspect, it signifies the native's wife is going to be difficult,[719] feral,[720] and inflexible. If however from the square or opposition, it signifies she is low-class and stinking [or foul] and tasteless.

Indeed if she were joined to Mars, it signifies she will be unlearned, unruly, understanding badly, unstable, and a devastatrix. Which if Mars were of good condition, it subtracts from the malice. And if he were of bad condition, it will add in malice and will make her a fornicatrix.

---

[715] This paragraph appears at the beginning of the next chapter, but I have moved it up above the chapter title (probably misplaced by the editors) since it continues 'Umar's descriptions of sexual proclivities. The next chapter begins with the type of wife.

[716] *TBN*, p. 68.

[717] But presumably over at least two of them, otherwise the definition would be overly broad. Note also that this cannot be a compound *al-mubtazz* over all, or else we would be calculating compound *al-mubtazz*es for every combination of places, which would still leave several candidates (and this sort of procedure is not attested to elsewhere in the literature). My sense is that he means we should see if Mercury is the Lord of the domicile, exaltation, and/or bound of the majority of them, especially if aspects are involved (that is, something akin to an equal-point *al-mubtazz*)..

[718] Reading *bonam* for *bonum*.

[719] *Laboriosam*, lit. "full of labor, toilsome, troublesome," *etc.*

[720] I.e., untamed or uncivilized.

Indeed if she were joined with Jupiter, with him not impeded, it signifies she is good, suitable, and proper; and shrewd and wise for the purpose of disposing familial matters.

Which if she were joined with Venus, it signifies she is full of jests, happy, and very beautiful. If however Venus (or Mercury) were impeded, what is signified will be below that which I said.

But if she were joined with Mercury, it signifies she is going to be fond of learning, and well attentive,[721] and intelligent.

And Ptolemy said[722] if Venus appeared with Jupiter or Saturn or Mercury, it will profit him enough in these things which pertain to life (namely a wife to a husband); she will even love him and the children much.

And 'Umar said[723] if Venus were in the domiciles of Saturn and Saturn were to aspect her, the native will be frigid in sexual intercourse; likewise if Saturn were to conquer[724] and were the al-mubtazz over the house of marriage. While [if] the Lord of the 7th does not aspect the 7th, and the Lord of the Moon the Moon, also the Lord of the Part of Marriage the Part of Marriage, and the Lord of Venus Venus, then the native will not taste the taste of women, and he will not marry. And he said, likewise if the al-mubtazz were the victor over the Ascendant and the Moon and the Sun, and the Part of Fortune, also the conjunction and prevention which was before the nativity, according to the condition which I said,[725] and more of the planets were feminine,[726] the native will be effeminate and soft. And if it were to conquer[727] in the aforesaid places in the nativities of females, the planets [being] masculine, a girl who was born then will be masculine practically like a male.[728]

---

[721] *Sollicitam.* This adjective also has connotations of being concerned, excited, and alarmed. Another synonym might be "solicitous."
[722] This seems to be a paraphrase of several types of statements in *Tet.* IV.5.
[723] *TBN*, p. 68.
[724] I am not sure what 'Umar means by this–perhaps that he "overcomes," i.e., that he is in the tenth from Venus.
[725] *TBN*, p. 69. It is unclear to me what conditions 'Umar means, although he seems (as above) to be referring to an equal-point *al-mubtazz.* Might he be referring to the *hīlāj?*
[726] Reading *femininae* (with 'Umar) for *fortunae.*
[727] Ptolemy does not use this word in *Tet.* III.15 (whence 'Umar has taken his version), but see above footnote on "conquering."
[728] *TBN*, p. 69.

On the aforesaid, through the Part of Marriage

You will even look at the Part of Betrothal,[729] and the Lord of the domicile in which it is, or its *al-mubtazz*–which if you were to find them in angles or in their succeedents, namely made fortunate and strong, joined with the benefics, this signifies that the native will be married with good and beautiful and suitable women. If however the Part were cadent, and the aforesaid planet sound, or the planet were impeded and the Part were sound, it signifies the middling character of the aforesaid. Which if the Part and the planet were cadent and impeded, nor did the benefics aspect them, it signifies that the native is going to consummate marriage with low-class and unclean women. If however the planet which were to aspect the Part of Betrothal or the Lord of the sign in which it remains, were a benefic, and it were in the angles, direct, it signifies that the native will contract marriage with many women, and with good women [who are] free of vices. Indeed if it were a malefic, and it were impeded (namely cadent, retrograde, or combust), it signifies that native is going to contract marriage with women of no usefulness, no goodness, no profit, and full of vices.

Which if Venus were to aspect Saturn then (and the more so, if the aspect were from the square or from the opposition), [and] either of them were cadent from the Ascendant, nor did Jupiter aspect one of them, it signifies the native is going to delight little in women; and if he were to marry, he will not particularly delight in sexual intercourse or pleasure, and practically not at all.

You will even see if Venus were in Taurus or Cancer or Libra or in Pisces: because this will signify that the native is going to contract marriage with women related to him.[730] If however Venus were in Sagittarius or Pisces, or Jupiter in Taurus or Libra, it signifies the native's betrothal [to be] verging more on the side of majority than minority,[731] and of goodness more than malice; and he will be praised by men with suitable praise. But if she were in Capricorn or Aquarius, it signifies the native is going to copulate in marriage with an aged woman. Which if she were in Gemini or in Virgo, it signifies he is going to contract marriage with an ignoble and low-class woman, or a waiting-woman or perhaps a female slave.

If however the planetary significator of the woman were free, in its own domicile or exaltation, it signifies he is going to contract a marriage with a noble

---

[729] *Partem desponsationis.* This must mean one of the Parts of Marriage, but Bonatti does not specify which he uses.
[730] *Propinquis.* Or perhaps, "nearby him."
[731] I.e., in age.

woman. If however it were in its other dignities, it signifies he is going to contract marriage with other women corresponding [in dignity]. If however it were received, it signifies he is going to copulate with a low-class one, but not much.[732] Indeed if it were peregrine, not received, it signifies he is going to contract marriage with a female slave. If however it were in Cancer, it signifies that the native will contract marriage with an unsuitable and malign woman, nor one permitting him to rejoice or have any rest.

And moreover, when Venus is in Taurus or Libra or Pisces, in an angle or in its succeedent, free from impediments (namely combustion and retrogradation and the conjunction and aspects of the malefics), say that the native is going to contract a good and fitting marriage, and that good will follow from thence; and the more so if Jupiter were to aspect her then, nor is he impeded in any bad way; and again more, if reception were to intervene. But if Venus were oriental, it signifies some kind of rulership of the wife over the husband, but by means of gladness and games and dancing. Indeed if she were occidental, or were in Virgo, it signifies the scarcity of the native's delight with his wives, and even with other women, unless perhaps Jupiter were then to aspect Venus. Which if you were to see her impeded (namely retrograde or combust, or cadent), say that the native's marriage will be delayed, and it will be with burdens and something contrary for him. If however the Ascendant were Aries or Scorpio, and Venus were combust, whether in front or from the back (but more from the back),[733] it signifies the native is going to contract marriage with a sick woman (but a hidden illness).

Chapter 4: On the time of the wife, when she will be taken, and on the number of wives, and on its durability in general

And the contracting of the marriage will be when the year of that nativity arrives to its 7th. Or, were its 7th the Ascendant of a revolution of the nativity, it signifies betrothal in that year. Or it will be when it is signified by the direction of the Moon to the planetary significator of the betrothal.

And Abu 'Ali said[734] if the [seventh] sign were movable, it signifies betrothal to many women. You would say the same if the Moon were joined to many

---

[732] I believe this means he will not copulate much (rather than that the low-class person will not be very low-class).

[733] By "in front" Bonatti means in a later zodiacal degree than the Sun; by "from the back" he means "in an earlier zodiacal degree."

[734] JN, p. 48.

planets in the same sign, or should she have *al-'ittisal*[735] with them, by a trine or sextile aspect. If however the sign were common, he will be betrothed to exactly [or only] two women. Indeed if it were a fixed one, or the Moon were void in course, or she were joined with, or had *al-'ittisal* with, only one planet, it will judge the native is going to contract marriage with only one woman.

You[736] will also look at the 7th and the 4th (if it were the nativity of a man), to see if one of the malefics stood in one of them. Because this signifies the death of the native's wives. If however it were the nativity of a woman, [it indicates the same] for her husband. Which if [Venus][737] were occidental, and were peregrine, joined to malefics, or in their square aspect or in their opposition, it signifies their hastened death.

You[738] will even see (in the nativities of males) if all the significators (or the majority of them) were feminine–because this will signify that the native will be low-class, effeminate, soft, stupid, idle, weak,[739] so that he will not seem to have any bones, and if [it is] wholly [so], he will be [a man of] passion.[740] And 'Umar said that the life of such people as these tend to be cut short on account of the multitude of moisture holding sway in their complexion. However, in the nativities of women, if the majority of their significators were masculine, the native will be vigorous,[741] practically like a man; for, apart from her sex, she could be called a man more likely than a woman, and the life of such people tends to be cut short on account of the multitude of dryness predominating in them.

On the marriages of women

Indeed Ptolemy said[742] that in the marriages of women we should consider the solar qualities in their nativities, saying: for it is necessary for us to see whether the Sun is found in one of the two eastern quarters (which are, as was

---

[735] Lat. *Ictisal.*
[736] *JN*, p. 47.
[737] *JN*, p. 47.
[738] *TBN*, p. 69.
[739] *Humidus*, lit. "moist." But the connotation is just like soup or beverages that are weak because they are "watery." Therefore it probably means weakness of character and will, not weak in physical strength.
[740] *Ac si totus esset caro.* This phrase is an elaboration of Bonatti's, and it is not altogether clear what he is trying to convey. It could also be translated as, "and if he is wholly flesh," or "and if [so], he will be a wholly stupid person," for example. In traditional thought, being a man of the flesh, being soft, and being stupid were connected ideas.
[741] *Virago*, i.e. a woman with masculine physical and/or moral qualities.
[742] *Tet.* IV.5.

said above, from the 10th up to the Ascendant, and from the 4th up to the 7th): because this will signify a female native is going to be betrothed by marriage to [an adult] man in her youth, or to a young man in her old age; and she will not take an old man for a husband. But if the Sun were between the Ascendant and the 4th, or between the 7th and the 10th, her marriage will be delayed, or she will marry an old man while she is a young girl.

Which[743] if the Sun were from the beginning of Aries up to the middle of Taurus, or from the middle of Leo up to the end of Virgo, or from the middle of Scorpio up to the middle of Aquarius, and the significator of the native were oriental, the aforesaid will come to be in her youth, or with a young man. If however the Sun were from the middle of Taurus up to the middle of Leo, or from the beginning of Libra up to the middle of Scorpio, or from the middle of Aquarius up to the end of Pisces, and the significator were occidental, they will come to be in her old age, or she will be conjoined with an old man.

And 'Ali said[744] that if the significator[745] were under the rays, it is signified that she will have none.[746] But if the Sun were in a fixed sign, it will signify she is going to copulate with only one man. (Which if some oriental planet were in that sign, you will announce he is going to be a young man, and it could be that she will acquire another after him. If however it were occidental, he will already have left his youth behind). Indeed if [the Sun] were in a common sign, you will pronounce she is going to have two husbands. (Which if some oriental planets are found in that sign, for each one of them you will adjoin another husband to them. But if they are not of good condition, they will signify fewer husbands.) Indeed if the Sun were in a movable sign, you will judge the female native is going to have many husbands.

Of what sort the bride's husband is going to be[747]

You[748] will even see if Saturn were to have partnership with the Sun then, from a trine or sextile aspect: because that will signify the female native's

---

[743] Source unknown. Note that this covers a huge amount of the zodiac.
[744] Again, I believe this is based on 'Ali ibn Ridwān's commentary on Ptolemy, not al-Rijāl.
[745] This probably refers to the *al-mubtazz* over the various places and significators of marriage—which again I take to be one by equal points, not a compound *al-mubtazz*.
[746] Reading *nullum* (masculine) for *nulla* (feminine).
[747] This section contains three different topics: the character of the husband by the luminary signifying him (the Sun), his character by means of Venus, and the future of the marriage by means of both luminaries. I have separated the paragraphs and organized the margins so these sections are evident and more readable.

husband is going to be wise, honest,[749] just in his deeds and concerned about others', and full of labor.

If however the Sun were united with Jupiter, this will signify the husband is going to be humble, gentle, magnanimous[750] and of good judgment.

But if the Sun is united with Mars, it signifies the husband of the girl is going to be unruly, cruel, cannot be pleased, disobedient, and of bad judgment.

Indeed if the Sun is united with Venus, it signifies her husband is going to be honest, decent and fine, and handsome.

But if the Sun were united with Mercury, it will demonstrate he is going to be full of labor and proficient [or profitable] in matters pertaining to the life of a man.

Which if Venus[751] were joined to Saturn, it signifies the husband of the female native is fatigued and holding himself back from venereal ways.[752]

Indeed if she is joined to Jupiter, it signifies her husband will be good, pure,[753] honest, and modest.[754]

If however she were joined to Mars, it signifies the husband of the female native will be of a hot complexion, a fornicator, freely engaging in, and soliciting, venereal experience.[755]

---

[748] *Tet.* IV.5. Ptolemy does not specify the sort of aspect, but since the indications here are good, Bonatti evidently feels free to say these terms apply to sextiles and trines.

[749] *Probum.* Or "proven," i.e., being experienced in life.

[750] Remember that being "magnanimous" was classified by Bonatti earlier as a serious vice in the chapter on infirmities of the soul. Here he is simply copying directly from his Latin edition of *Tet.*, which says *magnanimus*.

[751] *Tet.* IV.5, possibly combining indications from several paragraphs.

[752] *Cultu. Cultus* has the broad meaning of "cultivation, honor, taking care of, experience," or arrangements made for a way of life.

[753] *Castum. Castus* signifies being spotless and pure: chaste, upright, guiltless, *etc.*

[754] Or: "having a sense of shame."

[755] *Cultum.* See footnote above.

But if she were joined to Mercury, it signifies he will be inclined to loving his wife, but he will not be a firm lover, nor continuing well in his loving; however he will love his children and he will have affection toward them.

If[756] however the Sun and the Moon were to aspect each other from a trine or sextile aspect in the nativities of either (namely those of men and women), it signifies that the marriage (which the male or female native has contracted) will not be dissolved, unless this should happen for a great reason.

Indeed if the Sun and the Moon did not aspect each other, or they aspected each other from a square aspect or from the opposition, or the malefics were to aspect one of them, it signifies that there will be litigation or separation in their marriages.

For if the malefics were to aspect the Moon in the nativity of a man, there will be dissent on the side of the man. If however they were to aspect the Sun in the nativity of a woman, there will be dissent on the side of the woman.[757] And if the marriage were to remain in place, it will endure [but] with litigation and duress and contention and hatred.

But if the benefics were to aspect the Sun or the Moon, it signifies the marriage of the man (if the Moon) or the woman (if the Sun) will endure in jesting and happiness, delight and health. If however the malefics and the benefics were to testify at the same time to the Sun or Moon, it signifies the marriage is going to be dissolved, even if not simply–and after the dissolving it will be re-instituted [or repeated] and will endure in peace and in delight.

Which if the malefics were to aspect the Sun from a square aspect or from the opposition (unless they were to receive him, which takes away from their malice), it will signify that the divorce will be with a lawsuit [or accusations] and like harshness and great ferocity, and likewise complaint.

---

756 *Tet.* IV.5.
757 The idea here is that the luminary signifying the spouse will be afflicted, making that spouse the cause of trouble; therefore the native will be the one initiating the separation in reponse.

Whence if Mercury were to aspect the malefics then, then the divorce will be made public and will fall into the rumors of the people. Indeed if Venus testified to those malefics, it signifies that the divorce will happen with the suspicion of adultery or like things.

Chapter 5: How the marriage may be known by what is signified by Venus, Mars, and Saturn

In this matter,[758] look to see if Venus or Mars or Saturn are conjoined corporally or from good aspects, by means of a suitable admixture. Because this will signify that the male or female native will be joined by means of a good and useful and legitimate marriage.

Wherefore[759] if Venus is joined to Mars by a good aspect, and the Moon were to aspect Mars or Venus from the said aspect, it will signify [the male native] is going to contract marriage with a woman [who is] a young girl [or teenager].

Which if Venus is joined to Saturn, he will be betrothed to a wife [who is] a little old lady. And if the Sun were joined with them or with one of them, it signifies the female native is going to do the same with a husband [who is] a young man. Which if Mercury were joined to them, the aforesaid will happen openly and will likewise be made known. And Ptolemy said[760] that if for example [Venus and Saturn] were in signs common to each, like Capricorn and Libra,[761] it will signify that he will be conjoined to his own sister or his own relatives, or he will perpetrate a defilement with her.

Which if the Moon were joined with Venus, Mars, and Saturn in male nativities, it will signify that the native will commit something impure with two sisters or with two women related to him or being attached to a relationship by close intimacy.[762] If however, in the nativity of some woman, the Moon is found in signs common to Venus and Mars,[763] it signifies the native will conclude

---

[758] *Tet.* IV.5.

[759] *JN*, p. 47.

[760] *Tet.* IV.5.

[761] I.e., signs ruled by both of them, as Capricorn is ruled by Saturn and Libra by Venus; in addition (as Schmidt points out), Capricorn belongs to the watery triplicity (ruled in part by Venus), and Libra to the airy triplicity (ruled in part by Saturn).

[762] *Vel ex propinquitate parentelae attinentibus. Propinquitas* could also mean "kinship," but Bonatti's Ptolemy has already covered this in the previous clause.

[763] The passage in Ptolemy seems to pertain to situations where (a) Venus is in a (whole-sign) aspect to Mars, (b) they are in signs which they both rule (Ptolemy's example is Capricorn

something impure with two brothers or with two [men] of a tight blood-relationship.[764]

And[765] if Venus is joined to Saturn in the aforesaid signs, it signifies a suitable marriage and one that will last for a long time. And if, in addition, Mercury applies to Venus and Saturn, the marriage will be with profit, and likewise a good and proper usefulness. Which if, in addition [to the aforesaid], even Mars were joined with them, it signifies that the marriage of the male or female native will not be useful for the married [couple], nor durable, but more likely coming to an end quickly, and [being] harmful. If however the disposition of Venus were just like the disposition of Mars and Saturn,[766] and she were in the domicile or exaltation or bound or triplicity of one of them, or in a sign common to herself and him, it signifies that the woman will be married to a man of the same age as her. Which if they all appeared oriental, and Venus were more oriental from the Sun, it signifies the female native is going to cleave to a

---

and Pisces, which they rule variously by exaltation and triplicity), and (b) Venus is also in a (whole-sign) aspect to Jupiter. I note that the Moon does not play a role in this particular arrangement in the nativities of women.

[764] This paragraph is confusing because it seems to confuse two different types of indications in Ptolemy. On the one hand (a) if Venus and Saturn are in signs common to each (see above), "they make the sexual minglings be with relatives." This was the topic of the previous paragraph. But here, (b) with Mars and Venus in signs common to each (like Capricorn and Pisces), it again "causes sexual minging with brothers or relatives. In the case of (b), if it is a male nativity and Venus is in aspect to the Moon, it is with two sisters or relatives; but if it is a female nativity and Venus is in aspect to Jupiter, it is with two brothers or relatives.

[765] *Tet.* IV.5.

[766] This passage expresses a complicated thought, and I am grateful to Robert Schmidt for clarifying it. The issue here is how close and soon Venus is to the beams of the Sun, relative to Mars and/or Saturn. Suppose the Sun is in 0° Aries, and both Venus and Mars are in Pisces. (1) if Venus has not yet reached her second station by retrogradation, and is closer to the Sun than Mars, then she is more in a rising (i.e., pertaining-to-arising) condition than he is: the native will marry someone younger. (2) But if she has retrograded past Mars, even if she has not reached her station, then she's less in a rising condition than he is: the native will marry someone older. (3) But if she is very close to them, the native will marry someone of roughly the same age. (4) But even after she has turned direct, she will be less in a rising position than Mars, all the way up to the conjunction with the Sun, because her swift motion will soon make her pertaining-to-setting (again, signifying an older spouse). (5) But if Mars were in a later degree than the Sun (i.e., occidental), and she were going toward him in direct motion, she is in more of a rising (i.e., pertaining-to-arising) condition (signifying a younger spouse). (6) And if she passes Mars she'll still be in more of a rising position (i.e., pertaining-to-arising), since at that time Mars is being approached by the Sun and will soon be pertaining-to-setting. (7) But when she is retrograding toward the Sun, after passing Mars she will be in more of a setting position (i.e., pertaining-to-setting), because she will enter the beams first on account of her swift motion.

man younger than her.[767] If however it were the nativity of a man, it signifies he is going to take a wife younger than him. But if they were occidental and she were more so than the others, it signifies the female native is going to contract marriage with a man of greater age than her, and a man is going to be betrothed to a wife more aged than him.

And Ptolemy said[768] if Venus and Saturn are staying in signs common to them, like Capricorn and Libra, the marriage will be between blood-relatives. If however the Moon belonged to this aforesaid quality, and this quality were to stay in the Ascendant or the Midheaven,[769] the native will do wrong and make war against Venus[770] with his mother or stepmother or maternal aunt, [or] a woman with her own offspring, or father, or brother-in-law, or with her own son-in-law, or paternal uncle, or mother's husband. And he said if the Sun belonged to this aforesaid quality, and the planets were occidental, a male native will defile the beds of his own daughter, or of the brother or sister of a female native, or of the son of her own spouse.[771]

But if the aforesaid quality [were] in signs naturally masculine (which are Aries, Gemini, Leo, Libra, Sagittarius, and Aquarius) or in signs naturally feminine (which are Taurus, Cancer, Virgo, Scorpio, Capricorn, and Pisces), or in places accidentally masculine (which are the eastern quarters) or accidentally feminine (which are the western quarters), or in houses accidentally masculine (which are the 1st, 3rd, 5th, 7th, 9th, 11th) or accidentally feminine (as are the 2nd, 4th, 6th, 8th, 10th, and 12th), or in their own dignities, so that Venus is in masculine signs, Mars and Saturn in feminine signs, or the reverse,[772] it signifies that the male or female native will be subject to venereal experience more so than is

---

[767] Reading *natum* and *eum* as *natam* and *eam*, since the next sentence specified male nativities (and is in accord with Ptolemy).

[768] *Tet.* IV.5.

[769] Now we get the detail mentioned above, that the Moon must be in the Ascendant or the Midheaven. Here "quality" means "configuration."

[770] *Veneri militabit.*

[771] *Natus filiae vel wui fratris seu sororis natae aut proprii filii coniugis cubilia incestabit.* These relationships seem to have gotten jumbled. Ptolemy says: "daughters or the daughters of their sisters or with the wives of their sons, while it makes the women have intercourse with their fathers or the brothers of their fathers or their step-fathers." It is not necessary to have the correct list to understand the point being made.

[772] Reading *econtra* for *contra*. Ptolemy emphasizes that he is only speaking about situations where the planets are in signs (or quarters) opposite their own natural gender. Bonatti's desire to spell out all the signs and places makes him obscure this fact.

proper; neither the man in being active nor the woman in being passive, he will show himself to be burdened in all the ways by which he indulges.[773]

But if the aforesaid quality were near the fixed star Aldebaran, or near the end of the sign of Leo, or near the beginning of Cancer, it signifies that the male or female native will engage in venereal experiences in a foul and shameful and reprehensible way. If however it were in the Ascendant or in the 10th, his venereal acts will be made known immodestly among the people. And if it were in the 7th or the 4th, he will engage in his aforesaid acts as secretly as he can, or perhaps he will be found to be without the male genitals, or sterile. Indeed if Mars were found with them then in the aforesaid places, it will signify the penis of the man will be cut off, with the testicles—but it will judge the unsuitable female parts of the native, or [that] she will be castrated.[774]

Again,[775] if you find Venus being separated from Mars or Mars from Saturn, in the nativity of a man, and Jupiter testifies to them, it will signify the man is going to be in moderate sexual intercourse, nor will he engage in venereal acts except by natural means, and wanting [it] in the appropriate way, and appropriately.

But if Mars were then joined to Saturn alone, it will judge the native to be not eager, not willing, not violent, and lazy, in venereal acts.

If however Mars is united with Venus and Jupiter, it will demonstrate the native is easy for venereal activities, and willing to do it, even if he will repent of it [or deny it][776] from thence; and he will strive from thence to restrain as much as possible from his will and badness [but] cannot do it well, and he will pretend to abstain from impurities and foul things. And if Mars were joined with Jupiter and Venus at the same time, or with only one of them, nor did Saturn aspect them, it will seem that the native is going to be eager for and delight in adultery or debauchery; and that he will gladly use indulgent foods and drinks.

---

[773] *Modis omnibus quibus luxuriatur se gravari ostendet.* This does not quite seem right. Ptolemy says the native will willingly do these things.

[774] There seems to be some confusion in Bonatti's source text. Ptolemy says *tribadas*, which is the Greek equivalent to Bonatti's usual *fricatrices* (from *frico*), referring to women who masturbate or "rub themselves" with other women. Certainly Ptolemy's text states that a male native may be castrated.

[775] The following indications are rather closely based on Ptolemy *Tet.* IV.5.

[776] *Redarguat*, but "repent" seems more appropriate than "refute, contradict," unless perhaps Bonatti means he will deny everything.

But if Venus or Mars or Jupiter were occidental, and the other were oriental, it signifies the native is going to have a foul form of sexual intercourse, both with men and with women.

If however only Mars and Venus were occidental, and Jupiter were oriental, he will abhor the foulness of sexual intercourse with men, and he will engage in venereal acts with women.

Indeed if the aforesaid significators (namely Mars and Venus) are joined together in signs which are called feminine (or even in feminine quarters), it signifies he is going to submit himself to foul and wicked sexual intercourse.

Which if each (namely Mars and Venus) were oriental, the native will be inclined to do it with men more than with women.

Moreover, if the aforesaid planets appeared oriental and in masculine signs, and Mars were stronger than Venus, and she were more remote from the Sun, the native will postpone women in every way for men, and he will concern himself with engaging foully in venereal acts, sodomitically, with men.

But if they were occidental, and Venus were more remote from the Sun, the native will be inclined more to women, but he will gladly submit himself to low-class and ugly ones, even waiting-women and female slaves, more so than noble or beautiful ones.

If however Mars were more occidental than Venus, it signifies the native is going to cleave to noble women, or to married ones, or to his own mistress,[777] by means of a carnal connection.

Indeed if it were the nativity of a woman, look to see if Venus is joined at once to Jupiter and Mercury, because this will signify the female native is humble and modest in her own way of having sexual intercourse, and that she performs all of her venereal experience with cleanness.

---

[777] *Dominae*, i.e., a woman who is master over him—not a mere mistress with whom he commits adultery.

Which if Venus were joined to Mercury, or with the participation of Saturn, it signifies the native is going to cleave gladly to venereal experience, but with the remorse of conscience and with the restraint of her will, and the omission of every indecent foulness of sexual intercourse.[778]

But if Venus is joined only to Mars, or unites herself to him in some way, he will willingly engage in venereal acts, and will delight indecently in them.

If however Jupiter were to aspect them, and Mars were covered by the rays of the Sun, that female native will be much aroused in venereal acts, and she will engage gladly and freely in them, nor will she avoid low-class men or other servants or slaves, nor even strangers [or foreigners].

Indeed if Venus were found under the rays, with Mars, the female native will lay down with her own lord or with other nobles.

But if the aforesaid Venus and Mars appeared in feminine signs or quarters, and they appeared occidental, she will delight in sexual intercourse with men.

Indeed if Saturn is joined with Venus and Mars at the same time, it signifies that the female native will be horrid and wild. Which if Saturn were oriental, it signifies she is going to desire adultery, and is going to love men whom she finds in solitude.

And Ptolemy said,[779] however, Jupiter always mitigates these impediments. However, Mercury assists these delights, and likewise their foulnesses.

Chapter 6: What would happen to the native because of his partners and from his partners and those participating with him

Indeed, to know the condition of the native with partners and his participators, and what would happen to him because of them, look at the Ascendant

---

[778] *Omnisque indecentis coitus turpitudinis omissione.* Perhaps the "omission" means she does not disclose it to later sexual partners or to prospective husbands.
[779] *Tet.* IV.5.

and its Lord for the native (also the Moon), [and] the 7th and its Lord for his partners and participators. Indeed you will know what kind of being they are going to have in partnership and in participating, from the 10th and its Lord; but you will know the end [of it] from the 4th and its Lord.

For if the Lord of the Ascendant (who is the significator of the native)[780] and the Moon were in fixed signs, and the Lord of the Ascendant is a benefic, and the Moon is free, not impeded, it signifies that the native has partners with whom he will take part with a good and lasting participation, but he will not gain much wealth with them, nor they with him; however their wealth will be of some kind, namely below a middling amount. If however it were a malefic, and the Moon impeded, it will judge the contrary.[781]

Indeed if they were in common signs, it will signify that the native is going to have good and faithful partners, and he will gain wealth with them, and they with him, unless something else impedes; and everywhere it will go well for each of them, and [the partnership] will often be renewed (and more often their merchant dealings), and often with usefulness and wealth.

But if they were in movable signs, it signifies that this participation will not be uniform, but sometimes there will be litigation between him and the partners, and likewise suspicion and confusion; after this there will be reconciliation and durability between them.

Which if there were a malefic in the Ascendant impeding them, it signifies that pain and fraud, and a cause of separation and regret is going to come from the side of the native. Indeed if it were in the 7th, you could judge the same thing is going to come from the side of the partners and those participating.

Indeed if you were to see that there ought to be separation between them, and you wished to know what kind it is going to be, and what will be the means of it, look at the Moon. Which if she were joined to the Lord of the domicile in which she is, or to the planetary *al-mubtazz* in that sign, and he were of good

---

[780] This is an indication that Bonatti considers the Lord of the Ascendant the "significator of the *native*" (as opposed to the Lords of other houses signifying other people), but it is not clear whether it is also the "significator of the *nativity*" as a whole.

[781] I believe this means that little or no wealth will be created.

condition and well disposed, it signifies his separating from the partners or participants with delight and a full spirit, and with usefulness and wealth. Which if the Lord of her domicile (or its *al-mubtazz*) did not aspect her, or if he were to aspect and he were made unfortunate and badly disposed, it signifies the separation of the native from the partners or participants by means of their bad will, and by the suspicion (which one will have about the other) that he is deceiving him and will defraud him of his goods—and more strongly so, if the impeding malefics were below the earth: for then the evil estimation which one will have against the other, will be the reason for their separation; nor will they remain good friends, but they will turn their backs to each other.

And Sahl said[782] if the benefics were in the Midheaven, their wealth will be multiplied; indeed if malefics were in the same place [instead], it will be decreased. And he said if the Moon were joined to the Lord of her domicile and a malefic were joined to them in one sign or were to aspect them,[783] they will not be separated except by death.

Chapter 7: What would happen to the native from enemies openly turning against him, or because of them, and whether he is going to have them or not

However,[784] in the qualities [in] which must be perceived whether the native is going to have enemies openly turning against him, and what would happen to him because of them or from them, it is necessary for us to consider the indications which induce us to know it, namely the Ascendant and its Lord, also the 7th and its Lord; even the places[785] of the luminaries, and the place of the Part of Fortune and its Lord, even the Part of Enemies[786] and its Lord, Saturn and its Lord.

---

[782] *On Quest.*, 7th House, "A question on the partnership of two, and what its end will be." Bonatti evidently feels free to put testimonies from horary questions into material on nativities—which is understandable, since all branches of traditional astrology are fundamentally the same.

[783] This probably reflects the Hellenistic use of whole sign houses for conjunctions and aspects.

[784] In what follows Bonatti is broadly inspired by Ptolemy, but Ptolemy's methods are different and he uses a more restricted set of significators.

[785] *Loca.*

[786] See Tr. 8, Part 2, Ch. 15 for two versions of this. But it is probably the second one, that according to Hermes, since his version uses the degree of the 7th.

For if the said places[787] and the aforesaid significators (or a majority of them) were badly disposed, that is, that there are malefics in them, or with them, or they were to aspect them from the opposition or the square aspect (but the square aspect is less malicious than the opposition), or the Lord of the Ascendant and the Lord of the 7th were to aspect each other from the said aspects; or the Lord of the Ascendant were in the 7th, and the Lord of the 7th were in the 1st, and more strongly so if the Lord of the 7th were a malefic, or there were a malefic in the 7th or in the place of the Part of Enemies; or one of the aforesaid significators were a malefic or impeded by malefics, and it were to aspect the Lord of the Ascendant–it signifies the native[788] is going to have many enemies openly turning against him, and he will suffer from them and because of their contrarieties and harm and detriment. But if there were a benefic or a well disposed planet in the aforesaid places (or in some one of them), namely made fortunate and strong, and he were to aspect the Lord of the Ascendant, nor were he the Lord of the 7th, nor did the Lord of the 7th aspect the Lord of the Ascendant, it signifies the native is going to have few enemies openly turning against him.

Which if the Lord of the 7th or the *al-mubtazz* over the 7th were to aspect the Lord of the 1st, or the *al-mubtazz* over the 1st were to impede him, it signifies that harm and impediment and destructions will happen to the native from the enemies, and it seems that on that occasion he could be ruined–and the more so if the Lord of the 8th house [domicile?] were to aspect him then; and more again if the Lord of the 1st were to have some dignity in the 8th besides the [dignity of] face (which does not impede much), and the Lord of the 8th were to impede him, because then it signifies the death of the native by the hands of the enemies. And more certainly again if Mars were the Lord of the 8th house [domicile?], because then he could hardly ever escape it but that it will come to him, and this will happen more in war than elsewhere.

Indeed if the significator of the native, and the significator of his enemies, or the Lord of the Part of Enemies were distanced from each other beyond the seventeenth degree, nor were they staying in places aspecting each other from the noted aspects, or they were opposite each other at the same time, it will signify that the native is going to have public enemies, between whom there will be enmity lasting for a long time, and perhaps that it will not be ended at that

---

787 *Loca.* Here they seem to mean "signs."
788 Reading *natum* for *nato.*

time.[789] But if it were from the square aspect, it will judge a lesser enmity between them, and lasting less; and the root and beginning of the enmity will be envy, and due to the fact that one is going to make more money than the other.

You will even look to see if some noted aspect of one of the luminaries were with the aforesaid; because if there were no noted aspect (a trine or sextile) between them, or some harmony or partnership, it signifies that inextinguishable enmity will fall between them, and which will never be ended.

Likewise, you will see if the *hīlāj* of the native is being separated from the *hīlāj* of the enemies,[790] because this will signify that the native's enmities will be temporary, nor very lasting. Which if Saturn were the *hīlāj* of the native, and Mars were the *hīlāj* of the enemies, or *vice versa*, the enmities which there would be between them will happen practically for no reason, on account of the contrariety of their natures. But if Mars were the *hīlāj* of one, and Mercury the *hīlāj* of the other, it signifies that enmities will fall between them for reasons of knowledge and the like.

In the same way, you will consider, in the nativities of a native, concerning enmity.[791] Wherefore if the significator of the native were a malefic, and he impeded the significator of enmities, it signifies the native is going to have many enemies, but he will overcome and conquer them all, and evil and detriment will follow from that; his enemies will be endangered by his hands and they will be slain outright and they will perish.

Moreover,[792] you ought to look to see where the Part of Enemies falls; because the native will hate that sign, and what is signified by that image.

And[793] if Saturn (or Mars) were in the house of enemies, he will destroy them.[794] Or if he were to impede the house of enemies, the native will not cease

---

[789] I.e., at the end of the "long time."

[790] This passage may be based on ibn Ridwān's commentary on Ptolemy. Ptolemy mentions the typical places that are used in calculating the *hīlāj*, so ibn Ridwān (or the source of this passage) must believe that we are to compare the *hīlājes* of the native and his enemy–this is a synastry technique which Ptolemy uses for various planets in *Tet.* IV.7. But this interest in a *hīlāj* must also derive from the fact that Ptolemy wants us to use primary directions of multiple planets in one nativity to the positions of planets in the other–and the *hīlāj* in Ptolemy was supposed to be used in primary directions. But I note that Bonatti (or his source) does not mention all of the planetary combinations Ptolemy mentions (which are exclusively for primary directions), and instead picks only a couple of examples to be used in this synastry technique.

[791] This sentence suggests that the previous paragraph may have been lifted from another text in a different context.

[792] *TBN*, p. 86. Presumably this means that if the Part falls in Pisces, the native will hate fish and what is associated with Pisces; if Sagittarius, horses; and so on.

to rejoice over his enemies, and he will send them to their deaths before him, and he will see their ruin. Indeed if the significator of enemies were in an angle or one succeeding an angle, and it were to have some dignity there, it signifies the nobility and strength of the native's enemies over him. Which if it were peregrine or cadent from the angles, and were combust, or were in its own descension or fall, it will signify their lastingness and bad condition, and that they will fall into poverty and want, and [it signifies] the prosperity of the native, and his good state against them–and the more so if one of the malefics were in the house of enemies, or their significator were impeded by the malefics; because then the native will prosper over against them, to their detriment and adversity. Indeed if a benefic were found in the house of enemies, and their significator were joined with it, it will signify the prosperity and strength of the enemies, and of their overcoming over against the native. But if their significator were in the Ascendant or in the opposition of one of the luminaries, it will signify the native is going to have many enemies and even those who condemn him. Which if it were a malefic, it signifies that they will be inimical for great and famous things. If however it were not a malefic, it will be both for great and small and middling things, and sometimes their enmities will come as though for nothing at all.

---

[793] This paragraph is largely based on a combination of *TBN* (p. 86) and *JN* (p. 59). But I note that both 'Umar and Abu 'Ali follow Ptolemy in making the twelfth sign the domicile of enemies–not the seventh.
[794] Reading *eos* for *eam*.

ON THE EIGHTH HOUSE

Chapter 1: On the native's death, and on the accidents by which death tends to come

Mention having been made in what has preceded about the life of the native and his substance, about siblings, about the father, children, slaves and about his marriage, it seems fitting to me to treat in this chapter of his death and the occasions of its means.

And even though death is the last accident [in life] which can happen to the native, it is more suitable that it be put in the 8th (which is said by the wise to be of the house of death). Therefore you will consider those things which occur to be considered: and they are obviously the Ascendant at the hour of the nativity of any native, and its Lord, and likewise his *hīlāj* and the projection of the rays of the planets to [the *hīlāj*], and its arrival to the 7th of his nativity. Because if it is signified that death ought to arrive on account of the projection of the rays of the planets to that *hīlāj*, or by means of its conjunction with one of the killing planets, it is necessary for us now to consider the places[795] in which the *hīlāj* is conjoined with the killing planet: for the reason for death will be what is signified by that house in which that killer were to fall then, and the more so if such a conjunction or aspect were when the *hīlāj* reaches to the 7th of the nativity.[796]

You[797] will even look at the Part of Death,[798] and the planet in whose domicile you were to find it, and the eighth sign from the Ascendant of the nativity, and its Lord, and the planets which you were to find in the eighth, or which aspect [the sign] (whether they were benefics or malefics). Likewise you will look at the Lords of the triplicity of the 4th domicile[799] from the Ascendant of the nativity, and the eighth sign from the Sun (if the nativity were diurnal) or from the Moon (if the nativity were nocturnal), and the planets in whose

---

[795] *Loca.* See above.
[796] See especially the footnote below on these two places (the direction of the *hīlāj* to the location or aspects of a killing planet, and to the degree of the 7th).
[797] *JN*, p. 60.
[798] Taken by day and night from the Moon to the degree of the 8th, and project from Saturn.
[799] Abu 'Ali (*JN*, p. 60) says "the angle of the earth," which could mean the degree of the 4th (even if it is not in the fourth sign). But I have split the difference between Bonatti and Abu 'Ali, and read *domus* as "domicile" since Abu 'Ali focuses on whole sign houses.

domiciles you were to find them.[800] For if all of the aforesaid significators, or the majority of them, were of good condition, and well disposed, free from impediments (namely retrogradation and combustion and the conjunction of the malefics, and their aspects), or there were benefics in the 8th [domicile], the native will finish his life and will pass away in his own bed. But if the aforesaid places[801] and aforesaid significators, or a majority of them, were impeded, or one of the malefics were in the 8th [domicile], he will die a bad and horrible and strange death.

Which[802] if Saturn alone were stronger in the aforesaid places, and he were the *al-mubtazz* over the place signifying the native's death, [it signifies death] is going to come by cold and dry humors. If however he were impeded, it will signify the native's death from active or unnatural coldness and moisture[803] (like snow, ice, drowning) or from a chronic infirmity or catarrh or excessive weakness [or destruction] of the body, or on account of a long quartan fever (not a true one),[804] or a pain of the spleen, or dropsy,[805] and the like. And if it were a woman, it is going to come because of an illness of the womb or its orifice, and illnesses of this kind which tend to come on the occasion of great coldness. Nevertheless he (nor even one of the planets) could not be the sole significator of death, without the Lord of the bound (into which he fell) being a participator with him.

But if Jupiter were the *al-mubtazz* over the domicile signifying the native's death, and he is of good condition and well disposed, it signifies that death will seize the native on the occasion of a liver complaint, or inflammation of the lungs[806] or *stomatica*.[807] If however he were of bad

---

[800] Reading *ipsa* for *ipsos*. I.e., the planets ruling the domicile of the luminary whose authority it is.

[801] *Loca*. See above.

[802] The following planetary descriptions are based on *Tet.* IV.9 and *JN* pp. 60-61.

[803] *Ex actuali frigitate vel innaturali atque humidtate*, reading *innaturali* for *in naturali*.

[804] A quartan fever is one which recurs every four days (especially one due to malaria) on account of the periodic release and invasion of new parasites into the blood. Bonatti may be saying that the fever cycle will be longer than four days but close enough to four to mimic a quartan fever.

[805] *Hydropisim*. Dropsy is an accumulation of fluid in bodily cavities, hence its connection to the deaths by moisture indicated by Saturn.

[806] *Peripleumonia*.

condition and badly disposed, the named death will happen to him, man-dated by the king or another great authority, and even by the judgment of the people; or perhaps by a tertian fever[808]–especially the noted one,[809] or tonsillitis[810] or other suffering of the throat, or heart ailment[811] or bile[812] or the ilium,[813] or even from any other illness which can come on the occasion of much obstructed windiness; or from *synocha*[814] or another of those infirmities which tend to come on the occasion of an excessive overflowing of blood.

But if Mars were the sole significator of the native's death, and he were of good condition and well disposed, it will signify his death is going to come on the occasion of a tertian (or even quotidian[815]) fever, or maniacal behavior[816] or a suffering of *emoptoica*,[817] or some sudden or accidental death. If however he were of bad condition, and badly disposed, it will signify the native's death is going to be by the sword or some bellicose instrument.

Indeed if the Sun were the sole *al-mubtazz* over the domicile, and he were of good condition, and well disposed, it will signify the native's death is going to be on the occasion of a fever or overflowing of heat, or from any

---

[807] Perhaps pertaining to the mouth (Gr. *stoma*, "mouth")? I cannot quite connect this to Ptolemy, unless this is a serious misread for sore throats (*squinantia*), which Ptolemy does mention; or diseases that can be noticed through bad breath (also mentioned by Ptolemy).
[808] A tertian fever (a kind of malarial infection) is one which occurs every other day, and is very difficult to cure.
[809] *Nota.* I am not sure what is meant by this.
[810] *Squinantia.* Or simply, "sore throat," although Bonatti would seem to mean something more specific like tonsillitis, since it is contrasted with other suffering of the throat in the following clause.
[811] *Cardiaca.*
[812] *Cholica.*
[813] *Iliaca.* The ileum is the portion of small intestine which meets with the large intestine, just above the pelvis–but there is no reason to believe that Bonatti's anatomy was precise. The inclusion of bile and the ilium right next to one another suggests liver and digestive problems, perhaps understood in terms of the humors.
[814] A kind of continuous fever; according to my medical dictionary source, it was used ambiguously with *synochus*, when in fact distinct fevers were actually the cause.
[815] A quotidian fever is either a malarial fever with fevers every day, or else it involves infections by distinct parasites whose outbreak cycles overlap, again leading to fevers every day.
[816] *Phrenesis.*
[817] Unknown word, but it bears resemblance to the Gr. *hemitritaikōn*, which pertains to intermittent fevers of one-and-a-half days (mentioned by Ptolemy).

infirmity from an overflowing of blood coming over [him]. If however he were of bad condition and badly disposed, it signifies his death by reason of his own parents, or the king, or an authority, or some prince, or a heart attack,[818] or the end of his life is going to be imposed by a heat of the stomach. And Abu 'Ali said,[819] or he will die in horrible places.

Indeed if Venus were the sole *al-mubtazz* over the domicile signifying the native's death, and she were of good condition and well disposed, it will signify the native's death is going to be from a pain of the belly or from intoxication or drunkenness. But if she were impeded, it signifies the death of the native is going to approach from a poison given to him through women, or from an excess of venereal experience consuming him; or an illness of the stomach or liver, or a heart complaint,[820] or by excessive bloodletting by means of the above, or perhaps of fistulas or some blister, especially those which are born of bloody material, or from taking a poisonous potion; nor from these illnesses alone, but it is even going to come from any other things arriving by means of some badness and overflowing of the humors.

But if Mercury appeared [as] the sole significator of death, and he were of good condition and well disposed, then you could judge the native's life is going to end by means of a true frenzy[821] or by some diverse pains because of an overflowing mixture of diverse humors coming over him.[822] Which if he were impeded, you could announce the native is going to die from indeterminate pains and practically imperceptible ones. If however he were united [with another planet], he will commit what is his to his partner, and the life of the native will be ended according to the nature of [that other planet], or perhaps by means of a manic passion or a loss of his senses, or swooning[823] or wasting,[824] or (as Ptolemy says), a supera-

---

[818] *Cardiaca passione*, lit. "by a heart-suffering."
[819] Abu 'Ali actually says, "amidst an assembly or crowd of people, or among a crowd of bathers"–i.e., in a public place (p. 60).
[820] *Cardiaca.*
[821] *Frenesim*, or "mania," from Lat. *frenesis* or *phrenesis*, a transliteration of the Greek *phrenetis*. See the alternative spelling *phrenesis* in reference to Mars above. I use "frenzy" here to distinguish it from Mars's *phrenesis*.
[822] Uncertain of translation: *ex diversorum humoribus simul commixtorum superabundantia supervenientium.*
[823] *Sincopi*, from Lat. *syncope*, a transliteration of the Greek *suncopé.*
[824] Reading *phthisi* for *ptisi.*

bundance of phlegm[825] or jaundice[826] or even from any other illness which comes over him from an excess of dryness.

Indeed if the Moon were the sole significatrix of the native's death, and she were of good condition and well disposed, superabundant venereal experience or gluttoning on foods, or an inordinate way of taking foods, will lead death to the native. But if she were impeded by one of the malefics, it will indicate the death of the native is going to be according to what is signified by the impeding [planet]. If however the impediment were to arrive not from a planet but by other means, death will be judged to come over the native from sailing or from a hunt or from excessive fatigue, or from repeated change from place to place.

And Abu 'Ali said,[827] for if the aforesaid authors of death were in their own domiciles or exaltations, free from the malefics, his death will be among his parents and close kin. Indeed if they were impeded by the malefics [and] peregrine, his death will be on a journey. Which if they were cadent, it will signify the death of the native is going to be due to a fall from a high place. If however they were in their own descension, this will signify that his death will be in wells or pits or caverns or in deep waters. Indeed if the said ones were the significators of the nativity, death will come to him by reason of killing, because he will be killed or perhaps stoned.[828]

However,[829] other significators of death, whose significations will not devolve into actuality by the aforesaid means (but [those people] will pass away by natural means), are [those] over whom planets signifying a bad death are not elevated.[830] Because the death which supervenes against nature, and happens

---

[825] *Sputum.* That is, matter coughed up from the lungs, not phlegm in its broader humoral sense.

[826] *Hetica.*

[827] *JN*, p. 61.

[828] *Si quidem fuerint dicti significatores nativitatis, accidet ei mors occasione necationis, etc.* This sentence does not quite make sense, does not match Bonatti's usual style, and anyway does not match Abu 'Ali's next sentence, which says "And if they were retrograde, his death will be from suffocation or being crushed in a mob." My sense is that Bonatti's Latin should include the word *retrogradi*, to read: "Indeed if the said significators of the nativity were *retrograde*, death will happen to him," *etc.*

[829] Based on *Tet.* IV.9.

[830] In other words, if someone's planetary significator of death does not have a planet signifying a violent death (i.e., Mars or Saturn) in the tenth sign from its own place, then the native will die a natural death. Ptolemy (who is the source of this passage) adds that the planetary significator should also be in its "own or a familiar natural character." According to

apart from the aforesaid means, is when Mars and Saturn are both in the place signifying death, or they rule over that place, or they were to aspect it from the opposition or from the square aspect, or they ruled over[831] the place of the Sun or Moon,[832] or they were to aspect [those places] from the said aspects. If however any of the other planets were to aspect the aforesaid malefics, they will help [promote] the native's death according to [that planet's] nature, and according to the nature of the signs from which they aspect them. Moreover, if Saturn were staying in a fixed sign, nor were [the sign] in his own sect (nor of the sect of the Sun),[833] and he were in the square aspect or in [the Sun's] opposition, the native will be trampled by a rumor of the people,[834] or he will be strangled, or he will even be killed outright by the hand of one of the populace. The same thing will happen, if, while he appears setting,[835] the Moon approaches him,[836] and he appears as the Lord of the place signifying death.

Indeed[837] if he were to stay in Leo or Scorpio, it signifies the native is going to die of the bites of wild beasts. If however he were to appear in Aries, or Taurus, or the last half of Sagittarius, or Capricorn, it will signify he is going to die by reason of domesticated animals.[838] Indeed if you were to find him in Cancer or Pisces, you could announce he is going to die by reason of fish or animals spending time in water. But if he were in Scorpio, it will be signified [that] he ought to die by means of poisonous animals, whether terrestrial or aquatic.

Schmidt, this ambiguous phrase could mean "being in its own domicile," "being in the sign of a sect-mate," or perhaps something else; either way, being in a place of its own character is meant to enhance it.

[831] Again, in Ptolemy this refers to being in the tenth sign from the luminaries.

[832] Ptolemy says they may overcome either or both of the luminaries.

[833] This statement seems redundant, since both Saturn and the Sun belong to the diurnal sect; this extra phrase does not appear in Ptolemy. Perhaps Bonatti says this to emphasize that we are speaking of the diurnal sect, which is led by the Sun. At any rate, Ptolemy only says "when the star of Kronos [Saturn], *out of sect…*".

[834] *Vulgi rumore.* Bonatti must mean that public rumors will stir up a mob, since Ptolemy speaks of being crushed by a mob.

[835] Reading *occidentalis* for *orientalis*. Ptolemy says "if [he] should set," i.e., *occidentalis* or "setting."

[836] Schmidt says this means that the Moon is in the sign following his, so that she sets right after him.

[837] This paragraph is an expansion of Ptolemy, who simply says that if Saturn is in a sign having the form of an animal, the native will die due to wild beasts.

[838] Ptolemy speaks of the native dying in battles with wild beasts in public places–which must refer to public games. Since these games were no longer held in Bonatti's time, he must have felt free to adapt these animals to medieval customs.

Which if Jupiter is joined to Saturn then, and he were impeded, he will strengthen the badness of Saturn; he will even signify that the native will be killed likewise by the said wild beasts, [but] on a festival or religious day. Indeed if the Sun or Moon were to stay in the Ascendant, and Saturn were in its opposition,[839] it will signify the native is going to die by reason of prison. Indeed if Mercury is joined to Saturn in the figure of the nativity (and more strongly so if their conjunction were in Leo or Scorpio, or with the Tail of the Dragon),[840] it will signify the native is going to end his life by reason of poisonous or rapacious animals. If however Venus were to add her own powers on top of that, it will signify that the native will be subjugated to death by a poisonous potion given to him by women. Which if Saturn were in Gemini or Virgo or Libra, or in the first half of Sagittarius, or in Aquarius, or even in Pisces (as Ptolemy says),[841] and the Moon were united to him in the figure, the native will end his life by drowning. Which if the Moon were in Leo with the Tail, it will signify the native is going to die from a poison given to him with purgative medicines.[842]

And Abu 'Ali said[843] if the Lord of the triplicity of the angle of the earth, or the degree of the Ascendant, and its Lord, or the Sun (in diurnal nativities) and the Moon (in nocturnal nativities) were impeded, he will complete his life with a strange [or foreign] death. But if the significators of death were above the earth, or they were in airy signs, or Mars were in the 4th or the 10th, and he were the Lord of the aforesaid quality, this signifies the death of the native is going to come openly and publicly, or it will come to pass in a yoke[844] or in some piece of wood similar to yokes. And if he[845] were below the earth, and in an earthy sign, it signifies the death ought to be hidden, or perhaps it will be under some ruin. Indeed if he were in fiery signs, it signifies he is going to be burnt up, or is going to die by reason of some other form of fire.

But [Abu 'Ali said][846] if one of the benefics were in the 8th, or with its Lord, or in the 4th, or with its Lord, it will signify the death of the native is going to come smoothly. But if one of the malefics were in the aforesaid places or with

---

[839] I.e., in the Descendant.
[840] Ptolemy reads, "the serpents of the sphere," which Schmidt understands to mean the constellations *Serpens* or *Hydra.*
[841] Ptolemy only mentions Virgo, Pisces, and the (other) watery signs.
[842] Ptolemy does not mention this.
[843] *JN*, Chap. 37. Abu 'Ali does add more details for the types of death and types of signs.
[844] *Furcis*, a fork-shaped yoke (perhaps this means by being in display via public humiliation).
[845] Abu 'Ali says "they," but Bonatti seems to be speaking about Mars alone. Probably we should look to see where the majority are, or where the most significant planet is.
[846] *Ibid.*

their Lords, they will indicate the native is going to die a bad death. Which if the malefic were Mars, death will come to pass through iron or fire. If however it were Saturn, it will be from poison or a ruin or falling or the stormy inundation of the sea, or some other submersion.

But if Saturn were from the fourth degree of Sagittarius up to the fifteenth degree of Capricorn, or from the twentieth degree of Cancer up to the fifteenth degree of Leo,[847] or he were in Aries or Taurus, corporally joined to the Sun, or Mars were opposed to him, or that same Saturn were opposite the Sun, it signifies the native is going to die from a fall from some ruin. But if Saturn were in the 10th, also Mars in the 4th or joined to him corporally, and Mars were the Lord of the aforesaid quality [of death],[848] namely that he is the Lord of the domicile or the bound of the degree signifying death, it signifies the native is going to end his life from falling down.[849]

Which[850] if Mars were in the 4th from the Ascendant of the nativity, and he were the Lord of the quality of the native's death, or one of the luminaries were opposed to him, and he were outside his own sect, and he were in Gemini or Virgo or Libra, or the first half of Sagittarius, or in Aquarius, it will signify the native is going to enter a yoke on the occasion of a quarrel or altercation or a contingent death, to be born among his blood-relatives, or on the occasion of some other war, [and] he will not avoid having his head cut off. And Ptolemy said, either he would kill himself by his own hand because of a woman, or he will be killed at the hands of women. And he said, this will happen if Venus

---

[847] This seems to be inspired by a passage in *Tet.* IV.9 which speaks of Mars being out of sect and in the bestial signs; but I am not quite sure why Bonatti picks these precise portions of the zodiac.

[848] This seems to be Bonatti's interpretation of Ptolemy. Ptolemy says, "When the malefics are present together and in this fasion are diametrical [opposed] to one of the said places responsible [for death], they cooperate still more toward the affliction of the death, with the lordship for the quality [of death] coming to the star that possesses the destructive place itself." Schmidt says Ptolemy is speaking about enhanced conditions that show violent death. For the planet signifying the quality of death, we prefer a planet in the 7th *or* in (or perhaps aspecting or ruling) the place to which the *hīlāj* is directed. And the death will be violent if (a) the malefics are both in the same sign, and (b) they are opposed to that place of direction, or in the 7th. Obviously this could be a rare condition, but Ptolemy is using to illustrate general principles.

[849] Here Bonatti seems to be mixing two passages. The end of this sentence comes from an earlier passage in Ptolemy, which says "and if [the malefics] are culminating [in the 10th] or anti-culminating [in the 4th], it makes [natives] be thrown from a height."

[850] This is a misread of the Latin *Tet.*, which uses *quarto* to indicate a square aspect; Bonatti reads it as meaning the "fourth sign" from the Ascendant. Ptolemy says: "When the star of Ares [Mars], out of sect, is square or diametrical to the Sun or the Moon, if it is set in *zōidia* of human shape…"

again will testify to Mars. Which if Mercury is united to Mars in the figure, he will be torn to pieces by robbers and pirates and those lying in ambush. And he said, but [it will be] by the cutting off of limbs, were Mars in the Head of Algol or signs of incomplete forms, or with the Head of the Dragon;[851] and with him appearing as the Lord of the aforesaid quality, the head of the native will be cut off; or he will be undone by reason of the mutilation of some other limb. If however the signification of death were to appear in Taurus or Scorpio, and Mars were present in the same place with the aforesaid conditions, it will signify the native is going to be deprived of life by some burning or from cauterization or other amputations[852] or puncturings, or the cutting of doctors by means of a remedy presented to him, or perhaps by convulsion. But if Mars were in the Descendant[853] (or the seventh), and [he were] the al-mubtazz over one of them (and Saturn had testified to him from a fiery sign),[854] it signifies that the native will be sent alive into fire so that he might be burned. Moreover, Ptolemy said that if Mars were in quadrupedal signs, the native will be crushed by falling.[855] And if Jupiter testified to Mars, with [Jupiter] being made unfortunate, a judgment of death will be entered because of a king or authority, and this will be public, not hidden.

And if Mars and Saturn are joined in the place signifying the death of the native at the hour of the nativity,[856] or they were opposite each other (as was said above), or they were to have dignity [there], or one of them were the al-mubtazz over the place signifying death, the manner or quality of the native's death will be made severe, and the severity will be double what it would be if the aforesaid malefics were not so disposed; nor[857] will his corpse be buried (and

---

[851] Ptolemy does not say this.

[852] *Abscisionibus*, lit. "cutting-off."

[853] Reading *descendente* (following Ptolemy) for *ascendente*.

[854] Ptolemy does not add this remark.

[855] Ptolemy suggests it could be by the collapse of a house.

[856] Here we get a repetition of a passage from above. Bonatti wants the malefics to be in one of the places promising death, but Ptolemy wants them to be opposing it. Bonatti seems to be treating this joint condition of their position and aspects and rulerships as something to be broken down into a number of separate conditions.

[857] The rest is a garbled elaboration of Ptolemy based on *JN* p. 61, and it is probably easier simply to quote the rest of the paragraph directly from him, so the reader may note the differences: "Such persons are even left without burial; and they are devoured by wild beasts or birds when the malefics chance to be near *zōidia* of the same form, with none of the benefics testifying to the subterranean place [the fourth sign] or to the destructive places. The deaths happen in a foreign country when the stars occupying the destructive places fall in the declines [the cadents], and especially whenever the Moon also chances to be present with the said places, or square or diametrical [opposite] to them."

more truly so if a benefic did not aspect the aforesaid malefics, or one did not have a dignity in the place signifying death); and his corpse will become bait or food for ravenous, four-footed [animals], and birds living by plundering [dead things][858] (and the more so if the aforesaid malefics were in Leo or Scorpio or in other places in which the forms of the aforesaid birds are depicted). If however the benefics were to aspect the aforesaid places[859] or the said malefics, and [the benefics] were below the earth, it will not go as was said, but rather the native will die any death, and it will signify he will die by means of a meet and proper death. Indeed if the said killing planets were in the third or the ninth (and the more so if the Moon were staying in the aforesaid places[860] of journeys, or she were to aspect them from the square aspect or the opposition), this will signify the native is not going to die among his own blood-relatives, but among foreign [or strange][861] peoples.

And Ptolemy said,[862] look at the *al-mubtazz* over the place signifying the death of the native: because if it were impeded in the place which is called the Bold One[863] (which is near the head of Scorpio), or the Moon herself [were so impeded], it signifies the native will be deprived of his own life from the bite of a serpent or the blow of a poisoned sword, or poison offered to him by some trick. And if it were impeded near the place which is called the Falling Vulture,[864] which is in Capricorn, or the Flying Vulture,[865] which is at the end of Capricorn, his corpse will not be buried, but will be the food of crows and other birds living by plundering, like vultures, kites, and the like. And if it were impeded next to the Head of Algol[866] (which is in Taurus), the native will have his head cut off. Which if it were joined to the Sun or Moon in the aforesaid places, or to Jupiter, and they were impeded, it signifies the native's death is going to be the worst. And if they were opposed, it signifies the native is going to die at the hand of kings or other authorities.

---

[858] The Latin (*de raptu*) is more vivid and grotesque, referring to jerking and ripping movements, as crows and ravens make when they tear meat from a carcass.

[859] *Loca.* Here, too, whole signs seem to be indicated, since they are distinguished from the planets themselves.

[860] *Locis…ea.* This is identical to *loca.*

[861] *Extraneis.* This might simply mean they will be from some other clan or city–my sense is that it does not necessarily imply being in another country or being among people with unusual mores.

[862] This is from *TBN*, p. 87, and is an elaboration of the final paragraph in *Tet.* IV.9.

[863] *Audax.* I am not sure what star is meant.

[864] *Vultur cadens*, another name for the constellation Lyra.

[865] *Vultur volans*, another name for the constellation Aquila.

[866] *Caput Algol.*

ON THE NINTH HOUSE

Chapter 1: On the religion and faith of the native, and his knowledge, and likewise on his pilgrimages or long journeys

Since it was spoken sufficiently in the preceding chapter about the death of the native and its occasions, I consider it fitting to deal with the subject of his religion and faith, and likewise on his pilgrimages or long journeys.

Indeed, it is necessary for you to look at the Ascendant in the aforesaid nativity of the one you wished to investigate, and to see whether the Lord of the Ascendant and the Moon (or the stronger of them) is in the 9th or joined with its Lord (which signifies the native's faith and his knowledge and religion). For if each of them were as it was said, and it were in a good place of the circle, and particularly in the aforesaid good condition and well disposed, and it were a benefic, it signifies the native is going to adhere to a fitting and proper or lawful religion.

For if Saturn were the significator of religion,[867] it will signify he is going to adhere to a severe religion and one full of labors, especially to a religion whose followers believe themselves to be better and more worthy to God than all other religious people; and especially wearing black vestments.

If however Jupiter were the significator of religion, it signifies he is going to adhere to a religion whose followers are called secular clerics (as are bishops, archbishops, and others who are in charge of the Church) on account of that religion's largesse.[868]

Indeed[869] if the Sun were the significator of religion, it signifies he is going to adhere to a bountiful and noble religion (namely of religious people spending time between spiritual and temporal things, and the like).

---

[867] Below Bonatti defines the significator as being the *al-mubtazz* over the 9th.
[868] *Largitatem.*
[869] Mars is missing in Bonatti's text.

Which if Venus were the significatrix, it signifies he is going to adhere to a religion in which he could be in charge of women spending time in it, and the like.

Indeed if Mercury were the sole significator of religion, and he were of good condition, it signifies the native is going to adhere to a religion of young men, or lettered men and the wise, and the like.

But if the Moon were the significatrix of religion, it signifies he is going to adhere to a religion of unstable men, and of those easily and quickly changing from proposition to proposition, nor of those well observing their own religion.

If however the significator of knowledge or religion (namely, the *al-mubtazz* over the 9th house [domicile?]) were joined to Jupiter or Sun from a trine or sextile aspect, and with reception, and he were any one of the planets besides Mars, [and] he were in the first, it will judge [that] religion is going to come casually to the native, and with him not knowing [why], and from something unexpected–and this will happen almost inevitably.

Chapter 2: On the native's faith and the depth of his knowledge

In the investigation of the native's faith and the depth of his knowledge, you must look at Mercury, and see how he is disposed: because he, before all the other planets, is the *al-mubtazz*[870] over the signification of the native's faith and the depth of his knowledge. Which if he were oriental,[871] free from impediments, namely made fortunate and strong, he will signify the native is going to be of good faith, and adhering willingly to the sciences, and profound in them, and he will gladly keep company with the religious, and that he will love them.

Likewise look at the Part of Faith,[872] and the place in which you were to find it, and its Lord (to see how he were disposed). Because if [the Lord of the Part] were sound, and taken away [or exempt] from impediments, and the 3rd and 9th houses [domiciles?] and their Lords were free from impediments, and they and

---

[870] Here Bonatti is using *al-mubtazz* as a synonym for "universal significator," without reference to essential dignities.

[871] This may really refer to pertaining-to-arising.

[872] Probably the Part of Religion (Tr. 8, Part 2, Ch. 12), taken in the day from the Moon to Mercury (and in the night the reverse), and projected from the Ascendant.

the aforesaid houses [domiciles?] (namely the 3rd and the 9th, and the Lords of the houses [domiciles?] in which you were to find them) were made fortunate and strong (namely, free from combustion and retrogradation, and likewise fall [being cadent], and the aspects of the malefics), this will signify that the native will be (as I said) religious and very profound in the sciences, and distinguished (to whom few will be found like). But if you were to find the contrary, you could judge the contrary.

Which[873] if you were to find Mercury (as was said) free and made fortunate, and strong, and the significator of the native's religion and faith and knowledge free, see in which of the signs or in what planet's aspect [Mercury] were to fall.

For if he were in Capricorn or Aquarius, and Saturn were to aspect him[874] from a trine or sextile aspect, and Saturn were of good condition and well disposed, it will signify the native is going to be religious, and of good faith, and very profound and distinguished in the sciences; and he will commit those sciences to memory well, and he will gladly devote himself to reading and study, nor will be inclined to monetary advantage from those sciences; and if he were so inclined, he will not pursue it; and he will be a solitary man: he will flee temporal delights (like jokes, games, [and] worldly joys), nor will he desire them in any respect whatever, and he will go away from them in every way; he will even be humble, and practically all things which come to him, however much they were adverse, he will withstand them well, nor will he be saddened easily on such an occasion; and he will bear difficulties, tribulations, labors, [and] disturbances that are introduced, easily and in peace–he will not be concerned to avoid them.

Indeed if he were in Sagittarius or Pisces, and Jupiter were to aspect him from a trine or sextile aspect, and [Jupiter] were of good condition and well disposed (namely made fortunate and strong), it signifies the native is going to adhere to the civil and canonical laws, from which praises and honors and a good reputation will follow, and likewise high and famous clerical dignities; and in addition he will give plentifully, [and be] of good mind, and good faith, rejoicing in those things which he has (unless Mars worked to the contrary). Because if [Mars] did as-

---

[873] JN, p. 51.
[874] Reading *ipsum* for *ipsam*.

pect, it signifies that he would despise his law, and he is a transgressor[875] of it.[876]

If however he were in Leo, and the Sun were well disposed (namely made fortunate and strong), and he were to aspect him from the trine or sextile aspect, it signifies the native is going to be[877] wise, humble and discerning, and of good faith; he will love religion, be profound in matters of faith, and will understand them well, and will gladly keep company with religious people.

But if he were in Taurus or Libra, and Venus were to aspect him from a trine or sextile aspect, with her being well disposed (namely, made fortunate and strong), it signifies the native will adhere to a religion in which he will not persevere well, and it will hardly happen without him leaving it behind; nor will he gladly devote himself to study, nor will he go on at length[878] in the sciences, even if he is found to be of good belief. He will delight much in lively things.

Which if he were in Gemini or in Virgo, and Mercury himself were of good condition and well disposed (namely made fortunate and strong), and [he were] the sole significator, it will signify the native is going to be of good faith and religious, everywhere blessed by the gift of knowledge, and he will understand books of the sciences well, and wondrously expounding both the divine ones and the others; and praise and a good reputation will follow[879] from thence. And these

---

[875] The Latin (*praevaricator*) is a bit more precise: it means someone who violates his duty, especially through sham allegiance to it (while he is in fact in collusion with the opposite side). Traditional astrology frequently links hypocrisy and false piety with an afflicted Jupiter, which is the situation envisioned here.

[876] Again, the text omits Mars, but Bonatti uses Abu 'Ali's information on it in the next section, first paragraph. There, Bonatti presents the description as though it pertains to Mars aspecting the 9th; but in Abu 'Ali's text, it belongs here (not with the quadruplicities), when Mercury is in the domiciles of Mars.

[877] *Extiturum*, which I often translate as "appear" when it pertains to planets. Here, as in other cases when Bonatti uses this verb (*existo / exsisto*), "appear" does not mean "falsely appear." Bonatti is not saying that the native will *only* appear wise, *etc.*, while not *really* being wise; he means that the native's devotion will be public and will proclaim itself.

[878] *Profundabitur.* I.e., he will not speak at length.

[879] *Sequetur.* This is one case in which Bonatti's use of *sequor* is ambiguous. In this Treatise he tends to use it backwards, meaning "to follow" when his grammar says "to pursue" (i.e., to pursue praise and a reputation). But here it is unclear which sense he means.

things will happen to him more strongly so, if Jupiter were to regard[880] him–but with Jupiter of good condition (namely made fortunate and appearing free).

Indeed if he were in Cancer, and the Moon were of good condition and well disposed (namely made fortunate and strong), it signifies the native is going to be of good condition and good faith, and good be-lief, and will strive for a good reputation.

[The 9ᵗʰ by quadruplicity]

And Abu 'Ali said,[881] if the 9th domicile were a common sign, it signifies that the native will be unstable in the faith or religion to which he adheres, and[882] the more so if Mars were to aspect it from a trine or sextile aspect, because he will deride and despise the law or religion which he has assumed for himself, nor will he observe it well, but rather he will disparage[883] it and deride it. And again more, if Mars were made unfortunate and weak, aspecting it[884] from a square[885] aspect or from the opposition–because then it will take away all goodness from the native, and will make him a shedder of the blood of a stranger, and gladly inflicting injuries on others; and this after he has gnawed off the collar of the religion which he has assumed. If[886] however Mars (when he aspects it[887]) were free from impediments, the native will fashion many lies (even [with him] appearing in religion), which will never seem credible, nor will they be known to be invented by anyone else.

But if [the 9th] were a movable sign, and its Lord were in a movable sign, it will signify the native is not going to follow well in some faith, and that he will

---

880 *Intueris.* I.e., "aspect."

881 *JN*, p. 51.

882 The rest of this passage pertaining to Mars is not from Abu 'Ali. Moreover, there is some unclarity in the text, with a change in genders when the text speaks of Mars aspecting "it" (the 9th), suggesting either some editorial confusion or else some missing lines.

883 *Vituperans.* This and *vilipendens* ("despise" above) suggest that the native has objective criticisms and finds fault with it, not merely that he is blindly lashing out. Whether the criticisms are valid is another matter.

884 *Ipsum,* suggesting a whole sign.

885 Reading *quarto* for *sextili aut trino,* since Bonatti has already described the sextile and trine and would usually speak of the square and the opposition together.

886 Now Bonatti is using material from the section in Abu 'Ali pertaining to Mercury in the domicile of Mars.

887 *Ipsam,* suggesting either a house or domicile. 1491 says *eam,* so there has been some editorial tinkering in the texts.

be changed easily from one opinion to another, and quickly so; nor will he persevere well in any, nor will he know how to choose the better of them.

Indeed if [the 9th] were in a fixed sign, it will signify his constancy or firmness in the faith and religion to which he adheres, and he will do good in it, and he will be firm in his counsel and proposals, and even [in] a strange one because he perceives its truth,[888] unless Mars works to the contrary.

[Additional indications]

And Abu 'Ali said[889] if the Lord of the ninth (or third)[890] were in the Ascendant or in the Midheaven, free from the malefics, it signifies the rulership of the native over his partners,[891] and he will be of good sense and the best morals, and complete in faith, especially if Jupiter were the Lord of the ninth, or the Lord of the ninth were in the Ascendant, in the aspect of Jupiter.

And know that if it were just as was said, and Mercury[892] were pertaining-to-arising,[893] the native will do well and will observe [his] faith and law visibly and manifestly, and likewise the religion in which he spends time, and those things which are of that law and faith.[894] And if he were pertaining-to-sinking, he will hide and conceal his law and faith.

You[895] will even look to see whether Mercury is [in the 9th][896] in Gemini or in Cancer or in Virgo, with the Moon, and the Part of Faith or the Part of Knowledge[897] were with them in one of the aforesaid places: because this will

---

[888] *In alieno ex quo veritatem eius perceperit.* If this meant a strange religion, one would expect *aliena*; but perhaps he means he will accept the advice of a strange or foreign person. This phrase is not in *JN.*

[889] *JN,* p. 51, but Abu 'Ali does not mention the third sign.

[890] This addition is Bonatti's own.

[891] Abu 'Ali does not mention this part about having rulership over partners. Perhaps Bonatti means "over his fellow co-religionists"?

[892] Abu 'Ali says "the lord of the 9th."

[893] I am deliberately changing *orientalis/occidentalis* to "pertaining-to-arising/sinking," because this distinction is typical when speaking about public/private with respect to the Sun. Moreover, Ptolemy explicity uses these terms when speaking about Mercury as a significator of the mind (see material on the 1st house above)–which is probably why Bonatti substitutes Mercury here for the Lord of the 9th.

[894] Here our sources seem to be distinguishing between personal professions of subjective faith, observing the everyday customs of the way of life recommended by the religion, and actively participating in the public ceremonies and rituals.

[895] *JN,* p. 52.

[896] Bonatti omits this clause from Abu 'Ali.

[897] This is either a synonym for the Part of Faith, or perhaps a variant on the sixth Part of the 9th House, the Part of Histories and Knowledge, Rumors and Stories (see Tr. 8, Part 2, Ch.12)

signify the native to be profound in knowledge and wisdom, and likewise practically a prophet. Which if Jupiter were to aspect them from the noted aspects, or were joined corporally with them, it will signify the native is going to appear true and lawful, and experienced in profound, and exalted, high, and even great matters; a witness and trusted counselor.[898] And even if he were not that, still he will be believed and [people will] stand by his advice, nor will it be believed that another one in it might know better than he.

You[899] will look in the same way to see if the Head of the Dragon were in the ninth (in diurnal nativities), or in the third (in nocturnal ones),[900] because it will signify the native to be of good memory and firm in his own proposals, and he is going to observe his faith and law well; and the more so, and more fervently, if Jupiter and the Sun and Mercury were to aspect that place from the noted aspects: because then his goodness and reputation will be exalted on high, and will fly though many regions or provinces.

And Abu 'Ali said[901] if the 9th domicile were a domicile of Jupiter, and the Moon in it (in nocturnal nativities), it signifies that the native will be a wise astronomer, and announcer of divinations and things to be. Likewise if Mercury [were] the Lord of the ninth [or a star of the nature of Mercury appeared][902] in it.

And[903] if you were to find the Moon in the Ascendant, and[904] the Ascendant were a sign having a human form, it signifies that the native will have a horrible, bad mind. Likewise if the Part of Fortune,[905] in [diurnal and nocturnal] nativities, were in the Ascendant or in the angle of the earth.

---

[898] *Consultor*, i.e., someone who provides good counsel.

[899] *JN*, p. 52.

[900] This bit is an extrapolation (albeit a reasonable one) of Bonatti's. Abu 'Ali only says, "when the Head of the Dragon of the Moon is in the 3rd house in nocturnal nativities."

[901] *JN*, p. 52.

[902] Following Abu 'Ali. Bonatti's text reads, "Likewise if Mercury, the Lord of the ninth [sign], were to appear in it."

[903] Based on *JN*, p. 52.

[904] Abu 'Ali does not give any requirements about the type of sign.

[905] Bonatti says "Saturn," and omits the "diurnal and nocturnal" clause. Either this is a mistake on Bonatti's part, or else he did not see why the Part of Fortune should be so bad (especially since an angular Part of Fortune is a good thing), and substituted Saturn, thinking that *Abu 'Ali* had made an error.

[The Part of Faith]

You[906] will even see if the Part of Faith were with Saturn, because this will signify that the native will be an inquirer into profound and subtle things, and a subtle investigator of them, and he will be grave in speech, and likewise offering ponderous words, and full of opinions.

But if it were with Jupiter, it signifies that the native will be an observer[907] of a good law, of good faith, offering beautiful and honest words.

Indeed if it were with Mars, the native will be of a bad faith, bad opinion, and a shameful character [or mind].

If however it were with the Sun, and the Sun were then made fortunate and of good condition, it signifies that the native will be of a great appearance, even more so than is the truth of the matter; still, however, he will be of good faith, and a good law, extolling good religions.

Which if it were with Venus, it will signify that the native will be of good will, a lover of games and joys.

If however it were with Mercury, it signifies he will be excellent in the science of measuring, likewise in number and merchant activities.

But if the Moon were with the said Part, it will indicate the abundance of his mind, and the native's elegance.[908]

[Additional indications]

Indeed[909] if [1] the 9th domicile were Aries or Cancer or Pisces,[910] and [2] the Sun or Jupiter or Venus (namely the one of them who is the Lord of the

---

906 *JN*, pp. 52-53.
907 Or "preserver."
908 *Munditiam.*
909 *JN*, pp. 52-53.
910 Bonatti should have added "the Moon," because Abu 'Ali says "a domicile of Jupiter, or the exaltation of the Sun, the Moon, or Venus." This would include Sagittarius, Pisces, Aries, Taurus, and Libra. An alternate reading could be, "a domicile of Jupiter, or the exaltation of the Sun, [or a domicile of] the Moon or Venus." This second version would include

triplicity of the sign in which the luminary whose authority it was, is) is in a good place of the figure of the nativity, it signifies the native, on account of his way of life (on the occasion of his faith or law), will be good and honorable, and he will have or acquire the notice and praise and likewise the love of men; and more so and more strongly, if then one of the benefics were found in the 3rd or in the 9th [domicile];[911] and again more strongly if the Lord of the 9th domicile,[912] or of the 3rd, were sound and free from impediments.

And 'Umar said[913] if Mercury were the Lord of the 9th domicile, and he were to agree[914] with the Lord of the Ascendant, the native will be one contending in faith, and a disputer, having instruction in words. If however Mercury were then made fortunate and oriental,[915] there will be knowledge [for him] in this, and he will acquire substance from it, and good, and even his condition [will be] praiseworthy.[916] If indeed he were impeded, and occidental, evil will occur to him from this.[917]

And Abu 'Ali said[918] if Saturn were the Lord of the 9th, it signifies the native is wise, and especially if he were in the aspects of the benefics, not retrograde, nor under the rays of the Sun.[919]

And Bernardus[920] said a planet appearing in combustion in someone's nativity signifies the laziness and even the idleness [or leisure] of the native, and his illegality; indeed if it were retrograde, it signifies he is going to be a liar.

And Remigius[921] said, look at the third and the ninth sign, likewise their Lords, and the Part of Faith, and the Lord of the sign then holding [the Part]. If however these three planets were of good condition and well disposed (namely made fortunate and strong), free from the malefics and from the other impedi-

---

Sagittarius, Pisces, Aries, Cancer, Taurus, and Libra. Either way, Bonatti's list of signs is too short.

[911] Abu 'Ali specifies "sign."

[912] Following Abu 'Ali.

[913] What follows is a nearly verbatim quote from 'Umar.

[914] *Congruerit.* It is unclear what 'Umar's Latin translator means by this.

[915] It is unclear whether this refers to pertaining-to-arising, or not.

[916] 'Umar's text is slightly different: "And he will acquire substance from this, and his end will be good and praiseworthy." Since Bonatti's Latin is slightly odd here (and is missing the verb), his text must be a misread of 'Umar.

[917] My assumption is that "oriental" and "occidental" in this paragraph really have to do with pertaining-to-arising/sinking.

[918] *JN*, p. 53.

[919] Abu 'Ali adds: "for this planet, when it is under the Sun beams, signifies deception and concealment, but when retrograde, lies."

[920] Unknown source, but the passage roughly matches *JN*, p. 53. Abu 'Ali specifies *this* planet, i.e., Saturn.

[921] Unknown author, but again the passage continues the statements of *JN*, p. 53.

ments, it signifies the native is going to be of good faith and a good law, and likewise of good religion. If however they were impeded by the conjunction of the malefics or their square aspect or from the opposition (and especially in the ninth or the third), it signifies the native is going to be of bad faith and a bad law, and much corrupt insincerity, undertaking a commingled matter in faith,[922] and of no religion.

And Vettius [Valens] said[923] if Cancer were the 3rd or 9th house [domicile?], and the Moon or Mercury were in one of them, and Jupiter or Venus were in the Ascendant or in the 10th, and they were free from impediments, namely made fortunate and strong, this will signify the native is going to ascend to a great dignity or preferment because of his faith and his law and religion.

And Bernardus said[924] if you were to consider the condition [or nature] of the Lords of the triplicity of the Part of Faith aright, you could know in what third of his life the native will be[925] of better faith and better law and a better religion.

And 'Umar said,[926] look from the ninth or the third[927] and the planets which are in them, and from the Part of Faith and its Lord.[928] You will even look at the *al-mubtazz* over these places[929]–which if it were Saturn, and he were safe (namely from the malefics, from combustion and retrogradation) or it were Jupiter or Mars or the Sun (and they were free from the malefics), the native will be a worshiper of one God[930] without the dividing of [his] intention, and the

---

[922] *Moventem rem commixtam.* The sense seems to be that the native's faith will be an inconsistent patchwork of different ideas, and without real commitment.

[923] Again, this continues statements from *JN*, p. 53.

[924] Again, this continues statements from *JN*, p. 53; but it also closely matches a paragraph in *TBN* (p. 87). It could be that an early edition of Bonatti read *Tiberiades* and this was turned by the typesetters into *Bernardus*. Or, perhaps there really was an astrologer named Bernardus, like Bernard Silvestris/Silvester. See Introduction.

[925] *Extiturum*, lit. "appear." See note above.

[926] *TBN*, p. 86. But 'Umar says "from the ninth [sign] and its Lord, and from the bound...and its Lord, and from the planets who are in the bound and in the ninth [sign]; from the Part of Faith too, and its Lord. Also look at the *al-mubtazz* over these places [*loca*]."

[927] 'Umar does not mention the third sign at this point.

[928] 'Umar says: "Look from the ninth [sign] and its Lord, and from the bound, and its Lord, and from the planets which are in the bound [of the Lord?], and in the 9th; also from the Part of Faith and its Lord. You will also look at the *al-mubtazz* over these places [*loca*]."

[929] *Loca.* But it is unclear whether Bonatti or Abu 'Ali means an equal or weighted-point *al-mubtazz.*

[930] 'Umar says "he will be of the worshipers of one God" (not "one of the worshipers of God," as Hand reads it), and the clause about dividing one's intention underlines his monotheism. Enemies of polytheism (and indeed Muslim and Jewish critics of the Christian Trinity) charged that believing in multiple gods or even Persons divides the worshiper's mind, so that one is not wholly committed to a unitary God.

native will be saved because of that faith, and he will observe it, nor will he be changed to another.

Chapter 3: On the pilgrimages of the native and on his long journeys

Having looked (in what has preceded) regarding the faith of the native and his religion, I believe it will be fitting subsequently to explain somewhat regarding his pilgrimages and his long journeys.

Indeed[931] in the pilgrimages of the native and his long journeys, look at the 9th domicile[932] from the Ascendant of his nativity, and its Lord, and if any [planet] were in it, you will consider it likewise; and likewise Mars and the Part of Pilgrimage,[933] and the Lord of the domicile in which you were to find it; and see which of the planets is the *al-mubtazz* over those places, or over one of them (whether [the *al-mubtazz*] were one or more). And you will even see how they behave with the Lord of the Ascendant, or with its *al-mubtazz*, and of what kind is their simultaneous aspect or conjunction or application. Because if they were of good condition and well disposed (namely made fortunate and strong), well applied together or corporally joined, or they were to aspect each other by the noted aspects (and the more so if this were with reception), it will signify the native is going to engage gladly in pilgrimages and long journeys, and especially in regions far and remote from his own land; and again more if the Moon (in the figure of the nativity) appeared setting,[934] [or] removed[935] from the angle of the 10th house, and especially if she were in the 9th from the Ascendant of the nativity.[936] You could give a similar judgment if you were to find Mars in the 9th or 8th or in the 7th,[937] and he were in the opposition or in the square aspect of the Sun or Moon, but he will not be so fervently inclined to journeys or pilgrimages.

---

931 *TBN*, p. 76.
932 Since this paragraph is based on 'Umar, and 'Umar explicitly says the ninth *sign*, this should read "domicile."
933 Calculated by day and night from the Lord of the ninth sign to the degree of the 9th, and projected from the Ascendant. See Tr. 8, Part 2, Ch. 12.
934 This passage and what follows concerning Mars are from Ptolemy (*Tet.* IV.8). "Setting" means "in the seventh."
935 Here "removed" means "cadent."
936 Ptolemy does not specifically mention the 9th, but because of his wording regarding Mars, this is a fair assumption.
937 Ptolemy says "setting" (in the 7th) or "declined from the place at the peak [the Midheaven]" (in the 9th). Bonatti must be assuming that the 8th is part of the setting process, so he includes it here.

Which[938] if a benefic were in the 9th, or joined with the Lord of the 9th, or the Lord of the 9th were a benefic, or one of the benefics were to aspect the aforesaid places,[939] or it were to aspect Mars or the Sun or the Moon, this will signify his journeys [to be] safe and useful and beneficial, and that the native will return from his pilgrimages shortly and in good health, and with wealth, even if by chance he is not going to celebrate many journeys or pilgrimages. But if you were to find the contrary, you could judge the contrary: for his journeys will have to be believed [to be] burdensome and useless, and likewise full of labor, and likewise fearful, and having a delayed return.

Which if you were to find nothing of these things, say the native is going to avoid pilgrimages and the aforesaid journeys, and that he will look for his own wealth in his own places of habitation.

In[940] the same way you will look at the Lords of the triplicity of the domicile in which Mars is; and according to the place and disposition and condition of the one of them who is stronger and more fortunate and better disposed, you will pronounce [that] in the period of his life attributed to that planet, his pilgrimages will be better and indeed useful, and more profitable–and likewise the reverse. Still, if, outside the aforesaid places,[941] one of the benefics will be united with the aforesaid significators, they will increase good and decrease the evil. If however they were malefics, [it signifies] they will perform the contrary, and that harm and evil and the decrease of substance will come to the native because of his journeys; and that he will appear to be of little faith.

You[942] will even look to see if the Sun and the Moon were facing toward the Ascendant from the angle of the 10th house, or in the Ascendant, up to the angle of the 4th house: because they will signify his pilgrimages and his long journeys will mostly be toward the east and toward the south. Indeed if the aforesaid were from the aforesaid angle of the 10th house toward the west, up to the angle of the aforesaid 4th house, or in the 7th itself, they are going to toward the west and the south, you will not doubt.

---

[938] *Tet.* IV.8.
[939] *Loca.*
[940] *TBN*, p. 76.
[941] *Loca.*
[942] This is not an accurate report of Ptolemy (*Tet.* IV.8). Ptolemy says that if the luminaries "fall out in the declines of the eastern quadrants, the travel away from home is toward the orient and the southern parts of the inhabited world…[in] the western quadrants or in the Descendant itself, the travel is toward the northern parts and the [west]." In other words, from the Ascendant to the Midheaven and from the 7th to the 4th, is to the east and south (respectively); in the other quadrants, to the west and north.

Which[943] if the aforesaid 3rd or 9th domiciles were fixed signs, and their Lords were benefics, and likewise in the aforesaid domiciles, or in any others in fixed signs, and in good places from the Ascendant, this will signify that the native will not make much use of journeys or pilgrimages, and if he were to go on pilgrimage, he will go on pilgrimage intermittently. But if the aforesaid places[944] and aforesaid significators were in common signs, it signifies he is going to make use of journeys or pilgrimages. And if the aforesaid places were either the places of the Sun and Moon, Taurus, or Cancer, or Libra or Sagittarius or Pisces,[945] this signifies that his journeys and his pilgrimages will be according to what the native desired of them, prosperous and certainly safe.

And Abu 'Ali said,[946] look at the Moon on the third day[947] of the nativity: which if she were applied to Mars, or were in his domicile or bound, with him aspecting her, it signifies many pilgrimages and journeys. And he said[948] if the Lord of the Ascendant were contrary to[949] the Ascendant, and the Lord of the domicile of the Moon contrary to[950] the Moon, or the Lord of the Ascendant were in its own descension,[951] it signifies the native's livelihood is going to come from foreign regions. And he said, indeed if the Lord of the domicile of the Sun

---

[943] Based on *Tet.* IV.8.

[944] *Loca.*

[945] This is awkwardly phrased in Bonatti's Latin. Ptolemy says: "When Zeus [Jupiter] and Aphrodite [Venus] become lords of the places that cause travel abroad, and of the lights." According to Schmidt, this lordship means something like an *al-mubtazz*, i.e. an overall strongest ruler. Since the strongest rulers would presumably rule the places by domicile, this list would pertain to signs such as Taurus, Libra, Sagittarius, Pisces, and whatever signs the luminaries were in. It is not so much that the places of travel have these signs on them, but rather, for Venus or Jupiter to be the lords of the places, such signs would most likely be on them. Bonatti evidently adds Cancer because it is the exaltation of Jupiter.

[946] *JN*, p. 49.

[947] That is, counting the first day of birth as day one. According to Vettius Valens (*Anth.* I.14), the third, seventh, and fortieth days of the Moon after birth give indications for eminent births, depending on the balance of benefics and malefics aspecting the place of the Moon. I imagine that in this case, Mars is supposed to indicate restlessness, and will agitate the general tendency of the Moon to signify quick changes in matters.

[948] I believe we are now looking back at the natal figure, and not at the situation on the third day after birth.

[949] Abu 'Ali says "conjoined or in opposition to the place of the Ascendant."

[950] Abu 'Ali says, "conjoined to."

[951] Abu 'Ali says: "When the Lord of the ASC is conjoined or in opposition to the place of the ASC, or in a sign of contrary nature to the ascending sign, and the lord of the domicile of the Moon is conjoined to the Moon, and if the lord of the ASC is in its own fall." "Contrary" in Bonatti's text would seem to mean "of a contrary nature" to the Moon, but this is still unclear. And it is possible that Bonatti misread Abu 'Ali's *coniunctus* ("conjoined") as *contrarius* ("contrary"), but, not having access at present to Abu 'Ali's Latin text, I cannot say.

were contrary to the Sun,[952] it signifies that the native will proceed on many journeys. And if the aforesaid Lord of the domicile of the Sun were a benefic, the native will achieve good and profit from his journeys. Indeed if it were a malefic, you will judge evil. And he said if the Moon were applied to Mercury on the third day[953] after the nativity, and she[954] were impeded by Mars, it signifies that horrible things will happen to the native on his journeys. If however the Moon or the Lord of her domicile were in the angle of the 7th house, it signifies that the native will love journeys. Likewise, the Lord of the Ascendant, if it were in the 9th, or the Lord of the 9th, if it were in the Ascendant, signifies that the native will desire to go on journeys and to change [place] from region to region.

Chapter 4: Which planets aid journeys, and which not

And know that planets [sometimes] help journeys, and sometimes they impede them. For Saturn and the Sun, if they were of good condition and well disposed (namely made fortunate and strong), will help journeys made toward the east; if however they were impeded, they will work to their contrary. Indeed Jupiter offers his aid to journeys made toward the north. In the same way, Venus will help journeys which come to be toward the south. However, Mars and the Moon, which are toward the west, strive to strengthen journeys which are toward the west. Indeed Mercury offers support to journeys according to the nature of him to whom he is joined.

You will consider the aforesaid assisting planetary significators of journeys or pilgrimages which there are: because if Saturn himself were of good condition and well disposed, it will signify the native is going to be engaged in the services of great prelates, and especially of those clothed in black vestments, or old men, or Jews.

If however it were Jupiter, he will perform them in the services of great men and the wealthy and nobles or great and famous jurists,[955] or their friends.

---

952 Abu 'Ali says, "to the Moon."
953 Holden's Abu 'Ali says "in the third sign from the Ascendant."
954 Reading *ipsa...impedita* (with Abu 'Ali) for *ipse...impeditus.*
955 *Iuristarum.*

Indeed if it were Mars, he will labor in the services of the armies of belli-cose soldiers and generals.

Which if it were the Sun, he will be exhausted in the services of great kings and the wealthy who are fit for a kingdom.

But if it were Venus, his own peculiar service will exhibited[956] for great ladies and even their friends.

Indeed if it were the Moon, his own service will be exercised in the mass[957] of the common people and the low-class.

However Mercury will serve those to whom he is applied,[958] and he will even offer his support to the lettered, and to young men.

In the same way you will see if Jupiter or Venus assisted the aforesaid signifi-cators of pilgrimages or journeys, [and] whether Mercury is applied to them, with him being of good condition and well disposed: because this will signify that the native will pursue great good and usefulness because of the aforesaid journeys; and he will perfect them well and according to his wishes, and he will acquire honor and contributions from them.

But if the Sun and the Moon were to help the aforesaid significators, and they were in Aries or Scorpio or Capricorn or Aquarius, and Mars or Saturn were in their opposition, it signifies that great inconveniences and likewise impediments will happen to the native because of his journeys or pilgrimages. Which if then Mars tarried in Cancer or in its triplicity, the aforesaid will happen to the native from inundations of the seas or even other waters, or on account of the inconvenience and insupportableness of journeys, or on account of robbery or cutters of roads, or submersions.

But if they (namely Mars and Saturn) were in Gemini or in its triplicity, the aforesaid will happen from a strong blowing of winds. If however they were staying in Taurus or in its triplicity, they will portend them coming from ruins. Indeed if you were to find them in Aries or in its triplicity, say that impediments

---

[956] Reading *exhibebitur* for *exhibebit.*
[957] *Natione.*
[958] *Mercurius autem illis quibus serviet ille cui fuerit ipse applicatus.*

will happen to the native which will surround him because of a fall from a height, or because of an unexpected or accidental fall.

And Ptolemy said[959] if Saturn and Mars were in solstitial or equinoctial signs, we will not doubt [that] this will happen because of their things, by which they [will] have want, namely by a revolt and taking away of [their] men, and on account of the qualities of corrupt air bringing in illness.[960] If however they were in signs having the form of a human, we will say they will come because of cutters of roads and the aggressions of men, or insults or traitors or plunderers. And he said if they were in signs whose forms are likened to the forms of wild [or forest] animals, it will happen because of the rapaciousness of wolves, or by earthquake, or because of some matter which will fall down on him.

And Abu 'Ali said[961] if the Moon were in the third [sign][962] on the day of the nativity, applied to benefics, and she [were] in a good place, namely made fortunate and strong, it signifies the native's progress [or profit] in his journeys. Indeed if it were to the contrary, it will indicate the contrary. And he said, look at the ninth [sign]: which if a benefic were in it, or in its square aspect, or in its opposition,[963] it signifies the profit of the native because of journeys, especially if the Lord of the Ascendant were[964] a benefic, or the benefics were to aspect him. If however you were to see the contrary, you could judge the contrary, especially if the Lord of the 9th were a malefic, or a malefic were to aspect him. And if the Lord of the 9th were in the Ascendant or in its 10th, it signifies the love of the native in journeys.

Indeed if Venus were the Lady of the 9th, and she were in the Ascendant, it signifies the native's joy, and his betrothal, on his journey.

Indeed if Jupiter were the Lord of the 9th, and he were in the Ascendant or in the 10th, it signifies the native is going to acquire praise and a good reputation on his journeys.

---

959 *Tet.* IV.9.
960 Ptolemy simply says "through lack of provisions and disease-ridden conditions."
961 The rest of this chapter is based on *JN*, pp. 49-50.
962 This could mean means "if, on the *third day* of the nativity, she were applied…". See above.
963 I.e., by whole signs.
964 Reading *fuerit* for *fuerint*.

But if the Sun were the Lord of the 9ᵗʰ, and he were in the Ascendant or in the 10ᵗʰ, it signifies the native is going to acquire knowledge and the things of nobles and from nobles on his journeys.

Which if Saturn were the Lord of the 9ᵗʰ, and he were in the Ascendant or in the 10ᵗʰ, in the aspect of Jupiter, it signifies the native is going to acquire substance because of watery and earthy things, and beasts.

Indeed if Mars were the Lord of the 9ᵗʰ, and he were in the Ascendant or in the 10ᵗʰ, it signifies he is going to gain substance in his journeys because of bellicose soldiers, and those people by which wars are started, and [because of] an army.

And Abu 'Ali said,[965] indeed if the Lord of the domicile of the Sun did not aspect [the Sun], and the Lord of the domicile of the Moon did not aspect [the Moon], and the Lord of the Ascendant did not aspect the Ascendant, or Mars were in the 3ʳᵈ or the 9ᵗʰ, and the Lord of the Part of Journeys[966] were contrary to its own domicile, it signifies a multitude of journeys with labor and dread and the loss of substance.

And if the Part of Journeys were in one of the angles, joined to the Lord of the Ascendant and the Moon, it signifies that the native will love journeys and journeying.[967]

---

[965] *JN*, p. 50.
[966] This must be the Part of Pilgrimage.
[967] Abu 'Ali says "love affairs on trips."

ON THE TENTH HOUSE

Chapter 1: On the native's profession[968] and his work, and his duties, and his force,[969] likewise on [his] prosperity and kingdom, and on the condition of the mother

If you wished to be made certain about the matter of the native's profession,[970] also of his work (what kinds they will be), and on his force and prosperity, and his kingdom,[971] and likewise concerning his duties,[972] and on maternal matters.

Look at the Ascendant of his nativity, and see if one of the planets is found in it: because he whom you were to find in the Ascendant will have to be considered, and you will take the signification of the aforesaid from him. Which if there were not a planet in the Ascendant, then you will look at the 10th: if one of the planets were in it, the signification of the aforesaid is to be taken from him. However, the 7th will signify the laziness of the native in his work (likewise the 4th).[973] And let the aforesaid significators be oriental from the Sun and occidental from the Moon.[974]

---

[968] In this chapter (and in Latin culture) we have several terms to distinguish: *artificium* (trade, employment, activity), *magisterium* (mastery, profession), *officium* (one's duty or "office"), *opus* (action, deed, work). The various texts (and their translators) do not seem to make any systematic or technical distinctions between these insofar as it would affect delineation procedures.

[969] *Valitudine.* See my comments on this word in the material on the 4th House, Ch. 5.

[970] *Magisterium.* This refers to the native's "mastery," or special skill, which will be expressed somehow, but preferably through the native's official occupation. Medieval writers assumed it would be, but it should be kept in mind that in the modern Western market, people may switch jobs frequently without actually having a job whose title matches the *magisterium.*

[971] *Regno.* We often see Bonatti use this term in a generic way, to denote whatever the native "rules" over. It does not necessarily mean the sort of kingdom an actual king rules.

[972] *Officiis.* In classical Latin, an *officium* ("office, duty") was a duty that was often expressed through a specific social position or role. The Roman Stoics (principally led by Cicero) expanded this notion to include the responsibilities we have in terms of other roles, including as rational beings, as members of a particular profession, and as people with idiosyncratic skills and interests. Again, I do not see any philosophical or technical distinctions in the text which would tie *officium* (or *magisterium*, etc.) to any particular procedure.

[973] Lat. *Decima.* This notion comes from (*Tet.* IV.5). Ptolemy wants to base the native's action on the Midheaven (and planets in it), and the Sun (or rather, planets that are pertaining-to-arising). According to Ptolemy, needing to rely on other significators (or places) suggests that the native has only occasional pursuits, or is an inactive person. Bonatti's statement does not make this clear, and we should follow Ptolemy; therefore I have corrected the text to read *septima*, indicating the 7th (and the 4th).

[974] See Schmidt's footnotes to *Tet.* IV.5 for commentary on this–it is unclear exactly what sort of orientality/occidentality or pertaining-to-arising/sinking is involved here.

Which if one of the planets were not in the Ascendant, nor in the 10th, then look at the 4th or 7th.[975] If you were to find one of the planets in one of them, you could take what is signified by the native's work from it; however, the things signified by it are weaker than the aforesaid [houses]. Which if there were not any planet in one of the aforesaid places, look at the *al-mubtazz* over each of them, whether it is the Lord or *al-mubtazz* over the Ascendant, or over the 10th or the 4th or the 7th.

Then, look even at the planet to which the Moon is first joined after her corporal separation from the Sun (if the nativity were diurnal) or [look at] the planet which were first joined with the Part of Fortune (if it were nocturnal).

You would even look to see whether one of the planets is newly appearing from under the rays of the Sun, removed[976] from him by not more than 20° (if [the planet] were of the superiors, let it be oriental from him, if however it were of the inferiors, let it be occidental).[977] And see if that planet (which I have just mentioned), or he who were in the 1st, or the 10th, or the 4th or the 7th, has *al-'ittisal* with the Moon.

If however you were to find one of the planets (whether of the ones stated above, or of the others) to which two of the aforesaid accidents pertained, you will consider him only, [and] you will omit the others, because we will not care much about them.

Which if you were to find only one of them so disposed (namely, that he alone is in one of the aforesaid places with one of the aforesaid conjunctions, or he is the *al-mubtazz* over one of them), you will consider him, and you will take up the above-stated individual professions from him, and especially if you were to find Mars or Venus or Mercury in the Ascendant or in the 10th; and again more if it[978] were to have rulership or exaltation or bound or triplicity there (but the face, even though it does something in this, its signification will be much less than the aforesaid).

---

[975] Note that Bonatti consistently lists the 4th before the 7th, suggesting its priority over the 7th.

[976] Here, *remotus* clearly means "remote" or "distanced," as shown by the following clauses.

[977] Further evidence that the inferiors are in a better condition when they are occidental of the Sun.

[978] I believe this refers to Mars, Venus, or Mercury (whichever one is relevant), but the Latin makes it possible that it refers to whatever planet is most relevant.

And were one of the aforesaid three planets in one of the noted aspects with the Sun (lacking that, with the Moon), and more strongly so if reception were to intervene, this will signify that the native would want to adhere to any work or duty or profession; he could achieve it well and easily; and from any one of them he would want to accept [its] usefulness, and he will pursue wealth [that is] pleasing to him, according to how one of the planets were to signify it.

Which if there were more of the planets in the aforesaid places, you will prefer, to all others, him who had dignities of greater authority there, or more [of them].

Which if you were to find none of the aforesaid, and the nativity were diurnal, take the signification from the planet which is joined with the Sun. But if it were nocturnal, then you will take it from the planet with which the Moon is joined. Indeed if the Moon is not joined then with one, the signification will have to be taken from him from whom she was most recently separated) or from the Lord of the domicile in which the Part of Fortune is, or namely from him who is better disposed.

Which if [the resulting planet] were made fortunate, namely of good condition and strong (and the more so if Mercury were made fortunate and strong, and [Mercury] were to aspect him by a friendly aspect), it signifies the native is going to be of a good profession and good work and good mechanical works, and that he will progress in that profession, and because of it, and likewise he will pursue wealth and usefulness and great profit; and he will be learned in the science of numbers, and a subtle worker of writing [or Scripture], and fortunate in all the aforesaid, and he will have a good character [or skill] and a good intellect.

And if Saturn were to aspect the said significator of the native[979] by a praiseworthy aspect, and Saturn were of good condition and well disposed, namely made fortunate and strong, it will signify the native's fortune will prevail in the cultivation of lands and trees and in planting.[980]

---

[979] This undoubtedly means "the said significator of the native's *profession*," but in the 7th house Bonatti used this phrase to mean the Lord of the Ascendant.
[980] Reading *natum* for *nati*.

And if Saturn were to aspect from the 10ᵗʰ or in the 10ᵗʰ, it will signify the native is going to approach [or rise] to great rulerships and to great duties [and] great burdens.

Indeed if Jupiter regards him from the said aspects, it will signify (the native) to be honest and wise, and likewise a writer, [and he is] going to be distinguished above others; and he will be in the household of princes (namely kings and great men).

Which if Mars were to aspect him from the above-mentioned aspects and places, or he himself were the significator of the native's work, it will signify the native is going to be proven in medicine (and especially in surgery), and likewise in theology; and he will be of a common enough mind, and of [a mind] applying itself, nor with difficulty, to those things which he wishes; and he will be clever and ingenious.

And Abu 'Ali said[981] if the Sun were to aspect him or were with him in one sign, so that he did not burn him up, it signifies him [to be] of a high profession and great loftiness and a writer for kings, and of great value among them.

And if Venus were to aspect him or she were the significatrix of the native's work, it signifies the native is commingled with the women of kings and nobles, and will often have power among them, and will attain profit from them.

If however Mercury testified to him, he is going to be proven in the knowledge of writing [or Scripture] and in number and in [mercantile] exchange.

But if the Moon were to aspect him, it signifies the native's knowledge and complete fortune in those things which are ended quickly.

But if one of the malefics were to aspect it with a bad aspect, it signifies labor and exertion in the profession. For if it were Mars who aspected him, and [Mars] were of bad condition and badly disposed, or Mars himself were in the

---

[981] JN, p. 56.

Ascendant or in the 10th and the nativity were diurnal,[982] it will signify the native is going to incur harm and danger because of his profession, for he will be whipped and put in chains from thence, or he will be beaten or convicted. If however it were Saturn, and he were of bad condition and badly disposed, and he were in the 1st or the 10th, and the nativity were nocturnal, it signifies that the native will be bound for the aforesaid reason, and he will be fettered with strong fetters, and he will be incarcerated or hanged, or he will be tortured like a hanged martyr.

And Abu 'Ali said[983] that in the year in which the Ascendant of the root[984] were to arrive at the sign of the Midheaven ([that is,] if one of the planets signifying the profession were in [the Midheaven]), the native will renew his profession according to the substance of the planet which is there.

And Ptolemy said that if we were to take the signification of the profession and work of the native from the 10th [alone],[985] the native will be idle in his profession and his work; and that we should take what kinds the native's work (and his profession) will be, principally through Mars, through Venus and Mercury, and through the signs in which they are–I say secondarily through the other planets and places.[986]

For if Mars[987] appeared as the sole significator of the work and profession of the native, and he were in his own dignities, it will signify his profession and work will be perfected by iron or fire; and it will indicate he is going to know how to split[988] rocks and sculpt images.

But if Mars were in the dignities of Saturn, and Saturn testified to him, and were of good condition and well disposed, it will signify the profession of the native is going to be in the building of ships (and especially pirates' and plunderers' ships), and by means of robbers sailing the sea.

---

[982] This point about Mars in a diurnal chart and Saturn in a nocturnal chart (below) has to do with these planets' not being a member of the ruling sect in such charts.

[983] *JN*, p. 56.

[984] *Radicis*, i.e., the natal figure. Bonatti is referring to annual profections.

[985] *Tet.* IV.4. Ptolemy says this pertains to cases where there is no planet that is pertaining-to-arising or upon the Midheaven, so that we are left with only the Lord of the Midheaven for our judgment. The medieval procedure allows for planets to be on any of the angles (although we would prefer them to be in the Ascendant and/or the Midheaven). See footnote above.

[986] *Loca.* Here the parallel clearly suggests that a *locum* is a sign.

[987] Based on *Tet.* IV.4.

[988] Reading *scindere* for *inscindere*, but perhaps it means something like "inscribe," or even to cut stones for jewelry (but see below).

And Ptolemy said that he will be a navigator and swimmer, and painter, and that he will gladly tarry in great waters and in baths.

If however [Mars] were in the dignities of Jupiter, and Jupiter testified to him, and one of them were well disposed (and the other badly), it signifies his work in the military and in the inflicting of punishments, both in the guilty and the not-guilty; and he will pretend to be a host to travelers, and will gladly pilfer from them what he can. And likewise he will be a buyer of captives, so that he might appropriate something.

Which if he were in the dignities of the Sun, and the Sun testified to him, and in addition the Sun were weak, this will signify the action of the native and his profession is going to be in the kindling of fire and in those things which come to be by the kindling of fire, and especially of fire in which metals and minerals are founded.

Indeed if he were in the dignities of Venus, and Venus testified to him, this will signify the work of the native and his profession will be fulfilled by the ornaments of women and of metals (namely of gold and silver) and in games, and in the inventing of songs, and building musical instruments.

And if he were in the dignities of Mercury or the Moon, and one of them testified [to him], it signifies the work of the native and his profession will happen by the hollowing out of coin-molds and the making of rings and necklaces, and likewise in the sculptures of precious gems.

And Ptolemy said[989] if two planets were to come together in the profession of the native, and they were Venus and Mercury, he will engage in music or games (he said this because Venus signifies delights, and Mercury signifies number), or his exertion will be in songs or in the invention of songs, or in any manner of finding songs—especially however if they will be interchanged in their places: for then the native will be a joker (and especially if Venus were in the dignities of Mercury and Mercury were in the dignities of Venus) or an actor (as are those who use *barbastellis*[990] and the like), and he will be a composer or

---

[989] Continuing with *Tet.* IV.4.
[990] This probably means "fake beards," from Lat. *barba*, "beard."

maker of citharas,[991] viols,[992] drums, organs, *levitarum*,[993] and other musical instruments; and he will be concerned to deflower and deceive and delude women (but, as Ptolemy says, not to marry them). And he will be a painter and a good operator or maker of the aforesaid [forms of] trust; he will even be a predictor [or preacher], and a mixer of flattery and lies in his predictions [or preachings].

And Ptolemy said if Saturn will testify to them, so that he would be a participator in the profession of the native with the aforesaid significators, his work and profession will be with these things which were said above, in merchant activities, and he will sell those things with which women are adorned.

And he said, if Jupiter testified to them, and he were in the dignities of Mercury, he will be a pleaser, and he will always stay gladly in places with a congregating of men. If however he were in his own dignities, he will stay around royal doors, and he will teach boys. If however Jupiter were weak, he will be concerned with the matters of the vulgar.

And he said,[994] but if Mars and Mercury were to have rulership of the work of the profession, he will be learned in the making of images and arms, and he will be a sculptor in matters which divine houses use, and he will make images of animals, and he will be a wrestler, a doctor, a surgeon, evildoer, fornicator, and a falsifier of papers.

And he said if Saturn testifies to them, the native will be a killer and will tear off the clothing of others, and he will be a cutter of roads.

And he said if Jupiter will testify to them, that he will love arms and duels on account of Jupiter; he will even be a regent, an administrator [or estate-manager], and crafty (and this because one is a benefic and the other a malefic); he will love works, and will meddle concerning strangers, and he will earn money in this way.

---

[991] *Cythararum*. A precursor to the guitar.
[992] *Violarum*.
[993] A *levita* was a medieval deacon, but I do not know what kind of instrument this could indicate.
[994] Continuing with *Tet.* IV.4.

And Ptolemy said,[995] if however the significator of the native's work and profession were Venus, and Saturn and Mars (or at least Saturn) testified to her, and Venus were in one of the dignities of the Sun or the Moon or Saturn, and he[996] were of good condition and well disposed, it signifies the native is going to be a buyer and seller of gold and silver goods; and even though the luminaries would not signify particular things, they signify them universally (and especially in this case). If however Saturn were not of good condition, provided that he is not otherwise made unfortunate, it signifies he will be a dyer, a merchant of lead and iron and the like, and of other works which are handled through obscure things.[997] And he will likewise be a sacrificer to divine will, and a lamenter for the dead, and he will be attracted to funerals of the dead by dressing [the bodies] and preparing for the burial; and he will engage in funeral chants by lay means, and he will gladly spend time in hidden places, and likewise he will divine there by the method of *tyrisia* (*tyrisia* was a certain communing of diviners).[998]

If however she were in the dignities of Jupiter, and Jupiter testified to her, it signifies the native will frequent the houses of religion, and will gladly stay in them, he will contract a stay with the religious, and thence he will pursue his way of life and those things which are appropriately necessary for him. Likewise he will know how to handle marriage, and to lead it wisely to effect, and from thence to pursue usefulness; and he will even be an augur.

If however Venus were in the dignities of Mars, and Mars testified to her, it will signify the native is going to have power in medical science in a competent way; and that he will delight in the bearing of arms (however more likely [in bearing them] than in their use)–delighting in bearing them on account of Mars; he will not care much to use them, on account of Venus.

---

[995] This seems to be based on a variety of statements in *Tet.* IV.4, but also represents some elaboration and paraphrasing.
[996] I.e., Saturn.
[997] *Obscuras.*
[998] This does not appear in Ptolemy.

And not only do the planets signify the native's works or professions; indeed even the signs assist them (as Ptolemy says).[999]

For if the significator of the native's work or his profession were running through one of the signs which are likened to the figures of humans, every profession which pertained to the native will be aided by that.

Indeed if it were in a sign of quadrupeds, and the native were to stick to a profession of minerals or the merchandizing of metals (namely gold and silver, copper ore, lead, iron), constructions, also the use of a pickaxe and the like, he will know them perfectly, because quadrupedal signs together help the aforesaid (and particularly the domestic ones).

And Ptolemy said the equinoctial and solstitial signs assist the professions of translation and the variation of interpretation, geometry, and likewise the of the matters of the houses of oration.[1000]

And he said, but the signs whose figures are likened to wild beasts and aquatic animals aid the professions which are for moisture (like fishing, sailing) and in which moistening agents are put, like making fresh presses[1001] and the like, and they aid the expertise of herbs (like the custodian of gardens and harvests), and of the building of ships; salted things, like salting fish in any way, and things that salt, like making salt.

And he said, but if the Moon ruled next to the place of the profession (I say, that she would have dignity in the Ascendant or in the 10th),[1002] and were going out from under the rays of the Sun, [and] after the separation from him she were first joined to Mercury, and you were to find her in Capricorn or Taurus or Cancer, this will signify that the native will be wise in subordinate sciences like in auguries; and he will become a harus-

---

[999] *Tet.* IV.4.

[1000] *Orationis*, which undoubtedly pertains to courts and legislatures, but might also refer to prayer.

[1001] *Vegentes torcularia.* An uncertain phrase. *Vegeo* pertains to living things, so perhaps Bonatti is referring to the pressing of fresh produce like apples and grapes. This phrase does not appear in Ptolemy.

[1002] Ptolemy says, "if the Moon should occupy the place pertaining to action while making [her] way from conjunction with Hermes [Mercury]." Bonatti must be reading "conjunction" as "*the* conjunction," i.e., the conjunction with the Sun. Such phrases are identical in Latin.

pex, a geomancer, a hydromancer, chiromancer, *agurgusticus*,[1003] a spatulo-
mancer,[1004] an enchanter, conjurer and sacrificer, and this in this way: for
if there were a conjunction of the aforesaid significators of the native's
work and his profession, and of the Sun and the Moon in Taurus (because it is the domicile of Venus and the exaltation of the Moon), it will
signify that the native will be a soothsayer or augur. But if it were in Capricorn (because it is the domicile of Saturn and the exaltation of Mars, and
of the triplicity of the Moon), it signifies that the native will be a sacrificer.
Indeed if it were in Cancer (because it is the domicile of the Moon) it
signifies that the native will be a hydromancer. And Ptolemy said if it
were in Sagittarius or Pisces, he will divine by the dead and will act to
move malign spirits from place to place by his incantations. But if it were
in Virgo or Scorpio, he will become an astrologer and nigromancer, and
he will judge hidden things, and he will predict the future (even if not
much, or he had no knowledge of letters). Which if it were in Aries or
Leo, or Libra, he will be a prophet or wise and an interpreter of dreams.

And this is the way which (according to Ptolemy) he enjoins us to observe,
for knowing rationally the qualities of the native's professions and their kinds.

However, you will weigh carefully the qualities of the works or professions of
the native, by their planetary significators and by their disposition, if you
consider it well. For if you were to see them well disposed, namely made
fortunate and strong, oriental, direct, in angles (and especially in the 10th or even
in the 1st), or in one of their dignities (namely domicile or exaltation or bound or
triplicity), it will signify the works or professions of the native are going to be
from dignities and strengths, and rulerships. If however you were to see them
outside the aforesaid dignities, occidental, or cadent, you will pronounce that his
professions or works, and he himself in them, will be subordinated to others—
and more so and more strongly so, if one of the malefics were to aspect the said
significators, or were elevated above them:[1005] because the native's works or
professions will be signified to be low-class and contemptible and despicable,
and that he could not be secure in them, and he will be despised in them and

---

[1003] Unknown. *Augur* means an augur; the ending *–gusticus* suggests eating or tasting, so
perhaps it refers to augurs who eat the sacred meat?
[1004] Spatulomancy (or scapulomancy) is divination by the shoulder blades of sheep, where the
different parts of the bone and cartilage signify various things.
[1005] This refers to the Hellenistic "overcoming." See Introduction and footnote to Tr. 3, Part
2, Ch. 20.

from them, and because of them. Which if that malefic were Saturn, and he were of the same triplicity with the significator of the native's profession, it will signify that this will happen from idleness and his apathy, and a cold disposition badly complexioned. But if it were Mars, and he were in a suitable sign of his own nature, this will happen because of the native's timidness, and his vileness and faint-heartedness; and he will suffer evil and destruction from thence. Indeed if both the aforesaid malefics were impeding the significators of the native's work and profession, his works and his professions will be displeasing to practically everyone indifferently and always.

You will observe whether the native is going to have a multitude or scarcity of works or professions, and whether he will be called or not called to professions or works to be made or exercised, from the nature or the disposition of the significators of works. For if they were well disposed, they will indicate good; if, however, badly, they will promise the contrary. Indeed if the benefics were to aspect them or were elevated over them,[1006] the native's works and his professions will be signified to be suitable and likewise favorable, and that the native will be commended from thence, and he will be secure in them and because of them, nor will he suffer some shame or disgrace because of them, but [rather] honor and usefulness in proportion as the work or profession were in his own nature, and the more so if Jupiter and Venus were to aspect–and on that occasion he will be raised up, and will be called a master in virtue of it.

Chapter 2: On the force[1007] of the native and his prosperity, and on his duties and on his kingdom

If[1008] you wished to explore concerning the native's force and prosperity, and his duties and his kingdom, look at the Sun in diurnal nativities (indeed the Moon and Saturn in nocturnal nativities), and the 10th, and its Lord, and the Part of the Kingdom,[1009] and the planet in whose domicile you were to find [the Part]. And if you were to see the said significators (namely the Sun and the Moon, or either of them) in angles, namely made fortunate and strong, joined to benefics (or even to others well disposed), and with reception, and the oriental

---

[1006] This refers to the Hellenistic "overcoming." See Introduction and footnote to Tr. 3, Part 2, Ch. 20.
[1007] *Valedutine.* See previous footnote in Ch. 1.
[1008] Here Bonatti begins to follow *JN*, pp. 53*ff.*
[1009] This is probably the second or third or fourth Part of the 10th house (Tr. 8, Part 2, Ch. 13).

ones were aspecting the Sun, and the occidental ones were aspecting the Moon and Saturn,[1010] this will signify the native is undoubtedly going to be a king. Which if it were not as I said concerning the luminaries, then look at the Lord of the 10th, and the planet in whose domicile the Part of the Kingdom is, and look at the 10th and the Ascendant and the planetary al-mubtazz over the said places[1011] (whether [the al-mubtazzes] were one or more), and its commingling over the Ascendant or over the 10th, or with their Lords. Because if there were those things which I told you, or a portion of them, it will signify the native is going to be a king or prince similar to a king, and that his dignity will be found to last a long time. And if the benefics were to aspect the luminaries, as was said, and they were in angles, or they were to aspect some one of the aforesaid significators appearing in the 10th, and the significator were well disposed (namely, made fortunate and strong)–and the more so if the benefics aspecting him appeared above the earth; and more again if they were joined corporally with him in the 10th; and more strongly so if reception intervenes– and the luminaries were in masculine signs, and the said significators (or a majority of them) were well disposed, it will signify the native is going to have a great name and great force, and even great power, and likewise be a king (or even at least similar to a king). If however they did not aspect each other–the Lord of the Ascendant with the aforesaid al-mubtazz–it will signify the native is going to have little power and little force, and his interaction with kings and great men will be little.

If[1012] however other planets besides the luminaries were to appear in the angles, or they were to have a commingling with planets appearing in the angles, and the Sun were in a masculine sign and the Moon in a feminine sign, and only one of them were in an angle, it will signify the native is not going to be a king, but [rather will have] commands in which it will be permitted for him to pour

---

[1010] Abu 'Ali says, "oriental from the Sun and occidental from the Moon," not mentioning Saturn. This portion of the passage itself derives from Tet. IV.3., which reads "For when both the lights are in masculine zōidia, and again both of them, or even one of them, are pivotal [angular], and especially when the light of the sect also has the five stars spear-bearing, the Sun having those which are east, the Moon those which are west, the offspring will be kings." Clearly then this refers to Ptolemy's doruphoria (or dastūrīya), but the account here differs from Ptolemy's (and not just in the use of Saturn). Ptolemy is only concerned doruphoria in relation to the luminary whose authority it is, not with both luminaries: in the case of the Sun, he wants all five non-luminaries to be oriental of the Sun (rise before the Sun), and in the case of the Moon he wants all five to be occidental of her (set after the Moon). Thanks to Robert Schmidt (private communication) for his help on this point.

[1011] Loca.

[1012] Tet. IV.3.

forth the blood of the wicked and the guilty, and to hang and decapitate them, and he will be able to kill by all other methods by means of his command. And such people are those to whom kings commit their own positions in the affairs of a kingdom, and they make them their proxies, and they give them the authority of command, and [the kings] ratify what [the deputies] do.

Which if the aforesaid stars [planets] were not in the angles, nor the planets which testify to the luminaries, nor did the angles belong to their *haym*,[1013] this will signify the native is going to be renowned, but his force or his power will exceed[1014] the power of him who completely lacks a command, for his rulership will like that of him who wields [power] after the manner of a great and powerful lord.

Indeed if the luminaries were not in the angles, but there were planets in them who testified to them,[1015] or had a commingling with them, it will signify the native should not be of such great force in the aforesaid affairs, but he will be forceful[1016] in the command of cities and the like, and he will know even in a middling way how to set the order of his own house, and likewise his life.

Indeed 'Ali said[1017] if the luminaries were not in the angles, but very many of the stars were in them, surrounding[1018] or uniting with them, then the native will be of middling force;[1019] but if the luminaries were there and the surrounding stars [were] in their own dignities, he will be middling in the disposition of matters which pertain to cities. For example, if Mars were the giver of substance, he will be of middling acquisition, and in the harmonizing of the weights and measures of the city. If however it were Jupiter, he will be middling in practicing justice. Indeed if it were Saturn, he will be middling in the activity of building. Indeed if it were Venus, he will be middling in religion. Which if it were Mercury, he will be middling in writing.

[1013] See *Tet.* IV.3. I have let Bonatti's Latin stand, although he or his Latin translation of *Tet.* is confused. First Ptolemy implies that the luminaries *are* in the angles (contrary to Bonatti); then he says, "If however…the attendant planets are neither angular nor witnessing [testifying] to the angles…" I do not understand where Bonatti is getting the word *ayz* (*haym*).

[1014] Omitting *non*.

[1015] Ptolemy says "but most of the spear-bearing stars are either pivotal or configured with the pivots." We cannot know whether by "them" Bonatti meant "the angles" or "the luminaries," since Bonatti already assumes that *doruphoria* or *dastūrīya* will involve an aspect to the luminaries.

[1016] *Valens.* Or, "strong."

[1017] I believe this refers to 'Ali ibn Ridwān.

[1018] *Circumdantes.* This verb undoubtedly refers to the planets who act as the bodyguards or spear-bearers of the luminaries, as the Latin *Tet.* also uses this verb.

[1019] *Valentiae.*

And ['Ali] said[1020] if the luminaries and the surrounding stars were not in their own dignities, the native will be middling in his own condition, as for instance in merchant activities, and so with the rest of the duties.

And Ptolemy said[1021] if all of the stars which surrounded the luminaries held[1022] none of the angles, the native will be miserable and unlucky in his works. Which if the luminaries appeared neither in the angles nor in masculine signs, nor did even the benefics surround them, he will be in an extreme of wretchedness and a lack of prosperity.

And he said,[1023] therefore the path by which we must proceed in the investigation of these matters, this [path] is what we have shown, in the increase and decrease of [the native's] force. However, we must observe very many qualities which there are between increase and decrease, by those things which were found in that sort of particular variation[1024] which the luminaries have (and the stars [planets] which surround them, and who disposed in the surrounding ones). For if the [planetary] dispositors[1025] were the Lords of the sect (of the Sun or the Moon), or [they were] benefics, the native will last more in force. Indeed if the stars which were contrary to the sect of the luminaries were the dispositors,[1026] or they were malefics, the native's force will be weak, and will be ended quickly, and will easily pass away.[1027]

And Ptolemy said[1028] the matters of future force are to be observed from the peculiar qualities of the stars which surround the luminaries:

For if Saturn were the dispositor of the native's prosperity which is going to come to him, and he were of good condition and well disposed (namely made fortunate and strong), it will signify the native's fortune and

---

[1020] Again, I believe this is 'Ali ibn Ridwān.
[1021] *Tet.* IV.3.
[1022] Ptolemy says "associated with," so he must include whole-sign aspects, too.
[1023] *Tet.* IV.3.
[1024] *Alteratio.*
[1025] I.e., the spear-bearers.
[1026] I.e., the spear-bearers.
[1027] I have altered this sentence to match Ptolemy's meaning, since Bonatti or his Latin edition of Ptolemy has unintentionally garbled it. Bonatti's own sentence [using the full version of 1491] reads: "For if the [planetary] dispositors were the Lords of the sect [*ayz*] of the place of the Sun and of the Moon or they were the Lords of the sect [*ayz*] of another benefic, the native will last more in force." Ptolemy is saying we should see whether the luminary whose authority it is, is the Sun or the Moon–and see whether the spear-bearers for that luminary are (a) of that same sect, *viz.*, diurnal planets for the Sun in diurnal charts, nocturnal ones for the Moon in nocturnal charts, or (b) benefics.
[1028] *Tet.* IV.3.

his force and his prosperity [will be] because of inheritances which will fall back to him,[1029] and even because of another congregating or accumulation of substance. If however he were disposed weakly, what he signifies will be much below the aforesaid.

Indeed if Jupiter or Venus were to dispose the force and prosperity of the native, he will approach it in pleasant things and lively things, and donations given to him, and honors conferred upon him, and by his magnanimity.

Which if Mars appeared as its significator, it will signify his force and prosperity is going to come because of victory over enemies or those contrary [to the native] and because of those subject to him who fear him and respect him with cause.

But if Mercury were the ruler of the force, it signifies that he will be raised up because of his intellect and instruction and the arranging of matters, and he will be made prosperous, and will be held [to be] forceful.[1030]

You will even look to see whether the Lord of the first is joined with the Lord of the 10th, or *vice versa*. For if the Lord of the 1st is joined to the Lord of the 10th (namely so that [the Lord of the 1st] is lighter than [the Lord of the 10th]) by a trine or sextile aspect with reception (or without reception), or from a square with reception, it signifies the native is going to achieve good and usefulness and profit because of kings and from kings, but not without his own inquiries and petition. If however the Lord of the 7th were lighter and is joined to the Lord of the 1st from the said aspects, it signifies that he is going to achieve the aforesaid without his own inquiries or petition—and the more so, if reception were to intervene, nor were they cadent or otherwise made unfortunate.

And Abu 'Ali said[1031] if this application were from the angles (and especially if it were from the Ascendant or the Midheaven), the dignity which he will pursue will be great and be given a surname.[1032] And he said, if the

---

[1029] *Recasuris.*
[1030] *Valens habebitur.*
[1031] *JN*, p. 54.
[1032] This probably means an official title, like "Earl of ____."

Lord of the Ascendant were in an angle, and the Lord of the Midheaven cadent, it signifies the native will have a great name, and his work is low-class. And if the Lord of the Midheaven were in angles, and the Lord of the Ascendant cadent, it signifies the greatness of the work and he [himself] will be low-class. If however both were cadent, it signifies the lowness both of the native and of the work.

And he said[1033] if the Lord of the Ascendant were in the Midheaven, it signifies he is born of a family of kings (or his commingling).[1034] And if the aspect which were between them is a good one, it signifies there is friendship between the native and the king; and if it were a bad one, it signifies enmity and severity.

And [Abu 'Ali] said,[1035] if indeed there were no application between the Lord of the Ascendant and the Lord of the Midheaven, look at the application which is between the Lord of the Ascendant and the Sun, and judge upon that, just as you have judged upon the application of the Lord of the Ascendant and the Lord of the Midheaven above.

And [Abu 'Ali] said[1036] if the Lord of the Ascendant were conjoined to the Sun, it signifies that native is an intimate of the king, and faithful, and knowing his secrets, and received in his words toward him.

And [Abu 'Ali] said[1037] if the Lord of the Ascendant were one of the superior planets, and he were in the Midheaven, applied to its Lord, it signifies he is commingled both with nobles and kings, and at the ready, and prepared, or taking his place[1038] around their dignity. If indeed one of the inferior planets were the Lord of the Ascendant, appearing in the Midheaven, and applied to its Lord, it signifies he has some office [or duty] of the king below that which I said before.

And[1039] if there were an application between the Lord of the Ascendant and one of the luminaries, it signifies commingling with kings; and if it were with reception, he will attain the greatest good for that (but lacking this, not so).

[1033] JN, p. 54.
[1034] I.e., he mixes with royal people even though he himself is not royal.
[1035] JN, p. 54.
[1036] JN, p. 54.
[1037] JN, p. 54.
[1038] *Consiscari, conficere vel consistere.*
[1039] JN, p. 55.

And[1040] for the force of the native, look at the planet which has an application with the Lord of the Ascendant, or who is the Lord of the domicile in
which the Part of the Native's Work and His Kingdom[1041] is: which if you were
to find him in his own exaltation, it will signify the native will have force and
greatness and the title of his force, and a commingling with kings and great
men. But if he were in his own domicile, it will signify something below this,
and the commingling of the native with those who are below the aforesaid. And
if he were in his own bound, it signifies yet something below this. If however he
were in his own triplicity, it will signify again something below this. But if he
were in his face, it will signify yet something very much less than the aforesaid.
If however the Lord of the Part were void in course, it signifies much ferality[1042]
of the native, and his solitude, and that he will love solitary places, according to
the nature of the sign which he then occupied.

Then[1043] look at the Part of the Work of the Native and his Kingdom, and its
Lord: which if you were to find [the Lord] in a good place from the Ascendant,
free from the malefics and from other impediments, or he and the Lord of the
Ascendant [were] in the angles, free from the aforesaid impediments, it will
signify the native is going to be of much work and little rest.

And 'Umar said,[1044] also look at the Sun: which if he were in the eastern
quarters, the native will find honor and sublimity and a kingdom in his youth.
And if it were in western ones, this will be in his old age, and at the end of his
life. However, you will look at his being [or condition] in his work, and at what
time he will be of greater dignity and honor, from the Lords of the triplicity of
the Sun; which if all three were strong, his kingdom and honor will last for the
whole time of his life. If however you were to find all of them weak, say that he
will suffer detriment and weakness and misfortune for the whole time of his life.
If however the first appeared weak, misfortunes will surround him and he will
be of fragile memory[1045] in the first part of his life. Indeed if it were made

---

[1040] *JN*, p. 55.
[1041] Abu 'Ali calls this the Part of Work. According Holden (*JN* p. 55 n.108), this is taken
from the Sun to Jupiter by day (the reverse by night), and is projected from the Ascendant.
This agrees with Bonatti's Part of Work (Tr. 8, Part 2, Ch. 13, the eleventh Part of the 10th
House).
[1042] *Feralitatis.* Like *feralis*, this seems to have to do with a lack of social connections, rather
than with having destructive behavior.
[1043] *JN*, p. 55.
[1044] *TBN*, pp. 77-78.
[1045] This might mean that he will be unknown and not remembered by *other* people, since
honor and reputation depend on recognition by others.

fortunate in that same third, you will pronounce [that] prosperous things will happen to him; the same in the second and third.

And 'Umar said[1046] if Saturn were in an angle (at night), or Mars (in the day), and especially in the Ascendant or the Midheaven, there will not be a [social] association or work or kingdom up until the satisfying of the lesser years of the planet. Which if it were to go past the end [of the time allotted by the lesser years], it will be according to the ascension of the sign in which the planet is.[1047] And he said[1048] if Mars were in the angles (and especially in the Ascendant or in the Midheaven) in the day, the native will be endangered because of his work, and his body will be whipped, and he will die. And he said if the Sun were in the opposition of the Moon, the native will not direct a kingdom, nor a profession[1049] or a chief place; and if it were directed, the wealthy and great men of that region will act contrary to him.

And ['Umar] said[1050] if you were to see a work or profession or kingdom is signified for the native, look at the planetary al-mubtazz over the Midheaven and the Sun and the Part of Work or Kingdom. And see of what substance is that al-mubtazz over those places,[1051] because his work or kingdom or the native's duty will be according to what is signified by the aforesaid al-mubtazz. For if it were the Sun, the native will be a prince or king, and he will be a wise arranger of matters, and of good discretion. And 'Umar said you will speak likewise of the nature of this al-mubtazz and of those aspecting it, whether he were one or more (namely two or three). And he said, likewise look at the al-mubtazz and see which of the planets aspects him, and commingle the work of them with the work of the al-mubtazz, and speak according to this.

And Ptolemy said[1052] even that the native will then have a profession if there were an oriental planet in the morning in the Midheaven with the Moon, or [if] the al-mubtazz over the Midheaven were oriental; and if this [al-mubtazz] did not

---

[1046] TBN, p. 78.
[1047] A rare indication of the continued use of the Hellenistic "ascensional times" in medieval prediction.
[1048] Reading dixit for dixi ("I said").
[1049] Opus.
[1050] TBN, p. 79.
[1051] Loca.
[1052] According to TBN, p. 80; cf. Tet. IV.4. Ptolemy says we must consider "both that star nearest the Sun which has already made a morning appearance [i.e., oriental but not under the beams or combust], as well as the one upon the Midheaven, when this star has the application of the Moon most of all." Schmidt believes this latter clause means that if more than one planet is in the Midheaven, we are to prefer the one with the closest application with the Moon.

aspect so, there will not be a profession for the generality of those natives.[1053] And ['Umar] said: I however say that the *al-mubtazz* over the Midheaven, if he were commingled with the *al-mubtazz* over the Ascendant, or agreed [with it], they will not lack a profession; and better than that if the *al-mubtazz* were oriental from the Sun and from the Ascendant or from either. For in the substance of the profession, in general [the ancients] looked from the quality of Mars, Venus, and Mercury toward one another, and in their commingling and aspect. And he said the qualities[1054] are like when a planet is in the square aspect of another, or a sextile aspect, or with it in the same sign.

Indeed,[1055] certain sages wanted that the angle of the Midheaven should fall in the 11th,[1056] and they dreaded that it should fall in the 9th, for its falling in the 9th subtracts the quality of the dignity of the divisor, and its falling in the 11th increases its honor and its nature [or condition]. Likewise, all places,[1057] if they were removed toward the receding and great places[1058] (like the 6th and the 2nd and the 8th and the 12th), it will be bad; for the 11th in the 12th is bad, and in the Midheaven, good.[1059]

Chapter 3: In what way you should look in the matter of the mother

Since, in the matter of the father, it is looked at from the fourth of the nativity of the native, and for the wife it is looked at from the 7th from the house of the man, [therefore] should we want to look in the matter of his mother, it is necessary that in the matter of the mother we look from the 10th, because the 10th is the 7th from the 4th.[1060]

[1053] *Universitati eorum natorum non erit magisterium.*

[1054] Reading *qualitates* for *quantitates.*

[1055] *TBN*, p. 80.

[1056] *Angulus medii coeli in undecima.* Based on the previous account of the Midheaven being "removed," this must mean that it is acceptable for the cusp of the Midheaven to be on the same sign as that of the 11th. Likewise, it would be bad for the cusp of the Midheaven to be on the same sign as that of a cadent cusp (here, the 9th). But by itself the statement is ambiguous. If the Midheaven is the tenth whole sign, then this should refer to "the angle of the [tenth whole sign] in the 11th [quadrant house]." Or, if the "11th" means the eleventh *domicile*, then the sentence means "the angle of the [quadrant cusp of the] Midheaven in the eleventh domicile."

[1057] *Loca.*

[1058] *Magnalia loca.* This is a euphemism for the cadents.

[1059] These statements present special problems, since *loca* seems like it has been used to signify signs (in the Greek fashion)–but a sign cannot be in another sign.

[1060] For more on the mother, see the material in the 4th House, Chs. 4-7.

Whence, if it should happen that you must look in the matter of the mother, look at the *hīlāj* [of the mother] from the 10th and its Lord, likewise from the Moon and Venus, and likewise from the Part of the Mother and the planet in whose domicile it stood firmly in, and the planet who is the *al-mubtazz* over some one of the aforesaid places: because it will be regarded as the significator of the mother.

Then look to see which of the planets is the significator of the years of the mother,[1061] and if some one of the others furnishes some years or months to him, or subtracts from him from its own years or months.[1062] For if one of the benefics were to aspect [the significator of the years] from a trine or sextile aspect, and it were of good condition and well disposed (namely made fortunate[1063] and strong), and it were in the angles, it will furnish its own lesser years to him, and on top of that so many months as are his middle years; and more strongly so, if it received him. If however [the benefic] were in the succeedents, instead of years it will furnish months to him. Indeed if it did not receive him from the said aspects, it will furnish its own lesser years to him, but it will not furnish months. But if [the benefic] were impeded, it will not furnish years to him, but instead of years it will furnish months.

Indeed if the one who aspected him were a malefic, and it were to aspect him from a square aspect or from the opposition, it will subtract from him from its own years, according to the number of its own lesser years. Which if the malefic were of good condition and well disposed (namely made fortunate and strong), it will subtract from him only according to one-third of its own lesser years.

After this,[1064] you will look, in the status and force of the mother and of her condition or work or profession and dignity and her fortune, from the *dastūrīya* of the planets from the Moon. For if you were to see Mars or Venus in the *dastūrīya* of the Moon, or Mercury (if he were joined with one of them), and they were of good condition and well disposed (namely made fortunate and strong),

---

[1061] This paragraph is similar to those on the father in the 4th House, Chs. 6 and 8, and is derived from *JN*, p. 39. It is not made clear here, but Abu 'Ali instructs us to find both a *hīlāj* (from the various universal significators of the mother: Venus/Moon, the Part of the Mother, the degree of the Midheaven) and an *al-kadukhadāh* (in the usual fashion). The *al-kadukhadāh* is the "significator of the years" mentioned in this paragraph. But if none of these universal significators is able to be the mother's *hīlāj*, we are to direct the degree of the Moon to the benefics and the malefics to determine her longevity and quality of life.

[1062] In what follows, it is unclear to me whether we are looking for the absolute years of the mother's life, or perhaps for the number of years she will live after the native is born. See below.

[1063] Reading *fortunata* for *fortuna*.

[1064] Compare this paragraph with that on the father in the 4th House, Chs. 1 and 5.

this will signify the increase of the mother's dignity, and her exaltation, and the greatness of her value and honor. Then look at the *hīlāj* of the mother, and the planet from which you took it,[1065] and you will direct it to the places[1066] of the benefics and malefics; and in what place you were to see it reach to the benefics, judge good in all the aforesaid from what is signified by that house [domicile?]. If however you were to see it reach the malefics, the contrary of all the aforesaid will be judged to come to the mother from what is signified by that house.

And 'Umar said[1067] that if the Moon and the Part of the Mother were not in the place of the *hīlāj*, and you wished to know the place which you will direct for the mother, you will direct from the degree of the Moon: as often as it arrives at the malefics, it will signify danger and the death of the mother.

After this, look at the concord and love of the mother toward the son, and her hatred against him, from the *al-mubtazz* over the Ascendant and the *al-mubtazz* over the place of the mother. Which if they were harmonious between themselves and loving in turn toward one another, judge there will be love between them. If however they were hating each other, you will judge the contrary. You will even look regarding the harmony between the native's father and his mother, and you will pronounce according to what you saw the harmony of their significators between them was going to be.

However, concerning the death of the mother, whether it is in the near future or remote, Dorotheus said[1068] that it is signified by the entrance of the *al-mubtazz* [of the mother] below the earth. And Abu 'Ali said,[1069] in the life of the mother you will look (of him whose nativity is diurnal) from Venus: which if she were aspecting the Ascendant, direct her to the bodies of the malefics and their rays by degrees of ascension, giving one year to every degree. If however Venus did not aspect the Ascendant, and the Moon did aspect it, direct [the Moon] just as you would have directed Venus if she had been fit to direct. Indeed if the Moon did not aspect, then direct the degree of the Midheaven. And you will begin in diurnal nativities from Venus first, then from the Moon,

---

[1065] Bonatti seems to treat *hīlāj* here as a function, and the planet as the agent of that function–he does not seem to be speaking as two different planets.
[1066] *Loca.*
[1067] *TBN,* p. 64.
[1068] According to *TBN,* p. 64. Dorotheus himself (*Carmen* I.15) says this is to be taken by the primary motion of the heaven, not secondary motion through the zodiac. So if, by the rotation of the heaven the Sun goes below the earth first, the father will die first; if the Moon, the mother. But Dorotheus is interested in which parent will die first, not whether the death of the mother will come soon or not (besides which, Dorotheus has much more to say).
[1069] *JN,* p. 38.

afterwards from the degree of the Midheaven. Indeed in nocturnal ones, you will begin first from the Moon, then from Venus, afterwards from the degree of the Midheaven.

Then[1070] look to see if the years signified by the *hīlāj*[1071] were equal to the years signified by the *al-mubtazz* over the degree in which Venus is, or over the degree in which is the Lord of the domicile in which she is (in diurnal nativities); indeed in nocturnal ones, [the *al-mubtazz*] in the degree in which the Moon is, or in the degree in which is the Lord of the domicile in which she is, and also in the day and the night [the *al-mubtazz*] in the degree of the Midheaven, or in the degree in which is its Lord. For by this, the death of the mother of that native will be signified to be before the completion of one year from the day of the nativity.

However, you will look at the condition of the mother from the Lords of the triplicity of the sign that the Moon then possessed. For, according to how you were to see them disposed, you will judge according to that (namely concerning good or about the contrary of the good); because if all were of good condition and well disposed, made fortunate and strong, you will pronounce there will always be good for the whole time of her life. If however [they were disposed] badly, they will judge evil. Indeed if the first one, it will show its signification in the beginning of life, from the nativity of that native. If however the second one, in the middle of life. Indeed if the third one, you will predict that which it would signify, in the last part of the mother's life.

You will perceive by means of what death the mother will die (namely easy or burdened or unusual), from the condition of the Moon and from the Lord of the domicile in which she is, and likewise from the Part of the Mother and its Lord, and from the Part of the Death of the Mother[1072] and its Lord. Because if they were of good condition and well disposed, they will judge a common and praiseworthy death. Indeed if they were impeded and badly disposed, they will signify the mother is going to die by a bad and strange death. However, the significator of her death in her own nativity will interpose his portions.

You will perceive which one (between the father and the mother) will die first, from their significators. For the one which first felt the misfortune of

---

[1070] Compare with the material on the father (4th House, Chs. 6 and 7).
[1071] I believe this still refers to the mother's *al-kadukhadāh* or "significator of years," mentioned above. Abu 'Ali does not call this planet the *hīlāj* of the mother.
[1072] See Tr. 8, Part 2, Chap.13.

combustion, or who first approached the angle of the 4th house of the nativity of the native, it will signify[1073] that one is going to predecease [the other].[1074]

[1073] Reading *significabit* for *significabitur.*
[1074] See above note on Dorotheus.

ON THE ELEVENTH HOUSE

Chapter 1: On the native's friends, and likewise on his good fortune and his hope

Having looked, in the chapter which preceded this one, regarding the matter of the native's profession, and regarding his duties and his force, and likewise regarding the matter of the mother, *etc.*, it seems apt and fitting to me in this present chapter that we should treat of the matter of friends, and his good fortune, and regarding his hope, and to make mention of all these things.

Whence if you did not[1075] wish to be fatigued concerning of the aforesaid in someone's nativity, you will look in this way. Indeed you will consider the 11th from the Ascendant of the nativity of whatever native, and its Lord: also the Part of Friends[1076] and its Lord, and likewise Venus (who naturally signifies friends, because we delight in them). Likewise you will look at the planets which are in the 11th and in the house [domicile?] in which the Lord of the 11th is, and the Lord of the domicile in which [the Lord of the 11th] is, and [the Lord of the domicile] in which the Part of Friends is, and the [the Lord of the domicile in which is] the planet in whose domicile the [Part] is. Likewise you will look at the planet in whose domicile Venus herself is. You will even look at the luminaries and their Lords (namely of the Sun in the day, the Moon in the night).

Which, having inspected them, you will see which of the planets is the *al-mubtazz* over any of the aforesaid places, and which of them were of better condition and better disposition, because you could take from him the signification of the matter of the native's friends and his good fortune, and likewise his hope, by beginning first from the 11th and its Lord, then from the planet which is in the 11th, after that from Venus, then from the Part of Friends and its Lord, then from the Lord of the domicile in which Venus is, then from the luminary whose authority it was, indeed lastly from the Lord of the domicile in which that luminary is.[1077]

1075 Adding *non*.
1076 Taken from the Moon to Mercury (by day and night), and projected from the Ascendant. See Tr. 8, Part 2, Ch. 14.
1077 The two lists differ. What they have in common are the following nine items: (a) the 11th, (b) the Lord of the 11th, (c) planets in the 11th, (d) the Part of Friends, (e) Lord of the Part of Friends, (f) Venus, (g) the Lord of Venus, (h) the luminary whose authority it is, (i) the Lord of that luminary. But the first list also adds: (j) planets in the house [domicile?] where the Lord of the 11th is, (k) the Lord of the Lord of the 11th, (l) the Lord of the Lord of the Part of

For if there were benefics in the 11th, and there were a friendly commingling between the Lord of the 11th and the Lord of the Ascendant (or an application by conjunction or from any friendly aspect), and especially with reception (which would come to be from the domiciles or the exaltations, or from two of the other lesser dignities), it will signify the native is going to have a multitude of friends loving him—and the more so, if the 11th house [domicile?] were Cancer or Scorpio or Pisces. If however the 11th house [domicile?] were Aries or Taurus or Libra or Sagittarius or Capricorn or Aquarius, they will diminish the number of the native's friends by one-fourth. Indeed if the 11th house [domicile?] were Gemini or Leo or Virgo, they will diminish the number of his friends by one-third. And if there were no benefics in the 11th, but they were to aspect it from the noted (or praiseworthy) aspects, and the benefics were of good condition and well disposed (namely made fortunate and strong), they will signify practically the same that was said about the number or multitude of the native's friends. If however it was not what was said concerning the 11th house [domicile?], you will consider its Lord: for you will pronounce on the matter of the native's friends toward him, according to how you were to see [the Lord of the 11th] disposed, and [according to] the planet in whose domicile you were to find him.

You will even look at the Part of Friends and its Lord: which if you were to find them (or either of them) well disposed, you could judge concerning the matter of friends from him—for they will indicate that good will come to the native because of friends.

Then look at Venus: which if she were of good condition and well disposed, and she were aspecting the Ascendant or its Lord, or the 11th or its Lord by a friendly aspect, it signifies the native is going to have many friends, and for the most part of the feminine sex, from whom usefulness and good will follow,[1078] and the friends will be made fortunate in their own right.[1079]

Likewise, look at the Lord of the domicile in which Venus is, because he will assist what is signified in the good of the friends.

But if the luminaries [and] their Lords were well disposed, you will not doubt [but that it will] do the same. For if the Sun were of good condition, and well disposed, it signifies that the majority of the friends will be wealthy and noble, namely of those who are fit for a kingdom.

Friends. Surely, though, the inclusion of these extra items would further cloud the issue with too much information.

[1078] Following 'Umar. Again, Bonatti seems to be using this verb ungrammatically.

[1079] *Pro seipsis.*

If however the 11th house [domicile?] belonged to one of the seven planets,[1080] it signifies that the native's friends will be according to the substance and
what is signified by him whose house was the 11th.

For if it were the domicile of Saturn, the native's friends will be according
to the image and being and disposition of Saturn: for they will be old
men, slaves, Jews, and other low-class persons.

Indeed if it were the domicile of Jupiter, they will be according to his
being and disposition or image, and they will be nobles or bishops, and
those like Jupiter.

Indeed if it were the domicile of Mars, they will be according to the nature and disposition of Mars, and his image and his being–namely princes
and the bellicose.

But if it were the domicile of the Sun, they will be according to the nature
and disposition and being of the Sun and his image, and they will be
nobles, kings, and the wealthy, as was said.

And if it were the domicile of Venus, they will be according to the nature
and disposition and being of Venus and her image (like women and effeminate men).

But if it were the domicile of Mercury, they will be according to the being
and nature and disposition of Mercury and his image, and they will be the
wise and merchants and writers.

If however it were the domicile of the Moon, then the native's friends will
be signified according the nature and disposition of the Moon, and likewise her being and her image.

And if all of the aforesaid significators (or the majority of them) were in fixed
signs, it signifies that the native's friends will love him, and their friendship and
delight is firm and constant and will endure. If however they were in bicorporeal

---

[1080] This clause is stated oddly, but Bonatti is drawing on *JN*, p. 58. He means, "See to which
of the seven planets the 11th belongs; if it belongs to Saturn," *etc.*

signs, it will signify the middling [quality] of the aforesaid and their durability. But if they were in movable signs, it signifies that his friends will go away from his friendship quickly, and that they will be made contrary to him, and will be inimical to him.

And ʿUmar said[1081] if the *al-mubtazz* over the Ascendant were a malefic, and he were to harm the *al-mubtazz* over the house of friendship, evil will come to the friends from the native. And if it were to the contrary, say the contrary. And he said, indeed if these significators were made fortunate by one another, [judge] good and respect and profit. Then he said, if however the Lord of the 11th did not aspect the 11th, nor did Venus aspect the Lord of her own domicile, nor the Lord of the Part of Friends the Part of Friends, the native will be of those who have no commingling with friends, nor will be he sociable with men, but he will live mainly solitarily, [and] gladly. And if there were benefics in the 11th, then you could judge that his friends will be good and of good suitableness, and of good habits [or morals], and that they will abound in riches (and the more strongly so, if a benefic were in the 12th).[1082] If however there were a malefic in it, this will signify that the native's friends will be bad, and of much discord and want.

Chapter 2: On the kinds of friends

And Ptolemy said[1083] that friendships and enmities are of three kinds,[1084] namely either [1] on account of the harmony of spirits by which it is necessary [that] a man should love his partner;[1085] or [2] on account of profit, or [3] because joy or sorrow draws them together.

And he said[1086] those who love each other on account of a harmony of spirits, these are those in whose nativities it happens [thus], like if the Sun and the Moon have cross-changed from their places. That is, that the Sun

---

[1081] *TBN*, p. 82.
[1082] I.e, because the 12th is the 2nd from the 11th.
[1083] Per *TBN*, p. 83; but cf. *Tet.* IV.7 here and below.
[1084] This doctrine comes originally from Aristotle's *Nichomachean Ethics*.
[1085] Ptolemy is referring to Aristotle's "perfect" or "complete" friendship. In this sort of friendship, friends love each other for their own moral goodness and for the goodness they inspire in each other. Aristotle says such friends' souls and values are so intertwined that they are like two souls in one body—hence the synastry-based technique by Ptolemy below.
[1086] Per *TBN*, p. 83.

is in the sign or in the place[1087] in which the Moon was in the nativity of one of them, and the Moon is in the sign or in the place in which the Sun was in the nativity of the other;[1088] or their significators[1089] or luminaries are in trine or sextile aspect (and this will come to be more strongly if reception were to intervene). Then their friendship will be constant and naturally durable (and again more if one of the benefics were to aspect the said significators or the luminaries in the aforesaid nativities, without the aspect of one of the malefics).

Then he said,[1090] those whose fondness were on account of joy or sorrow, will be those to whom it will come [thus], like if their Ascendant is one and the same sign, or the [ascending] sign of the nativity of one were to aspect the [ascending] sign of the nativity of the other from a trine or sextile aspect, and the benefics were to aspect the sign of each nativity from a trine or sextile aspect, with the aspects of the malefics being completely removed.

However, those whose friendship were harmonized [or united] on account of profit, are those in whose nativities the Part of Fortune is in the sign of one, in which it is in the nativity of the other (or in its triplicity, or in its trine or sextile aspect); and there will be concord between them, and they will make money from one and the same matter or merchant activity, and each will be eager to make money and profit from thence, and their friendship will come down [into being] for that reason, and delight will fall between them. Or, something unlucky will happen to them (or to either of them) from one and the same cause, because of which each one will be in pain, and one will have compassion for the other,[1091] and for that reason they will become friends—which will happen if the benefics

---

[1087] It is unclear whether "place" is a synonym for "sign." Since Hellenistic astrologers called the whole sign houses "places," could this mean that the Sun is in the 3rd "place" (whole sign house) of one, and the Moon is in the 3rd "place" of the other? Or does he just mean "in the same sign"?

[1088] In other words, just as the Sun and Moon pertain to life and the soul, and form a natural pair, so such people have the ability to form a natural pair and enjoy united souls.

[1089] Perhaps this means the *al-mubtazz* of the figure, the *al-mubtazz* of the Ascendant, or else even the *hīlāj?*

[1090] *TBN*, pp. 83-84.

[1091] *Compatietur.* This verb, like compassion, means "to suffer with."

were to aspect the Ascendants of their nativities or their significators, without the aspect of some malefic.

Moreover, if the *al-mubtazz*[1092] of each nativity were to aspect each other from the noted aspects, they will be friends and love each other (and the more strongly so, if each were to receive the other). Which if their aspect were from the square or the opposition (and especially if they did not receive each other), evil wills will fall between them for one and the same reason–and the more strongly so, if one of the malefics were to aspect those significators; and again more if the aspect were to come between [them] without reception; and more and more, if it were from the square or from the opposition, or the conjunction were corporal.

Indeed if the malefic which aspected[1093] were Saturn, and he were in some sign in the nativity of each of them, such that it is the domicile (or exaltation, or bound or triplicity) of the significator of the nativity of one of them, and [it is] some dignity of the other one (namely of the aforesaid [dignities]), and the aspect were a trine or a sextile (and more strongly so if reception intervened), there will be friendship between the natives by reason of waters or lands or another estate, or on account of old men or old age, or on account of fathers who will be the occasion for their friendship, or on account of other suitable things or familiarities coming between them. But if the aspect were from the opposition or square aspect, or it were a corporal conjunction (and more strongly so if the conjunction or aspect were without reception), enmities will fall between them, and likewise discords and contentions because of the aforesaid reasons.

1092 It is unclear what Bonatti means by this (or indeed what his source means). This passage seems to be drawn from *Tet.* IV.7, where Ptolemy wants us to compare the mutual configurations of four places between the two friends' charts: the places of the luminaries, the Lot of Fortune, and the Ascendant. Bonatti and later writers seem to have taken this to be an instruction to compare one of three things: (1) the *hilājes* of each chart (since the *hilāj* is typically gotten through one of these). But why didn't Bonatti use the word *hilāj*? Or they thought (2) we are to find the most authoritative planet or *al-mubtazz* of all of these places. Or, (3) something like the *al-mubtazz* of the figure is meant (though note that Bonatti never describes how to find it, if he even recognizes it). Of course, Bonatti could simply be calling the Lord of the Ascendant an *al-mubtazz*.

1093 Although he has just spoken about malefics, the following list shows that Bonatti wants to expand the description to include all possible *al-mubtazzes*.

If however it were Mars, the aforesaid will happen by reason of something of those things which are signified through Mars.

Which if one of the benefics were to aspect him,[1094] and it were Jupiter, the friendships and agreements between them will happen by reason of substance or the acquisition and money, or some other of the things signified by Jupiter.

Indeed if it were the Sun, they will happen on the occasion of some lay dignity or profession, or duty [or office], or raw gold, or something else of the matters which are signified by the Sun.

Indeed if it were Venus, they will happen on the occasion of marriages, or some delightful matter which is signified by Venus.

But if it were Mercury, they will happen by reason of writing or sculpture or merchant business, or the exchange of a moneychanger, or some other thing of the sciences which are signified by Mercury.

But if it were the Moon, the above said [matters] will happen by reason of legates or mandates to be imposed upon them, or some other distinguished function, or for some reason of those things which are signified by the Moon. And you will look at the things signified by her, according to her disposition in the quarters and dichotomies of every lunation.[1095]

You will even consider the condition and disposition of the aforesaid benefics, because the aforesaid ought to come about according to how they were disposed.

And Ptolemy said,[1096] but in the matter of the native's friends, and of his friendship, [there are] four places[1097] in the figure of his nativity which are called greater, or greater things, namely those [places] which have more rulership and more power over the nativity and [his] friends: which are the place[1098] of the Sun and the place of the Moon, even the place of the Lord of the Ascendant

---

[1094] By "him," Bonatti seems to mean "the *al-mubtazz* of either nativity."
[1095] Again, for Bonatti a "dichotomy" is the endpoint of a lunar quarter.
[1096] *Tet.* IV.7.
[1097] *Loca.*
[1098] *Locus*, both for the Sun and the rest of the places listed.

and the place of the Part of Fortune.[1099] For if all the places[1100] (or a majority of them) were in one sign, or the places[1101] were to exchange with each other, namely so that the Sun in the nativity of one is in the place in which the Moon was in the nativity of the other, or *vice versa*, or the Lord of the Ascendant of the nativity of one is in the place of the Part of Fortune of the other's nativity, or *vice versa*, and there were 7° or less between them and the places,[1102] this will signify the love between the natives is going to be[1103] fixed and unfailing and inseparable. If however the said significators or the Lords of the said places were to aspect each other from a trine or sextile aspect, they will signify friendship between them, but not so true as the aforesaid [kind] will be.

But if the *al-mubtazz* of the Ascendant, with the *al-mubtazz* of the 11th or even with the *al-mubtazz* of the 7th, were to regard[1104] each other from a trine or sextile aspect, and especially with reception, nor were they otherwise made unfortunate or impeded, you will pronounce indubitably a future friendship between them by joy and gladness.[1105]

Which if you were to see one of the planets transferring the light or virtue between the significators of the two nativities,[1106] and it were of good condition and well disposed (namely made fortunate and strong), you could judge a friendship happening, even if it will not last forever, but [only] for a time (but not very short).

If however you were to discover Jupiter or Saturn as the significator of the friends or the native's friendship, and one were to cross over from his own domicile into the domicile of the other, or from the place in which he was into the place in which the other was, they will signify that the friendship between them will be by reason of estates or some other durable matter; or, if the significators were fit for this, by reason of agriculture.

But if Saturn were the *hīlāj*,[1107] and Venus,[1108] and you were to find them so disposed that one is striving to occupy the place of the other, friend-

---

[1099] Ptolemy often tries to reduce all considerations to these places.
[1100] *Loca* again.
[1101] *Loca.*
[1102] *Loca.*
[1103] *Adventurum.*
[1104] *Respixerint.*
[1105] This is probably the same as the friendship by "joy and sorrow."
[1106] This must mean, between the *degrees* held by the significators, since obviously the planets at the time of the nativities themselves were in different places.
[1107] Here we get a hint that perhaps Bonatti considers the *hīlāj* itself to be the *al-mubtazz* mentioned above.

ship will happen between [the one] native and [the other] native because of blood-kinship, but in a short time it will be terminated because one is a benefic and the other a malefic.

Indeed if Saturn appeared as the significator of the native,[1109] and Mercury as the significator of friends, and he were joined to him, you will pronounce friendship between them because of merchant activities, because of giving and taking, and the like; and this, because their domiciles aspect each other from a trine aspect.

And [Ptolemy] said[1110] if Jupiter and Mars were the *hīlājes* this will happen by reason of riches or some rulership, because their domiciles likewise aspect each other from a trine aspect.

If however Jupiter appeared as the significator of the nativity with Venus, and he were to have a commingling with the *al-mubtazz* of the 7th or 11th, friendships will happen between them because of women or another delightful matter, or because of divine obedience or religion, or the construction of the houses of the religious, or the like.

But if Jupiter were the *hīlāj* with Mercury, with an application of the *al-mubtazz* of the 7th or 11th, they will love each other of their own free will by reason of the science of the *trivium* or the *quadrivium* and philosophy.

And he said, if Mars and Venus were the *hīlājes*, and they were with the aforesaid *al-mubtazzes*, as was said, there will be delight between them because of venereal activity, namely fornication or adultery or perhaps the wicked foulness of the sodomite; nor however will their friendship last

---

[1108] He must mean that Saturn is the *al-mubtazz* (or *hīlāj*) of one native, and Venus that of the other.

[1109] I.e., as the "*hīlāj*" named in the paragraph above. The synastry-like pattern above repeats itself.

[1110] *Tet.* IV.7. Again, Ptolemy is saying this in the context of primary directions. Since Ptolemy already assumes the two natives will have a friendship, these planetary combinations are supposed to say *when* and *why* the friendships will come to be. Ptolemy does not characterize the friendships themselves by the planets, only the occasions for them. He follows the Aristotelian classification of friendships into those of pleasure, utility, and complete friendship.

for a long time: which will happen to him because Mars is a malefic, but Venus a benefic.

Which if Venus and Mercury were the significators of the nativity, or the *al-mubtazz* over the Ascendant, and [they] were with the aforesaid significators, as was said, they would have a commingling because of women, or perhaps the study of music or books, or by reason of victuals which men use for their nourishment; friendship will be confirmed between them.

You will consider all of these aforesaid things, according to how you were to see the said significators to be of good condition and well disposed (namely made fortunate and strong), and in the good aspects with the Sun and the Moon, or in the Ascendant, or with its *al-mubtazz*, or with the Part of Fortune, because according to how [the conditions of] the aforesaid four were, or according to how they were to aspect the four aforesaid places,[1111] what is signified by them will appear according to that. And if they did not aspect them, what is signified by them will wholly disappear.

[1111] *Loca.*

ON THE TWELFTH HOUSE

Chapter 1: On the matter of hidden and jealous enemies, and on the considerations which it is necessary for you to have in the significations of the twelve houses, and likewise in judgments which result from the aforesaid significations

[Hidden enemies]

Look, in the matter of enemies and the jealous, at the 12th house [domicile?] from the Ascendant,[1112] and see of what sort is the condition of the *al-mubtazz* of the 12th with the *al-mubtazz* of the Ascendant. You will even[1113] look at Saturn and the Part of Enemies,[1114] and its Lord, to see how they are disposed.

For[1115] if the *al-mubtazz* over the 12th or over the domicile in which the Part of Enemies (or Saturn) is, is of bad condition and badly disposed, or some malefic were to impede one of them (and more strongly if it impeded the Lord of the Ascendant or its *al-mubtazz* or the Moon; and again more strongly if the impediment were from the opposition or from the square aspect), or the *al-mubtazz* of the 12th were in the Ascendant or in the opposition of some one of the luminaries, it will signify the native is going to have many hidden enemies and many jealous ones, and that they could secretly hurt him much, and they strive to harm, and they will harm, and the more so if the malefic were to have some dignity in the 12th–and again more if the one impeding the *al-mubtazz* over the Ascendant were the Lord of the 12th. If however the *al-mubtazz* over the 12th did not aspect the *al-mubtazz* over the Ascendant, nor the Moon, or one of the benefics were to aspect them, or one of them were the *al-mubtazz* over the 12th (nor were it impeded), it signifies the native is going to have few hidden enemies and few jealous ones.

[1112] I have omitted the following parenthetical phrase, which is identical to the title of Ch. 2 and really belongs there: "and likewise the judgments which result from the significations of the houses and their Lords."

[1113] Reading *etiam* for *enim*.

[1114] In this case, Bonatti is probably referring to Abū Ma'shar's first Part of Enemies using the 12th House: see Tr. 8, Part 2, Ch. 15.

[1115] *TBN* p. 85.

Which if Saturn were the *al-mubtazz* of the 12th, it signifies that the native's hidden and jealous enemies will be old men, Jews, low-class people of the crowd, religious men wearing black vestments, and uncultured men, and those from the forest, and the like.

If it were Jupiter, they will be men who will appear wise, and jurists and secular clerics and even middle and lesser nobles, and the like.

If however it were Mars, they will be bellicose men, evildoers, whisperers, and those speaking evils, and the like.

But if it were the Sun, they will be nobles and magnates and the like, and the more so if the *al-mubtazz* of the 12th were in an angle and in one succeeding an angle, in which he had some dignity.

But if it were Venus, they will more often be women and effeminate men, and drunks and gourmands, and the like.

If however it were Mercury, they will be literate men, young men, writers, and the like.

Indeed if it were the Moon, they will be unstable men, and common and low-class persons, and the like.

If however the *al-mubtazz* of the 12th were retrograde or combust or besieged by the malefics, or peregrine, or in a cadent from an angle, or in its own fall or in its own descension, or it were in a cadent from the Ascendant or in the 2nd or 6th or in the 8th, or the *al-mubtazz* of the Ascendant were to impede him, or one of the malefics were in the 12th (who was impeded by the malefics), it signifies that the native will prevail over all his hidden and jealous enemies, and he will trample them, and that they will be able to harm him little or practically not at all, but he himself will impede them. And if the Lord of the Ascendant were a benefic, and it were to impede the Lord of the 12th or its *al-mubtazz*, they will suffer harm and detriment from him. Indeed if Saturn or Mars (or either of them) were in the 12th, and they were of bad condition and badly disposed; or [the malefic in the 12th] were to impede the Lord of the 12th or its *al-mubtazz*, it signifies that the native will see, regarding his own hidden enemies and the jealous ones, what they are inclined to see from him.[1116]

Chapter 2: On the judgments which result from the significations of the twelve houses and their Lords[1117]

Having looked in what has preceded concerning the matter of the native's hidden enemies and those jealous of him, now it remains to see about the judgments which result from the significations of the twelve houses[1118] and the appearance of the planets in them (which are comprehended under this chapter), and concerning the manner which it is necessary for you to observe in them, according to what our ancient, wise predecessors seem to have advised. For it seemed to them that we ought to look at the aforesaid houses and their Lords, and to judge concerning them according to their disposition.

Whence you ought to look at all the houses in the nativity of any native, when you have erected the figure of that nativity, and see in which houses the planets are received, and how they are disposed, and what kind of condition they have (both of the benefics and the malefics). For in whatever house you were to find a benefic, or whatever house it were to aspect with a friendly aspect (namely a trine or a sextile), and it is free, namely made fortunate and strong, nor beset by any impediment, nor were there one of the malefics in the place

---

[1116] I believe this means they will harm each other.

[1117] In both this and the following ones, Bonatti is drawing largely on *JN*, Chs. 38-45.

[1118] This introductory section is ambiguous and reflects our ongoing attempt to sort out medieval Latin procedures. For (a) its connection with the following sections on the individual planets shows that Bonatti is ultimately interested in planets in the various domiciles. But (b) the general framework in the introductory paragraphs works equally well with quadrant houses. Saturn will produce Saturnian difficulties in whatever quadrant house (or whole sign house) he is in. In addition, (c) the passages on the individual planets are explicitly put in terms of their being the "significator of the nativity," and (d) do not reflect what one would expect when taking into account the dignities which are necessarily connected with being in a given sign. For instance, Saturn in the domicile of the Sun (i.e., Leo) is bad for Saturn because he has his detriment there; but Bonatti's description is wholly positive for diurnal nativities. Now, if Bonatti had meant merely "domiciles" in the introductory section, then it would have been hard for him to say that the native will receive good or ill from "what is signified by the domicile" in which that planet is, since by themselves the signs do not signify wealth, siblings, the father, etc. They only signify these things in their role as houses or topical places (or by universal signification). And the significations he later gives are said to affect the native in particular because the planets there are assumed to be the "significators of the nativity," not as rulers of this or that house, or as being present in a given topical house. Therefore I have translated *domus* in the introductory section as "house," and in the following sections as "domicile."

which the benefic aspects, nor even were a malefic to aspect that place, and the superior benefics were oriental (indeed the inferiors occidental), nor otherwise impeded, and the Part of Fortune of good condition and well disposed, free (namely from the conjunction of the malefics and their aspects)–this will signify (out of what is signified by those houses in which the aforesaid are found) good things and benefit and prosperity are going to come.

If however the said significators were not made fortunate (provided they were not made unfortunate), they will still signify the native's good and benefit, but much less than what was said. And if they were impeded, they signify some benefit, but little, and with an admixture of many contrary things.

If however they were malefics, and they were aspected by the benefics, nor otherwise impeded, and in their own dignities, made fortunate and strong, they will signify again some good is going to come (out of what is signified by the houses in which they are, or which they were to aspect by good aspects), but with such fatigue, and likewise complications, and burdens, that it will hardly seem to the native that he is profiting. But if they were impeded, they will signify [that] all evils, all contrary things, together with unlucky things, together with harms, and likewise misfortunes (out of what is signified by those houses of that native) are going to come to that native.

On Saturn in his own domicile

Which if the nativity were diurnal, and Saturn were the significator of that nativity,[1119] and he were of good condition and well disposed (namely made fortunate and strong), and he were in Capricorn or Aquarius or Libra, and in the Ascendant,[1120] this will signify that nobles and magnates and the wealthy themselves will make friends with the native willingly, and that he will remain in a sound and good bodily and mental condition; and it even will signify that he will come to be a great accumulator of substance (and the more so if [Saturn] had a commingling with the Part of Fortune or with the Part of Substance in the Ascendant or in the 2nd or in another praiseworthy place of the figure). Indeed if his disposition were contrary to the aforesaid, it will indicate a multitude of

---

[1119] Now we see that Bonatti wants to talk about the planets in the domiciles solely in terms of their signifying the native. But it is unclear whether, by the "significator," he means the *al-mubtazz* of the Ascendant, the *hīlāj*, or what. Earlier, the significator of the *native* was the Lord of the Ascendant, but in the context of the Lords of the other houses. Here we have the significator of the *nativity*.

[1120] This requirement is not consistently repeated below, so again it is unclear what situation (and what planet) Bonatti is envisioning.

illnesses of the body and mind, and likewise the contrary of all of the aforesaid [indications].[1121]

On Saturn in the domicile of Jupiter

And if he were in Sagittarius or Pisces, and the nativity were diurnal, it signifies the native will be of a beautiful body, beautiful stature, and a child of truth, and an accumulator of substance because of [something] just and suitable and licit. Indeed, in a nocturnal nativity it signifies the native will willingly stay with nobles or great men and the wealthy, and that he will send his own father to death before him.[1122]

On Saturn in the domicile of Mars

Indeed if he were in Aries or Scorpio, it will signify the native is going to have strong proposals, a hard heart, little pity (or practically none), no compassion, [and] be very liable to anger. And if the nativity were nocturnal, he will be found doubly worse and cruel.

On Saturn in the domicile of the Sun

Indeed if he were to stay in Leo in a diurnal nativity, it will indicate the native (and his father) to be fortunate, unless the nativity of the father (in his own peculiar affairs) works against it. If however it were nocturnal, they will portend the contrary of the aforesaid, and it will show their depression.

On Saturn in the domicile of Venus

Indeed if you were to find him in Taurus or Libra, both in diurnal nativities and the nocturnal ones, it will show the native will pass the time in venereal acts, and especially with low-class women, and he will suffer harm because of them, and he will be badly complexioned,[1123] and often practically half-sick, and he will be of a bad faith.

[1121] Note that Bonatti does not say what Saturn would indicate in a nocturnal nativity.
[1122] *Praemittet sibi proprium patrem in morte.* The verb *praemitto* makes it sound like the native will be responsible; but Abu 'Ali's text simply says that the father may be killed.
[1123] I.e., in terms of health–his humors will be badly mixed.

On Saturn in [the domicile] of Mercury

Which if you were to find him in Gemini or Virgo, whatever kind of nativity it was, it will signify he is endowed with the investigation of the sciences and the inquiry into books, and he will lay open their secrets. And you could say that his tongue[1124] will be impeded from much study and much exhaustion over these things; and often the labor and that study will overflow to his own harm, and his being reproached. And he will be made unfortunate by men, and especially from those whom he serves, who, not wanting to respond to his services, will find pretexts for speaking ill about him and criticizing him, thinking he has committed evils (which he has never devised), on the occasion of which he will be made to have a bad conscience[1125] and bad thoughts and a bad soul.[1126]

On Saturn in the domicile of the Moon

And if you were to find him in Cancer (because Cancer is the sixth sign from his domicile [Aquarius]), it will signify the native will be burdened often by infirmities, and his mother will incur a bad illness on the occasion of his birth, or perhaps the native will destroy her goods while she is alive, and will disperse her substance in a bad way, or perhaps he will kill her.

On Jupiter in the domicile of Saturn

Which if Jupiter were in Capricorn or in Aquarius, and he appeared as the significator of the nativity, free from impediments, it signifies the native is anxious, gasping for breath, distressed about making money, and always showing himself to be in need and a pauper to [other] men, and living a low-class and a miserable life, and always thinking bad thoughts, and low-class and an imbecile in all things by which men have force; and because of that, many inconvenient things will come down to him.

On Jupiter in his own domicile

And if he were in Sagittarius or Pisces, and the nativity were diurnal, it signi-fies the native is wealthy and fortunate in substance, and he will accumulate it in

---

[1124] Or, "his language." For example, overeducation can make someone incomprehensible.
[1125] *Conscientiae.* In other words, it will spoil his sense of himself and others.
[1126] I cannot help but wonder whether Bonatti is describing himself here–see his comments about being persecuted, especially in Tr. 5.

a great quantity, and he will even be a discerning man, knowing how to succeed among the nobles and great men and the wealthy. If however the nativity were nocturnal, it signifies that he will be fortunate in the aforesaid, but much less than what was said; still, he will be in the household of the religious and those worshiping God, and he will gladly stay with them.

On Jupiter in the domicile of Mars

Indeed if he stayed in Aries or Scorpio, whatever kind of nativity it was, it signifies the native is made fortunate among kings and nobles and magnates, and bearers of arms; and he will be a man of great stability and much constancy, and the more so if Jupiter appeared then in the angles or their succeedents, and in a masculine sign; and he will be a good warrior,[1127] and likewise a good combatant, and producer[1128] of an army (and particularly of great and famous armies).

On Jupiter in the domicile of the Sun

Indeed if you were to find him in Leo, appearing in a diurnal nativity, it will signify he is going to be noted, famous, wise and of deep skill, and that he will gladly stay with kings, and that he will be loved (even if not much) when serving them—and not only by great men, [but] even by the common people. And Abu 'Ali said, if in addition he were in the angles or the succeedents, free from the malefics and impediments, he will be more fortunate, namely a king or someone like a king—but his lineage having been considered, because he will transcend it more than men had expected. But if the nativity were nocturnal, the aforesaid will come to be, but much less than what was said, but still with him appearing fortunate and well disposed.

On Jupiter in the domicile of Venus

Indeed if the nativity were diurnal, and Jupiter were in Taurus or in Libra, say that he will willingly cling to noble and wealthy and financially endowed[1129] women, and he will consummate marriage with them, and he will be made rich from thence. Indeed if it were nocturnal, he will willingly live with the religious,

---

[1127] *Guerrizator.* This word has broader connotations of being able to carry out war effectively.
[1128] *Productor.* This might also have a financial connotation in relation to raising armies.
[1129] *Dotatis,* with the added connotation of a dowry (*dos*).

and he will be a possessor of good faith, and for that reason he will make money, and become rich.

On Jupiter in the domicile of Mercury

If however he were found in Gemini or Virgo, free from impediments both in diurnal nativities and in nocturnal ones, he signifies he is going to be a great accumulator of substance, and for that reason he will be preferred to many other men, and will seem almost to be a king.

On Jupiter in the domicile of the Moon

Which if you were to find him in Cancer, namely made fortunate and strong, and well disposed, the nativity being diurnal, it will signify he must be a man made fortunate practically beyond measure, and the more so if he were in the angles or in the succeedents of the angles. But if the nativity were nocturnal, the aforesaid will come to be, but this will be much below what was said; still he will be a man having a great name and a great reputation, nor however will he pursue the benefit from that reputation which would be very profitable to him.[1130]

On Mars in the domicile of Saturn

And if Mars is found in Capricorn or in Aquarius, and he were the significator of the nativity, and of good condition and well disposed (namely appearing fortunate and strong), it will signify the native is going to be magnanimous and bold, and overbearing together with arms; and whatever he might think in his heart he will want to bring about; and many of those things which he would wish to begin, he will perfect and complete; and his reputation will be exalted, and he will bear a royal manner. And if he were of a stock for which it is fitting, he will be made king, and his reputation will fly to faraway parts, and he will be a great disperser and dissipater of both his own and strangers' substance. And if he were to have older brothers, he will send them to their deaths before his own, or perhaps he will be the reason for their death, and especially if the Lord of the 8th aspected their significators, or were joined corporally with them.

[1130] *Nec tamen ex illa fama sequetur utilitatem quae sibi multum prosit.* The sentence seems to mean that he will not take advantage of the benefits of his reputation.

On Mars in the domicile of Jupiter

Which if Mars were in Sagittarius or Pisces, and he were the significator of the nativity, and he were made fortunate and strong, whatever kind of nativity it was, it will signify the native is going to have a commingling with kings and magnates and the wealthy; and that he will be loved very much by them, for they will prefer him to their own tradesmen and to the generals of their own armies (and the more so, and more strongly so, if then Jupiter appeared in Aries or Scorpio, made fortunate and free).

On Mars in his own domicile

And if Mars were staying in Aries or in his other domicile (and the more so if the nativity were nocturnal), it will signify the native will be a master of instruments of war, like *trebuchets*,[1131] war-machines, and the like, and [he will be] very clever, and likewise acute with geometrical reason. If however the nativity were diurnal, and he were oriental in the world[1132] or from the Sun, nor did one of the benefics aspect him, it will signify the native to be bad, diabolical, a whisperer, an injurer of men, and he will appear as gladly applying himself in their evils; and he will be sick with hidden illnesses (like hidden cancers and the like); and if he were in Aries, he will fall from a height; and because of that fall he will injure his body according to the part attributed to the ascending sign. Which if he were in Scorpio, his malice will be lessened.

On Mars in the domicile of the Sun

Indeed if Mars were in Leo, and he appeared as the significator of the nativity (whether the nativity were diurnal or nocturnal), it will signify that inconveniences are going to happen to the native, and destruction to his person and his matters, and that illnesses of the eyes will beset him (and especially the right one); and his illnesses will even thrive in his stomach, and his professions will be more in those things which operate by iron and fire; and likewise it will signify that he will die an unexpected or sudden death, or perhaps he will be decapitated or hung (and the more so if Mars were then in the 10th), or he will

---

[1131] *Trabuci.* A *trebuchet* was a powerful medieval catapult used in sieges. Using weights to propel their loads, they were capable of slinging as much as a 300-pound missile for 300 yards.

[1132] I.e., in one of the "eastern" quadrants–either between the Ascendant and the MC, or between the 7th and the 4th.

be killed by another means, at the hands of men. And Abu ʿAli said, either he or his father will die on a pilgrimage.

On Mars in the domicile of Venus

Which if Mars were in Taurus or Libra, and he were the significator of the nativity, it will signify the native to be wanton, fornicating, a sodomite, and wicked in all venereal abuses, and even a deceiver, and a deceiver of women (and he will be deluded and deceived by them), and he will be betrothed to some in order to be able to commit adultery with them, and he *will* commit adultery with some, and afterwards he will be betrothed to them; and he will observe a bad method in all of these, and those like them, and he will suffer harm and detriment from thence. And Abu ʿAli said that if he were in Taurus, it signifies the native will be a traitor, false, malign, a maker of threats, and a fornicator. Indeed if you were to find him in Libra, it signifies he will suffer wounds in hidden places and in the private parts of his body; or perhaps he will be burned in some part of his body.

On Mars in the domicile of Mercury

And if you were to find him in Gemini or Virgo, whatever kind of nativity it was, it signifies the native is going to be neglectful, but still, "he is carnal who is occupied with temporal things";[1133] and he will be clever, nor very legal, and he will strive to make money however he could, both by furtive means and other illicit ones; if he were to stick to writing he will be made a good writer; he will learn foreign languages easily, and he will even understand books of diverse discourses well, and he will make their meanings clear, and he will be of a very good mind, and perceptive in sciences beyond others who study with him.

On Mars in the domicile of the Moon

Indeed if you were to find him in Cancer, it signifies that he will be inconstant, easily changing from proposition to proposition; he will have a profound mind in all sciences, and he will progress in them, and he will be eager and willing [to commit] bad acts. And Abu ʿAli said that he will suffer an evil or impediment in hidden parts of his body; he will die an unexpected death; and he

---

[1133] *Erit tamen carnalis qui circa temporalia versabitur.* This reads like a proverb, but I do not know its source and do not know why it is stated here. The quotation marks are my own.

will dissipate his mother's goods; his mother will suffer a long infirmity because of the birth of that nativity.

On the Sun in the domicile of Saturn

Which if the Sun were the significator of someone's nativity, and you were to see him staying in Capricorn or Aquarius, I say with the nativity being diurnal, it signifies the native will be of good quality, and benevolent, eager, of good commerce, of good social contacts,[1134] even if delighted with some burden, and making others to be delighted, and perfect in administrative functions[1135] or mechanical arts, if he wished to get involved with them. If however the nativity were nocturnal, it will signify the native to be unstable concerning every matter which he might wish to do or begin, and quickly changing to something else.

On the Sun in the domicile of Jupiter

If however you were to find the Sun in Sagittarius or Pisces, and the nativity were diurnal, it will signify the native is going to be the more excellent one of all of his relatives [or neighbors], and very famous among men; and he will freely have a commingling with nobles and magnates; however he will assent to venereal experience beyond what is fitting, so much so that for that reason he will be called a fornicator, and he will commit something unclean, nor will he avoid fornicating with the wives of his neighbors, nor even with his own stepmother.

On the Sun in the domicile of Mars

Indeed if you were to find the Sun in Aries, and the nativity were diurnal, and he appeared as the significator of that nativity, appearing of good condition and well disposed (namely made fortunate and strong), it will signify the native will be fortunate and exalted and have a great name, and especially among kings and nobles and great men wanting gladly to go to war; and this will last for him as long as he shall live, unless a Lord of the triplicity of the Ascendant worked against it (which, even if it could not abolish the aforesaid, still it could diminish them). If however the nativity were nocturnal, it will signify the aforesaid will be one-third below what was said above. Indeed if you were to find him in Scorpio in a nativity (I say, diurnal), it will signify he is not going to be fortunate, unless

---

[1134] *Commixtione*, what I have usually translated as "commingling."
[1135] *Ministeriis.*

the Lords of the aforesaid triplicity offer support. But whatever kind of good fortune it is, it will signify he is going to have illness of the joints, and likewise liver complaints. And Abu 'Ali said his father will be weighed down by the worst death. Which if the nativity were nocturnal, it signifies the aforesaid will be weighed down or increased according to the disposition of the Lords of the triplicity.

On the Sun in his own domicile

And if the Sun were in Leo in someone's nativity, and he were the significator of the nativity, and he were of good condition and well disposed in an angle (and chiefly in the 10th) or in a succeedent to an angle (and especially to the 10th), it will signify the native is going to be a great king and strong and exalted king (if the native were of such a stock that great offices or any higher dignities were fitting for him). If however the native were of a middling stock, even if he does not reach to the ultimate kingdoms, still he will reach to the greatest honors, and the greatest dignities, and riches, and unexpected appointments. Which if he were of a low-class progeny, he will reach great offices and great dignities, concerning which men are very much amazed, but it will be feared that on that great occasion, inconveniences will come to him. And Abu 'Ali said, in nocturnal nativities it signifies the stupidity of the father, and he will be seized by a sudden death, and will achieve good in pilgrimages.

On the Sun in the domicile of Venus

Indeed if you were to find the Sun staying in Libra or Taurus (whether the nativity were diurnal or nocturnal), and he appeared as the significator of the nativity, it signifies the native will be good and truthful, an interpreter of dreams and of secret things, and even a discoverer of hidden things; however he will sin in shameful sexual intercourse.

On the Sun in the domicile of Mercury

And if you were to find the Sun in Gemini or Virgo, in the nativity of someone (it being diurnal), and he were the significator of the nativity, it will signify the native is going to be very proven in the sciences, and a perfect teacher of them beyond all other teachers of his time, and likewise [a teacher] of good morals, and good works. And Abu 'Ali said, perhaps that he will be a noted and loved astronomer among kings and nobles. Indeed if the nativity were nocturnal, it will signify he is in need, and unfortunate, [and] will gladly do bad things. And Abu 'Ali said, indeed in his youth he will be a pauper, but were he to reach middle age he will abound in riches; [and] pains will happen to him in the aforesaid and in a hidden part of his body; [and] he will be an exorciser, making men be loosened from a slip into demoniacal works.[1136]

On Venus in the domicile of Saturn

If Venus stood in Capricorn or in Aquarius in someone's nativity, and she appeared as the significatrix of the nativity, whatever kind of condition she had or what her disposition was, and whatever kind of nativity it was, it signifies that the native will desire low-class women, nor even will he abhor ugly ones; and he will easily acquire them for himself, and will be betrothed to them; and that he will send his first wife to the grave before him.[1137]

On Venus in the domicile of Jupiter

If however you were to find Venus in Sagittarius or in Pisces in someone's nativity, with her appearing as the significatrix of the nativity, it signifies in a nocturnal nativity that the parents of that native will hate him, and without just cause; but it will signify he is going to attain riches by means of noble women, or belonging to the nobles, or even by means of wives or marriage or by his own mother-in-law or aunt. If however it were diurnal, the aforesaid will happen, but weaker and below them.

On Venus in the domicile of Mars

Which if you were to find Venus in Aries or Scorpio, whether the nativity were diurnal or nocturnal, and whatever kind of condition she had, with her appearing as the significatrix of that nativity, it signifies that the native will be unyielding toward women, not living with them well, and he will make much use of low-class and foul and unsuitable women, and many harms and inconveniences will follow from thence, and he will hardly or never marry; and if he were to marry, he will pursue it with difficulty and complications, and because of it he will incur many contentions and quarrels, and on the occasion of those conten-

---

[1136] *Faciens homines in lapsum operum daemonicacorum labi.*
[1137] Again, this does not mean he is responsible for her death.

tions, many unlucky things will happen to him, and he will fall into suspicion of his wife, and it will be possible that by reason of that suspicion he will kill her.

On Venus in the domicile of the Sun

And if Venus were standing[1138] in Leo, and she appeared as the significatrix of the nativity, whatever kind of condition she had, and likewise whatever kind of nativity it was, it signifies that the native will burn in the love of women, and that he will abound in venereal experience, and that he will be tastelessly wanton, and will be inclined to abuse boys.

On Venus in her own domicile

Indeed if you were to find Venus staying in Taurus or Libra, whatever kind of nativity it was, and she was appearing as the significatrix, and whatever kind of condition she had, it will signify the native is going to be inclined to wicked women, and those who call out[1139] and those gladly whoring and fornicating; and those making others be harlots; and from thence he will be defamed, and his infamy will be made public. And Abu 'Ali said that he will be made fortunate, and good will follow in all the times [of his life].[1140]

On Venus in the domicile of Mercury

Indeed if she were found in Gemini or Virgo in someone's nativity, the nativity being diurnal, and she of good condition and well disposed, and she were the significatrix of the nativity, it signifies that the native is going to be a painter of diverse paintings, and likewise a writer, and will know how to make the ornaments of women, and of womanly works, and [those] of effeminate men,[1141] and will live under a certain kind of false sanctity with the religious, but he will be oppressed by the vice of luxury. Indeed if the nativity were nocturnal, and she were of bad condition and badly disposed, the native will know how to do none of the aforesaid good things, but he will more willingly act on the bad ones.

[1138] I.e., if she "were in" Leo–the Latin does *not* mean she is in one of her stations.

[1139] *Affaturatrices*, from *adfor*, to call out or speak out. This must mean a street prostitute who calls out to passersby.

[1140] This is quite a contrast between Bonatti's opinion and that of Abu 'Ali.

[1141] It is unclear to me whether this comment about womanly works and effeminate men refers to what the native knows how to make, or to his writing and painting.

On Venus in the domicile of the Moon

Again, if Venus dwelt in Cancer, and she were the significatrix of the nativity, whatever kind of nativity it was and whatever kind of condition she had, it will signify the native is going to be unstable and quickly changing from thing to thing and from place to place; [to be] full of vices, earning money shamefully, and being shamefully wanton.

On Mercury in the domicile of Saturn

And if you were to find Mercury staying in Capricorn or Aquarius in someone's nativity (both diurnal and nocturnal), and he appeared as the sole significator of the nativity, whatever kind of condition he had, it will signify the native is going to be of a bad suspicion and a grave tongue, but he will gladly have a commingling with the religious and the wise.

On Mercury in the domicile of Jupiter

If however you were to find Mercury in Sagittarius or Pisces in someone's nativity, and he were the significator of the nativity, and the nativity were diurnal, and he appeared in good condition and of a good quality, it signifies the native is going to have the commingling of kings, and the disposition of their matters, and [he will handle] men's [legal] cases, and he will be wise in judgments and in judging. Indeed if the nativity were nocturnal, whatever kind of condition he had, it will signify this, but they will be very much below the aforesaid.

On Mercury in the domicile of Mars

Which if you were to find Mercury in Aries or Scorpio, whether the nativity were diurnal or nocturnal, of whatever condition of that nativity he were the significator, it signifies the native to be a thief, a wooer, false, a liar, clever, and everywhere surrounded by all malice, and many evil things will follow from that.

On Mercury in the domicile of the Sun

Indeed if you were to find Mercury staying in Leo, with him appearing in good condition and well disposed, and as the significator of the nativity, whatever kind of nativity it was, it will signify the native is going to acquire the friendship of magnates and the nobles, and he will willingly stay among them. Which if you were to find him badly disposed, whatever kind of nativity it was, it will signify he will appear to be a wooer and inept.

On Mercury in the domicile of Venus

And if you were find Mercury in Taurus or in Libra in someone's nativity, whatever kind of nativity it was, and he appeared as its significator, it will signify the native is going to be lively and humorous, and knowing all the sciences and all matters because of which and in which men delight.

On Mercury in his own domicile

Indeed if you were to find Mercury staying in Gemini or in Virgo, and he appeared as the significator of the nativity, and were of good condition and well disposed, it will signify the native is going to be proven and perfect in all the sciences, both in the trades and the theoretical ones.[1142]

On Mercury in the domicile of the Moon

If however you were to find Mercury staying in Cancer, and he were the significator of the nativity of good condition and well disposed, it will signify the native knows well (and gladly) how to prepare items for a banquet and for eating, and is of good will, not delighting himself in venereal experience, faithful and benevolent.

On the Moon in the domicile of Saturn

Which if you were to recognize that the Moon is staying in Capricorn or Aquarius, and she were well disposed, and the nativity were nocturnal, and she [were] the significatrix of the nativity, and in the decrease of her light, it will signify the native is going to suffer illnesses of the eyes and pains of the kidneys, and often will suffer because of the aforesaid. If however the nativity were diurnal, he will be troubled less by the illnesses than what is said above. In each nativity, whatever kind of condition she had, it will signify that the native is not commended by men, but they strive to blame him and speak evil about him, even if he is doing the good and speaking good.

[1142] *Tam in disciplinabilibus quam doctrinalibus.*

On the Moon in the domicile of Jupiter

If however you were to see the Moon appearing as the significatrix in Sagittarius or Pisces, in each [kind of] nativity, it will signify the native is going to prevail among all of his blood-relatives, and that he will be seen as practically a king among them with respect to them; and his reputation will be exalted; but he will be defiled with the vice of wantonness, and he will be wanton with prohibited women.

On the Moon in the domicile of Mars

Indeed if you were to find the Moon in Aries or Scorpio, and she appeared as the significatrix of the nativity (whatever kind of nativity, and whatever her condition was), it will signify the native to be a wooer, a thief, avoiding good works, eager for bad things, willingly staying with robbers and other wicked men, and inclined to live with them.

On the Moon in the domicile of the Sun

Indeed if you were to see the Moon remaining in Leo, in either [kind of] nativity, with her appearing as the significatrix of the nativity, it signifies the native is going to have a commingling with kings and the wealthy, and great men; and the more so if the Moon will be abiding in the first or last bound of Leo.

On the Moon in the domicile of Venus

Which if you looked around at the Moon in Taurus or Libra (whatever kind of nativity it was), and she were the significatrix of the nativity (but with her not appearing impeded), it signifies the native is going to burn in the love of women, and he will be delighted to have fun with them; [and] good and usefulness will follow from them.

On the Moon in the domicile of Mercury

And if the Moon stood in Gemini or Virgo, and likewise she were the significatrix of the nativity, it signifies that the native will be benevolent, observing a good life, and eager to harm no one, of good understanding, and a good skill [or character], [and] he will gladly be wanton with girls and young women.

On the Moon in her own domicile

Indeed if you were to look around at the Moon in Cancer, and she were of good condition and appeared as the significatrix of the nativity, it will signify that the native is going to have a commingling with kings and magnates, and he is going to pursue good and usefulness and profit from them. And Abu 'Ali said if she were conjoined or applied to malefics, it will signify diverse illnesses of the native. Indeed if she were conjoined or applied to the benefics, it signifies the soundness of the body and [its] good temper.

Chapter 3: On the years of the *firdārīah* and their dispositors[1143]

The ancient sages considered certain years in nativities which are not called greater, nor middle, nor lesser ones, but they called them years of the *firdārīah*[1144]–that is, disposed years. For every planet disposes its own portion of the native's life, according to its own portion of the years of the *firdārīah*, in this way: because, whatever kind of nativity it was, the disposition of the years of the *firdārīah* will begin from the luminary whose authority it is. And that [luminary] will dispose the native's life according to the quantity of years of its own *firdārīah*, but not without the participation of the other planets.[1145]

For if the nativity were diurnal, it will begin from the Sun (who is the diurnal luminary), who will dispose the native's life according to the years of his own *firdārīah* (which are 10), with the participation of all the other planets. But he will obtain the principal place, and especially in the first one-seventh of those years.

In the second part [of the Sun's *firdārīah*], Venus (who succeeds him in the order of the circles) will participate with him in the disposition of the native's life.

1143 This section is based on al-Qabīsī, IV.20.

1144 Lat. *firdaria*, from Ar. فرداريه, itself deriving via Persian from some paronym of the Gr. *periodos* ("cycle, periodic recurrence").

1145 The assignment of planets and years to the *firdārīah* is puzzling. Most puzzling to me is why the planetary numbers begin with 7 (see below). But I see the beginning of two possibilities for the order or grouping of the planets. (a) In terms of sect, the nocturnal planets have 7, 8, and 9; the diurnal planets have 10, 11, and 12; and Mercury, who is convertible, stands alone with 13. (b) If we begin from Aries, then Mars (who rules it) is the first planet; Venus is opposite him; and the Moon is the remaining member of the sect. Skipping Mercury (who does not belong intrinsically to a sect), the next planet is the Sun; Saturn is opposite him; Jupiter is left over. Mercury comes last.

In the third one-seventh, Mercury (who succeeds Venus in the order of circles) will participate with him.

In the fourth one-seventh, the Moon (who succeeds Mercury in the order of the circles) will participate with him.

In the fifth one-seventh, Saturn (who succeeds the Moon circularly in the order of the circles) will participate with him.

In the sixth one-seventh, Jupiter (who succeeds Saturn in the order of the circles) will participate with him.

In the seventh and last one-seventh, Mars (who succeeds Jupiter in the order of circles, and is the seventh planet from the Sun) will participate with him.

After this, Venus (who succeeds the Sun in the order of the circles) will dispose the native's life, according to the quantity of the years of her *firdārīah* (which are 8), and all the other planets will participate with her in the disposition of those years, each one according to its one-seventh, as was said about their participation with the Sun.

Then Mercury will dispose according to the quantity of the years of his own *firdārīah* (which are 13), and the others (namely each of them) will participate with him according to its own one-seventh of those years.

Then the Moon will dispose according to the quantity of the years of her own *firdārīah* (which are 9), and each of them will participate according to its own one-seventh of those years.

Then Saturn will dispose according to the quantity of the years of his own *firdārīah* (which are 11), with the participation of the others, just as was said regarding the Sun.

Then Jupiter will dispose according to the quantity of the years of his own *firdārīah* (which are 12), with the participation of the other planets, as was said about the others.

Then Mars will dispose according to the quantity of the years of his own *firdārīah* (which are 7), with the participation of the other planets, as was said above.

Then the Head of the Dragon will dispose according to the quantity of its own *firdāriah* (which are 3). Then its Tail will dispose according to the quantity of the years of its own *firdāriah* (which are 2).

After this the disposition reverts to the Sun, by going (as was said) successively up the end of the native's life.

Concerning a nocturnal nativity

Which if the nativity were nocturnal, the disposition will begin from the Moon (who is the nocturnal luminary), and it will come to be in all and by all (as was said when the disposition begins from the Sun), both concerning the participation of the planets with her, and their succession in the order of the circles. And all the aforesaid significators or dispositors will dispose according to what the condition and disposition of each of them was–like if they were well disposed, by increasing good fortunes and diminishing misfortunes; and if they were badly disposed, by increasing misfortunes and diminishing good fortunes. And this is a very labor-intensive matter, but one well to be observed, because some of the astrologers, avoiding labor, sometimes do not consider it in their judgments, whence they slide into deception.

And these years of the *firdāriah*, collected all together, are 75, which sometimes (though it rarely happens) are all given to some natives; nor are they the years then given to the native by the *al-kadukhadāh*; for it could be of such weakness, that it will not suffice for giving the years which are given by the *firdāriah*–whence sometimes an astrologer, in perceiving the number of the native's years, can be deceived if he does not watch himself (nor is it surprising).

**Chapter 4: On the eminence[1146] of the planets,
or the transit of one over another**

Indeed in the eminence of the planets, or of the transit of one over another,[1147] al-Qabīsī said[1148] that you ought to look at the average course of any

---

[1146] *Eminentia*, "eminence, standing out, prominence." This word also has the connotation of being over or above others, which is perhaps why Bonatti is linking it with planets at higher or lower parts of their epicycles.
[1147] This is apparently meant to be an astronomical way of determining which of the planets in a transit will predominate over the other.
[1148] Al-Qabīsī, IV.21.280-85. Al-Qabīsī simply calls this "transit."

[superior] planet,[1149] and likewise the place of its equation.[1150] For if its equated place were less than the average course of the planet, that planet will be ascending from the middle of its epicycle to its summit, by approaching to the farther distance [or longitude]. And if its equated place were more than its average course, the planet will be descending from the middle of its epicycle to its lower part, by coming toward the nearer distance [or longitude]. But if they were both equal, the planet will be in the middle of its epicycle, namely between the farther distance [or longitude], and the nearer distance [or longitude], the which having been found truly and most certainly, subtract the lesser of them from the greater, and what is left over you will multiply by 7, and what comes out of that, divide by 22,[1151] and what comes out for you by division, will be the quantity of the ascending or descending of the planet in its circle.

On Venus and Mercury

Al-Qabīsī said[1152] that you ought to take what there is between the place of the Sun and the place of Venus, and likewise what there is between [the Sun] and the place of Mercury, and subtract the lesser from the greater, and multiply [by 7] and divide [by 22] just as was said above. Because by this we will know which of them is stronger in the circle. And he said if Venus and Mercury were oriental, and the equated place of one of them were less than the place of the Sun, we ought to take the remainder which is between the place of the Sun and its place, and do with it (in terms of multiplication and division) just as was said above for the superior planets.

And he said[1153] that the signification of the planets would be stronger and nearer while they go away above each other (namely one over the other), in the conjunction. But in the [opposition],[1154] and in the square aspect, their signification will be weaker and less apparent. And if one of them were ascending, and

---

[1149] As Bonatti points out below, this paragraph pertains to the superior planets. The next paragraph will deal with Venus and Mercury.
[1150] By "average course" and "equated place," Bonatti means the "mean position" and the "corrected" or "exactly computed" position. This calculation pertains to Abū Ma'shar's theory of transits as reported by al-Qabīsī. Readers should consult Abū Ma'shar's *Abbr.* II.6 and *OGC* VI.1 (and pp. 597-98), as well as al-Bīrūnī's *Instruction*, §§151-52. See also Kennedy (1958).
[1151] 7 divided by 22 is a very close fractional equivalent to the inverse of π.
[1152] Al-Qabīsī, *ibid.*
[1153] Al-Qabīsī, *ibid.*
[1154] *Praeventione*, "prevention." I say "opposition" because Bonatti typically reserves "prevention" for Full Moons.

the other descending, then the ascending one goes over the descending one. And he who has the lesser descension, goes above him who has the greater descension, when both are descending. But if both are ascending, the one who has a greater ascension goes over him who has the lesser ascension.

On another manner of elevation of a planet over another one

And a planet is said to be elevated over [another] planet in another way (even though I have touched on this for you elsewhere),[1155] and it is stronger than [the previous way]. For if one planet were northern [in ecliptical latitude] and the other southern, the northern one goes above the southern one. And if they were both northern, he who is more northern, goes above the one who is less northern. If however they were both southern, he who is less southern goes above him who is more southern. And therefore it is said that the Moon goes above all the planets,[1156] and any one of the others goes above all the others, in these two ways.

Likewise, if one planet were in the middle of its own epicycle (that is, in the most extreme distance [or longitude], farther or nearer), or it were in its own *jawzahirr,*[1157] then the one ascending in the epicycle goes above him who is in the farther distance [or longitude] or the nearer one, and the northern goes over the southern, and even above the descending one, and over him who is in his own *jawzahirr;* and he who is in his own *jawzahirr* goes above the southern one, and even over the descending one, and over the one who is in the nearer distance.

Chapter 5: On the opening of the gates, according to al-Qabīsī[1158]

The "opening of the gates" follows the aforesaid, and this is when two planets whose domiciles are opposed, are joined together–like Saturn and the luminaries, Jupiter and Mercury, Mars and Venus[1159]–when the lighter one of

---

1155 I.e., in Tr. 3, Part 2, Ch. 2.
1156 Al-Qabīsī (IV.21.293) says only "it is said that the Moon passes above Jupiter in both these computations."
1157 Al-Qabīsī says "or has no latitude," confirming that the Nodes are just special cases of the *jawzahirr* which all planets (except the Sun) have.
1158 Al-Qabīsī, IV.22. Bonatti also refers to this phrase in Tr. 3, Part 2, Ch. 23; and also in Tr. 10.
1159 These examples are not found in al-Qabīsī, but they are found in John of Seville's edition of a text called the *Apertio Portarum* (called "Opening of the Doors" by Burnett 2000, pp.

these is joined with some heavier one of the aforesaid,[1160] and he finds him in his own domicile or exaltation, or in two of his other lesser dignities, he receives him. And it is called opening the gates for him, just as one would do who, if he found his enemy in his own house, he will honor him, nor would he act like a rustic to him,[1161] provided that it was not a mortal enemy (unless he was an impudent or uncivilized or wild man who did not have a household relation with men, as was that Ezzelino da Romano, who spared neither sex, nor age, nor rank, nor dignity). And what was said above, is called the opening of the gates.

Chapter 6: On the twelve hours of the Sun and of the Moon, which are applied to the Sun

Then what comes next is of the 12 hours of the Sun and Moon, which al-Qabīsī calls the *al-bust*,[1162] which follow immediately after the separation of the Moon from the corporal conjunction of the Sun. And al-Qabīsī said that the ancient sages triply divided these 12 hours, that is into three equal parts, of which each consists of four unequal[1163] hours, the which 12 hours they applied to the Sun. And they judged concerning those hours according to the Lords of the triplicity in which the Sun had been at the hour of his conjunction with the Moon, by beginning from the Sun, by giving to [the Sun] the first four hours; by giving the second Lord of the same triplicity the second four; and [by giving] the third Lord of that triplicity the last four hours.

Then the aforesaid ancient sages gave to Venus (after the 12 hours of the Sun) another 12; and they divided them into three divisions (as was said concerning the Sun), and they judged concerning each of those divisions, by giving the first four hours to [the first Lord of the triplicity of] Venus, the second four hours to the second Lord of the triplicity of Venus, and the last four hours to the third Lord of that triplicity. And they judged according to how the aforesaid Lords of the triplicity, and the others, were disposed.

385*ff*. Since the opening of the gates is usually found in the context of weather prediction, someone (though probably not Bonatti) has expanded the range of its meaning in delineation as we see here. For Bonatti (at least in this Treatise), it occurs when one planet receives another whose natural domicile is opposite its own.

1160 This is where al-Qabīsī's definition stops.

1161 *Nec faceret ei rusticitatem*. This must mean something like "having bad manners."

1162 Lat. *Albuim*. See footnote in Tr. 4, Ch. 7. Earlier he called this the *duodena* of the Moon, not *al-bust*, and moreover had a different way of organizing the planetary rulers.

1163 Why unequal? Al-Qabīsī does not say this.

They did the same thing with Mercury and with the Lords of his triplicity. Likewise with the Moon and the Lords of her triplicity. Then with Saturn and the Lords of his triplicity, and likewise with Jupiter and Mars and with the Lords of their triplicities. Then [after 84 hours][1164] the circle reverts to the Sun [and so on again] until the next conjunction.

On the twelve combust hours after the conjunction

And al-Qabīsī said[1165] that certain people used to say that the *bust* is this: namely that after the conjunction of the Sun and Moon there are 12 unequal hours which are called "combust," and behooves someone not to begin any work in them.

On the 72 incombust hours

And after the 12 combust hours were 72 incombust hours,[1166] and after the 72 incombust hours are another 12 combust ones likewise, and so on with each individually up to the next conjunction which follows.

After this, they divided the aforesaid 12 combust hours into three equal divisions, and they said that one who begins to go do war in the first four hours, will have to fear the loss of his soul. And one who begins in the second four hours, will have to fear the detriment of his body without the loss of his soul. And he who begins to plow[1167] in them will have to fear great detriment in all things which he possesses, and in his own body, without the loss of his soul; and ruin will be feared for those who belong to him. And one who begins [such actions] in the last four hours, will have to fear the detriment of his substance, just as was touched on elsewhere.

[1164] According to al-Qabīsī. Four hours multipled by seven planets with three triplicity rulers apiece makes 84.

[1165] Al-Qabīsī, IV.24. This is a repetition of material in Tr. 4, Ch. 7.

[1166] During which (according to al-Qabīsī's report) it is good to begin actions.

[1167] There is an error here. Al-Qabīsī's example does not mention plowing, and continues on to the final four hours, during which everything will be lost (which Bonatti attributes to the middle four hours while plowing). The bottom line is that the last four hours are the worst.

Chapter 7: On the profection of years,
both of the world and of nativities

Having made mention above about the number of years which are attributed to every native, it seems fitting to me, and right, to speak next about the profection of their years. But a profection[1168] is something signified which results from those things which happen from the sign which immediately succeeds the sign which was the Ascendant of the nativity, and its Lord—whether good, or bad, or middling, just as was said for the superiors. For indeed it is called an "advancement" because it advances by changing every year by one sign, following the continual succession of signs, whose Lord offers assistance to the significator of the year of the [solar] revolution, both for good and bad, sometimes increasing one, sometimes decreasing—whose interpretation is the *sālkhudāy*,[1169] which is a participator in accidents which will come to the native in every year of any revolution of his. The knowledge of the discovery of which is this:

You will consider the year, day, month, hour, of any nativity you wish, and you will see how many solar years the native has already completed. And you will take one sign[1170] for every solar year from the Ascendant of the nativity. And you will begin from the hour of the nativity of that native, according to the succession of the signs, by giving one sign to each year, and where the number were ended, the sign which immediately succeeds is the sign of the profection from the Ascendant of that nativity, and it will be the Ascendant of the profection of the year which then follows (which you did not yet send [forward] in your number); and the profection of that year will be in such a degree of that sign as was the kind of the degree of the Ascendant at the hour of the nativity.[1171] And understand this for every profection, because in every year it will always be in such a degree of the sign (in which were to fall) as it was in the sign which preceded it in the year which has just immediately passed by. You seek

---

[1168] *Profectio*, lit. "advancement." See below. I retain the term "profection" because it has passed into common usage as a particular technique.

[1169] Lat. *alcochoden* (a misread), Ar. السالخذاي (al-Qabīsī, IV.19). According to al-Bīrūnī (*Instruction*, §520) it is derived from Persian, meaning the profected "Lord of the Year."

[1170] For Bonatti, a sign is to be taken in two ways: (a) as the named zodiacal signs, like Cancer or Leo; (b) as any 30° section of the ecliptic. Here he means (b). In other words, if the native has lived 2.5 years, this will be equal to 75° from the degree of the Ascendant, since 2.5 multiplied by 30° equals 75°.

[1171] That is, the Ascendant of any given year will have the same degree of the current sign as it did in the previous sign the previous year (e.g., 5° 41' Taurus, 5° 41' Gemini, 5° 41' Cancer, *etc.*). See Bonatti's explanation which follows.

this [degree], and the planet which is the Lord of that sign is called the *sālkhudāy*, which is the helper of the planet which is the Lord of that sign which was the Ascendant of the revolution of the year which you are revolving.[1172] And by such a planet [i.e., the *sālkhudāy*] will be shown to you the disposition of the standing of the native in that year, even if it should happen that, in [that year], you must make more revolutions.[1173]

Indeed for the honors and annual dignities of the native, you will look at the sign of the profection from the Sun (namely one complete sign for every solar year), so that you might see his profection.[1174]

For the condition of the body and soul of the native, you will look at the sign of the profection from the Moon.

For his professions and offices, you could look at the sign of the Mid-heaven.

But for knowing his wealth and prosperity, you could look at the sign of the profection from the Part of Fortune, and from the sign of the house of substance.

For the profection of brothers, you will look from the sign of the profection from the house of brothers.

For the profection of fathers, you will look from the sign of the profection from the house of fathers.

[1172] In other words, when doing a native's solar revolution, we ought to combine the significations of the profected Lord of the year (the *sālkhudāy*) and the Lord of the Ascendant of the revolution.

[1173] This phrase pertains to the use of mundane revolutions. If the ascending sign of the Aries ingress is either common or movable, then additional charts have to be cast for the year; if the sign is fixed, that chart will apply to the whole year (see Tr. 8). So far as I know, no medieval writer recommends multiple revolution charts in a given year for individual natives, if in fact Bonatti is suggesting that. So Bonatti is saying that this profected *sālkhudāy* will be a partner for the Lord of the Ascendant in the solar revolution, even if (in the case of mundane revolutions) there will be multiple Lords due to having multiple charts.

[1174] In other words, we can make specialized profections by profecting from other degrees in the chart–subject to the provision, of course, that the natal figure itself promises the good or bad things we are looking for. We cannot predict something (like great fame) that is denied by the natal figure.

For the profection of children, you will look from the profection of the sign of the house of children.

For the profection of male and female slaves, you will look from the sign of the profection from the house of slaves.

For the profection of wives and partners and enemies, you will look from the sign of the profection from the house of wives.

For the profection of [the wives'] substances, you will look from the sign of the profection from the house of the substance of wives.

For the profection of the religious, you will look from the sign of the profection from the house of the religious.

For the profection of kings, you will look from the sign of the profection from the house of kings.

For the profection of friends, you will look from the sign of the profection of the house of friends.

But for the profection of hidden enemies, you will look from the sign of the profection of the house of hidden enemies.

And know that a profection is a certain way of altering the revolution, which is individually according to the succession of the signs. For whatever kind of Ascendant it was, the profection does not come to be except from [one] sign to the sign which follows immediately, which does not happen so in a revolution.

And a profection alters a revolution according to this method: that if a good is signified by the revolution in that year, and a good is signified by the profection, the good that is signified by the revolution is increased. If however the contrary is signified by [the profection], the good which is signified by the revolution is decreased. Indeed if an evil is signified by the revolution and the profection, the evil which is signified by the revolution is increased. But if an evil is signified by the revolution, and a good by the profection, the evil which is signified by the revolution is decreased. And so, according to this, the profection is a different revolution.

Chapter 8: The order of the profection

The order of the profection is this: let us put it that someone is born with Aries rising by 10°. In the following year, Taurus will be the sign of the profection, by 10°–but it will not be the Ascendant of the revolution; but in a certain way it will bear itself toward it. In the third year, Gemini will be the sign of the profection, by 10°, but it will not be the Ascendant of the following revolution. And so on in order, up to the end of the signs. After finishing the twelve signs, the profection will revert to the first sign, and so you will order it up to the end of the native's life. And therefore I will give you a certain true example.

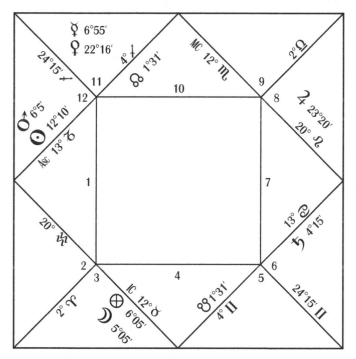

Figure 1: Nativity of Bonatti's Nephew

A certain nephew of mine was born in the era of the Arabs, in the 665th year, third month, nine days–and in the era of Christ 1267, the 6th day of the entrance into January.[1175] The ascending [sign] of whose nativity was Capricorn, 13°; and Mars in it, 6° and 5'; the Sun in it, 12° and 10'. The 2nd house was Aquarius, 20°. The 3rd house Aries, 2°. The 4th house Taurus, 12°, the Moon in it, 5° 5'. The Part of Fortune, 6° 5'. The 5th house Gemini, 4°. The Tail in it, 1° 31'. The 6th house Gemini, 24° 15'. The 7th house Cancer, 13°. Saturn in it, 4° 15'. The 8th house Leo, 20°. Jupiter in it, 23° 20'. The 9th house Libra, 2°. Scorpio the 10th house, 12°. Sagittarius the 11th house, 4°. The Head in it, 1° 31'. Mercury in it, 6° 55'. Venus, 22° 16'. The same Sagittarius [was] the 12th house, 23°.[1176]

Whence, when he had already passed five solar years, I looked at a certain revolution of his.[1177] And the fifth year from the Ascendant of his nativity arrived [by profection] at Gemini (which is the sixth sign from Capricorn), to its thirteenth degree; and the profection of the Sun likewise to its thirteenth degree. And Mercury was the *sālkhudāy*, or the Lord of that year or revolution. And the profection of Mars arrived at Gemini, to its seventh degree, and the profection of the Moon to the sixth degree of Libra (and it is the sixth sign from Taurus), and the profection of the Part of Fortune to the seventh degree of Libra, and the profection of Saturn arrived at the fifth degree of Sagittarius (which is the sixth sign from Cancer), and the profection of Jupiter arrived at the twenty-fourth [degree] of Capricorn (which is the sixth sign from Leo). The sign of Virgo was enclosed.[1178] And the profection of Mercury arrived at the sixth [degree] of Taurus (which is the sixth sign from Sagittarius). And the profection of Venus arrived at the thirteenth degree of Taurus. And the profection of the 10th house arrived at the twelfth degree of Aries (which is the sixth sign from the degree of the Midheaven of the nativity).

[1175] Bonatti's nephew could easily have been born in Forlì (44° N 13', 12° E 03'), especially since the relation between the Midheaven and the Ascendant gives a latitude very near 45°N latitude (unfortunately he does not give us the exact longitude of these cusps). Using Janus software I have cast a chart very close to these values, for December 27, 1267 JC (or January 3, 1268 GC), 7:41:00 AM LAT, at Forlì. Alchabitius semi-arc house cusps get us all of the intermediary cusps within a few degrees of longitude. But all of the planetary values are somewhat off. It is also unusual to see Bonatti mentioning all of the intermediary cusps, and here we can see him clearly use *domus* to mean quadrant houses, not domiciles.

[1176] Here we have a clear example of two cusps on a sign.

[1177] Unfortunately Bonatti does not provide the figure of the revolution–nor does he interpret the profections. But it does show that he could not have finished this section of the book until 1273 GC (1272 JC).

[1178] *I.e.,* intercepted.

To say what things happened to him in that year would already take a long time to narrate, wherefore I will not pursue it,[1179] but I will proceed to more useful things.

Therefore you will consider every profection of whatever kind you wish, because it will always be in such a degree (in the sign in which you were to find it), as the kind it was in, in the sign in which it was at the hour of the nativity, by changing it from one sign to the next one that immediately and successively follows it, in each year (namely the solar one), by one complete sign. And the planet which is the *al-mubtazz* over that place, or the one which is in it, or which projects its own rays to it, will be called the co-helper of the significator of that revolution[1180] with the *sālkhudāy*. But [the other planets listed] will not be called the *sālkhudāy*, except for the one who is the Lord of that sign. And if some one of the planets were in it, or its rays, and you wished to know when the profection will arrive at it or to its rays, al-Qabīsī said[1181] that you should look to see what there is between the degree to which the profection of the year has reached, and the planet (in terms of degrees and minutes), and you will multiply that by twelve and one-sixth of one day,[1182] and what results will be the days of that year in which you are.

Chapter 9: On the profection of the years of the world

But the profection of the years of the world varies somewhat from the profection of the years of a nativity.[1183] For the profection of the years of nativities is taken from the Ascendant of someone's nativity, then it is changed every solar year by one complete sign, just as was said. However, the profection of the years of the world is taken from the first minute of Aries, or even [from the first minute] of any inception of another great matter (like some kingdom or some empire, or some sect, or some religion)–like when the kingdom of Nebuchadnezzar began, or the kingdom of Ptolemy began, and the kingdom of Philip, and the kingdom of Alexander, and the kingdom of King Yazdigird,[1184] and the

---

1179 This is very disappointing.
1180 The "significator of the revolution" is obviously the Lord of the Ascendant of the revolution, based on what was said above.
1181 Al-Qabīsī, IV.8.
1182 Al-Qabīsī does not add "of one day" (*unius diei*).
1183 Again, Bonatti is following al-Qabīsī. But I note that while Bonatti mentions the reign of Yezdigird (see below), he adds Greek and Latin kings, and omits Muhammad.
1184 Undoubtedly the reign of Yazdigird III (r. 632-642), the last of the Sassanid emperors. He was defeated by the Arabs and lived in exile until he was assassinated by his troops in 651.

kingdom of the Romans [i.e. the Byzantines]; and just as it was when the sect or religion of [Saint] Augustine began, and the sect of [Saint] Benedict, and the sect of the Minor Brothers [the Franciscans], which began in the era of the Arabs in the 609th year,[1185] the month of the latter *Rabi*,[1186] in the era of Christ, 1211 years[1187]—the beginning of which was such an Ascendant that it will undermine[1188] all other sects and the other Orders existing under the Roman Church; but I do not dare to state its end, out of fear that I might fall into the rumor of the people. However, it was very public when it arrived, and the rumor about it immense.

And [for] like things (whose beginnings are had), their accidents will be generally be known forever; and by their annual revolutions will be known annual [accidents], having considered its beginning. And the profection interposes portions according to its nature (sometimes by adding, sometimes by diminishing, or by taking away from the revolution). By considering it from sign to sign, successively (as I said), the accidents of that matter (whose revolution you wished) could be known in that revolution. Nor however is this profection simply of such beginnings, as is the profection of the years of the world, but it is likened to it in a certain manner, on account of its long durability.

However, concerning the advancement[1189] from the Ascendant of the profection, and concerning a significator which is in one of the angles, or in one of the other places besides the angles, and concerning the significator of the right circle, and concerning the significator of the oblique circle, and concerning certain other things which are in the fourth chapter of the *Introduction* of al-Qabīsī for the judgment of this art,[1190] I do not speak just now, since it is determined enough concerning all of these in that Treatise, in a long discussion, so that it is not necessary that I should sweat about them now; and even because this work, even should it be useful and deep in knowledge, still it

---

[1185] See following note. Perhaps Bonatti is measuring by lunar years (which was standard for the Muslim calendar), as 609 years added to the Christian equivalent (622 AD) yields 1231, many years after the Franciscans were established.

[1186] Lat. *Rabae ultimi*. I take this to be the fourth month of the traditional Arab calendar (*Rabi al-thani* or *Rabi II*), described with its festival days in al-Bīrūnī (*Chron.*, p. 329). There are two months called *Rabi*, this one being the second one.

[1187] According to modern sources, the Order received its first Rule in 1210—another reminder that we cannot be completely confident with the dates Bonatti gives us. I note that his years are often 1 year off.

[1188] *Subradicabit*, treating it as *sub* + *radico*, i.e., "uproot" or "undermine."

[1189] *Profectione*. I do not find this particular phrase in the Latin edition of al-Qabīsī. Perhaps Bonatti is referring to the mundane material following in Ch. 14.

[1190] See Ch. 10 below.

renders something of greater labor than obvious benefit; but I will resolve the things which are more obviously useful.

It was spoken above concerning the direction according to the Lords of the bounds in the Second Part [of this Treatise], in the chapter on the knowledge of the life of the native and his condition.[1191] Therefore let it be spoken below about the significators to be directed, and in what way, and how we ought to direct them.

Chapter 10: On the direction of the significators to be directed in the circle, and how many are the significators which we must direct, which are directed by the wise

The significators which are directed, are seven, namely: [1] the degree of the Ascendant, [2] the degree of the Sun, [3] the degree of the Moon, [4] the degree of the Part of Fortune, [5] the degree of the Midheaven, [6] the degree of the conjunction, and likewise [7] the degree of the prevention.

And the degree of the Ascendant is directed for knowing the accidents which are going to come to the native in his own person[1192] (namely good, or bad or middling). For if you were to see the direction come to the good planets, say that there will be good accidents of his body. If however it were to arrive at the malefics, you will judge the contrary. If indeed to the bicorporeal or convertible ones,[1193] or to those having a middle disposition, you will pronounce the mediocre quality of the accidents (this is, neither truly good, nor truly evil).

Indeed the Sun is directed for knowing to what dignities or exaltations (which seem to pertain to honor and lay reputation) the native ought to come. Whence if the Sun were of good condition and well disposed, and the direction were to arrive at benefics well disposed, it will signify the native is going to come to great and famous honors. And if you were to find the contrary, you could judge the contrary. If however the Sun were disposed in a mediocre way, or the benefics to which the direction arrived

---

[1191] Part 2, Ch. 6.
[1192] Bonatti always uses *persona* to mean the physical body.
[1193] Bonatti probably means Mercury and the Moon, which are classed as "convertible" because they tend to take on the qualities of the planets with whom they are joined.

were disposed in a mediocre way, it will signify the native is going to come to some kind of dignities, but not very famous ones.

Indeed the Moon is directed for knowing the disposition of the native's body, and the quality of his soul, and likewise his marriage. Which if the Moon were of good condition, and well disposed, and the direction were to benefics well disposed, it will signify that the disposition of the native's body will be good and praiseworthy, and the quality of the soul, and that he will be well married (if the Lord of the 7th were of good condition and well disposed, and in a good aspect with the Lord of the Ascendant or with the Moon herself, or with the Lord of the Part of Marriage).[1194] But of the contrary you should observe the contrary; of what is mediocre, say what is mediocre.

The Part of Fortune is directed for knowing the native's wealth, and the advancement [or profit] of his monies, [and] even his acquisition. Whence if the Part of Fortune were well disposed, and the direction were to come to benefics well disposed, it signifies the native is going to acquire and accumulate much money by good means. If however the benefics were impeded, it signifies that he will acquire it, but after the acquisition he will dissipate it. But if you were to see the contrary, you could judge the contrary. If however you were to find mediocrity, pronounce mediocrity.

But the Midheaven is directed for knowing the native's works and his arts or professions (as al-Qabīsī says)[1195] and for all particular dispositions[1196] and their nature. Whence if the Lord of the Midheaven is well disposed, or the Midheaven itself, and the direction were to arrive at well-disposed benefics, the native will conduct himself well with respect to professions and with respect to duties [or offices], and to all work-projects[1197] and lay matters, and those things which pertain to them.

[1194] This last point illustrates an important principle–one cannot predict something that is not allowed already by the natal figure.

[1195] Al-Qabīsī, IV.12.200ff.

[1196] *Dispositiones particulares.* Bonatti is following John of Seville's translation of al-Qabīsī. Burnett's translation of the Arabic says "particular conditions of management."

[1197] *Fabrilitates. Fabrilis* and its paronyms have to do with tools, implements, and the activity of artisans.

But the degree of the conjunction is directed for generally knowing ahead of time and for considering, all the aforesaid up to the middle of the native's life (if the nativity were conjunctional). Whence if it were well disposed, it will increase the signification of those things signifying good, and will decrease what is signified by those signifying evil. If however it were badly disposed, it will increase the signification of those things signifying evil, and will take away from what is signified by those signifying good.

You could say the same about the degree of the prevention after the middle of life (if the nativity were preventional), and you will join the aspects of the benefics or the malefics with the *al-mubtazz* over the aforesaid degrees and their significators, because they will add or subtract according to their nature [or being], and according to their dispositions.[1198]

Indeed these aforesaid [significators] must be considered in nativities generally, and in the beginnings of other matters of which [some] end is expected.

Indeed if you wished to give attention to the aforesaid in the revolutions of years (both of the world and of nativities), look at the Ascendant of any one of those years. For if you wished to direct for the year of the world, al-Qabīsī said[1199] that for knowing the condition of the rustics ahead of time, we must direct the degree of the Ascendant of the revolution, and give one day to every 59' 8". And according to how the direction were to arrive at the benefics or at the malefics, you could judge according to that regarding their condition and status in those days, up to the end of that revolution—and this [is] according to the oblique circle.

If however you wished to look into the direction of kings, you will look for them from the degree of the Midheaven according to the right circle, by giving one day to every 59' 8", and thus you will know the accidents which ought to happen to kings in that revolution, in [the affairs] in which they are kings. But for their own personal affairs, and in their persons, you must look for them just as for other individual persons, and according to how you were to see the

---

[1198] Bonatti's view seems to be, then, that (a) conjunctional births can only direct the degree of the conjunction (and likewise for preventional births); and (b) we can only direct the degree of the *syzygy* for half of any native's life. Al-Qabīsī does not talk about directing the syzygies.

[1199] Al-Qabīsī, IV.13.

direction arrive at the benefics or at the malefics, you will judge according to that concerning the condition (whether good or bad or mediocre), both for kings and the rustics.

You could say the same for the nature [or being] of revolutions of nativities–nevertheless it is necessary that you consider revolutions of nativities from the Ascendant of nativities, and from the Ascendant of the revolution. But revolutions of the world [must be looked at] from the Ascendant of the revolution of the years of the world to know the condition of the common people according to the oblique circle; but the revolutions of kings according to the right circle for knowing their condition, according to what was said.

Chapter 11: On the nature of the degrees of the signs in any sign

And[1200] there is something else to be known, that the ancient sages (and especially the Indians) considered in nativities and questions and the beginnings of matters,[1201] and they said it was of the twelve planets and domiciles, or the twelve signs. For every sign is divided into twelve divisions, each of which consists of two-and-a-half degrees. And these divisions are given to the twelve signs, so that every sign has its own twelfth-part [1202] in each sign, and in that twelfth-part it signifies that sign to which is attributed that which pertains to the peculiar quality of its own nature, according to how Abū Ma'shar[1203] seemed to want it.

Whence, if you wished to know in the nature of what sign may be some degree of some sign, just as he will say,[1204] take the degrees which are from the beginning of the sign[1205] up to the degree whose twelfth-part you seek, and multiply it by 12, and divide what remains in this way, namely by giving 2° 30' to

---

[1200] Al-Qabīsī, IV.15.
[1201] I.e., in elections.
[1202] *Duodecima.* These are what John of Seville calls both *duodenariae* and *duodecimae* in his translation of al-Qabīsī and the *Gr. Intr.*
[1203] See Abū Ma'shar, *Gr. Intr.* V.18.
[1204] In what follows Bonatti gives a confusing version of al-Qabīsī, and he clearly does not care to tell us much. It helps to know that the first twelfth of each sign belongs to sign itself–i.e., the first 2° 30' of Leo belong to Leo, the second to Virgo, and so on in order in increments of 2° 30' up to the end of Leo. The procedure is more clearly spelled out in *Abbr.,* IV.32. The procedure is as follows. Let the degree of the planet whose twelfth we want, be at 1° Leo. Multiply 1° by 12 (=12°). Now cast out this 12° from the beginning of Leo, and see in what sign the counting stops. Obviously the counting stops while still in Leo–therefore the twelfth that rules 1° Leo, is that of Leo itself.
[1205] Reading *signi* with al-Qabīsī, for *signorum.*

each sign.[1206] And see where your number will have led you, because there will be the nature of the same degree of the sign in whose twelfth-part it fell.

[This] seems to certain modern sages to be understood thusly, namely that the degree of the Ascendant (or any other house, according to what that house signified) of whatever sign is taken, and it would be multiplied by twelve, and to what is collected are added the degrees of the ascending sign (or the house of which it were the beginning), and it is projected by 30, namely by giving 30 [degrees] to every sign or house. And this number is projected from the Ascendant or from the domicile in which you wished to begin, and where the number were finished, there will be the signification of the twelve signs and planets. Then look to see in the twelfth-part of which sign the number fell, because that sign and its Lord will offer help to the Ascendant or to another domicile (and its Lord) from which you might begin. Whence if that sign and its Lord were well-disposed, they add something in the good, and the subtract something from evil, namely by one-twelfth of each.[1207] If however the sign and its Lord were badly disposed, they will add something in evil, and will subtract something from the good, by one-twelfth. Which if the sign were well disposed and its Lord badly so (or *vice versa*), they will add or subtract in the good or in the evil by one twenty-fourth. But if one were well or badly disposed, and the other neither well nor badly, but mediocre, they will neither add nor diminish. And all of these are according to what there was concerning the nature of that sign or that planet.

And the sages understood this to be the twelfth-part of the planets and domiciles. And even though this chapter might not seem to be of great usefulness, and it may be difficult, still it is appropriate that you know it. For in a certain manner it renders you more fluent.[1208]

[1206] Here I think we see that Bonatti is using a different method to yield the same results. Let the same planet be at 1° Leo again. Multiply its position by 12, to yield 12° again. Divide this result by 2° 30', which yields 4° 48'. This treats each full degree as being one sign, with the remainder pertaining to the sign whose twelfth we want. If we start from Aries, we see that the first 4° are taken up by the first four signs (Aries, Taurus, Gemini, Cancer). The remainder (48') falls in the next sign Leo, which was the result we got using Abū Ma'shar's method.

[1207] Adding or subtracting one-twelfth of the good or bad does not seem like much, and hardly worth the trouble to figure out.

[1208] *Facundiorem.* This must mean, "more fluent in the literature of the ancient sages."

On the ninth-parts[1209] *of the signs, and what they would signify*

Mention having been made above in the preceding chapter concerning the twelfth-parts of the signs (or concerning the nature of the twelve signs in each sign), their ninth-parts should not be overlooked. For indeed the ancient sages said that we must know how much a planet has walked in the sign in which you were to find it, in terms of degrees and minutes, or how many degrees have ascended of the house[1210] whose ninth-part you wished to know.

Then, divide the sign into nine divisions, each of which consists of 3° 20', and you will begin to project from the beginning of the sign in which is the planet or the degree of the house from which you began. And see in which ninth-part that degree were to fall, and you will give that ninth-part to the Lord of the movable sign of that triplicity of the Ascendant, or of the aforesaid domicile, and you will give the second ninth-part to the Lord of the sign which immediately succeeds the Ascendant or aforesaid house. And the third [ninth-part] to the Lord of the third sign which succeeds the second, and the fourth to the Lord of the fourth sign which succeeds that one, and the fifth to the Lord of the fifth sign which succeeds that one, and the sixth to the Lord of the sixth [sign] which succeeds that one, and the seventh to the Lord of the seventh sign which succeeds the first [sign], and the eighth to the Lord of the eighth sign which succeeds the first one, and the ninth one to the Lord of the ninth sign which succeeds the first one.[1211] And you should always do this until you were to find a planetary ruler of that ninth which you seek, by the following example:

The Ascendant or the domicile from which I began was Aries or Leo or Sagittarius. So Mars is the Lord of the first ninth-part, because he is the Lord of the movable sign of this triplicity (namely, Aries). Venus is the Lady of the second ninth-part, because she is the Lady of Taurus, which is the second sign from the first one (namely from the ascending one), and it succeeds it immediately. The third ninth-part is Mercury, who is the Lord of Gemini (which is the third sign from the first one). The fourth ninth-part belongs to the Moon, who is the Lady of Cancer (which is the fourth sign from the first one). The fifth ninth-part belongs to the Sun, the Lord of Leo (which is the fifth sign from the first one). The sixth ninth-part belongs to Mercury, the Lord of Virgo (which is

---

[1209] *Novenariis*. A *novenaria* is the equivalent to one version of the Arabic *nawbahrat*, called the *navamsa* by the Indians. Bonatti's description is right out of al-Qabīsī, IV.16-17.

[1210] This could also be read as "domicile." The point is that we can look to see in what ninth of a *domicile*, the cusp of a *house* falls, just as we do with a planet in a domicile.

[1211] This procedure has the effect of granting all three members of the triplicity rulership over a ninth: in the first, the middle (the fifth) and the last ninths.

the sixth sign from the first one). The seventh ninth-part belongs to Venus, the Lady of Libra (which is the seventh sign from the first one). The eighth ninth-part belongs to Mars, the Lord of Scorpio (which is the eighth sign from the first one). The ninth ninth-part belongs to Jupiter, the Lord of Sagittarius (which is the ninth sign from the first one).

On the second triplicity

If however the Ascendant or aforesaid house were Taurus, Virgo, or Capricorn, the first ninth-part will belong to Saturn, the Lord of Capricorn. Indeed the second ninth-part will belong to Saturn, the Lord of Aquarius. The third ninth-part to Jupiter, Lord of Pisces. The fourth to Mars, Lord of Aries. The fifth to Venus, Lady of Taurus. The sixth to Mercury, Lord of Gemini. The seventh to the Moon, Lady of Cancer. The eighth to the Sun, Lord of Leo. The ninth to Mercury, Lord of Virgo.

And understand thusly about the third and fourth triplicity, if the Ascendant or some house were some sign of the said triplicity, always by starting from the movable sign of that triplicity of the Ascendant or house, and by proceeding in order, as was said.

Therefore you should see an example of the aforesaid:[1212] therefore let it be put that some planet, or the beginning of some house from which you wished to begin, is in the twenty-first degree of Taurus. You would divide all of Taurus into nine divisions. Therefore the first division, i.e., the first ninth-part, will belong to Saturn, the Lord of Capricorn, and you will have 3° 20' of Taurus. The second ninth-part belongs to the same Saturn, Lord of Aquarius, and thus you have 6° 40' [total]. The third ninth-part will belong to Jupiter, Lord of Pisces, [and] behold you have 10 full degrees. The fourth ninth-part belongs to Mars, the Lord of Aries, and you have 13° 20' [total]. The fifth one belongs to Venus the Lady of Taurus, and you have 16° 40' [total]. The sixth one belongs to Mercury the Lord of the Gemini, and you have 20 full degrees. The seventh one belongs to the Moon, the Lady of Cancer–and behold, you have 23° 20'.

Thus the planet or the degree of the aforesaid house falls necessarily into the ninth-part of the Moon, whence it is necessary that the Moon be the Lady of that ninth-part. And according to how the Moon were then disposed, so will she [either] offer support to the Ascendant and its Lord (or to the house from which you began the matter), or the *al-mubtazz* of the nativity (or of the

---

[1212] Omitting a redundant *exemplum ad praedicta.*

question, or of any other inception)—or she will take away from him from what he signifies. For if she were well disposed, and the Ascendant well disposed, she will support by approximately one-seventh in the good. If however each were badly disposed, she will take away from him according to a like portion. But if one were well disposed, and the other badly, they will neither add nor diminish.

However, you will always consider the Lords of the triplicities and the bounds, because they will always remain in their own condition, and in their own significations, just as was said above.

Concerning the *ad-darijān*,[1213] I do not say anything here, because it seems to pertain to a consideration of the faces, concerning which it was sufficiently and broadly discussed above in the First Treatise, in the chapter on the faces.

Chapter 13: On the Lord of the circle or of the orb of the signs[1214]

You will consider, in nativities, the Lord of the orb or circle of signs in this way. Indeed you will look at the Lord of the Ascendant of the nativity of whatever native, and at its first hour, and you will give the Ascendant, and its Lord, and the Lord of its hour, to the first year of that native, because these two will signify the condition [or being] of the native, of what kind he is going to be in the first year of his life. Whence if both were well disposed, his condition will be good in that year. If however it were the contrary, you will judge the contrary. But if one were well disposed, and the other badly, then you could announce the condition of the native is going to be mediocre, unless the Moon or the Lords of the triplicities or of the bounds work against it. You could say the same about the good and bad condition of his body. Then you will look at the Lord of the 2nd house [domicile?], and the Lord of the second hour, to see how they were disposed; for if their disposition were good, the substance of the native will be well disposed in the second year; concerning the contrary, you will judge the contrary. Which if one were well disposed, and the other badly, the substance of the native will be disposed in a middling way. After this, look at the Lord of the 3rd house [domicile?], and the Lord of the third hour, to see how

---

1213 Lat. *dorungez*, from the Arabic الدريجان, either a term of art or meaning "[two] degrees/steps" (al-Qabīsī, IV.18; see also al-Bīrūnī, *Instr.* §451). This is an alternative way of assigning rulerships to the faces. Instead of them being ruled successively by the planets (in descending Chaldean order), the faces of each sign are ruled by the Lords of three signs of the triplicity to which that sign belongs. So the faces of Aries are ruled (in order) by Mars, the Sun and Jupiter.

1214 Based on al-Qabīsī, IV.19. Al-Qabīsī calls this the "lord of the period in nativities."

they were disposed. For the condition of the brothers in the third year will be disposed according to [these Lords'] condition [in the nativity]. And so on in order, by proceeding according to disposition and the condition of the Lords of the houses [domiciles?] and of the hours, up to the twelfth, you will judge concerning the significations of all of the houses [domiciles?] in his years, according to the aforesaid method, which was now stated for the 1st, 2nd, and 3rd house [domicile?].

Chapter 14: On the Lords of the twelve leftover hours

But[1215] concerning the Lords of the twelve hours left over after the aforesaid [hours], you will consider in this way successively, just as you considered the aforesaid and their Lords. For indeed you will give the thirteenth[1216] hour and its Lord to the 1st house [domicile?] and to the Lord of the first hour, for it will offer support to the Ascendant and its Lord, in the increase of good by a twenty-fourth part, if they both (that is, the hour and the Lord of the hour) were well disposed–and even the Ascendant and its Lord.[1217]

If however the Ascendant and its Lord were badly disposed, it will subtract from their malice by one-fourth. But if the Lord at the thirteenth hour were badly disposed, it will subtract one-twenty-fourth of the good, and it will increase the evil by the same amount in the first year–and understand thusly concerning the rest of the hours successively, by proceeding, in order. For according to how he and their Lords are disposed, so will they assist or impede the disposition of the other significators, according to the significations of the twelve houses in his years, just as even according to natural things it can happen in those years–just as was said concerning the thirteenth and its Lord, which are given to the Ascendant and its Lord, so the fourteenth and its Lord[1218] are given to the 2nd house [domicile?] and so on in order.[1219]

1215 This ought not to have been made a separate chapter, as it simply continues al-Qabīsī's text from above, and on the same topic.

1216 Reading *tredecimam* for *duodecimam*, following al-Qabīsī.

1217 That is, if the Ascendant and its Lord were also well disposed.

1218 Reading *dominus* for *domino*.

1219 To put it briefly, the technique is very much like profections, except that the Lord of the planetary hour takes the place of the Lord of the sign of the profection. The (a) planetary lord of each hour will testify to the condition of (b) the relevant natal house and (c) the relevant year of the native's life. So when the native is in his third year (age 2), the third planetary hour Lord will testify as to the native's third year and the condition of the brothers; in the next year, the fourth planetary hour Lord will testify as to the native's fourth year and the condition of the parents; and so on. Since the signs form a cycle of 12, and the planets a cycle

And according to this method you will look ahead to all houses, and their Lords, and to all hours and their Lords. For every Lord of these houses and these hours (as al-Qabīsī testifies), is a Lord of the orb, and it has a signification for every year over everything signified in that year to which it is deputed, according to what the *sālkhudāy* has,[1220] and it disposes the significations of the native according to how he were well or badly disposed, by adding or subtracting in good or evil, by the above-named portions.

And al-Qabīsī said that certain ones of the astrologers make the Lord of the Ascendant of the root of the nativity the Lord of the orb in the first year; and in the second [year] the planet who succeeds him (just as was said for the Lord of the hour)–and it seems to me this could appropriately be upheld; not that they are the Lords of the orb pure and simple, but they are co-helpers of the aforesaid.[1221]

[More on profections]

I would even say certain things according to what he handed down, which seems to be appropriate for you to know; and even though it has more labor than usefulness, still it renders you more profound in the science of profection. And [al-Qabīsī] spoke[1222] about the profection of certain ones of them, and even of certain other matters, as I will recite to you in what follows.

For indeed the said philosopher said, that al-Kindī said,[1223] that between the year of the conjunction which signified the sect of the Saracens and the year of the Hijra (which was the first year of the years of the Arabs), there were 51 [complete] solar years.[1224] And the Ascendant of the year of the conjunction of

---

of 7, this technique quickly gives rise to a great multiplicity of combinations (as opposed to the more common profection method).

[1220] I.e., because the years follow the order of the profections.

[1221] In other words, these other astrologers look at the ecliptical ordering of the planets, instead of the order of the signs or hours. Suppose the Lord of the Ascendant is Jupiter, and he happens to be in the 9th, with Saturn somewhere after him, and the Moon somewhere after Saturn, and so on. Then the native's first year will be ruled by Jupiter; the second, by Saturn; the third, by the Moon; and so on. Like the planetary hour scheme, the rulership would return to the same planet after seven years.

[1222] The following material is based on al-Qabīsī, IV.9ff.

[1223] Al-Qabīsī later gives an alternative view derived from Abū Ma'shar's *OGC*. See below.

[1224] Al-Qabīsī is using the following dates. The year of the Saturn-Jupiter conjunction heralding the "sect of the Saracens" or the rise of Islam was in 571 AD. The year in which the Hijra took place (forming the actual beginning of Islam) was 622 AD. Al-Qabīsī's text says 52 years, because since the Hijra took place in the middle of 622, only 51 had been completed and the 52nd year was still in effect.

the aforesaid sect [in 571 AD], in that region, was the sign Gemini. And the profection of that same year arrived at Virgo.[1225] And between that first year of the years of the Arabs [in 622 AD] and the first one of the years of Yazdigird (the King of the Persians), were 3,624 days.[1226] Therefore if you wished to have knowledge of this matter, take the years of Yazdigird, and turn them into days (just as was done in the book of the courses of the planets),[1227] and add from above the days which there are between the first one of the years of the Arabs and of Yazdigird, and divide this by 365 days and one-fourth of a day, and how many divisions come out, the solar years will be that many; and how many remain in terms of months and days, will be of an incomplete year.[1228] And what is conjoined or collected together in terms of years, those are the solar years from the beginning of the years of the Arabs. Therefore project one sign for every year, and begin from Virgo, and to whatever sign the number were to lead you, that will be the sign to which the year of the world (from the ascension of the conjunction of the aforesaid sect) will have arrived.[1229]

However, to others (like Abū Ma'shar and his followers)[1230] it seemed that we would add on top of the years of Yazdigird, 61[1231] complete years and two months, and 12 days, and 16[1232] hours from the years of the Persians (which are without fractions and without a one-fourth day),[1233] and they extended these

---

[1225] I.e., profecting from Gemini through 51 complete years brings us into Virgo, which was the profected Ascendant for that Great Conjunction in the 52nd (ongoing) year in which the Hijra took place.

[1226] The beginning of the period of Yazdigird, was June 16, 632 AD. See Burnett's notes to al-Qabīsī, pp. 119ff. Bonatti mistakenly says 3,124, but I am taking al-Qabīsī as being more accurate.

[1227] The *Zij*, according to al-Qabīsī.

[1228] Al-Qabīsī is simply saying that we should subtract the date of the Hijra from the date of the first year of Yazdigird's reign, to give us an exact number of years, months, and days between the two. In the solar calendar, this gives 9 years, 11 months, 2 days (using 30-day months to get the days). Abū Ma'shar (*OGC* VIII.8) has 9 "Persian" years, 11 months, 9 days.

[1229] Now we see that he is simply trying to get us to practice profecting–since we already know that the Hijra happened when the years of the world were profected from Gemini to Virgo, we now profect from the Hijra to see what sign the profection reaches to at the beginning of the first year of Yazdigird. By my reckoning, the profected Ascendant for the year 632 (Yazdigird) is Cancer.

[1230] Al-Qabīsī IV.10, *OGC* VIII.8.

[1231] Reading *61* (with al-Qabīsī) for *51*.

[1232] Reading *16* (with al-Qabīsī) for *18*.

[1233] This seems to be poorly phrased in al-Qabīsī. Abū Ma'shar is simply adding the years from the Great Conjunction to the Hijra (= 51 years, 3 months, 3 days) to the years from the Hijra to Yazdigird (= 9 years, 11 months, 9 days, according to Abū Ma'shar), to yield 61 years, 2 months, 12 days, 16 hours. This is not really a different sort of calculation, it is just

years into days, and they turned those days into solar years (as was said), and they began to project from the beginning of Libra.[1234]

Which if you wished to know the [terminal point of the] profection from the sign of the conjunction of such a sect, let the projection be from Scorpio, because the conjunction of the planets which signified the sect [of Islam] began from Scorpio.[1235] Indeed if you wished [to know] the [terminal point of the] profection from the ascension of the kingdom [of the Abbasids],[1236] subtract from the complete years of Yazdigird 118 complete years, and turn them into solar years, just as was said, and begin to project from Virgo.

(Here, however it must be known that Muhammad[1237] was not the aforesaid king, but a prophet, and so the kingdom [of the Abbasids] did not begin from his own time, but it began long after [the Great Conjunction], perhaps by 117 Persian years, and the Arabs began to reign. And the Ascendant had returned to Virgo, and it seems that there may be an error in this literature. For this is not so, but then the kingdom of the Arabs changed to the blackness of that day;[1238] and this is had in the second figure of the three figures of the last section of the book of *Alalraren*.)[1239]

The profection from the Ascendant of the change[1240]

On the other hand,[1241] if you wanted [the terminal point of the profection] from the Ascendant of the change of the conjunction from the watery triplicity to the fiery triplicity, subtract 176 years from the complete years of Yazdigird, and turn those which remain into solar years, and begin the projection from

---

Abū Ma'shar pointing out that we can profect right from the Great Conjunction to Yazdigird (skipping the Hijra) by adding together the intermediary years.
[1234] Abū Ma'shar says that the Ascendant of the Great Conjunction was Scorpio, but he seems to think that the Ascendant of the year for the Hijra was Libra (not Virgo). There seems to be a difference in the method of counting between Abū Ma'shar and al-Kindī.
[1235] See above footnote.
[1236] See footnote to al-Qabīsī, IV.10. The Abbasid dynasty began in 750 AD.
[1237] Lat. *Machomethus*.
[1238] I do not understand what Bonatti means, unless this is a criticism of Islam (which is certainly possible).
[1239] Unknown word or title. Since the above material based on Abū Ma'shar comes from the last sections of *OGC*, maybe the book had a different title (composed of Latinized Arabic) in Bonatti's edition.
[1240] Reading *ascendente* for *ascensione*, and *mutationis* for *profectionis*, following al-Qabīsī and my amended rendering of Bonatti below. The "change" is the mutation of the Saturn-Jupiter conjunctions from the watery triplicity into the fiery one.
[1241] I have substituted the correct words and some brackets to make Bonatti's Latin clearer, as this passage comes directly out of al-Qabīsī but with some confusion in the first sentence.

Leo. And to where the number were to arrive in that same sign, will be the [terminal point of the] profection of each beginning, of those which were said.

Chapter 15: On the direction of a significator[1242]

And after this, the direction of a significator. This is that you direct the significator which you wanted, to some place of the signs. And you should know what there is between them (in terms of degrees of the direction), and you will take one year for every degree.

[1] Therefore if you wished to know this, and the significator which you want to direct to some part of the circle were in the Ascendant,[1243] subtract the ascensions of the degree (in which the significator is) by the ascensions of the region,[1244] from the ascensions of the degree to which you wished to direct him. And what remained will be the degrees of the direction.

Which if the significator were in the opposite of the ascending degree, subtract the ascensions of the opposite degree (in which the significator is), from the ascensions of the opposite degree to which you wished to direct him in that region (because the setting of some one sign agrees with the risings of its opposite one).[1245]

And[1246] it must be known that the degrees of the direction (for which one year is taken for each), are the degrees of the equatorial day. And the degrees which are directed, and to which the direction is, are the degrees of the oblique circle.[1247]

[1242] Much of this material consists of verbatim quotations from the Latin edition of al-Qabīsī, IV.11. Bonatti merely inserts a sentence or synonym here and there. But when it comes down to the details of the math, Bonatti rushes through a few details and then refers the reader to al-Qabīsī's clear and full account (see below).

[1243] Here there is ambiguity between whether the Latin edition means the "degree of the Ascendant" or the "ascending sign," but al-Qabīsī makes it clear he means the actual degrees of the Ascendant and Descendant.

[1244] Here Bonatti means "by oblique ascension."

[1245] This is a bit garbled. Al-Qabīsī is trying to provide a shortcut. Since the oblique descension of a significator on the Descendant is 180° from the one on the Ascendant, he is suggesting that we use the already-known degrees on the Ascendant to figure out the arc. So if the Descendant is 5° Libra and we want to direct it to some other degree (say, 5° Scorpio), we could simply calculate the arc using 5° Aries (the Ascendant) to 5° Taurus (using oblique ascensions, of course).

[1246] This paragraph is Bonatti's own.

[1247] Bonatti is reminding us that while we are interested in directions between zodiacal positions ("degrees of the oblique circle"), they must be converted for timing purposes into degrees of right ascension on the celestial equator ("degrees of the equatorial day").

[2] Indeed if the significator were in the 10th or the 4th,[1248] you will subtract the [right] ascensions of the degree of the significator from the [right] ascensions of the degree to which you wished to direct him; but the ascensions of the right circle, and how many were to remain, will be the degrees of the direction.

[3] But if the significator which you wished to direct were not in one of the angles, you will look at its distance[1249] from the angle from which he is less distant (namely from the angle of the 10th house, or from the angle of the 4th house). Which if he were between the Ascendant and the 10th, subtract the ascensions of the degrees of the 10th house from the ascensions of the degree of the significator, by the right circle. And if it were between the 7th and the 10th, subtract the ascensions of the degree of the significator (by the right circle) from the degrees of the 10th house (likewise by right circle). And what remained from any one of these places, you will divide it by the parts of the hours of that day of the degree in which the significator is. And what were to come out of that division, will be the "hours of the length from the angle."

And if it were between the Ascendant and the 4th house, you will subtract the ascensions of the degree of the significator (by the right circle) from the [right] ascensions of the [degree of the] 4th house. On the other hand, if the significator were between the 4th and the 7th, you will subtract the [right] ascensions of the degree of the 4th house from the ascensions of the significator (by the right circle). And what remained of each of those places, you will divide it by the parts of the hours of the night of the degree in which the significator is. (And this is if the significators are in one quarter of the circle and not in different ones.)[1250]

And if the significator were in the middle of the eastern circle (which is from the 10th up to the 4th, from those which succeed the Ascendant),[1251] subtract the [right] ascensions of the degree in which the significator is, from the ascensions

---

[1248] The Latin edition of al-Qabīsī says "in the Midheaven or the angle of the earth." Al-Qabīsī is clear that this means the *degree* of the Midheaven and the *Imum Coeli*, not just anywhere in the 10th or 4th.

[1249] I am following the critical edition of al-Qabīsī in reading "distance" for "longitude" (*longitudo*).

[1250] That is to say, if both the significator and the promittor are in the same quadrant (e.g., between the Ascendant and the degree of the Midheaven). If they are in different quadrants, al-Qabīsī (IV.12) says we simply use methods [1] and [2] above to move the significator to the angle between them, and then from the angle to the promittor, adding the two sums together. For instance, if the significator is in the 9th house and the promittor is in the 11th, we measure the right ascension between the significator and the Midheaven, and add that to the distance in right ascension between the Midheaven and the promittor.

[1251] I.e., in the eastern half of the chart.

of the degree of the one to which you wished to direct (by the right circle), and what remained, will be the "significator of the right circle." Save this.

After this, subtract the ascensions of the degree in which the significator is (by the [oblique] ascensions of the region) from the ascensions of the degree to which you wished to direct him (by [oblique] ascensions of the region), and what there was, will be the "significator of the region."

After this, you will look at the [numerical] remainder which there is between the "significator of the right circle" and the "significator of the region,"[1252] and you will take one-sixth of the remainder, and you will multiply [it] by the "hours of the length from the angle." And what comes out, will be the "equation." That is, if the length were of one hour, you will take one-sixth. And if it were more, you will take more sixths, so that you will take one sixth for every hour. And if the "significator of the right circle" were less than the "significator of the region," you will add the equation on top of the "significator of the right circle." And if it were greater, you will subtract the equation from it. And what remained, will be the degrees of the direction.[1253]

And if the significator were in the middle of the western circle, you will do at length as al-Qabīsī says (who gives fully the method of directing).[1254]

[1252] Reading *regionis* for *regionum*.
[1253] I.e., the arc of the direction that gives the time in years.
[1254] Al-Qabīsī repeats the method for significators and promittors on the western half of the chart.

BIBLIOGRAPHY

Abu Bakr, *Liber Genethliacus* (Nuremberg: Johannes Petreius, 1540)

Abū Ma'shar al-Balhi, *The Abbreviation of the Introduction to Astrology*, ed. and trans. Charles Burnett, K. Yamamoto, and Michio Yano (Leiden: E.J. Brill, 1994)

Abū Ma'shar al-Balhi, *Liber Introductorii Maioris ad Scientiam Iudiciorum Astrorum*, vols. VI, V, VI, IX, ed. Richard Lemay (Naples: Istituto Universitario Orientale, 1995)

Abū Ma'shar al-Balhi, *The Abbreviation of the Introduction to Astrology*, ed. and trans. Charles Burnett, annotated by Charles Burnett, G. Tobyn, G. Cornelius and V. Wells (ARHAT Publications, 1997)

Abū Ma'shar al-Balhi, *On Historical Astrology: The Book of Religions and Dynasties (On the Great Conjunctions)*, vols. I-II, eds. and trans. Keiji Yamamoto and Charles Burnett (Leiden: Brill, 2000)

Abū Ma'shar al-Balhi, *The Flowers of Abū Ma'shar*, trans. Benjamin Dykes (2nd ed., 2007)

Al-Biruni, Muhammad ibn Ahmad, *The Chronology of Ancient Nations*, trans. and ed. C. Edward Sachau (London: William H. Allen and Co., 1879)

Al-Biruni, Muhammad ibn Ahmad, *The Book of Instruction in the Elements of the Art of Astrology*, trans. R. Ramsay Wright (London: Luzac & Co., 1934)

Al-Fārābī, *De Ortu Scientiarum* (appearing as *"Alfarabi Über den Ursprung der Wissenschaften (De Ortu Scientiarum)*," ed. Clemens Baeumker, *Beiträge zur Geschichte der Philosophie des Mittelalters*, v. 19/3, 1916.

Al-Khayyat, Abu 'Ali, *The Judgments of Nativities*, trans. James H. Holden (Tempe, AZ: American Federation of Astrologers, Inc., 1988)

Al-Kindī, *The Forty Chapters (Iudicia Astrorum): The Two Latin Versions*, ed. Charles Burnett (London: The Warburg Institute, 1993)

Al-Mansur (attributed), *Capitula Almansoris*, ed. Plato of Tivoli (1136) (Basel: Johannes Hervagius, 1533)

Al-Qabīsī, *Isagoge*, trans. John of Spain, with commentary by John of Saxony (Paris: Simon Colinaeus, 1521)

Al-Qabīsī, *The Introduction to Astrology*, eds. Charles Burnett, Keiji Yamamoto, Michio Yano (London and Turin: The Warburg Institute, 2004)

Al-Rijāl, 'Alī, *In Iudiciis Astrorum* (Venice: Erhard Ratdolt, 1485)

Al-Rijāl, 'Alī, *Libri de Iudiciis Astrorum* (Basel: Henrichus Petrus, 1551)

Al-Tabarī, 'Umar, *De Nativitatibus* (Basel: Johannes Hervagius, 1533)

Al-Tabarī, 'Umar [Omar of Tiberias], *Three Books of Nativities*, ed. Robert Schmidt, trans. Robert Hand (Berkeley Springs, WV: The Golden Hind Press, 1997)

Alighieri, Dante, *Inferno*, trans. John Ciardi (New York, NY: Mentor, 1982)

Allen, Richard Hinckley, *Star Names: Their Lore and Meaning* (New York: Dover Publications Inc., 1963)

Aristotle, *The Complete Works of Aristotle* vols. I-II, ed. Jonathan Barnes (Princeton, NJ: Princeton University Press, 1984)

Bloch, Marc, *Feudal Society*, vols. I-II, trans. L.A. Manyon (Chicago: University of Chicago Press, 1961)

Bonatti, Guido, *Decem Tractatus Astronomiae* (Erhard Ratdolt: Venice, 1491)

Bonatti, Guido, *De Astronomia Tractatus X* (Basel, 1550)

Bonatti, Guido, *Liber Astronomiae: Books One, Two, and Three with Index*, trans. Robert Zoller and Robert Hand (Salisbury, Australia: Spica Publications, 1988)

Bonatti, Guido, *Liber Astronomiae Part IV: On Horary, First Part*, ed. Robert Schmidt, trans. Robert Hand (Berkeley Springs, WV: The Golden Hind Press, 1996)

Boncompagni, Baldassarre, *Della Vita e Della Opere di Guido Bonatti, Astrologo et Astronomo del Seculo Decimoterzo* (Rome: 1851)

Brady, Bernadette, *Brady's Book of Fixed Stars* (Boston: Weiser Books, 1998)

Burnett, Charles, ed., *Magic and Divination in the Middle Ages* (Aldershot, Great Britain: Ashgate Publishing Ltd., 1996)

Burnett, Charles and Gerrit Bos, *Scientific Weather Forecasting in the Middle Ages* (London and New York: Kegan Paul International, 2000)

Carmody, Francis, *Arabic Astronomical and Astrological Sciences in Latin Translation: A Critical Bibliography* (Berkeley and Los Angeles: University of California Press, 1956)

Carmody, Francis, *The Astronomical works of Thābit b. Qurra* (Berkeley and Los Angeles: University of California Press, 1960)

Dorotheus of Sidon, *Carmen Astrologicum*, trans. David Pingree (Abingdon, MD: The Astrology Center of America, 2005)

Grant, Edward, *Planets, Stars, and Orbs: The Medieval Cosmos, 1200–1687* (New York, NY: Cambridge University Press, 1994)

Haskins, Charles H., "Michael Scot and Frederick II," *Isis*, v. 4/2 (1921), pp. 250-75.

Haskins, Charles H., "Science at the Court of the Emperor Frederick II," *The American Historical Review*, v. 27/4 (1922), pp. 669-94.

Hermes Trismegistus, *Liber Hermetis*, ed. Robert Hand, trans. Robert Zoller (Salisbury, Australia: Spica Publications, 1998)

Holden, James H., *A History of Horoscopic Astrology* (Tempe, AZ: American Federation of Astrologers, Inc., 1996)

Ibn Labban, Kusyar, *Introduction to Astrology*, ed. and trans. Michio Yano (Tokyo: Institute for the Study of Languages and Cultures of Asia and Africa, 1997)

Ibn Sina (Avicenna), *The Canon of Medicine (al-Qanun fi'l tibb)*, ed. Laleh Bakhtiar (Great Books of the Islamic World, Inc., 1999)

Kennedy, Edward S., "The Sasanian Astronomical Handbook Zīj-I Shāh and the Astrological Doctrine of 'Transit' (Mamarr)," *Journal of the American Oriental Society*, v. 78/4 (1958), pp. 246-62.

Kunitzsch, Paul, "Mittelalterliche astronomisch-astrologische Glossare mit arabischen Fachausdrücken," *Bayerische Akademie der Wissenschaften Philosophisch-Historische Klasse*, 1977, v. 5

Kunitsch, Paul, trans. and ed., "Liber de Stellis Beibeniis," in *Hermetis Trismegisti: Astrologica et Divinatoria* (Turnhout: Brepols Publishers, 2001).

Kunitzsch, Paul and Tim Smart, *A Dictionary of Modern Star Names* (Cambridge, MA: New Track Media, 2006)

Latham, R.E., *Revised Medieval Latin Word-List from British and Irish Sources* (Oxford: Oxford University Press, 2004)

Lemay, Richard, *Abu Ma'shar and Latin Aristotelianism in the Twelfth Century* (Beirut: American University of Beirut, 1962)

Levy, Raphael, "A Note on the Latin Translators of Ibn Ezra," *Isis*, v. 37 nos. 3/4 (1947), pp. 153-55.

Lilly, William, *The Starry Messenger* (London: Company of Stationers and H. Blunden, 1652). Reprinted 2004 by Renaissance Astrology Facsimile Editions.

Lilly, William, *Anima Astrologiae*, trans. Henry Coley (London: B. Harris, 1676)

Lilly, William, *Christian Astrology*, vols. I-II, ed. David R. Roell (Abingdon, MD: Astrology Center of America, 2004)

Long, A.A. and D.N. Sedley, *The Hellenistic Philosophers*, vol. I (Cambridge: Cambridge University Press, 1987)

Māshā'allāh *et al.*, *Liber Novem Iudicum in Iudiciis Astrorum* [Book of the Nine Judges], ed. Peter Liechtenstein (Venice: 1509)

Māshā'allāh, *De Receptione* [*On Reception*] and *De Revolutione Annorum Mundi* and *De Interpraetationibus*, in *Messahalae Antiquissimi ac Laudatissimi Inter Arabes Astrologi, Libri Tres*, ed. Joachim Heller (Nuremberg: Joannes Montanus and Ulrich Neuber, 1549)

Māshā'allāh, *On Reception*, ed. and trans. Robert Hand (ARHAT Publications, 1998)

Maternus, Firmicus Julius, *Matheseos Libri VIII*, eds. W. Kroll and F. Skutsch (Stuttgard: Teubner, 1968)

Michelsen, Neil F., *The Koch Book of Tables* (San Diego: ACS Publications, Inc., 1985)

Mantello, F.A.C. and A.G. Rigg, eds., *Medieval Latin: An Introduction and Bibliographical Guide* (Washington, DC: The Catholic University of America Press, 1996)

New Oxford Annotated Bible, ed. Bruce M. Metzger and Roland E. Murphy (New York: Oxford University Press, 1994)

Pingree, David, "Astronomy and Astrology in India and Iran," *Isis* v. 54/2 (1963), pp. 229-46.

Pingree, David, "Classical and Byzantine Astrology in Sassanian Persia," *Dumbarton Oaks Papers*, v. 43 (1989), pp. 227-239.

Pingree, David, *From Astral Omens to Astrology: From Babylon to Bīkāner* (Rome: Istituto italiano per L'Africa e L'Oriente, 1997)

Pseudo-Ptolemy, *Centiloquium*, ed. Georgius Trapezuntius, in Bonatti (1550)

Ptolemy, Claudius, *Tetrabiblos* vols. 1, 2, 4, trans. Robert Schmidt, ed. Robert Hand (Berkeley Springs, WV: The Golden Hind Press, 1994-98)

Ptolemy, Claudius, *Tetrabiblos*, trans. F.E. Robbins (Cambridge and London: Harvard University Press, 1940)

Ptolemy, Claudius, *Quadripartitum* [Tetrabiblos], trans. Plato of Tivoli (1138) (Basel: Johannes Hervagius, 1533)

Sahl ibn Bishr, *Introductorium* and *Praecipua Iudicia* [The Fifty Judgments] *De Interrogationibus* and *De Electionibus*, in *Tetrabiblos*, ed. Girolamo Salio (Venice: Bonetus Locatellus, 1493)

Sahl ibn Bishr, *De Electionibus* (Venice: Peter of Liechtenstein, 1509)

Selby, Talbot R., "Filippo Villani and his Vita of Guido Bonatti," *Renaissance News*, v. 11/4 (1958), pp. 243-48.

Seneca, *The Stoic Philosophy of Seneca*, ed. and trans. Moses Hadas (New York: The Norton Library, 1968)

Stegemann, Viktor, *Dorotheos von Sidon und das Sogenannte* Introductorium *des Sahl ibn Bišr* (Prague: Orientalisches Institut in Prag, 1942)

Thomson, S. Harrison, "The Text of Grosseteste's *De Cometis*," *Isis* v. 19/1 (1933), pp. 19-25.

Thorndike, Lynn, *A History of Magic and Experimental Science* (New York: The Macmillan Company, 1929)

Thorndike, Lynn, *The* Sphere *of Sacrobosco and Its Commentators* (Chicago: The University of Chicago Press, 1949)

Thorndike, Lynn, "A Third Translation by Salio," *Speculum*, v. 32/1 (1957), pp. 116-117.

Thorndike, Lynn, "John of Seville," *Speculum*, v. 34/1 (1959), pp. 20-38.

Utley, Francis Lee (review), "*The Legend of the Wandering Jew* by George K. Anderson," *Modern Philology*, v. 66/2 (1968), pp. 188-193.

Valens, Vettius, *The Anthology*, vols. I-VII, ed. Robert Hand, trans. Robert Schmidt (Berkeley Springs, WV: The Golden Hind Press, 1993-2001)

Van Cleve, Thomas Curtis, *The Emperor Frederick II of Hohenstaufen: Immutator Mundi* (London: Oxford University Press, 1972)

Weinstock, Stefan, "Lunar Mansions and Early Calendars," *The Journal of Hellenic Studies*, v. 69 (1949), pp. 48-69.

Zoller, Robert, *The Arabic Parts in Astrology: A Lost Key to Prediction* (Rochester, VT: Inner Traditions International, 1989)

Zoller, Robert, *Bonatti on War* (2nd ed., 2000)

INDEX

Lightning Source UK Ltd.
Milton Keynes UK
UKOW06f0158060315

247337UK00001B/19/P